41 Major Bible Themes Simply Explained

Herbert Lockyer

Fleming H. Revell
A Division of Baker Book House Co
Grand Rapids, Michigan 49516

© 1975 by Herbert Lockyer

Published by Fleming H. Revell
a division of Baker Book House Company
P.O. Box 6287, Grand Rapids, MI 49516-6287

One-volume edition published 1997

Previously published by Baker Book House under the titles *Selected Scripture Summaries: From the Whole Bible,* volume 1 and *Selected Scripture Summaries: From the New Testament,* volume 2

Printed in the United States of America

All rights reserved. No part of this publication may be reproduced, stored in a retrieval system, or transmitted in any form or by any means—for example, electronic, photocopy, recording—without the prior written permission of the publisher. The only exception is brief quotations in printed reviews.

ISBN 0-8007-5637-1

To
Dr. E. Schuyler English,
gifted expositor of the Word, who was among my earliest friends
in America, and who, when editor of *Our Hope,* encouraged me to
write about some of these themes for that renowned periodical
now, unfortunately, defunct

After all, the chief proof that the Bible is good food is the eating of it.

General Gordon

Contents

Preface   9

Theme 1   The Presence of Humor   11
Theme 2   The Emphasis on Determination   18
Theme 3   The Divine Inability   31
Theme 4   The Virtue of Thoroughness   40
Theme 5   The Significance of Singularity   48
Theme 6   The Wondrous Hiding of God   57
Theme 7   The Gospel of Nevertheless   64
Theme 8   The Spiritual Depths   75
Theme 9   The Aspects of Fear   85
Theme 10   The Features of Depression   95
Theme 11   The "North Side"   110
Theme 12   The Repetition of Surnames   113
Theme 13   The Divine Tenderness   116
Theme 14   The Divine Guidance   124
Theme 15   The Number of Probation—Forty   134
Theme 16   The Blessed Trinity   142
Theme 17   The Antagonism of Satan   159
Theme 18   Romance and Redemption in Ruth   167
Theme 19   The Twelve Gates in Nehemiah   180
Theme 20   Divine Providence in Esther   190
Theme 21   Wisdom in Proverbs   211
Theme 22   The Church in Solomon's Song   224

New Testament
Theme 23   The Reputation of Christ   233
Theme 24   The Gifts and Glory in John 17   251
Theme 25   Acts: The Atmosphere of Prayer   258

Theme 26	Romans: The Teaching of Salvation	286
Theme 27	Galatians: The Wondrous Cross	295
Theme 28	Ephesians: The Unfolding of God	301
Theme 29	Ephesians: The Unfolding of Christ	309
Theme 30	Ephesians: The Unfolding of the Spirit	317
Theme 31	Ephesians: The Unfolding of Grace	326
Theme 32	Philippians: The Portrait of Christ	337
Theme 33	Thessalonians: The Second Advent	350
Theme 34	2 Timothy: The Christian Worker	359
Theme 35	Philemon: Christian Courtesy	370
Theme 36	Hebrews: Better Things	386
Theme 37	Peter's Epistles: Suffering	396
Theme 38	1 Peter: The Features of Judgment	403
Theme 39	John's Epistles: The Rapture	410
Theme 40	Jude: The Apostasy	422
Theme 41	Revelation: The Lamb	437

Preface

For well over sixty years it has been my great privilege to preach and teach the Word over the British Isles, and also throughout America, in churches and mission halls and in Bible colleges and institutes. In turn, it has been my joy to serve as an evangelist, pastor, and for the last thirty-five years, as Bible teacher-at-large.

My great, undying passion has been prayerfully and carefully to study God's incomparable Word, and to communicate to others truth revealed to my own mind by His Spirit. And in all kinds of opportunities, one has been encouraged by the absorbing interest of believers in a sane and satisfying exposition of Scripture. In an extensive Bible conference ministry, often with the use of a blackboard to carry outlines of themes presented, it has been most gratifying to watch the delight of an audience as these were expounded.

For over half-a-century I have amassed a quantity of material on many Scriptural subjects, and now, conscious as I am that, having gone well beyond the "four score years," heaven is not too far distant, I felt that a host of Bible searchers would like to share some of the treasures I discovered in God's inexhaustible storehouse—the Bible, the brightest and most precious gems in the crown of literature. May your meditation of these outlined truths be as sweet to your taste as they were to mine! As for my estimation of the

9

Holy Scriptures, I add a hearty Amen! to the lines of Robert
Pollock—

> This Holy Book, on every line
> Marked with the seal of high divinity,
> On every leaf bedewed with drops of love
> Divine, and with eternal heraldry
> And signature of God Almighty stamped,
> From first to last.

Theme 1
The Presence of Humor

You may wonder why we have chosen such a theme to introduce these Scripture summaries. The simple reason is to show that although the Bible is God's Word, divinely inspired, yet it is written in human language, and its humorous element reveals how closely it is related to human life, particularly, human emotions. In her *Northanger Abbey*, Jane Austin reminds us that "the liveliest effusions of wit and humor are conveyed to the world in the best chosen language." This observation is certainly true of the Bible brand of humor. Samuel Butler, who boasted, "The phrase *unconscious humor* is the one contribution I have made to the current literature of the world," contends that "the most perfect humor and irony is generally quite unconscious." It would seem that this is so with those in the Bible who used the humorous and ironic in the service of truth.

Humor is defined as "a mental quality which apprehends and delights in the ludicrous and mirthful." Some men are naturally humorous. Others, quite unconsciously, are capable of exhibiting a dry humor. Jonathan Swift in a letter to Mr. Delany, had the lines—

> Humour is odd, grotesque and wild
> Only by affectation spoiled;
> 'Tis never by invention got;
> Men have it when they know it not.

C. H. Spurgeon, that Prince of Preachers, knew he had such a gift and used it wisely and well. Cicero expressed the sentiment that "joking and humor are pleasant and often of extreme utility." Spurgeon's preaching and teaching sparkled with humor which he could also use to great advantage, as his *Lectures to Students* and *John Ploughman's Talks* reveal. The story is told of a minister who called to see Spurgeon about a member of his church who was strongly opposed to his ministry. This troublemaker always sat in the front row of the church, and as soon as the minister announced his text, this man put his fingers in his ears, and so continued to the end of the sermon. The distracted preacher asked Mr. Spurgeon what he should do in these trying circumstances, and he replied, "If I were in your plight I think I would ask the Lord to send a fly to light upon his nose." The troubled minister saw the humor of the situation, and found relief in a hearty laugh.

It may be open to question whether there is any intentional humor in the Bible. Without doubt, many of its writers had a sense of humor, yet such a natural expression of mirth is by no means conspicuous in what they wrote. The Bible makes no reference to court jesters, clowns, or funny men. Certainly there are references to "laughter," but it is usually associated with scorn, mockery, derision, rather than with unadulterated merriment. When God is referred to as laughing it is in derision (Ps. 2:4). What divine sarcasm there is in the scorn of the impotence of those who try to overturn His throne! Who, with a watering pot, is able to put out the stars, or roll back the burning orb of the midday sun into night (Ps. 37:13)? God laughs at all human folly and awaits the day of retribution.

When God fashioned man, He gave him face muscles with which to laugh. "God hath prepared laughter for me" (Gen. 17:17; 21:16, margin); " . . . ye shall laugh" (Luke 6:21; see Job 9:23; Ps. 126:2). Solomon reminds us that there is "a time to laugh," as well as cry, even though he later added that "sorrow is better than laughter." This king who wrote that "a merry heart doeth good like medicine," would never have subscribed to the Ordinance of the Second Council of

Carthage—"If any monk or clerk utters jocular words causing laughter let him be excommunicated." Can we not detect a touch of humor in some of the figures of speech Solomon employed to drive home a truth? For instance, what bitter contempt is found in the statement applied to the slacker, "Go to the ant, thou sluggard, consider her ways and be wise" (Prov. 6:6). Here the ant is before us as an example of industry and energy and economy—a contrast to humans who are lazy and indolent (see Prov. 26:14-15). Then there is the illustration about the crib being clean where no oxen are found (Prov. 14:4). This is an extension of the lesson of the ant and the sluggard. It is easy to be lazy, hard to go hungry. If a farmer has no oxen, of course, the crib will be clean—no fodder to furnish and no litter to clean out. But think of what is lost by not having the strength of the oxen to plow the field and pull the loads! Monks may return to a monastery for a life of contemplation and be clear and clean of the dust and turmoil of the world, but the world suffers from their absence from it and their work in it.

Solomon also used the figure of a living dog being better than a dead lion (Eccles. 9:4). Dead, the king of beasts loses its strength and majesty. The dog, although held in low esteem in the East, is superior to a dead lion in that it can be tamed and made to fulfill a good purpose. Humor is likewise found in the allegory Solomon gives us of a great king who came against a city and besieged it, and how one poor wise man within the city delivered it by his cunning (Eccles. 9:14-18; see also 10:10). Throughout the Bible, then, the many facets of humor—wit, satire, irony, retort, ridicule, and other forms of the ludicrous can be traced. Discussing this humorous element in Scripture, Dr. A. T. Pierson observes—

> Humour has its legitimate place, province, and office, even in sacred things. Being one of the faculties in man, it affords a medium and a channel of approach and appeal. Ridicule is sometimes a keener

13

and more effective weapon than argument—the only answer which some assaults on truth or errors in teaching and practice deserve. But like other sharp weapons, it requires careful handling, and it is one of the marks of perfection in the Word of God that we are instructed by example as to its proper uses and the avoidance of its abuses.

The Gospels tell us that "Jesus wept," but are silent as to His laughter and wholesome humor. Surely He must have had an engaging smile to attract the children to His knee. He knew that sarcasm was a potent weapon and He used it most effectively. But He never employed humorous, ironic figures of speech merely for effect. The humor He used did not draw attention to itself, or exist only for its own sake. Think of His metaphor about a camel trying to go through the eye of a needle; or of blind men leading the blind, and all falling into a ditch; or of describing Herod as a cunning cruel fox! For withering irony our Lord's somewhat humorous illustrations are incomparable.

Going back to the Old Testament, can we not detect intentional humor in the spectacular and impressive conflict between Elijah and the prophets of Baal on Mount Carmel (I Kings 18)? The pagan prophets called in vain for fire to kindle the sacrificial bullock. Elijah, mocking them, said, "Cry aloud: for he is a god; either he is talking, or pursuing, or he is in a journey, or *peradventure he sleepeth and must be awaked!*" The sting is in the tail of such an ironic taunt, for how could a *god* talk so loud as not to hear the cry of his suppliants, or fall into a dead sleep and not be able to hear?

Another bit of unconscious humor can be traced in Gideon who had *seventy sons.* No wonder! "He had many wives" (Judg. 8:30)! We moderns may smile at some of the quaint language of the old translators of the Bible, but humor is there. We are told that Asa was diseased in his feet and that the disease spread, so much so that he sought, not the Lord,

14

but the physicians for relief from his loathsome malady. With what result? "Asa slept with his fathers" (II Chron. 16:12-15). Had he sought the Lord, the implication is that he might not have joined his departed relatives so soon. The same touch of humor is seen in the incident related by Jesus of a woman suffering for twelve years from an issue of blood, and who "suffered many things of many physicians," and who when she had spent every penny she had was worse than before (Mark 5:25-26). They were physicians of no value (Job 13:4).

The same quaint touch can be found in the account of the slaughter of the Assyrians who became *dead corpses* (II Kings 19:35). How expressive is the redundancy here! David, too, knew how to use terms humorous yet ironic. We have, for example, his protest to Saul about pursuing him as a *dead dog,* and as a *flea* (I Sam. 24:14; 26:20). These homely but vivid similes are readily understood by Orientals. Nothing was so loathed by the Hebrews as a dead dog, and David accuses Saul of treating him as such. As for the figure of the flea, the original is more emphatic, "a single flea." Fleas were a universal pest in Palestine where they abounded in a degree not known elsewhere. Saul was hunting for David as "one flea"— description of extreme insignificance. David was a flea not easily caught, one who easily escaped, but who, if he had been caught, would have been poor game for the royal hunter.

Samson stands out in Scripture as an example of the mischievous *abuse* of the ludicrous. Dr. A. T. Pierson speaks of him as "the representative wag of Scripture, in whom humour runs mad, the element of the ridiculous in this case being carried to the extreme, as if for warning. Samson's riddle about the carcass of the lion has an element of wit about it, just as bitter sarcasm is found in his condemnation of the Philistines for plowing with his heifer—a reference to his wife (Judg. 14:14-18)." After his slaughter of the Philistines, Samson celebrated his victory by an utterance in

15

which he skillfully played on words. "With the jawbone of an ass, heaps upon heaps, with the jaw of an ass have I slain a thousand men" (15:16). The original Hebrew for "ass" is almost equivalent to that of the word for "heaps." Wordsworth reproduces the verse, "With the jaw bone of an ass, a mass, two masses," etc. But a Jewish writer suggests as an approach to the witty original the setting—*"I ass—ass—inated them."*

Another humorous incident can be found at the fords of Jordan where the Gileadites forced the Ephraimites to pronounce the Hebrew word *Shibboleth.* They had difficulty, however, in pronouncing the *sh,* just as a German friend of mine has difficulty with the English *w* and always pronounces it as a *v,* so "wonderful" is "vonderful" to him. Because the Ephraimites could not frame to pronounce Shibboleth right and said "Sibboleth," the loss of the *h* cost them their lives (Judg. 12:6). Dr. Pierson remarks that "this word has passed into our language to indicate the test word, pet phrase, or trifling peculiarity, which becomes the watchword of a party or the test of orthodoxy, and may give rise to bitter warfare between sects and persecuting bigotry and intolerance."

Isaiah's account of the abysmal folly of idolatry cannot be equaled. What humor, in the form of irony, the prophet manifested when he described the idolator as one feeding on ashes as out of part of a tree he carves out a god to worship (see Jer. 10:1-16), and another part he burns to warm himself and to cook his food. Thus, "the log he burns and turns to ashes is identical with the god he adores" (Isa. 44:9-20). Further, there is a hint of comedy in poetic retribution as in the case of Adoni-bezek who was paid back in his own coin (Judg. 1:5-7); and in the experience that befell Haman when he perished on the gallows he had prepared for Mordecai (Esther 8:7). Paul likewise knew how to use divine sarcasm. In many of his paradoxes he also betrayed a sense of humor, as, for example, when he wrote about "idle tattlers and busybodies"

(I Tim. 5:13). They were idle in all that was good, but industrious in evil. "Hands hanging down for want of work, but tongues always swinging with gossip—active in meddling and mischief making." Paul's illustration about "itching ears" has a humorous touch about it as he employed it as a ludicrous rebuke in his exposure of error and vindication of the truth (II Tim. 4:3). An itch in the ears is as bad as in any other part of the body, perhaps worse. Behind the apostle's amusing metaphor is a reference "to swine that, having the scurvy, seek relief for itching ears by rubbing them against stone heaps." Thus Paul ridicules those who like to hear false teachers who give them mere pleasure (Acts 17:19-21) and do not offend by truths that grate on the ears and disturb the conscience. It was Horace, the Roman poet and satirist who said—

> For a man learns more quickly and remembers more easily that which he laughs at, than that which he approves and reveres.

Q: What am I determined to be, to know, to do, to accomplish?

A: God's will

Theme 2
The Emphasis on Determination

All who read the Bible carefully are impressed by the fact that certain words stand out like a range of mountain peaks against the sky of Scripture. And such a word study is most profitable as we gather together references to an outstanding word, noting the significance of each peak as we pursue our search. One such word is a strong, resolute, and forceful term occurring in some form or other over thirty times in the Bible. It is the word *determination*. *Termination* implies an ending, but *determine* means to set down limits or bounds to something, as when you determine to perform a task. From the several places where this compelling word occurs we have divine determination, satanic determination, and Christian determination.

Divine Determination

The idea of fixity, inflexibility, tenacity of purpose is characteristic of the nature of God. His resolution to stand by or adhere to His promises and prophecies is prominently featured in Scripture. "I am the Lord, I change not" (Mal. 3:6). Here is a summary of some of the passages dealing with this specific trait in the divine character. "God hath determined to destroy thee" (II Chron. 25:16).

The word translated "determine" in this instance carries the idea of giving counsel. The unknown prophet declared the doom of Amaziah because of his idolatry. God had given His counsel and He would abide by it because of His intense hatred for the graven images which robbed Him of His glory

18

and honor. With ruthless determination He was out to destroy all that aspired to the place He alone should occupy on the throne of the human heart. This is the thought expressed by the prophet Isaiah in these pages—"For the Lord God of Hosts, shall make a consumption, even determined, in the midst of all the land" (10:23). "He hath determined against it" (19:17). "A consumption, even determined upon the whole earth" (28:22). Godly reformers, burdened about the social evils of their times, have reflected something of this divine determination to exterminate them. "Seeing his days are determined" (Job 14:5).

The term as used here means "to move sharply," "cut off." This reveals the true thought of the passage, namely, that the days of the patriarch were measured, appointed, cut off. As "God is the length of our life and days," then, seeing He is the Lord of life, He determines how long a man shall live. If it is His purpose to take away a child from any home, then no power can withhold the fair flower from being removed. As He gave, so He can take away. If it is His desire that a person should go the whole length of the allotted span, or beyond it, then He cannot be robbed of His purpose. Our span of life is as long as God determines. We stay or go at His pleasure and bidding—"He hath determined the times before appointed, and the bounds of their habitation" (Acts 17:26).

Luke the historian uses the word *horigo* for the English "determined." The implication at this point is that the seasons referred to which God ordained for seedtime and harvest, summer and winter, day and night which are fixed by divine decree, make the earth a fitting abode for men. He also fixes, or determines, the bounds of their habitations, or where they cannot dwell. This is why different nations live in different parts of the globe. Thus God determines not only how long a man shall live but where he shall live. "Seventy weeks are determined . . . desolations are determined . . . that determined shall be poured upon the desolate . . . then that that is determined shall be done" (Dan. 9:24, 26-27; 11:36).

19

The Revised Version gives the word *decreed* for *determined*. These passages in Daniel's prophetic book revolve around the stupendous truth relating to the end of Gentile reign or dominion on the earth. While it is not possible to outline in this present summary all that is involved in the various aspects of Gentile rule and overthrow as Christ returns to usher in His glorious reign, the truth emphasized by the prophet is that the Stone out of the mountain—the type of the power of Christ in judgment—is the divinely decreed method of the consummation of Gentile history.

As the righteous judge, He will be inflexible, unwavering, unyielding in His purpose to abolish all that is wrong, and to diadem that which is right. Meantime, amid the increasing corruption of the world, we are to be patient seeing the Judge is at the door (James 5:9). "My determination is to gather the nations . . . to pour upon them mine indignations" (Zeph. 3:8). All the glories awaiting the redeemed, and all the desolations involved in the overthrow of the anti-Christian forces by the all-conquering Christ must be fully realized, seeing He has decreed them. "The Son of man goeth, as it was determined" (Luke 22:22).

Horigo is also employed in this passage related to divine determination. This word means "to mark out, to divide, make, or set a boundary." It is the foundation of our English word *horizon*, implying "that which bounds." Here, *determination* is linked with *termination*, or *conclusion*, "the end of the way." Luke expresses the same truth of Christ's determination to die, and of the firm resolve of cruel men to crucify Him. "Him, being delivered by the determinate counsel and foreknowledge of God" (Acts 2:23); and "to do whatsoever thy hand and thy counsel determined [Revised Version, "foreordained"] before to be done" (Acts 4:28).

The Greek word *proorigo*, means, "to mark out beforehand," here the Revised Version translation "foreordained." Christ came as the Lamb slain *before* the foundation of the world. *Born* a Saviour, He was actually "born crucified."

20

Such a death as Jesus died was, therefore, irrevocable, for God had decreed it from the past eternity as the means of the sinner's salvation. The divine and human factors involved in the death of the cross is expressed by Peter in his sermon— "Him, being delivered by the determinate counsel and foreknowledge of God, ye have taken, and by wicked hands have crucified and slain" (Acts 2:23).

When we read that Jesus set His face steadfastly toward Jerusalem, we have evidence of His cooperation with God in such a decreed death. There must have been the look of unshakeable resolve on that strong face of His as He walked so assuredly to Calvary. Christopher Smart, of the seventeenth century, in his majestic poem "Song of David," hints at this in the last verse—

> Glorious—more glorious is the crown
> Of Him that brought salvation down
>   By meekness, call'd Thy Son;
> Thou that stupendous truth believ'd,
> And now the matchless deed's achiev'd
>   Determined, dared, and done.

Perhaps a word or two are in order as to the two distinct aspects of the mystery of the cross referred to in Peter's declaration.

The Historical Aspect—"Ye have taken and by wicked hands have crucified and slain."

This blackest crime of all history was perpetrated by those who were morally responsible for the dark deed of the cross. Jew and Gentile alike took part in a cruel action, as deliberate as it was diabolical. They would not have this Man to reign over them. Peter declared that Pilate was determined to let Jesus go (Acts 3:13), but that the Jews desired a murderer in His place. Pilate pronounced Jesus innocent, and knew

21

that it was not right to keep Him as a prisoner; yet he allowed his determination to weaken, evaporate, and parted with Christ against his better judgment.

The Divine Aspect—"Delivered by the determinate counsel . . . of God."

The cross, then, was no afterthought on His part but was "marked out beforehand." In the dateless past, "love drew salvation's plan." Peter makes no effort to demonstrate the logical consistency of these two aspects, but simply presents them as facts. Later on we read, "For of a truth against thy holy child Jesus, whom thou hast anointed, both Herod, and Pontius Pilate, with the Gentiles, and the people of Israel, were gathered together, for to do whatsoever *thy* hand and *thy* counsel determined *before* to be done" (4:27-28). Such a passage indicates that God made the passions which the enemies of Jesus indulged in, and perverted, to be the instruments of working out His will. When men suppose they are choosing their own way, the end is shaped by God, rough hew them as men will. Yet they must bear the blame for their misdeeds in spite of the fact of God's foreordained purpose.

(Prov. 16:9) The mind of man plans his way, but the Lord directs his steps.

Satanic Determination

If fixity of purpose is characteristic of God's purpose in the extermination of evil, and in the preservation of His redeemed children, Satan is just as determined to destroy all divine aims and to further his own diabolical ends. He is unshaken, unwavering, immoveable, and staunch in his plan to go to eternal doom dragging as many deluded souls with him as he can. Saul is a tragic example of satanic resolve, as a casual glance at his career quickly proves. Saul's constant hatred toward David is a reflection of Satan's antagonism toward Christ and His own.

22

"Evil is determined by [Saul]" (I Sam. 20:7, 9; 5:17). The threefold repetition of this phrase indicates how deep-seated Saul's determination to kill young David was. Because King David is a fitting type of Christ in many ways, we can see in Saul's decided effort to slay David, a glimpse of the hatred Satan manifested toward Christ in the days of His flesh.

"Evil is determined against our master" (I Sam. 25:17). "Evil is determined against [Haman] by the king" (Esther 7:7). Several passages emphasize the association of *evil* with determination, and they all prove how the enemy of our souls is unyielding in his persistence to rob us of the best God has for us. But in this fact we can rest that if we are truly the Lord's: Satan cannot rob us of Him for we are His forever, and no one—not even Satan—can pluck us out of His hand. What he does strive to do is to plunder us of the fullness of blessing the Lord seeks to bestow upon His own. Therefore, it is imperative for us to be constant in our endeavor to live near Calvary, for He who died there is our only shelter from the dark, sinister, and persistent forces of evil to impede our spiritual progress.

Christian Determination

Constancy and resoluteness are to be the hallmark of the saint, as well as of the Saviour, and, in a wrong sense, of Satan. A group of passages outline our need of the same constant, unbending, immoveable attitude toward all that is of God. It is a most unworthy kind of determination when a Christian is set in his purpose not to put wrong things right, or not to fully obey every express command because of his own preconceived ideas and prejudices. But Scripture extols the right kind of determination which is as a flame from the divine beacon.

> His way once chose, he forward thrust outright
> Nor turned aside for danger or delight.

Asahel, who refused to turn aside from following Abner, sealed his dogged perseverance not to turn aside to the right-hand or to the left with his heart's blood (II Sam. 2:19-24). No wonder those who passed the spot where Asahel fell down dead because he would not budge, stood still in reverence. May fixity of purpose, tenacity, courage to adhere to the truth of God through thick and thin, be ours!

"And Solomon determined to build an house for the . . . Lord" (II Chron. 2:1).

The Revised Version gives us "purposed to build." It was the ambition of Solomon's father, David, to erect such a house of worship, but he was divinely prohibited to accomplish this worthy aim because he had shed blood. Yet, before his death, David made full provision for the building of the temple, and when Solomon came to the throne he manifested a deep-seated determination to erect a magnificent structure for the worship of God.

Solomon presents us with an expressive type of the present, undiverted purpose of the Holy Spirit to complete the building of the church which is the Lord's body. For almost two millenniums now, the Spirit has been unceasing in His efforts to consummate the expressed purpose of Jesus to build His church. As the shadow of judgment appears to be falling upon the world, and the rapture of saints not far distant, it would seem as if the last living stones are being added to the building of God, His habitation through the Spirit. May a similar dogged perseverance be ours in the work of the Lord! Let us not be like the man Jesus pictured who began to build but was not able to finish. *Luke 14:30*

"The disciples determined to send relief unto the brethren which dwelt in Judea" (Acts 11:29).

The church today could do with a little more of the determination of the church at Antioch as it sought to help the

24

needy saints elsewhere. In the last few years there has been a tremendous upsurge to relieve the distressed, famine-stricken, and impoverished millions in various parts of the world. Christian and secular organizations have been, and are, conspicuous in saving many from starvation. Luke, however, was writing of the Christian community at Judea in dire need of relief, and, as the Lord's, we must not forget our prior responsibility to relieve our brothers and sisters in Christ who are in severe distress, physically and financially. We must set our minds to do good to those in the household of faith who are afflicted in many ways. If we cannot send relief to the brave, persecuted saints in China and Russia, we can intercede for them that God will rebuke the persecutors for the sake of His own.

"They determined [Revised Version: "appointed"] that Paul and Barnabas . . . should go" (Acts 15:2).

A question of most vital importance is associated with the appointment of Paul and Barnabas by the church at Antioch to go up to Jerusalem. God had opened the door of faith to the Gentiles, independent of the observance of ceremonial rites and laws. But many of the Jews were unwilling to cast aside the prejudices of the old religion of Judaism, and were thus unwilling to receive the Gentiles freely. But the church had been brought into existence through the free, unmerited favor of God, and as the apostles had nailed their colors to such a mast, they were determined never to surrender them. We cannot but admire the unyielding perseverance of those early saints to magnify the grace of God, and to doggedly maintain that salvation was without works. The word used here for "determined" means to arrange, or set in order as soldiers. God has arranged the truths of His free grace, and dying love, in orderly fashion, and it is our solemn responsibility to declare to legal-bound souls the freedom salvation imparts.

25

"Barnabas determined to take with them . . . Mark" (Acts 15:37).

The Greek and some of the best authorities give the weaker word "wished," or as the margin of the Revised Version puts it, "was minded," for the stronger term "determined." There must, however, have been a most resolute purpose on the part of Barnabas to take John Mark, although he had proved himself somewhat unsatisfactory for missionary service. Because of the sharp division over this matter, two very close and splendid workers separated. John Mark, of course, was the nephew of Barnabas, and as blood is thicker than water, the family relationship may have perverted Barnabas's better judgment.

Both Paul and Barnabas were equally determined not to give way on the matter of Mark, yet it would seem as if Paul was right in his resolve, seeing the church commended his decision. The sorrowful feature is that from that cleavage, Barnabas passed out of sacred history and is never heard of again. Often an unbending and decided attitude on certain matters between friends where a vital principle is at stake results in a lamentable separation. If the honor of Scripture, and the glory of God are involved, then there must be an unflinching stand, no matter how great the cost of such consecrated determination. This was the spirit of Martin Luther when he chose to leave Rome—"Here I stand! God help me! I can do no other."

" . . . it shall be determined [Revised Version: "settled"] in a lawful assembly" (Acts 19:39).

According to E. Bullinger, the word employed here for "determined" implies "to let loose (as dogs), of letters to break open, to solve." The town clerk's judicious handling of the uproar preserved Paul from a rough mauling by a mob of enraged Ephesians. A legal mind saved Paul by urging the complainers to take the matter in question to a court where it could be rightly decided.

"For Paul determined to sail by Ephesus" (Acts 20:16).

The reason behind the apostolic resolve was the desire to be in Jerusalem on the Day of Pentecost—a day of great memories. Would that we had the same impelling motive to remember the Lord in His appointed way, and to prosecute His command to evangelize the lost!

"I have determined to send Paul" (Acts 25:25).

Back of the pompous declaration of Festus regarding Paul's appearance before King Agrippa was the fulfillment of God's prophetic utterance at Paul's conversion. "He is a chosen vessel unto me, to bear my name before . . . kings" (Acts 9:15).

"It was determined that we should sail into Italy" (Acts 27:1).

In this instance we have an illustration of how God used a human agency to bring the apostle Paul to Rome, thereby fulfilling His servant's great desire "to see Rome also," and also to give him the opportunity of preaching the gospel in the then "mistress of the world." Determination brought Paul to Rome where ultimately he died for the Lord he dearly loved.

"For I determined not to know any thing among you save Jesus Christ and him crucified" (I Cor. 2:2).

This forceful word, occurring so often as it does in Paul's life, proves him to have been a man of resolute will, and of unshakeable convictions. Renan, the brilliant French skeptic,

27

referred to Paul as "the ugly little Jew." But he must have had a face that, once seen, was never forgotten, a face bearing the imprint of inflexibility, tenacity, and fixedness of purpose. The photograph of David Livingstone, the renowned Scottish missionary to Africa, is a study of unflinching courage. What an unbending, unwavering, and determined countenance! After that dramatic meeting between Livingstone and Stanley in the dark continent, the resolute explorer-missionary refused to return to England in spite of Stanley's plea. "I still have much work to do," Livingstone said, and on he trudged until one day just before dawn the natives found his lifeless form kneeling by the crude bed, his head resting upon his gnarled, clasped hands.

Can you not picture Paul's face as he condemned the Corinthians for their puffed-up pride and fleshly wisdom, and recorded the great evangelical determination "not to know any thing, save Jesus Christ, and him crucified"? Not only was Paul bent on refusing to speak on any other theme, but he will *know* no other. It was without controversy a portentous determination to have the crucified Saviour fill the whole horizon of his mind and heart.

Among all the "determinations" of Scripture this, surely, is the immediate and abiding one—a dominating ideal we must never surrender if we, too, would be true knights of the crucified Son of God. Probably, the determination of Paul to limit his Christology to "even him as being crucified" represents a temptation conquered, a soul-conflict won. To such an one as the apostle, it would be a trial of spirit to contemplate service in such a city as Corinth. As Dinsdale T. Young expresses it—

> Corinth was a centre of fashion. Shall he essay to appeal to the fashionable crowd with Christ *crucified* as the central theme? Will he not repel them thus? May he not emphasize other aspects of Christ which will be attractive and not repellant? Thus the

28

evil one would ply him. But the God of peace crushed Satan under his feet and his splendid, "I determined" rings out. Corinth was an aesthetic city. Its architecture is a proverb still, and its brasses are famous now. Corinth was an intellectual city. Its typical Greek love of philosophy all men know.

Corinth was an opulent commercial city too. Shall he not soften the truth and smooth his message? Will not taste, and culture, and materialism, and wealth resent the preaching of "Him" crucified? But, "I determined" cries this hero of the cross. He will cry out and shout in the delicate ears of Corinth nothing but the crucified Lord.

Corinth, with all its art and culture and affluence was abominably corrupt. To "Corinthianize" was a synonym for lust. The city seethed with guilt, and was sodden with sin. Its cheek was painted gaily, but its heart was diseased.

Corinth was "a hyperbole of sin," and Paul was a good physician able to diagnose accurately and prescribe unerringly. He knew that to dilate on Christ's teachings and character and lovely deed, would not effect the salvation of the gay town. Only Christ "as having been crucified" could accomplish such a miracle.

There are those who reject this brave determination of Paul as a very narrow one indeed. But such a message of dominating verity is by no means circumscribed, but one "spacious with firmamental infinity. The very catholicity of God breathes in this evangelical determination to preach a crucified Christ." If you read through the apostle's two Letters to the Corinthians you will find that he wrote to them on some twenty different subjects, yet here he is affirming that the *redeeming* Christ is the true center of Christian preaching. May we be found swearing new devotion to Him

29

who died on that wondrous cross for our redemption! May we share Paul's great evangelical determination to preach a crucified Christ, and to live a crucified life!

"I determined this with myself, that I would not come again to you in heaviness" (II Cor. 2:1).

The matters on which Paul had made up his mind and had set himself out on his resolute course to follow was the subject previously stated when he had been called upon to exercise severity of discipline upon a sinning brother. He resolved to remove all such irregularities, so that his visit might be mutually agreeable. The church at Corinth had been too lax in condoning things the early church had to deal with in a drastic manner in order to preserve its spiritual influence in heathen surroundings. In these apostate days, when the professing church seems so impotent to arrest the rising tide of infidelity and iniquity, all because of her departure from the faith as delivered to the saints, leaders need something of the apostolic determination to lovingly discipline those who openly flout the authority of Scripture.

"I have determined there to winter" (Titus 3:12).

Why Paul had firmly made up his mind to winter at Nicopolis we are not told. The name means "City of Victory," and the town was built in honor of the victory Augustus achieved over Mark Antony at Actium. Perhaps the apostle was impressed with the tremendous spiritual need of the place, and because of this determined to spend the winter months there, making it a city of victory for his Lord. Amid the winter of sin, bitter antagonism, and personal trials, he positively decided to live in that city. When winter comes, no matter in what shape and form, may it be our unending desire to live in our spiritual *Nicopolis*—Calvary, our city of continual victory over the world, flesh, and the devil.

30

Theme 3
The Divine Inability

It may come as a surprise to you to learn that the Lord God Almighty is found saying, "I cannot" (Isa. 1:13). Faith delights to feed upon the ability of God, and to rest in the affirmation of Job concerning Him, "Thou canst do every thing" (Job 42:2). Yet, as we are to see, there are some things that God cannot do. The story is told of Napoleon who wanted cannons conveyed over the Alps and consulted his engineers as to the project. They said that the task was impossible. "Impossible," snapped Napoleon, "never mention that hateful word in my presence again. It is not in my vocabulary." But we know from what followed that the word was very much there.

"Impossible" *is* a word in God's vocabulary. Certainly His power is unlimited in the material world. He could roll back the sea for Israel, make the sun stand still for Joshua, and turn it back on its course for Hezekiah. The miracles of Jesus prove that "all power in heaven and on earth" was His. In the material and natural realms, "the sweet omnipotence of love" is clearly manifest. But when it comes to the moral and spiritual realms, God is confronted with glorious impossibilities, as Joseph was when he said to his lustful temptress, "I cannot do this great wickedness." G. Bernard Shaw, in *Man and Superman* has the phrase, "He who can, does. He who cannot teaches." God can do mighty things—and does. But there are some things He cannot do, and this teaches us the significance of His inability.

31

He Cannot Endure Hypocrisy

> "The new moons and sabbaths . . . I cannot away
> with; it is iniquity, even the solemn meeting" (Isa.
> 1:13).

The evident teaching of the narrative is that certain religious observances and ordinances were intermixed with sin and iniquity, and that God abhorred such a mixture. It was hateful to Him, and He could not, therefore, sanction or condone unreal ceremonialism or hypocrisy. The same severe condemnation is found in the scathing denunciation of the hypocrites by Jesus in Matthew 23. If there is anything heaven cannot stand it is sham, or mere make-believe. Those who profess to be holy must be honorable. Life must be pure if it is to be pleasing to God.

Our modern age is one of unreality, superficiality, a mixture of true and false, and there is dire need of preachers to cry out with Jeremiah, "Cursed be he that doeth the work of the Lord deceitfully" (48:10). As we diagnose the seemingly religious life of many today we find that some go to church and assume a religious exterior in order to advance their social, material, and financial position. Others go to cover up their shortcomings. A garment of religion covers unholy transactions. Church associations divert attention from unworthy practices. Then there are those who connect themselves to a church, not out of any deep need of personal worship, but simply out of habit. There are others who minister in holy things, but who are yet unregenerate, and hostile to deeply spiritual service. The sons of Eli were priests *before* the Lord, but not *of* Him, for they knew Him not.

Isaiah records the divine inability to have anything to do with the "solemn meeting," simply because the lives of those attending it robbed it of any real solemnity. Did not Jesus say of some who taught in His name, "I know you not"? He had to condemn the church at Laodicea because it had kept

Him outside its so-called sacred precincts. "I stand at the door and knock." What a travesty—a church without the Christ! To a very large degree, modern religion must be hateful to God, and He cannot condone it.

He Cannot Condone Sin

"Thou art of purer eyes than to behold evil and canst not look upon iniquity [Revised Version: "perverseness"] " (Hab. 1:13).

This estimation of the divine character does not mean that God cannot see sin. He does see it as no other can, and is grieved. When Jesus beheld the gross sin of Jerusalem, He wept. A skeptic said to a Christian worker, "If I could see what your God sees, my heart would break." The reply was, "God's heart did break at Calvary over all He saw." What the prophet means is that God cannot look upon iniquity with approval, or countenance anything alien to His holy mind and will. Pitying our failures and weaknesses, He cannot wink His eye at them, or gloss them over.

How grateful we should be that we have a God who cannot be lenient with sin! He cannot approve evil because of its dire results, and because of all it cost Him. In these days of growing laxity multitudes have no idea of the sinfulness of sin. Writers, artists, and playwrights make fortunes by appealing to the animal in man. The production of anything suggestive is the best-paying business on the stage and screen. As Christians, we have become so accustomed to sinful sights that we do not feel the shame and abhorrence of evil that we ought to. James tells us, "God cannot be tempted with evil" (1:13). But, alas! we do not share the divine hatred and disapproval of iniquity in any shape or form. Yet to be Godlike is to loathe sin, yet love the sinner, seeking to win him for the One who died to save him from all iniquity.

In these days of intense pornographic pressure, it is increasingly difficult not to look upon iniquity or to behold evil. May purer vision be ours! Said Job, "I have made a covenant with mine eyes." May the Lord enable us to guard our eye-gates so that nothing shall pass through them to destroy our purity and peace of heart.

> O Holy Spirit, keep us pure,
> Grant us Thy strength when sins allure;
> Our bodies are Thy temple, Lord;
> Be Thou in thought and act adored.

He Cannot Consider His Own Comfort

Another glorious impossibility can be found in the taunt flung at the Saviour as He died upon the tree—"He saved others: himself he cannot save" (Matt. 27:43). The foes paid Him an unwitting tribute when they said, "He saved others." What self-abnegation was His! The giving of Himself to others in His ministry among men reached its climax when, at Calvary, He gave His life to save the lost. He gave Himself for our sins. But those rejectors greatly erred when they said, "Himself he cannot save." Because of all He was in Himself as the Mighty God, and Creator of the wood on which He hung, and of those who nailed Him to it, He could have called fire down from heaven upon His crucifiers and stepped down from His cross a triumphant victor.

To those around the cross it appeared to be true—"Look at that blood-spattered man, unable to do anything for Himself, although in the days of His flesh, He was the miracle-worker." But such a limitation was self-imposed. Jesus did not use the power He possessed to relieve Himself from the anguish He endured. He denied self-action. Did He not say that power was His to lay down His life and to take it up again? Therefore, His life was not forcibly taken by cruel men; rather, it was freely given. He could have saved Himself,

34

but, glory to His name, He did not. Had He saved Himself we would have been of all men most miserable. The only way by which Jesus could atone for sin and deliver us from it was to hang there—and hang He did!

The nails that kept Him on that tree were not those made of wood or metal. Those rough spikes were only the symbols of these nails—satisfying the claims of the broken Law, and of God's holiness, justice, and righteousness; self-abnegation, and obedience to the Father's will; passion to redeem man from sin; love, unfathomable love for sinners; determination to conquer the devil and hell. He knew that He would conquer death by dying. These, then, were the nails that kept Him from saving Himself. In his most moving chapter on "Why Do the Innocent Suffer?" Bishop Fulton Sheen, in *Life Is Worth Living,* has the paragraph—

> At the broken Person of Christ on the Cross, we begin to see the full gravity of sin. We see there our own autobiography. The Cross is the desk upon which it is written, His blood is the ink. His nails the pen. His flesh the parchment. We see our evil thoughts in the Crown of Thorns, our avarice is the Hands that are pierced with nails, our wanderings away from the path of goodness is the Feet pinned with nails. And all our false loves are the open and rent side.

Because Jesus did not save Himself, His death was a voluntary one. He did not consider His own comfort, but willingly surrendered Himself to men to do their worst. Does the principle of willing sacrifice govern our lives, or are we prone to save ourselves from identification with His cross? Did not Jesus say that trying to save our lives, we lose them, but that, in losing them for His sake we find them?

> Live for self—you live in vain;
> Live for Christ—you live again.

35

He Cannot Be Inconsistent with Himself

It was Paul who used the pertinent phrase of Jesus, "He cannot deny himself" (II Tim. 2:13)—of which Bengel, the renowned expositor said, "This impossibility is worthy of praise"—and so it is! In the context, Paul contrasts God with ourselves, "If we deny him . . . he abideth faithful: he cannot deny himself." We deny Him and prove to be inconsistent toward God, ourselves, and others, but there has never been the least flicker in the lamp of divine faithfulness. What a helpless, hopeless world ours would be if an inconsistent God controlled it! How we should give thanks at the remembrance of His unstained holiness! Had there been the slightest flaw in His divine character, then God would not be infallible, or have any right to act as God.

But the Almighty, Perfect One cannot act contrary to His own being and nature. He must be righteous and just in all His ways. "Your Father in heaven is perfect," was the testimony of His Son. He cannot, therefore, be untrue to Himself. He would be inconsistent if He treated saved and unsaved alike, failing to punish sin. (The laws of our country demand justice—shall we deny to God what man himself demands?) He would be inconsistent if He allowed those redeemed by the blood, and regenerated by the Holy Spirit to be finally lost, seeing that Jesus said, "No man is able to pluck them out of my Father's hand."

He would be inconsistent if He did not heed the penitent cry of a lost soul, for He said, "Whosoever shall call upon the name of the Lord shall be saved." He would be inconsistent if He did not answer prayer in accordance with His will, for He promised, "Ask, and ye shall receive." Too often, our bonds and promises are quickly made, and as quickly broken, but God can never go back on any promise He has made.

The greatest hindrance in effective Christian witness today is that of inconsistency. Equity has fallen upon the streets. What we are often contradicts what we say. We deny our-

36

selves. May God grant that our character and conduct will ever be harmoniously blended, of one piece, as was the garment Jesus wore!

He Cannot Lie

The idea of God's inability to depart from truth pervades Scripture. "The Cretians are always liars," Paul says, and by way of contrast, "God . . . cannot lie" (Titus 1:12, 2). "God is not a man that he should lie" (Num. 23:19). "The strength of Israel will not lie" (I Sam. 15:29). "It [is] impossible for God to lie" (Heb. 6:18). What a great comfort it is for the saint to know that, as he continues living in a world of liars, he has a God who cannot lie! Scripture often reminds us that He is the God of truth and, therefore, hates all forms of lying, dishonesty, deceit, and craftiness.

"Lying lips are an abomination unto the Lord: but they that deal truly are his delight" (Prov. 12:22). It might have been in haste that David said, "All men are liars," but is it not true that such an estimation describes present day humanity? We have business and commercial lies; political lies; religious lies, such as Ananias and Sapphira were guilty of. But God cannot lie—the Word declares it; the fulfillment of His promises confirms it; experience affirms it. Among those finally excluded from the Kingdom are "liars" (Rev. 21:8, 27). May we be constantly delivered from all semblance of lying—even from telling what we call "white lies"! By His grace and power we must aspire to be like Him—a God that cannot lie!

He Cannot Save Apart from the Human Will

The reason sin intruded into God's fair universe was because, when God created man, He did not fashion him as a machine with no power of choice. God endowed man with

37

freedom of will, and the history of sin is the use of this gift against the Giver.

> Our wills are ours, we know not why.
> Our wills are ours, to make them Thine.

But Adam and Eve became sinners when they willingly thwarted the divine will. God could not keep our first parents in that original Paradise against their will, seeing He had endowed them with liberty of choice. Jesus recognized this aspect of divine inability when He said of those who rejected His love and mercy—"How often would I have gathered thy children together . . . and ye would not" (Luke 13:34). Then we read that when He came into His own country "he did not many mighty works there because of their unbelief" (Matt. 13:58).

When it comes to the deliverance of a soul from the tyranny of sin, the battle is fought in the region of the will. God is willing to save. The preacher seeking to win souls manifests the divine will. The devil, however, exerts his will against the divine will, and works upon the will of the one who hears the gospel. Once a soul is willing to be saved, the battle is won. An awful responsibility, therefore, rests upon the sinner to say, "I will arise and go to my Father." But if he lingers in his sin, and is indifferent to the divine entreaty, then the sinner seals his own doom, for God cannot save him against his will. He never forces an entrance into the human heart. "*If* any man open the door . . . I will come in to him."

In Tonbridge, Kent, there is a monument to a company of gypsies, who, after picking hops in a field, set out to cross from one side of the Medway to the other when the river was in flood. They were drowned. A young man crept into a trench where the bodies were laid out, and kneeling down beside one corpse cried, "Mother, mother, I tried to save you; I did all a man could do to save you, but you would not let me." Is this not also the divine wail? Think of the Master's sob of unwanted love over Jerusalem sinners when, in effect,

38

he bemoaned, "I did all a God could do to save you, but you would not let Me." But what instant emancipation there is when the sinner reaches the point of surrender, and cries—

> Nay, Lord, I yield, I yield
> I can no longer hold.
> I sink by dying love compelled,
> And own Thee—Conqueror!

Theme 4
The Virtue of Thoroughness

One of the arresting features of Scripture is the way simple, ordinary phrases seem to leap out of the page and compel us to stop to discover sublime truths from the homely words that go to form them. For instance, after Joshua assumed the leadership of Israel we read that "he left nothing undone of all that the Lord [had] commanded Moses" (Josh. 11:15). The phrase, "he left nothing undone," testifies to the thoroughness with which Joshua carried out the divine instructions committed to his late chief, Moses, the servant of God. He did not complete *some* of those commands but *all* of them. As a true soldier, Joshua's love of obedience would not allow him to rest until he had fulfilled every detail of the last words of Israel's lawgiver. Conscientiousness in carrying out the divine will is, therefore, the conspicuous trait in Joshua's character. But the sentence "he left nothing undone" bristles with most suggestive thoughts and applications.

The Perfection of Creation

In the divine record of creation we read, "Thus the heavens and the earth were finished and all the host of them" (Gen. 2:1). On the seventh day, the Creator rested from His work, and as He looked at the completed product said, "It is very good." It was thoroughly perfect, with no loose ends to be tied up. In the adaptation of both man and beast to the world in which they were to live, God left nothing undone, even down to the minutest details. It is not difficult for faith to believe that the world and man, formed by a

40

definite creative act, were perfect as they came from the hand of the Creator. Nothing was forgotten or overlooked. Thoroughness stamps creation.

The Completeness of Provision

Once settled in the Land of Promise allocated among the tribes of Israel, Joshua recorded, "There failed not ought of any good thing which the Lord had spoken unto the house of Israel; all came to pass" (Josh. 21:45). Here again is evidence of thoroughness in divine dealings. What the Lord had promised with His lips, He fulfilled with His hands. There was the total fulfillment of all He had declared. He had left nothing undone in respect to provision for the pilgrim journey of His people. And what is descriptive of God's dealings with Israel is true of our individual lives, for each of us daily enjoys the totality of His benefactions. If we find ourselves in straits, facing varying needs, God reveals Himself as Jehovah-Jireh who has left nothing undone in all that is necessary for our well-being.

The Finality of Revelation

The solemn warning about adding to the words of Scripture, or taking away any of its words, is proof that the Bible is the complete, final, and authoritative revelation of the mind of God to the mind of man (Rev. 21:18-19). "The Law of the Lord is perfect," for He left nothing undone when He inspired holy men of old to set forth "the prophecy of the Scriptures" (II Peter 1:20-21). All we need to know about God, the Saviour, sin, the human heart, life beyond the grave, the destiny of earth, are set forth with a thoroughness we cannot escape. The reason why the Bible is so up-to-date is because God left nothing undone in His description of the world, present, as well as past. Possessing greater wisdom than the wiseacres of today, God knew all about our twen-

41

tieth century when He inspired the prophets and apostles to set down the truths He wanted the world to read. Momentous happenings of our time were predicted millenniums ago, and prove how absolute Scripture is in its panorama of the ages.

The Fullness of Redemption

When it came to our deliverance from the guilt and power of sin, and the awful consequences of rejecting divine claims, Jesus left nothing undone in the matter of our salvation and security. As He died on the cross, He cried, not as a victim but as a victor—"It is finished!" The superb work of emancipation for the sin-bound was superbly and thoroughly accomplished. Once and for all, by His death and resurrection, Jesus made a full and final provision for a sinning race. Now, all that a sinner can do is to accept by a naked faith the perfect redemption so freely provided. Nothing can be added to such a matchless gift of grace.

> "It is finished!" Jesus cries,
> I will trust! I will trust!
> As He bows His head and dies!
> I will trust! I will trust!
> All my load on Him is laid;
> And my debt He freely paid;
> He my peace with God has made;
> I will trust! I will trust!

The Ideal of Service

The old adage that if a thing is worth doing it's worth doing well certainly sums up the thoroughness in the attainment of aims on the part of many Bible saints, none of whom left anything undone. Receiving full and complete instruc-

42

tions as to the creation of the tabernacle and the institution of its services, we read that "Moses finished the work," even down to the formation of the necessary tent pins. With such an accomplished task the glory of God filled the sanctuary, for He always crowns the perfect with honor. Boaz certainly did nothing by halves when it came to the redemption of Ruth and the security of her as his bride. "He did not rest until he finished the thing" (Ruth 2:18). To Solomon was granted the privilege of building a temple for the Lord, and through the years of erection, the king was most thorough in the provision of all that was necessary for such a task, and labored on till he "built the house and finished it" (I Kings 6:9, 14). Nehemiah was another who left nothing undone until his vision of a restored city was realized: "So the wall was finished," and that in spite of sneers and scoffs (Neh. 6:5). Paul, inspired by the dying declaration of Jesus—"It is finished" (John 17:6)—could come to his own end by affirming, "I have finished the course" (II Tim. 2:7). How we need the same thoroughness in our service for the Master! Yet how sadly we miss.

The Inspiration of Life

It was the renowned Cicero who said, "Let us do nothing in a spiritless fashion, nor anything timidly, nor anything sluggishly." Ovid, another Roman philosopher, remarked, "Finish thoroughly the work you have set yourself." Would that these words could form your epitaph and mine—"He left nothing undone"! What an inspiration for a full, God-honoring life this reputation that Joshua achieved is for us! Too often, things we have done should have been left undone. All of us are conscious of mistakes and failures we would not make if we could live our life over again. On the other hand, there are some things left undone we should have done. All of us need to join in the Confession contained in *The Book of Common Prayer*—

43

We have left undone those things which we ought to have done; And we have done those things which we ought not to have done; And there is no health in us.

We are guilty of sins of omission as well as of commission. When David spoke of "secret sins," he referred to those he had committed unconsciously. Whether we are cognizant of it or not, all of us are guilty of partial obedience, imperfect consecration, and defective allegiance. There is a lack of thoroughness, or stickability, about our efforts. We are like the man the Master referred to in one of His peerless parables who "began to build but was not able to finish" (Luke 14:30). Near the town of Ancrum is a site known as "The Baron's Folly," so-named because the nobleman set out to build a magnificent castle but relinquished the task, and the few stumps of stone testify to his lack of constancy.

The historic city of Edinburgh was determined to erect a monument on Calton Hill to the memory of the Scottish soldiers who fought in the Peninsular War and at Waterloo. Such a memorial was to have been a reproduction of the Parthenon at Athens, at a cost of some fifty thousand pounds—a large sum in those days. Out went the appeal, but the response was meager, and after sixteen thousand pounds had been spent the work was suspended. The twelve great pillars, standing out in the skyline and costing one thousand pounds each, look like some ancient ruin. Although admired by architects and builders who have a "feeling for stone," that uncompleted memorial is referred to as "Pride and Poverty," or as "Scotland's Disgrace."

Are we not guilty of beginning to build but not being able to finish? Is not our pathway through life strewn with broken pillars where there should have been a worthwhile edifice? What God expects of us is what He Himself manifested at creation, namely, *consummation*. There are three observations to be made in connection with the fact that our sins of omission prevent completion—

First, they are many in number.

In his *Diary,* the revered Andrew Bonar wrote at the conclusion of one year, "This year omissions have distressed me more than anything." As we come to the end of a year or a life, we have need to be distressed over what we have left undone. The biographer of Charles Darwin said of the renowned scientist, "He never wasted a few spare minutes from thinking that it was not worth while." His golden rule was, "Take care of the minutes," hence, he became rich and accurate in many realms of knowledge.

Do we not think of some things we might have done—tears we might have dried, loads we might have lifted, heartaches we might have eased, souls we might have saved, time we might have used more profitably? Too often, we leave little acts undone in the home and neglect those we should have helped before death claimed them. We evade manifest obligations and work which we ought to face. With what fiery energy the bees, birds, and butterflies carry out their special commission entrusted to them in the natural realm. But we, alas! have gaps, inertia, laziness, procrastination, imperfection, lack of thoroughness, stumps where there should be a stately castle.

Second, they are not to be slighted.

Things left undone are often of great consequence. Mighty issues hang on little things. Emerson speaks of "the science of omitting as a necessary science if things are vulgar, unseemly and nonessential." But to treat some of the small things of life as trivial is suicidal. "A little thing is a little thing: but being faithful in a little thing is a great thing." Did not Jesus say that "he that is faithful in least is faithful in much"? And the former is the gateway to the latter. Too often, however, we leave undone large and noble matters and concentrate on the inferior and unnecessary. We strain at gnats but swallow camels. For instance—

> We shirk work demanding courage and sacrifice, and condescend to please our own pride, or further our own selfish pleasures.
> Great principles are left out of character, because they seem difficult to acquire and maintain.
> Great duties are ignored because they involve heroism, suffering, and self-sacrifice.
> Great opportunities are forfeited because they demand endeavor, resolution, thoroughness, and promptitude.
> Great service is declined because it entails separation from worldly pleasures and pursuits, and utter consecration.

Third, they are to be accounted for.

Can it be that we are as deeply concerned as we ought to be over the things we have done amiss, but less troubled about the things we have left undone? God will hold us responsible for what we have not done, as well as what we have done. It is useless to say we have no gifts, no time, no opportunity to serve, for this is but a way of glossing over the shirking of personal responsibility. Each of us, no matter how simple and ordinary we may be, has a God-given task to complete that no other can do.

> There's a work for Jesus
> Ready at your hand,
> 'Tis a task the Master
> Just for you has planned,

46

Haste to do His bidding,
  Yield Him service true;
There's a work for Jesus,
  None but you can do.

May grace be ours to crowd into life more passion, purpose, perseverance, and precision! Let us strive to be more prompt, definite, resolute, and thorough. Having put our hand to the plow may we never halt till the end of the furrow is reached. Then, when we reach heaven, it will be said of us as it was of Joshua, "He left nothing undone"!

Theme 5
The Significance of Singularity

The adjective *singular* means, "individual, distinctive, exceptional, peculiar to oneself." These ideas are embedded in the recurring phrase, "as for me." Doubtless you have observed the frequent occurrence of this arresting triad in the lives of various saints in Bible days, and noticed how they sparkle like gems in the crown of Scripture. These three words bring before us a certain contrast, or separation, as the speaker places himself apart from others. Looking around he sees other men following this and that line of thought and action, and they appear to be in the majority. Their sentiments have all the weight and force of fashion behind them, for what they do has been done from time immemorial. Therefore, he cannot help it if he takes another line under divine compulsion, and risks being thought odd.

However singular, opposite, or peculiar it may seem to say, "As for me," all of those who uttered these words felt that they must set out on another road, or pursue a different course than that the others were taking. Let others live and act as they may, but, "as for me," it must be otherwise. For instance, when David said, "As for me," his life was like a star, dwelling apart. That such a singularity is Godlike is proven by the first occurrence of the phrase where it is applied to God—"As for me, behold my covenant is with thee" (Gen. 17:4). No matter how Abraham had been selfishly treated by Lot, and Abraham himself had been guilty of deception, God was different in that He had set His heart upon Abraham as the progenitor of a mighty race. As we are to find, the quotation marks a strange and forceful spiritual

48

singularity in the lives of those who used it. In *Twelfth Night,* Shakespeare has the line, "Let not thy tongue tang arguments of state; put thyself into the tricks of singularity." But as used by Bible saints, singularity has no trick, but is a conspicuous feature of decision and character.

> Each the known track of sage philosophy
> Deserts, and has a byword of his own;
> So much the restless eagerness to shine,
> And love of singularity, prevail.

The Individuality of Devotion to God

"As for me and my house we will serve the Lord" (Josh. 24:15).

Joshua, the ancient leader of Israel is a fitting illustration of the necessity of the personal element in singularity when it comes to spiritual matters. At Shechem he placed before the nation the nature of loyalty to God, and the obligations of such an expected loyalty, and then challenged them to a choice, a choice that must be their own, and not one that even Joshua, loved and honored though he was, could make for them. It would seem as if the people wavered in their choice, and so we reach the climax of Joshua's appeal in the phrase, "As for me and my house." Whatever else he might do for him and his, the die was cast—"We will serve the Lord."

Having firmly established the things of God in heart and home, whether such an action was singular or no, Joshua was determined to abide by his distinctive choice. Yes, and his declaration has had a long and active life, seeing it became the watchword of many a Christian home in which it can still be found as a motto. May such personal devotion to God be ours, although the way of the world runs otherwise, and

49

other homes are ordered by other, less worthy principles. Our hearts and homes are thrice happy if the things of God are as deep springs in individual daily thought and action. Although the world may be against us, let the spiritual singularity of Joshua be ours—"As for me I will serve the Lord"!

The Individuality of Prayer

The compelling phrase we are considering occurs often in the Psalms. Here, for instance, is its triple association with prayer—"As for me, I will come into thy house" (Ps. 5:7). "As for me, I will call upon God" (Ps. 55:16). "As for me, my prayer is unto thee, O God" (Ps. 69:13).

Once again we have the determination of the speaker to stand out from all others, odd though his position may have been thought to be. This "as for me" of dependence upon God contrasts sharply with the way of others. In the first two verses above we have the psalmist's proposal, "I *will* come . . . call," but in the third verse his proposal becomes practice, "My prayer *is* unto thee."

Is not the growing need of our day for men and women to preserve this individuality of prayer, seeing they are surrounded by myriads of prayerless people, even those to whom waiting upon God has no appeal? Let others try to live their lives apart from God, and fashion their own ways—ours must be the determination to watch and safeguard singularity in respect to fellowship with God. Because prayer is contagious and pleaders win pleaders, we must ring out our "as for me" as a holy, personal ambition and save others, thereby, from the sin of prayerlessness. Further on, we have the psalmist saying, "It is good for me to draw near to God" (73:28)—good, not only for ourselves, but also for others as we intercede for them. May Samuel's resolve be ours as we think of saints and sinners "standing in the need of prayer": "As for me, God forbid that I should cease to pray for you" (I Sam. 12:23).

The Individuality of Eternal Satisfaction

"As for me, I will behold thy face in righteousness: I shall be satisfied when I awake, with thy likeness" (Ps. 17:15).

Within this Psalm there is sketched for us with awful vividness, the individuality of worldly men, each of whom were satisfied with the pursuit of their own selfish and sensual desires. But in the verse before us the psalmist isolates himself from all worldly and carnal aims, contrasting them in a powerful way with immortality and its satisfaction of mind. Men of the world receive their satisfaction in this life, but the saint is content to wait for his complete gratification in heaven—"*shall* be satisfied."

Thus the truth to be gleaned from the psalmist's particular and peculiar aspiration is, let worldly men of low degree be pleased and satisfied with earthly store; but let ours be the personal hope and eternal pleasure of seeing the King in all His beauty. Let others live for their carnal joy, their earthly possessions, their gold; let them thirst after pursuits which bring a passing contentment. Such people are to be pitied if they die without Christ, for their present pleasures form the only heaven they will ever have. Bless God, those who through faith in the redeeming grace of Christ may appear odd, singular, or peculiar to world-lovers, have a glorious prospect of never-failing satisfaction once they cross the narrow sea of death and see Him whom their hearts have loved since first they met Him.

The Individuality of Christian Forgiveness

David, in another Psalm, describes a most unusual aspect of his spiritual singularity. "As for me, when they were sick, my clothing was sackcloth" (35:13). The "they" he speaks of were the people who had treated him with gross and persistent injustice, and who became "sick," or chastened by God, as they deserved to be. But what about David's attitude? Was he jubilant? Did he say, "Serves you right for the way you treated me"? No, he returned good for evil, and thus foreshadowed the spirit of Calvary. He bewailed their trouble by clothing himself in the garb of mourning and by fasting and praying for them. Others might have been glad to see them suffer, but not David—his clothing was "sackcloth."

What an example of noble spiritual individuality David left us! We need more of this distinctiveness in forgiving those who have wronged and ill-treated us! How do we treat those who offend and hurt us and how do we feel when they suffer? Is ours an inward gratification to see them being paid back in their own coin? If so, let us stand rebuked by the psalmist's "As for me . . . sackcloth." Others may believe in keeping up the old grudge, never forgiving, remaining aloof, and being glad to see those who ill-treated them afflicted. But as for me, a blood-washed, divinely forgiven sinner, it must be the Calvary way, for the cross reveals the very heart of God with whom is forgiveness that He may be feared. Symbolically, we must put on the sackcloth when we see our enemy sick, seeking, thereby, to win him from his antagonism. May the Lord enable us to cultivate, more than ever, this feature of singularity, and turn the other cheek! To forgive those who despitefully treat us may appear odd, but it is the way the Master went and we must follow Him.

The Individuality of Divine Support

Still in the Psalms, we find another instance of spiritual singularity, this one related to what God is able to do for those who, in their desires and aims, are separate from sinners. "As for me, thou upholdest me in mine integrity" (41:12). Under what circumstances did the psalmist prove that God was able to uphold and sustain although it appeared that he had been left to fight his own battle? Why, he was on a bed of languishing, surrounded, not by kind sympathetic

52

friends consoling him as ministering angels, but encircled by enemies, deaf to his cry for succor and impatient to see his end. As if to add extra infusion of gall to his bitter cup, his own familiar friend had turned his back upon his anguish.

What a picture of unrelieved suffering this Psalm presents! Yet there is no such a thing as unrelieved suffering with the saint of God, because as he gives himself to prayer, he proves the personal divine support available to him in his hour of need. John Wesley used to speak of "the old unfashionable medicine of prayer," and such effective medicine can sanctify and transform a sickbed, making it administer blessing to the afflicted one. Every child of God may know this singular, individual support God offers to all who are upright in heart. The Good Shepherd never forgets even the poorest lamb in His flock. No matter how humble and insignificant we may be, He has us on His heart at all times. Let us, then, lay hold of this precious "as for me," and determine to know God as our personal support, stay, strength, and song! While multitudes around may be ignorant of divine sustenance and feed on their own ways, may ours be the serenity that comes through knowing that God cares for us.

The Individuality of Satan Assault

In an autobiographical psalm, Asaph reveals how narrowly he escaped from falling into a net the wily tempter had set for his feet: "As for me, my feet were almost gone; my steps had well-nigh slipped" (73:2). The psalmist was envious when he saw the prosperity of the wicked and arrogant and almost fell into the temptation of complaining over his own impoverishment as he saw the wealth of others. Is there not an individuality and singularity about the terrible temptation some people face? Each of us has a special kind of temptation, and no saint can hope to escape. Some, of course, are more susceptible than others to the approach of the enemy. May we be delivered, however, from the peculiar temptation of Asaph, namely, that of envy over the prosperity of others. How we need to beware of covetousness, especially if we do not have much of this world's goods!

When you look at others, with their lands and gold,
Think that Christ has promised you His wealth untold.

Gold and grandeur can do nothing for a man beyond the veil. If it could, then Dives, the rich man, would not have gone to hell. The child of God has One who is able to supply all that is necessary for the manifold needs of life. "Be content with such things as ye have: for he hath said, I will never leave thee, nor forsake thee" (Heb. 13:5). Do you know that this is one Scripture that if read backwards means the same—"Thee forsake nor thee leave never will I." If we have yielded to Asaph's temptation and our feet are almost gone, let us hasten to the cross and humbly and repentantly ask for forgiveness and complete deliverance from the tempter. God's delivering grace is for each and all, and He gives individual grace to resist every individual temptation.

The Individuality of Divine Revelation

Although there are many other verses that contain the phrase "as for me," which Bible lovers can pursue with profit, we conclude with these two references from the Book of Daniel.

"As for me . . . this secret is not revealed to me for any wisdom that I have" (2:30). "As for me . . . my cogitations much troubled me" (7:28). There are two phrases in the second chapter of this prophecy, which provide a vivid contrast, "As for thee O King"—"As for me" (2:29-30). Nebuchadnezzar's dream came in the silence of the night, and he was to discover that there was a God in heaven able to reveal secrets. The revelation of the structure of the dream, and also

54

its significance was granted to Daniel, who had no wisdom of his own to interpret it. It was divinely revealed that the thoughts of many hearts might be made bare. The Chaldean astrologers sought to interpret the king's dream by the aid of natural reason, but failed. Daniel was exceptional, singular in that he alone was able under God to unfold the mystery and message of the dream. Is there not an "as for me" in respect to a true unfolding of the Word and ways of God? Is not the Holy Spirit able to take you and me aside and reveal the inner significance of truth? What we receive may be contrary to the accepted theories and ideas of men, but with Daniel we must be singular in saying, "As for me, this secret is revealed unto me, and I must accept, believe, and declare it." Daniel said that his "cogitations" troubled him, and often we are compelled to stand aside and tremble at the overwhelming revelation of truth granted.

As we conclude this particular summary it is necessary to remind ourselves what "as for me" does not mean. Never for a moment is the Christian called to isolation, detachment, singularity for their own sakes, but always for the sake of God and of others. It is the believer's business to be most considerate, sympathetic, courteous, and companionable within the orbit of the will of God. If this is not remembered, the absence of prayer and of sanctified common sense can make one disagreeable, unwelcome, objectionable by their oddity, singularity, mistaking this as fidelity to a principle.

It is imperative to keep a sacred place in the heart for the aim "as for me," when it means consideration and sympathy as different as possible from drift and compromise. If our lives are absolutely governed by a personal surrender to the will of God, then there will come the abandonment of all worldly methods of living and acting, and of all alluring fashions of thought and practice. If the "as for me" of Bible saints is conspicuous in our lives, then, with our feet planted firmly on the revelation that God's Word provides, we will be content to let others live as they may.

Let the multitudes drift into indifference to His Word, His sanctuary, His Holy Day.

Let even those who bear His name be ignorant of His express commands as to the Ordinances, and to personal self-discipline of habits and the need of holy living.

Let it be out of fashion, even in religious circles, to witness definitely for Christ, to seek the salvation of the lost from sin and hell.

"As for me," it must be otherwise. Without pride trumpeting self-exaltation, we must be spiritually singular. I am not my brother's judge as to what he should not do, but my Master's servant whose call I must obey, and so, "As for me, I must serve the Lord."

Theme 6
The Wondrous Hiding of God

Can we own a God who
. . . Hides Himself so wondrously
As if there were no God?
He is least seen when all the powers
Of ill are most abroad.

Evidently the saintly and seraphic Isaiah, known as "The Evangelical Prophet" could own and love such a God for he, it was, who challenged Him by saying, "Verily Thou art a God that hidest thyself, O God of Israel, the Saviour" (Isa. 45:15). To the prophet, God appeared to remain incognito. From the narrative it would seem as if Isaiah condemned the Lord for neglecting His people when they were in exile and bondage. Somehow He had forgotten them, or they, Him; yet now with clearer light it is possible to trace His footprints. Although apparently unseen and indifferent, prophet and people alike came to discover that the unseen One was actively ruling and overruling in all their past history. The verse before us pulsates with great thoughts, so let us try to take some honey out of this piece of the rock of impregnable Scripture. We love and serve a God who delights in hiding Himself in order that our discovery of Him may enrich our lives.

His Being

God, in His own divine essence, no human being has seen. He dwells in glory inaccessible, and hides Himself from the gaze of inferior beings, as Paul indicates in his letters to

57

young Timothy, "Now unto the King, eternal, immortal, invisible" (I Tim. 1:17). " . . . the blessed and only Potentate, the King of kings, and Lord of lords, who only hath immortality dwelling in the light which no man can approach unto; whom no man hath seen, nor can see" (I Tim. 6:15-16). Then John declares that, "No man hath seen God at any time . . . " (1:18). The nearest any human has come to seeing Him who is invisible is Moses, for on that mount, God said to his honored servant who desired to see Him, "Thou canst not see my face: for there shall no man see me and live. . . . Thou shalt see my back parts: but my face shall not be seen" (Exod. 33:20, 23). Even the seraphim in His august presence have to veil their faces before the blinding glory of His radiant holiness. We have a faint idea of the dazzling glory of Deity at the Transfiguration when the disciples were partially blinded through the inherent glory of Jesus flashing forth.

> True Image of the Infinite
> Whose essence is concealed,
> Brightness of uncreated light,
> The heart of God revealed.

His Creation

Solomon reminds us that "it is the glory of God to conceal a thing" (Prov. 25:2); and the prophet says, "There was the hiding of his power" (Hab. 3:4). What are the great discoveries of men in the realm of science but the unfolding of what God originally hid in the universe. He, it was, who deposited the gold, silver, diamonds, coal, and other minerals and beneficial treasures in the earth, leaving man to find what He had hidden. "There is nothing new under the sun" because all was known to God who placed it there. This is what man is continually doing, bringing to light by laborious search what God stored away in His creation. Kepler said, as he made fascinating studies of the starry heavens, that he was only "thinking God's thought after Him," or, discovering what God had hidden.

His Book

As we think of Scripture, the description of Isaiah is most apt, "Verily thou art a God that hidest thyself." The prophet also witnesses that God reveals the unseen and unknown, "I have showed thee new things from this time, even hidden things" (48:6).

David prayed, "Hide not thy commandments from me" (119:19). He did not want God to keep the inner, hidden sense of divine truth from him. Often it seems as if He hides Himself in His Word and "showeth himself through the lattice." Prejudice, disobedience, and sin can keep Him hidden from our gaze. It is only as we are obedient to the voice of the Holy Spirit that He can enable us to trace the Lord.

> Beyond the sacred page,
> I seek Thee, Lord.

In the days of His flesh, Jesus made it clear that unbelief prohibits revelation: "But they understood not this saying, and it was hid from them" (Luke 9:45). "If thou hadst known . . . now they are hid from thine eyes" (Luke 19:42). It is one thing to read the Book of God superficially, as literature, but a different thing altogether to know and love the God of the Book, and knowing the Author enables us to see the glory gilding the sacred page. The psalmist prayed, "Open my eyes, that I may behold wondrous things out of thy law"—things that have always been in the Word since it was written, but which the Holy Spirit alone can enable us to find. And when we do, then we rejoice as those finding great spoil. Further, quietly and unseen by others and unobserved by ourselves, our life, loves, beliefs, and habits are changed through the sanctifying Scriptures.

59

His Providence

There are times in your experience and mine when it does seem as if Isaiah's words are true, about God hiding Himself. In the midst of his anguish Job cried, "O that I knew where I might find him!" (23:3). To the patriarch it seemed as if God had either departed from him, or was veiling His face from the eye of faith.

Take Mystery

The frequent complaint of saints of old is that expressed by David, "Why hidest thou thyself in times of trouble?" (Ps. 10:1; see 44:24; 88:16). When in dire need Mary and Martha sent for Jesus, He delayed His journey to Bethany and hid Himself, as it were. Why? Why is God silent in the hour of grief? Thanks be to the Saviour Himself who at Calvary cried, "Why?"—"My God, my God, why hast thou forsaken me?" There are mysteries, perplexities, and problems in human life that our finite minds cannot explain, and hidden purposes in many experiences that no skill can unravel. It is consoling, however, to walk in the dark with God. Moffatt translates Isaiah's estimation of the divine character, "Verily thou art a God that hidest thyself," as "Yours indeed is a God of mystery, a God that saves." Even in the mystery, He is working out His beneficent, saving purpose. Now, we live in a world of mystery, but the Paradise of Revelation awaits us, as Paul reminds us in the comforting words, "For now we see through a glass, darkly; but then, face to face." But although God may veil His aims in all He permits, He never makes a mistake as we shall discover when He unrolls the canvas and explains the reason why.

> Judge not the Lord by feeble sense
> But trust Him for His grace;

> Behind a frowning Providence,
> He hides a smiling face.

Take Prayer

David urges God to give ear to his prayer, and not to hide Himself from his supplication (Ps. 55:1). In a daring way, the psalmist pleads with God not to turn His face away as if resolved not to listen to his cry. Are there not times when it seems as if the divine ears are not open to our supplication? Have we not experienced the problem of unanswered prayer? Have we not prayed for necessary, legitimate things, yet received no answer? Although the Scripture assures us that He is the God who hears and answers prayer, somehow it appears as if He has hid Himself from our need, and has forgotten to be gracious. In spite of our agonizing cry, He does not hasten to relieve us of our adversity or trial.

What we must not forget is the fact that there can be a radical cause for God hiding Himself from our supplication. We cannot expect to have the smile of His face and His ears open to prayers if our life is displeasing to Him. If we regard iniquity in our hearts, then He cannot hear us. Lack of divine favor, then, should lead us to search our ways. "Thou hidest thy face, they are troubled" (Ps. 104:29). In spite of His miraculous ministry, many people did not believe Jesus, and He departed from them, and hid Himself from them (John 12:36-37). May we so live that His ears will always be open to our prayers! If, however, some remain unanswered, when we see Him we'll know the reason why.

> Unanswered yet? Faith cannot be unanswered,
> Her feet are planted firmly on the Rock;
> Amid the wildest storms she stands undaunted,
> Nor quails before the loudest thunder shock.
> She knows Omnipotence has heard her prayer,
> And cries, "It shall be done"—sometime, somewhere.

His Christ

When we come to the Saviour, God's beloved Son, we touch the deepest truth of Isaiah's word about God hiding Himself, for in Christ, God truly hid Himself. "God was in Christ reconciling the world unto himself." To Moses, God said, "There shall no man see me and live." It is only as we see God in Christ that we can live both now and in eternity. "No man hath seen God at any time; the only begotten Son, which is in the bosom of the Father, he hath declared him" (John 1:18). Jesus Himself could say, "He that hath seen me, hath seen the Father," for He came as the culmination of the revelation of God. Often in the Old Testament God veiled Himself in angelic form, and appeared to men, but He became incarnate in Jesus. "Veiled in flesh, the Godhead see." The only One privileged to see the face of God is the One who reveals the divine character. He came as the express image of God's person. Does He not live and have His being in a silent, hidden, mysterious way in your heart and mine? Are we not indwelt by the unseen blessed Spirit? Conversely, our lives are hid with Christ in God.

His People

Paul reveals a mystery hid from the ages: "Christ in you the hope of glory" (Col. 1:26-27). There is the veiling of Him in our own being. The world cannot see the Father, Son, and Holy Spirit; yet all three are resident in your life and mine, for every true believer is a mysterious cabinet of the Trinity. When Jesus was here among men, He "could not be hid," and when He appeared it was quickly noised abroad that He was in the house (Mark 2:1; 7:24). We cannot hide the fragrance of a rose, the heat of a fire, the glory of a sunset. Thus it is with Christ and ourselves. If we are living in unbroken fellowship with the three Persons of the Blessed Trinity they are bound to express their hidden presence through our lives, and those around us will swiftly discern the charm of our God-possessed life. Let us pray that He will bury Himself deep in our being, and then reveal His love through us to a world of sin.

Theme 7
The Gospel of Nevertheless

A good, serviceable Bible concordance is the best commentary when it comes to word study. Dr. A. J. Gordon, one of the outstanding Bible expositors of the last generation, wrote, "In Scripture, words, like blazed trees in a forest, are sure guides through the labyrinth of Revelation. *Lamb, blood, faith, forgiveness, peace*—these are God's words: and whoever will take one of them and trace it through the Bible, threading together on this single word, as on a cord, the various texts where it occurs, will find both a wondrous continuity, and a wondrous unity thereby established."

It is this excellent advice we are taking with the word *nevertheless.* It occurs some thirty times in Holy Writ, and is actually three words in one, Never-the-less, meaning, "not the less," or "notwithstanding," or "however," or "none-the-less," or "yet." Scattered throughout the pages of the Bible, this cheery word, *nevertheless,* challenges our thought and invites meditation. As S. E. Burrow put it—

> In the dark patches of life—when things are difficult and clouds darken the horizon—it speaks to us, either of a possible alternative or an ultimate advantage. There may be a night of failure, but the morning shall find the nets full to overflowing! It bids us not to be wholly concerned with the present, for there is a "nevertheless afterward" in the programme for which it is worth waiting. It is a friendly word—is this *nevertheless*—for it urges us to look out for the brighter side, and to wait for the compensa-

64

tion which the all-loving Father holds in reserve for His children, so that all things shall work together for good.

As we examine many of the references where *nevertheless* appears, we shall find how the word is associated with the various aspects and experiences of Christian service.

As used by Nehemiah, the model worker, the word represents difficulty in service, for this exile in Babylon was not only deeply concerned about his fellow-Jews in faraway Jerusalem who were suffering "great affliction," but was equally distressed concerning the city of his fathers—"the walls of Jerusalem broken down, and the gates burned." Nehemiah not only wept and mourned, but fasted and prayed. God heard His servant's cry, and moved the heart of the king to grant Nehemiah leave of absence that he might repair the walls and encourage his brethren. But setting about the task, he met with much opposition and ridicule, and found the going hard. What did he do—compromise with the foes who tried their utmost to stop the rebuilding plan? Let Nehemiah himself answer, "Nevertheless we made our prayer unto our God, and set a watch against them day and night" (4:7-9). Here we have the *Nevertheless of Steadfastness*. Satan tries in so many ways to discourage the child of God, and often faith is sorely tried; but victory is secured as he shelters behind the "nevertheless" of Nehemiah, and just goes on working, watching, and praying.

While there are other Old Testament references to this word, wealthy in meaning and content, let us confine ourselves to many of its appearances in the New Testament.

"The King was sorry, nevertheless for his oath's sake" (Matt. 14:9)

This was the *Nevertheless of Doublemindedness*. Herod was more afraid of the taunt of assembled guests than he was

65

of the voice of conscience. The careless oath he made should have been broken, for a holy man's life was at stake. While John's cruel death reminds us of the cost of fearless discipleship, he should not have died, and would not have been murdered if Herod's last struggle with conscience had not created a false regard for public opinion. Associated with this "nevertheless" is not only the doom of the Baptist, but the gross licentiousness of Herod and his court.

"Nevertheless not as I will, but as thou wilt" (Matt. 26:39; Mark 14:36)

The circumstances surrounding this *Nevertheless of Surrender* are familiar. Jesus was born to die, for He came as the Lamb slain before the foundation of the world. Virtually, then, He was born crucified, and during His public ministry He often spoke of the decease He was to accomplish at Jerusalem. Conscious of all that awaited Him, He did not falter, but set His face steadfastly toward His cross. His cry for the removal of the bitter cup was but the natural cry of human weakness, and it was quickly followed by submission and surrender to the will of His Father. Because God is infinitely wiser than we are, knowing what is best for us, this Gethsemane "nevertheless" must condition all our petitions.

"Nevertheless, I say unto you, Hereafter shall ye see the Son of man sitting on the right hand of power, and coming in the clouds of heaven" (Matt 26:64)

The contrast before us in the context is most impressive. Jesus had been standing before Caiphas, and, wrongly accused, He was sentenced to die. Defiantly, however, He rings out the truth that the tables would be changed and that He would sit as the righteous judge, and sinners would be made to stand before Him to receive, not false justice as had been heaped upon Him, but only what their sin truly deserved. His foes gave Him a cross, but that was to be the way to His throne. "Nevertheless . . . hereafter"! How comforting is the *Nevertheless of Glory!*

"Nevertheless at thy word I will let down the net" (Luke 5:5)

Peter, the spokesman of the apostolic band, as an experienced fisherman knew that night was the right time to fish, even though on this particular night not one solitary fish found its way into his net. So when the sun rose and shone upon the waters—the wrong way to fish—Peter was a little amazed when Jesus said to these discouraged fishermen, "Put out to sea again, and let down your nets for a draught." Yet, although he might have questioned the wisdom of his Master, there came his *Nevertheless of Obedience.* With what result? Because he was willing and humble enough to forego his own judgment and ignore his fishing knowledge and experience and obey his miracle-working Lord, he reaped a bountiful harvest from the sea that fine morning. Peter was obedient to Christ's command even though it was contrary to the accustomed order of things. The fisherman's wrong time for fishing was Christ's right time.

"Nevertheless I must walk to day, and to morrow, and the day following" (Luke 13:33)

Is there not something defiant and challenging about this *Nevertheless of Immortality?* Herod, "that fox," as Jesus called him, tried hard to kill Him before His time to die on the cross, but He knew that He was immortal until His work was done. The time and manner of His death had been planned in a past eternity, and not even a bloodthirsty king could quicken His end. Let Satan, demons, and men do their utmost to thwart Calvary, He knew that He would walk "today, to morrow, and the day following," and then die as

67

decreed. Do we believe that if we live in obedience to the will of God we too are immortal until our course is finished?

"Nevertheless when the Son of man cometh shall he find faith . . . ? (Luke 18:8)

The original is a little more emphatic and explicit—"Shall he find *the* faith?" When Christ returns He will find plenty of faith—faith in heresies, in superstitions, in self-righteousness and self-sufficiency, and, conversely, personal faith in Himself by the few in comparison to those who are iniquitous and apostate. But the question is, will He find "the faith," . . . that is, adherence to the whole body of revealed truth, to " . . . the faith which was once delivered unto the saints" (Jude 3)? Is not this *Nevertheless of Loyalty to the Fundamentals,* scorned even in religious circles today? Apostasy is responsible for the evident spiritual impotence of the church in a world of need. By the time Christ returns, "the faith" will be a very scarce commodity indeed.

"Nevertheless let us go unto him" (John 11:15)

The word, as used here by Jesus, marks an interruption and transition, and indicates a reference to something else. He knew all about the fatal sickness of Lazarus whom He loved, yet He did not hasten to his relief. He said to those who were mourning the death of Lazarus, "I am glad for your sakes that I was not there, to the intent ye may believe"—meaning that His delay was not a denial, even though His friend had died. Thus, there came the *Nevertheless of Glorious Assurance,* and you will see that nothing can defy the Lord of power. Sometimes we are confronted with what seem to be gigantic or impossible tasks, but when, nevertheless, we go to them in the power of Him who conquered death, faith is amply rewarded.

68

"Nevertheless among the chief rulers also many believed on him" (John 12:42)

How the heart of Jesus must have been cheered as some of the chief rulers declared their willing acceptance of Him as their Messiah! In spite of the spiritual blindness of the Jewish nation as a whole, there were those whose eyes were opened to see in Him the One eagerly anticipated, and who manifested the *Nevertheless of Acceptance.* There has always been the remnant who recognize the validity of the spiritual.

"Nevertheless I tell you the truth" (John 16:7)

The emphasis here is on the pronoun, *"I,* who knoweth all."* As the truth, He could not do anything else but tell the truth. What He had told them filled the hearts of the disciples with sorrow, for He spoke of His departure. They were also perplexed by His statement that it was "expedient," or a good thing for Him to leave them. Too often, we cannot see the beneficial purpose in some things God takes from us, and how even the most untoward experiences of life work together for our good. As scholars in His school we have to learn the lessons associated with the *Nevertheless of Expediency.*

"Nevertheless he left not himself without witness" (Acts 14:17)

Paul and Barnabas, in restraining the people of Lystra who wanted to worship them as gods because of their miraculous power, thundered out against the nation's idolatry, utter godlessness, and selfishness, and then declared that even amid such God had not left Himself without witness. Divine goodness was not only manifested in nature, but in the darkest scene there is something to remind the darkest heart of God as the Creator. In our corrupt time, as the shadow of judgment gathers around a world far from God, He has not left Himself without a witness among people in every walk of life. There are still the thousands who have not bowed the knee to Baal, and who are embraced in the *Nevertheless of Testimony.*

"Nevertheless the centurion believed the master and owner of the ship, more than those things which were spoken by Paul" (Acts 27:11)

Perhaps it seemed more natural to trust an expert than a missionary. But Paul had a divine intuition, and so advised against the advice of the owner of the ship. His warning, however, was not accepted and the *Nevertheless of Rejection* resulted in disaster. The centurion in charge of the prisoners, who would not accept the word of a man of faith, must have been humiliated when Paul's prophecy came true. We do not doubt that the centurion showed all due deference to Paul, nevertheless he believed not the apostle, but the master of the ship. He came to learn that God often works contrary to experience.

"Nevertheless we have not used this power; but suffer all things lest we should hinder the gospel of Christ" (I Cor. 9:12)

How noble and sacrificial is this *Nevertheless of Self-denial!* As Jesus never performed a miracle to bring personal relief in time of need, so the apostles were embued with the same spirit. Paul could have taken what was justly due, but he exercised a self-imposed poverty in order that his self-abnegation might make the gospel more effective. In the cause of Christ, it is not a matter of what we can get out of it that counts, but what we can put into it in the shape of self-sacrifice. Later on, Paul has another "nevertheless," proving that he never made gains out of those he ministered to.

70

" . . . nevertheless, being crafty, we caught you with guile" (II Cor. 12:16). The more he spent for them, and loved them, the less those Corinthians seemed to spend on Paul. Yet, with inspired craftiness, he won many of them for his Master.

"Nevertheless God . . . comforteth those that are cast down" (II Cor. 7:6)

In Macedonia Paul found himself troubled on every side, with fightings without and fears within. There was so much to discourage and distress this brave herald of the cross, but he took fresh heart when he saw Titus. Not only was Paul divinely consoled in spite of his trials, but in the coming of Titus, a brother was born for adversity. No matter how black the night, there is always the *Nevertheless of Consolation,* someone whose presence is a balm and benediction.

"Nevertheless I live, yet not I" (Gal. 2:20)

The word as used here makes an antithesis, and is conspicuous as an injunction. Death and life are joined together. Among the paradoxes of our Christian faith there is the most pertinent: Dead yet alive! Crucified yet existent! Are we sharing in this *Nevertheless of Co-Crucifixion and Co-Resurrection?* Are we dead indeed unto sin, and fully alive unto God?

"Nevertheless I am not ashamed . . . " (II Tim. 1:12)

Living in the "Nevertheless what saith the Scripture?" (Gal. 4:30), Paul was never ashamed of, nor apologized for his forthright witness. Remember that at this time, Paul was a prisoner in Rome. He knew there was no release for him, and that as a prisoner he was doomed to die. As the end drew near for him to be offered, the past came up before his mental vision. There were many things in his old life as a persecutor he deeply regretted, but they were all under the blood. He never regretted, however, his sacrificial and faithful ministry as a preacher. He was never ashamed of the gospel of Christ, and could face martyrdom resting on the *Nevertheless of Satisfaction.* "I have fought a good fight."

"Nevertheless the foundation of God standeth sure . . . " (II Tim. 2:19)

Paul could foresee the trials facing the church, and the hurt and damage before her because of apostacy and persecution, but he had no fear as to her continuance. He knew that because she is eternal she is indestructible. Even the gates of hell cannot prevail against her. The *Nevertheless of Safety* here seems to suggest that although many would be shaken by false teaching, yet God's firm foundation would stand immovable. What a bracing "nevertheless" this is for the days of spiritual declension in which we live! The vast majority neglect the church, others deem it to be an outworn institution, and so despise and condemn it. Yet in spite of seeming decay and the hostility of men, His true church stands secure. Individual, material church buildings may vanish and denominations cease to be, but the church of the living God composed of born-anew souls can neither wither nor perish.

"Nevertheless afterward it yieldeth the peaceable fruit of righteousness" (Heb. 12:11)

The writer to the Hebrews tells us that there is a loving purpose behind the discipline of life. "Whom the Lord loveth he chasteneth." Such chastening may come in different ways—the pain of loss, of failure, of disappointment—the keener pain of being slighted by friends, of being misunderstood, and consequently misjudged by them—the sorrows and trials of life. What unspeakable comfort it is to know that

72

Jesus passed this way before us when He lived our life on earth. "He was tested in all points like as we are," and is therefore "able to succour those who are tested." Is it not balm to our soul to remember that He endured the contradiction of sinners against Himself?

Our peril during a season of testing is to dwell unduly upon it and become resentful and bitter of spirit, and thus lose our joy and become powerless for service. We must never forget that all chastening is parental, and for our present and future good. Our all-loving Father has us under His watchful eye, and designs that we should become not only like Him, but also like His beloved Son "who learned obedience by the things which he suffered." While for the moment divine chastening is not joyous but grievous, there is the *Nevertheless of Enrichment*—a spiritual enrichment resulting from submission to the divine will, even when it seeks our highest good through pain.

"Nevertheless we, according to His promise, look for new heavens and a new earth, wherein dwelleth righteousness" (II Peter 3:13)

Presently, as Peter makes clear in the context, we live in an age of scoffers, and of those who walk after their own lusts, and who challenge the promises of Scripture, and make light of its doctrines, particularly that of Christ's return with its consequent bliss for His own and terrible judgment for His foes. Concerned and distressed as we ought to be over the utter abandonment of the world to the lustful pursuit of carnal pleasures, we must face the future undismayed, for Peter gives us the *Nevertheless of Hope*. Things may be dark and distressing today, but God has promised a universe in which righteousness will prevail. The worldling being "without God" is "without hope." But those of us who are Christ's through His atoning work "look beyond this vale of tears to that celestial hill" with glad and grateful assurance. Peter's glorious "nevertheless" keeps us calm and confident amid the chaos, turmoil, and dissolution of things of this world.

"Nevertheless I have somewhat against thee, because thou hast left thy first love" (Rev. 2:4)

In His first letter to the churches, our Lord has some admirable things to say about the church at Ephesus. It was an almost perfect church. It had borne much for His sake. It had manifested superb patience. It had not become weary in well-doing. Yet the Lord had this *Nevertheless of Complaint* against her. She had *left,* (not "lost") her first love—and this was no little thing to fail in, no slight fault. Paul makes it clear that the decay of love is the decay of that without which all other graces are as nothing (I Cor. 13).

After parading the commendable virtues of the church, Christ intervenes with His "nevertheless." No person or church bearing His name is absolutely good or utterly bad. He marks the worst in the best, and the best in the worst and gives credit where it is due. What does He see to commend or condemn in you and me? Has He anything against us as His professed followers? May we so live that He will never have to write this "nevertheless" over our spiritual experience!

74

Theme 8
The Spiritual Depths

Among the 150 psalms forming the Psalter, one of the most remarkable is Psalm 78, proving as it does that its composer was a most unusual historian. Faithful in descriptive details, he reviews the providential dealings of God toward the children of Israel as they journeyed through the wilderness. How he delighted to dwell upon the wonders of that pilgrimage from Egypt to Canaan, when miracles were wrought for the physical welfare of the people almost every step of their passage through desert land! One instance of divine provision for the host is found in the phrase, "[God] . . . gave them drink as out of great depths" (78:15).

This observation emphasizes one aspect of the goodness and power of God; for what the psalmist had in mind was not a mere trickle, which satisfied the thirsty travelers for a little, but a boundless, inexhaustible supply of fresh water. It is this fact that we want to use as an illustration of the infinite supply God has for His pilgrims today. If the supply is limited it is from our side, not from His. We can have as much of God as we desire. Has the wonder, then, of His marvelous fullness flashed upon our minds? Are we to be found drinking out of the great depths?

> Praise to the Holiest in the height,
> And in the depth be praise;
> In all His words most wonderful,
> Most sure in all His ways.

Before we come to examine some of the depths of Scripture, there are two introductory thoughts worthy of emphasis—

75

Superficial Days

What a superficial age ours is! People, alas! are easily satisfied. Small pools suffice for the majority. These are days of flimsy beliefs and behavior; days of flippancy and frivolity, and of a shallow experience. Too many are all show, lacking depth. We have a scarcity of deep characters. Robert Burns, the Scottish poet has a verse which, perhaps, is self-revealing—

> Good Lord, what is man! for as simple as he looks,
> Do but try to develop his hooks and his crooks.
> With his depths and his shallows, his good and his evil,
> All in all, he's a problem must puzzle the Devil.

In our Lord's Parable of the Sower, He spoke of the seed withering away because it had "no depth of earth." How descriptive this is of multitudes today! They do not "dwell deep" to use Jeremiah's words (49:8, 30). We fear that even in Christian circles there is too much superficiality, especially now among some young believers who crave pop-music for hymns, and a very light spiritual fare. But they will never achieve much for the Kingdom unless they launch out into the deeps of the precious things of faith and of the Spirit. The man whose house stood when the floods came was the one who "digged deep" below the sand (Luke 6:48). Job was asked the question by Jehovah—"Hast thou entered into the springs of the sea? or hast thou walked in search of the depth?" (38:16). May we ever be found walking in "search of the depth"—digging, dwelling, drinking, drawing deeply of His bountiful springs!

Satisfying Depths

One sweet thought which emerges from this beautiful Psalm of Pilgrimage is the display of the splendor of divine provision. Imagine Israel crowding round that smitten rock saying, "This cannot last long. The gushing stream will soon dry up." But when they discovered that in spite of the vast quantity they drank, the water still flowed on, glad and grateful surprise possessed their hearts. The spring was inexhaustible, for what the people could see was fed by channels they knew nothing about and could not see. Thus it is with grace! The idea behind the psalmist's allusion to "great depths" is that of striking or boring through rock to the great ocean on which the earth was supposed to rest—great depths are the reservoir of water hidden in the earth. (See Gen. 7:11; Ps. 33:7; Prov. 8:24.)

The refreshing supply, gushing up from earth's innermost storehouses, never ceases to run. Those streams in the desert were so plentiful in quantity because they were miraculous in origin. Torrents, not driblets, came from the rock, and so the psalmist was lost in admiration at the abundance God provided. When Abraham cast out Hagar, the bondwoman, he gave her a bottle of water. When it was exhausted, God gave her a well. Our supplies are never exhausted because their origin and source is God and, being fathomless and boundless, they remain to satisfy the saints in succeeding ages. Giving never impoverishes God, nor does withholding from us enrich Him. The story is told of Archbishop William Temple when he was a student at Rugby. "Are you not," one of the masters asked him in discussing one of his schoolboy essays, "a little out of your depth here?" "Perhaps, sir," was the confident reply, "but I can swim." The waters that flowed from the sanctuary which Ezekiel mentions, commenced as a trickle but became waters deep enough to swim in. Let us, then, think of some of these deep waters, out of our depth altogether, but in which we can swim.

Depth of Life's Experiences

Tennyson, in *The Princess*, wrote of

> Tears, idle tears, I know not what they mean,
> Tears from the depth of some divine despair.

Is this not the sentiment of the psalmist when he penned the words, "Out of the depths have I cried unto thee, O Lord" (130:1)? Who has not with the writer, some time or other, out of the great depth of soul-need cried to heaven? How often we are made to drink of the depth of sorrow, disappointment, or anguish over sin. Paul commended the churches of Macedonia because in spite of their "deep poverty" they were conspicuous for the riches of their liberality (II Cor. 8:1-2). The blind unbelief of the Pharisees caused Jesus to sigh "deeply in his spirit" (Mark 8:13).

David speaks of "deep calling unto deep" (42:7), and from the depths of our human need we must ever draw from the depth of divine grace. In his appraisal of Shakespeare, Coleridge said, "The body and substance of his works came out of the unfathomable depths of his own oceanic mind." But our unfathomable depths are not in ourselves, but in Him who is the boundless source of every precious thing. Our cares, tears, trials, toils, and graves may be some of the depths we plumb, but life's experiences, although adverse, must not sink us in the depths of despair, depression, and doubt. They should send us for spiritual refreshment to the great depths of God's love, grace, and sufficiency. "He led them through the depths" (Ps. 106:9). No matter what deep trials we may encounter, we can constantly drink of the Rock who follows us (I Cor. 10:4). Wordsworth in *Laodamia* says—

> The gods approve
> The depth, and not the tumult of the soul.

Of this we are confident, God our Father approves when in spite of the tumult of the soul, we are found drinking out of the great depths of His provision.

Depths of Satan

Scripture has a triad of passages relative to these satanic depths that Jesus knew something about. "Her guests are in the depths of hell" (Prov. 9:18). " . . . deeper than hell" (Job 11:8). "Which have not known the depths of Satan . . . " (Rev. 2:24). Have we had experience of the depths of Satan that our Lord drank from in those fierce temptations in the wilderness? Saintliness and satanic attacks go together. The more we drink of the great depths of divine grace and power, the greater will be the assaults of Satan. But He who emerged from the depths of Satan more than a conqueror is able to make us sharers of His victory. The only souls He uses to roll back the tides of iniquity in the world are those who have met and conquered the devil in their own lives.

We are exhorted not to be ignorant of the enemy's devices and wiles, and of the terrible blight he causes. General William Booth startled his officers one day, when speaking to them on evangelism, by saying, "I wish I could send you all to hell for a fortnight." What he meant was that if they could live for two weeks amid the groans and moans of the damned in the depths of hell, they would return to earth with a passion for souls. It was said of Dante, that as he moved silently along the street, people would say, "He has seen hell." Knowing of the diabolical purpose of Satan to ruin our beings, corrupt our desires, cripple our testimony, blast our lives, let us drink continuously out of the great depths of Calvary's victory over his dominion. Christ was manifested to destroy the works of the devil, which He did through His death and resurrection. Therefore, as a defeated foe he can be resisted by faith.

Depths of Scripture

Having reached the period of widespread apostacy predicted in the New Testament, we are not surprised at the way the Bible is being treated in religious circles. Its inspiration is denied; its authenticity, ridiculed; its authority, despised. Historical persons and events are treated as myths. Facts are dealt with as fiction. Of itself, the Bible says, "Every word of

God is true," but many theologians scorn such a claim. By the time he takes out of the Word all the supposed myths, legends, discrepancies, inconsistencies, suppositions, and errors, the Modernist has little left save the covers. How refreshing and consoling it is to turn from the ramblings of apostates to the psalmist's wonderful estimation of God's works and words: "O Lord, how great are thy works, and thy thoughts are very deep" (92:5).

Those of us who love and revere Scripture, deeming it to be the divine revelation of God, are yet sometimes guilty of a light, cursory, casual, and superficial reading of it. We do not seem to have the time or inclination to explore its sublime depths. Scripture is not like the shallow, trashy literature of today—too muddy and polluted to offer a refreshing draught for thirsty minds. Within Holy Writ are unfathomable depths we can never plumb, truths and thoughts too high for us to reach. But all we need to know, the Holy Spirit is willing to show us. Further, the more immersed we become in its teachings, the more we are known as "a people of a deeper speech" (Isa. 33:19). The Spirit who searcheth the deep things of God is with us to reveal the deep and secret things (Dan. 2:22; I Cor. 2:10).

Scripture is not a set of petty maxims. It has no surface views of God, man, sin, and judgment. Its truths, themes, and doctrines are the deepest to engage the greatest intellect ever made. Here is knowledge too high for man to attain (Ps. 139:6).

> Here may the wretched sons of want
>> Exhaustless riches find;
> Riches above that earth can grant,
>> And lasting as the mind.

We believe the Bible to be the Word of God, not merely containing it, but His Word, in its entirety, and that "*all* Scripture is given by inspiration of God." The Greek word for "inspiration" means "God-breathed," the breath of God

80

being used as a symbol of His power as He acted upon those who wrote the Bible, guiding them as to what they should write or speak. It is a significant commentary on the doctrine of inspiration in any age of the church, that the nearer one lives after the pattern of the holy men who wrote the Bible, the more devoutly one clings to their view of inspiration (I Cor. 2:13; II Tim. 3:16). Without doubt—

> A glory gilds the sacred page,
>> Majestic, like the sea:
> It gives a light to every age;
>> It gives, and borrows none.

> The Hand that gave it still supplies
>> The gracious light and heat:
> Its truths upon the nations rise:
>> They rise, but never set.

Depths of Deity

When we come to the blessed Trinity, we reach an ocean that is boundless in extent and fathomless in depth, for in each Person "the fulness of the Godhead bodily" can be found (Col. 2:9). It was F. W. Faber who taught the church to sing—

> My God, how wonderful Thou art!
> Thy majesty how bright;
> How beautiful Thy mercy-seat
> In depths of burning light!

Let us see if we can descend into the luminous depths of Deity by separating the three members of the Godhead.

The Grace of God

> Depth of mercy! can there be
> Mercy still reserved for me?

Yes, such a depth can never be exhausted. Micah tells us that God is able to cast all our sins into the depths of the sea of His forgetfulness (7:19). In this depth, our sins are beyond the reach of man or devil. "Thy judgments are a great deep" (Ps. 36:6), and God can cast your sin and mine into the depth of the sea, because sin was deeply embedded in the sacred body of Jesus at Calvary where He bore our judgment and drank the bitter cup for us. In some mysterious way He was made to drink of the wrath of a righteous God.

> None of the ransomed ever knew,
> How deep were the waters crossed

and He plunged into them for our sake, and by His stripes we are healed. At the cross, the Rock was struck, and out of its riven side streamed oceans of grace and forgiveness. Are we experiencing the deep and ever-deepening grace of God? It would seem as if for many the experience of His saving power is so shallow that they merely dip a toe in the lake, when they should be swimming in the mighty sea. With the woman of Samaria they say, "The well is deep and I have nothing to draw with." But they can draw out of the never-failing depths if only they are willing to obey and surrender. The full purpose of grace, however, is not completed when the Lord rescues us from the depths of sin. Through His matchless, boundless grace, we are to be raised to the heights of glory. "I will bring my people again from the depths of the sea" (Ps. 68:22). The sea can be used as a type of our restless, agitated world, and out of its depth of sin and sorrow we are to be caught up to meet the Lord in the air. Even the actual sea will give up its Christian dead.

The Love of Jesus

What a fathomless ocean we have in Jesus who came as the personification and revelation of the love of God for a world of sinners lost, and ruined by the Fall! No satanic depth can

82

separate the blood-washed from such inexhaustible love (Rom. 8:38-39). Paul prays that those who have Christ deep in their hearts by faith may comprehend all the dimensions of the love of Christ—its breadth, length, depth, and height. Then he has this paradox, " . . . to know the love of Christ which passeth knowledge" (Eph. 3:17-19). How can you know the unknowable? O the depths of the riches of divine love!

> O Love, that wilt not let me go,
> I rest my weary soul in Thee;
> I give Thee back the life I owe,
> That in Thine ocean depths its flow
> May richer, fuller be.

Not only is the Saviour's love a bottomless abyss, but all His words, works, and ways spring from the depths of His deity, and well up out of the vast reservoir of His untainted holiness. We may drain a vessel of its contents, but we can never exhaust the hidden springs from which the vessel is filled. Samuel Rutherford expressed it thus, "How little of the sea can a child carry in his hand? As little as I am able to take away of my great Sea, my boundless and running over Christ Jesus." May we ever be found drinking deeply of His love, His self-abnegation, His sacrifice, His glory and majesty!

> Oh, the deep, deep love of Jesus,
> Vast, unmeasured, boundless, free;
> Rolling as a mighty ocean
> In its fullness over me.
> Underneath me, all around me,
> Is the current of Thy love;
> Leading onward, leading homeward,
> To my glorious rest above.

The Ministry of the Spirit

Paul indicated something of the inexhaustible depths in

the sacred Third Person of the blessed Trinity when he said, "But be filled with the Spirit" (Eph. 5:18). What a limitless ocean He is! In Scripture, water is a type of the refreshing ministry of the Holy Spirit; so when Ezekiel wrote of a river that could not be passed over, waters constantly rising, waters to swim in, he gave us a fitting illustration of the fullness of the Spirit (47:5). Then the prophet asked the pointed question, "Son of man, hast thou seen this?" Have we experienced the fullness of the blessing of the gospel of Christ the Spirit can make possible? Because He is the reservoir of power, limitless in supply He does not want us to be content with water to our ankles, or up to our knees and loins. His purpose is to fill us with His fullness. But have we an ever-increasing thirst for the rivers of living water to be found in Him? Listen to Him as He says, "Drink abundantly, My friends." In one of his hymns on *The Holy Spirit*, Charles Wesley writes,

> God, through Himself, we then shall know
> If Thou within us shine;
> And sound, with all the saints below
> The depths of love divine.

Theme 9
The Aspects of Fear

Cervantes, the fifteenth century novelist, tells us that "fear has many eyes." Wordsworth, the eighteenth century poet, wrote—

> Fear hath a hundred eyes, that all agree
> To plague her beating heart.

The simile of several eyes is but another way of describing the quantity of fears that plague the human heart. But that there is victory from all fettering fears is proclaimed by David, "I sought the Lord, and he heard me, and delivered me from all my fears" (34:4). The setting of this psalm gives a preacher sufficient material for a sermon on cowards. Pursued by King Saul, David was smitten with fear. Then we read that "sore afraid of Achish," he pretended he was mad while in the presence of the Philistine king (I Sam. 21:12-13). But in the psalm, David tells us how he turned to God when at a dead end, and He emancipated him from the fear of both Saul and Achish. A peculiarity of the psalm is the labor the author bestowed upon it, for in the Hebrew its twenty-two verses are cast in alphabetical order, and uses fear in five different ways in four of its verses (34:4, 7, 9, 11). Four different meanings are likewise given of the word:

Terror

It is this agitated emotion that we find in passages like "Fear and dread shall fall upon them" (Exod. 15:16). "Then the men feared the Lord exceedingly" (Jonah 1:16). This

85

idea of terror can be used in a wrong way, as, for instance, when we read that the shepherds were sore afraid, and that the angels told them not to fear (Luke 2:10). Such a terror-stricken condition is unhealthy, and robs the soul of peace, trust, confidence, and power. But *terror* is also used in a right way. We are not to be "highminded, but fear" (Rom. 11:20). We must "serve God acceptably with all reverence and fear" (Heb. 4:1; 12:28).

Reverence

Several times the word *fear* implies reverence of soul—a reverential trust with hatred of evil. This is filial fear, the holy feelings of the renewed heart toward God. "The fear of the Lord" is a common phrase used often (Ps. 111:10; Prov. 3:7; 8:13, etc.). Such a fear produces trust, loathing of sin, reverent submission to divine providences, and a ready obedience to all God's gracious commands. It also bids us keep our heart tender, our soul safe, and our life continuously adjusted to the divine will.

Timidity

In writing to young Timothy as he commenced his ministry as an evangelist, Paul reminded him that God had not given him "the spirit of fear," but of "power" (II Tim. 1:7). The veteran preacher counsels the young man just beginning to preach to be firm, courageous, and not timid or hesitant in the face of foes. He must never be guilty of drawing back, but launch out into the deep, and thus fully commit himself to the cause of Christ.

Caution

Noah, we read, "moved with fear" (Heb. 11:7), went on building the ark. In spite of the ridicule and unbelief of the

86

multitude to be drowned by the Flood, Noah went on quietly, cautiously with his God-given task. Christ's intercessions were heard of God "in that he feared" (Heb. 5:7). Daily, it was His concern to be cautious as to the accomplishment of God's will. When the mob threatened Paul's life, the captain dealt with the unruly crowd in a cautious, tactful manner. The Latin word for "caution"—*lavere*—means "to be on one's guard." *Cautious,* says Webster, implies "attention to examine probable effects and consequences of acts so as to avoid danger."

Idle Fears

Aesop says that we might—"better die once for all than to live in continual fear." But the tragedy is that the majority of our fears are imaginary. We live in dread of experiences that never come to pass. The psalmist describes those who were in "great fear, where no fear was" (Ps. 53:5). How foolish it is to be troubled over troubles that never appear, and to worry over things that never happen! Never trouble trouble, till trouble troubles you, is sound advice. How useless it is to try to cross bridges before we come to them! The good Lord deliver us from the fear of what may overtake us, and give us grace to live in the present, even moment by moment, knowing that the future is His concern.

> Lord, for tomorrow, and its needs
> I do not pray:
> But keep me, guide me, hold me, Lord,
> Just for today.

Those heartbroken women at the tomb of Jesus entertained an idle fear when they asked, "Who shall roll us away the stone from the door of the sepulchre?" But when they looked, the stone was out of its groove, the door was wide open, and an angel was seated on what the women had feared. A physician, who was also something of a psychologist, and who knew that many of his patients made themselves ill by worrying over the future, displayed a large motto in his consulting room for all to see and read—

DON'T WORRY,
IT MAY NOT HAPPEN

If we truly believe that our times are in the Lord's hands, then we also believe He knows all about the future and will suffer no trial to overtake us without His permission. And what He allows, no matter how grievous, is for our good and His glory.

Ye fearful saints, fresh courage take;
The clouds ye so much dread
Are big with mercy, and shall break
In blessings on your head.

Fear of Things

This aspect is more tangible than the one just considered in that we know that inevitable dreaded consequences are associated with certain experiences. Scripture gives us many instances of the "hundred eyes" of fear.

Fear of Physical and Material Loss

Cried Job, "For the thing which I greatly fear is come upon me" (3:25). The loss of work, of money, of health, are foreseen by many and bring despair. But if we are God's children, why worry in the day of adversity? Have we not the promise about there being no want to them who fear Him (Ps. 34:9-10)?

Fear of Opposition and Hatred of Others

Because of His stern condemnation of the Pharisees, Jesus

knew that animosity would accrue, but He had no fear, for in spite of demons and men, He finished His course. Our allegiance to Him, and spirituality of life are bound to arouse the antagonism of a godless world, but we have nothing to fear for He will preserve our life from the enemy (Ps. 64:1). The Angel of the Lord is encamped near us, and is, therefore, at hand to deliver us when assailed (Ps. 34:7).

Fear of Calamities

Out on those storm-tossed waves, thinking they would perish any moment, the disciples might have been justifiably afraid, but Jesus rebuked them, "Why are ye so fearful, O ye of little faith?" They should not have been alarmed, seeing "the Master of ocean, and earth, and sky" was in their boat. Faith and fear cannot live together. When the storms of life are raging, if Jesus is at the helm of your little craft, then all will be well.

Fear of Persecution and Death

It must have seemed hard for the disciples to accept the fiat of Jesus, "Fear not them which kill the body" (Matt. 10:28). He knew that His own body would be killed, but He had no fear. He could reecho the declaration of the psalmist, "I will not fear what flesh can do unto me" (Ps. 56:4). Similar defiance can be ours, if we believe that God is ever at hand to protect us from our foes. With boldness we can say, "The Lord is my helper" (Heb. 13:6).

Fear of National and Political Changes

Describing the end-time period of Gentile history Jesus said that, "Men's hearts [would fail] them for fear" (Luke 21:26). Are we not living in this predicted fear-driven world? Whether we think of statesmen and rulers or industrialists and workers or parents and children, hearts are possessed by fear as to the condition of human society. But for those who rest in their omnipotent Lord, there is the confidence that though the earth be removed they need not fear (Ps. 46:2). They have a courage born of truth, and a grace of fearlessness which springs from the revelation of God's almightiness. Such courage is the helm that keeps the soul according to the divine compass, and makes us safe regardless of adverse events.

Fear of Man

Solomon reminds us that "the fear of man bringeth a snare" (Prov. 29:25). Such a phase of fear is common to saint and sinner alike. It was characteristic of many in the New Testament as well. There were those Galileans who came to believe in the fearless Christ—"Howbeit no man spake openly of him for fear of the Jews" (John 7:13). Joseph of Arithmathea, who sacrificed his new tomb for the burial of Jesus, was "a disciple . . . , but secretly for fear of the Jews" (John 19:38). After the resurrection, "the disciples were assembled together for fear of the Jews" (John 20:19). The psalmist could say, "Whom shall I fear . . . of whom shall I be afraid?" (Ps. 27:1). Alas! many are secret disciples for fear of what the worldly minded around them may say. They have the light, but keep it under a bushel. Such fear is a sign of a craven, cowardly heart. But God is able to impart courage, or nerve which enables us to do His bidding in spite of ridicule and contempt. As they looked upon John Knox after his death, and passed by his coffin, people said, "There's the face that never feared the face of man." If we fear God we have no reason to be afraid of any man.

When professed believers realize their obligations of being more pronounced in their witness and more committed to the Lord, but withhold their full allegiance because of the fear that this will interfere with business prospects, they are guilty of keeping back part of the price. When a Christian feels he should be separated from worldly pleasures and pursuits, but fears to make the break in case he is laughed at or snubbed for a seeming holier-than-thou-attitude, then his fear of man is a snare. Peter was afraid to own His Lord in the hour of His suffering, but Pentecost made all the difference, for on that historic day he so condemned the Jews with the crime of history that as they witnessed his boldness they marveled. No wonder they were amazed, knowing of his previous denial of Jesus. There are others who are almost persuaded to become Christians, but cowardice keeps them back from surrendering to Christ. They are afraid of the jeers they may receive, and so, lacking the courage of their convictions, the fear of man keeps them in the peril of dying without the Saviour.

Slavish Fear of God

Scripture makes it clear that there are wrong ways, as well as right ways, of fearing God. Job confessed, "Therefore am I troubled at his presence, when I consider, I am afraid of him" (23:15). But Paul reminds us that we "have not received the spirit of bondage again to fear" (Rom. 8:15). When the psalmist said, "But there is forgiveness with thee, that thou mayest be feared," he referred to a holy, reverential fear—the mark of one whose many sins have been forgiven. Filial fear of God is a duty, and causes us to shrink from sin, keeps us from straying, and enables us to avoid all that is offensive to our Holy Father. Servile fear, or dread of God, drives us from Him, as it did our first parents. But this is not the sort of fear that can make us holy. This aspect of fear springs from selfishness.

Often dread of God is based on ignorance of God's nature and a wrong conception of His character. He is not a God with a mailed fist, a tyrant, a despot, a hard Being bent on the vengeance and destruction of sinners. Once we receive the

Spirit of adoption we cry, "Abba, Father!" What a glorious change from cowering before Him! In his exaltation of the Saviour, after the birth of his son, Zacharias exclaimed, " . . . that we being delivered out of the hand of our enemies might serve him without fear" (Luke 1:74). Here the concept of dread is meant, for the saints must ever serve the Lord with reverence. Such fear is the beginning of wisdom. Are you afraid of God? "I remembered God and was troubled," the psalmist confessed. Sinners are half-way on the road to salvation if they are afraid, or troubled, as they remember the thrice Holy One. But such fettering fear vanishes when they come to know Him as the God of love who gave His only begotten Son for their salvation. This loving, gracious God is our God for ever and ever.

> Fear Him, ye saints, and you will then
> Have nothing else to fear;
> Make you His service your delight,
> Your wants shall be His care.

Fear of Death

Doubtless this is the most common aspect of fear. Sometimes even true believers are afraid to die and fail to fear the grave as little as they do their bed. The writer of Hebrews speaks of those "who through fear of death were all their lifetime subject to bondage" (2:15). Death, of course, is the greatest fact of life. As soon as we are born we start our journey to God's green acre, but whether death is a friend or a foe depends upon our relationship to God. Sinners are afraid to die, and have good reason to be. Those who are not ready, through grace, to die, have cause to dread the grave. Conscience makes cowards of many, who blatantly rejected God, when they come to the swelling of Jordan.

Christ, through death, destroyed him who had the power of death. Willingly, He tasted death for every man, and

92

robbed it of its sting (I Cor. 15:35; Heb. 2:9, 14). Why, then, fear man's last enemy since the sting is gone? Our relationship to Christ determines our attitude to death. To those who live and die without Him as Saviour, death is a terrible foe ushering them into a Christless eternity. But if He has been received as "the resurrection and the life," then death is a kind friend leading us into the presence of Him who is alive forevermore.

> I fear no foe, with Thee at hand to bless;
> Ills have no weight, and tears no bitterness:
> Where is death's sting? Where, grave thy victory?
> I triumph still, if Thou abide with me.

Fear of Hell

It was a sermon on hell that convicted the renowned missionary, Mary Slessor, of her sin and led her to accept Christ as her Saviour. It is to be regretted that this solemn truth of Scripture is seldom preached today. Yet the fear of hell is deep and real in many hearts. Would that we could have more of such fear in these materialistic days! How dare we be silent about warning the lost of "the blackness of darkness for ever," when we have Scriptures like these? "Fear him which is able to destroy soul and body into hell" (Matt. 10:28). "The rich man also died . . . in hell . . . in torments" (Luke 26:22-23). "But a certain fearful looking for of judgment and of fiery indignation" (Heb. 10:27). "It is a fearful thing to fall into the hands of the living God" (Heb. 10:31). "But the fearful . . . shall have their part in the lake which burneth with fire and brimstone: which is the second death" (Rev. 21:8). "The wicked shall be turned into hell, and all the nations that forget God" (Ps. 9:17).

Men may try to do away with future judgment, or treat hell in a jocular manner, but because it was a grim reality to Jesus, and He died to save sinners from such a doomed, eternal abode, it is a subject that should be preached with all the compassion of the Saviour. This fear of hell is tormenting, but perfect love can cast out such fear (I John 4:18). Submission to divine claims removes all fear of perdition. "There is therefore now no condemnation to them which are in Christ Jesus" (Rom. 8:1). Faith kills fear. Trust casts out terror. After seeking the Lord, David was delivered from *all* his fears (Ps. 34:4), even the fear of death for although he would have to walk through death's dark vale, he would fear no evil. Through grace, may our song be—

> The fear of hell has gone forever,
>   No more to cause my heart to grieve.
> There is a place, I do believe,
>   In heaven for me, beyond the river.

Theme 10
The Features of Depression

Florence Nightingale, The Lady of the Lamp, tells how on her way to the Crimean War she heard from the sailors a weird story of birds with black wings, and blue breasts that flew over the Black Sea during stormy weather. Sometimes they perched on the masts of the ship, but they never were caught. On dark nights they would go to Mohammedan grave-yards and roost among the green boughs of the cyprus trees, mingling their doleful notes with the sighing of the wind, making thereby weird, eerie sounds. Moslems declared that the spirits of the wicked lived in the birds and that the sorrowful notes were the wailing of the dead.

To most lives, these birds with their black wings and blue breasts come, and we hardly know from whence they come. They are hard to capture and destroy, and almost turn hearts to the cemetery. Sad, heavy-hearted, we are not able to define the burdens depressing us. In other words, fits of depression, despondency, melancholy overtake us and we have "the blues"—a colloquial expression for deep despondency and depression of spirit. It is said that "blues" is a contraction of "Blue Devil," or an evil demon. In the opening verses of Psalm 77, it would seem as if the writer knew all about "the blues," and also their radical cure. Read the first nine verses and you can hear the flutter of a whole flock of those birds with their black wings. It would seem as if God allowed the author of the psalm to have "the blues" in order that he might give us a divine analysis of his state of mind. Having diagnosed the disease, he gives the cure—how to pluck the feathers out of the black wings of the blue-breasted birds symbolizing a melancholy frame of mind and despondency of heart.

The more we read the Bible the more fascinated we are by its relevance to human life. In a most impressive way it covers the whole gamut of feelings and emotions common to mankind and takes account of human frailties. For instance, some of the outstanding characters are portrayed as being subject to spiritual depression, heaviness, and dejection. As C. Ernest Tatham puts it,

> One might think of some of God's picked servants of old, men whose names come down the centuries perfumed with Heaven's aroma and who have affected the lives of myriads for blessing. We are not to think of these as sort of demi-gods or even supermen, but rather that they themselves were compassed about with infirmity, men of like passions with us. In spite of their accomplishments for God and His glory, they were quite imperfect vessels.

Biblical Illustration of Depression

Many of the best men of the Bible, because of their periodic lapses into "the blues," reveal that they were only men at the best. They were touched with the feeling of our infirmities.

Take Moses

This outstanding figure of the Old Testament, a giant among men, the great lawgiver and instrument of divine miraculous power, surely knew nothing about gloominess or despondency. Such a friend and servant of God must have had a continuous mountaintop experience, and no downcast valley. But think of the complaint he poured into the ears of God when he succumbed to the feeling of despair, "Wherefore hast thou afflicted thy servant? And wherefore have I not found favor in thy sight, that thou layest the burden of all this people upon me. . . . I am not able to bear all this people alone, because it is too heavy for me" (Num. 11:11, 14).

Men of lesser grit would have fainted under such a burden long before Moses did. In his downcast frame of mind, he momentarily forgot that it was Jehovah who had been bearing the multitude of murmuring Israelites for so long. Looking at the horde of complainers and taking his eye off God, Moses gave way to the feeling of discouragement. Often excessive labor results in a wearied body, exhausted frame, and a tired brain. Such a condition can rob the harp of the sweet music of joy. If one has had extra strain in caring for and nursing others, with all that this entails in loss of regular hours, irregular meals, and loss of sleep, it is not to be marveled at if the nerves become overstrung and a feeling of dolefulness ensues. Ian Maclaren, the Scottish novelist loved to use the bright motto—"Be kind. Everyone is fighting a hard battle." Those who are hard-pressed need all the sympathy we can offer.

Take Elijah

The stern, rugged figure of this prophet dominates the theocratic period of Israel's history. What a stalwart defender of faith in Jehovah he was! Solitary yet brave, he stood alone, and when he called down fire to consume the sacrifice, 850 defiant priests saw the nation forced to its knees sobbing, "The Lord, he is the God; the Lord, he is the God." We would have expected such a champion to follow up such a tremendous conquest with a terrible onslaught upon the hosts of evil. But the physical exhaustion of building an altar, dividing the bullock, running miles, and the psychological tension of his confrontation with the maniacal priests of Baal, were too much even for this strong, fearless prophet, and so we see him plunging into the deepest valley of reactionary melancholy and depression.

After Carmel there came the juniper experience, with its reaction to the contest with the priests of Baal, and Elijah's yielding to the feelings of despair. Sitting under the tree with dejected countenance, he mournfully laments, "O Lord take away my life; for I am not better than my fathers." While on the mountain, defying the godless priests, he spoke about "Jehovah, God of Israel." Now under, the tree of despondency, he laments, "I, even I only." After his life had been so remarkably used of God, he now begs Him to take away his life; yet he was afraid that Jezebel might oblige instead. He was defiant on Mount Carmel, yet he ran away from the threat of an evil-minded woman. How would you react in similar circumstances?

Take David

The Psalms are full of sighs, moans, and laments. Perhaps it is because of what they have to say about depression and melancholy feelings that we love them. How true to life they are! A depressed age like ours has need to face the question— "Why art thou cast down?" David not only wrote about spiritual despondency, he experienced it. From the time he was a shepherd-lad when he tackled and killed wild beasts attempting to destroy his father's sheep and slew Goliath the Philistine giant, noble exploits had been his. Forced to flee because of Saul's jealousy, God covered David's head in the day of battle, and was his shield. All plots against him failed.

But even such a warrior experienced that human endurance has its limitations, and one day he failed to see Him who is invisible, and who was able to undertake for him to the end. So he dejectedly moaned and mourned, "I shall now perish one day by the hand of Saul: there is nothing better for me than that I should speedily escape into the land of the Philistines; and Saul shall despair of me to seek me any more

98

in any coast of Israel: so shall I escape out of his hand"
(I Sam. 27:1).

A quaint writer says of Psalms 42 and 43, which are credited to David and are one in style and sentiment, that in
them, "David is chiding David out of the dumps." As can be
seen, these two doleful psalms form a soliloquy, which means
a person talking to himself about himself. Tossed and ruffled
within his soul and with turbulent waves destroying his inner
peace, David asks himself why he is in such a dark, sad state.
"Why art thou cast down, O my soul?" There was no reason
why he should be disquieted within for he had a thirst for
God and was the recipient of His loving-kindness (42:1).
Robert Louis Stevenson once wrote, "The world is so full of
a number of things, I'm sure we should all be as happy as
kings." But David, although a king, was not happy.

Do not these two psalms fully express the frequent feeling
of many, and should we not, like David, seek to chide ourselves out of a fit of depression? For nothing is so detrimental to health and happiness as unrelieved despondency and
downheartedness. This is the state of mind which Shakespeare could describe only as "the dumps, so dull and
dreary." Three times over David asks himself the reason for
the melancholy emotion surging within his soul. Twice he
asked in vain, for trouble and anxiety came rolling back in
spite of a moment's respite, but the third time the answer
came in the form of triumph—"I shall yet praise him, who is
the health of my countenance."

Take John the Baptist

This Elijah-like prophet that Jesus so highly commended
exercised a remarkable ministry as the forerunner of Him
whom he acclaimed as "the Lamb of God who taketh away
the sin of the world." Although he lived and labored in the
desert, he gathered a great congregation in his wilderness
habitat. (Modernistic preachers turn a congregation *into* a

wilderness. Giving stones instead of bread, they empty churches of hungry souls.)

The Baptist's magnanimity is seen when Jesus entered His public ministry, and John's task as the forerunner was ended—"He must increase but I must decrease." Because of his fearless preaching on sin and repentance, the Baptist found himself in prison, and it seemed as if, for the time being, all his hopes of the establishment of the Kingdom he had taught were fast disappearing. So he dispatched two of his disciples to Jesus with the question, "Art thou he that should come, or look we for another?" What a doubtful question to ask, especially as John himself had introduced Jesus as the Lamb who had come into the world to die for sin!

Mystified, perplexed, downcast, and depressed, and sensing the brutal death before him, this greatest of all the prophets (Matt. 11:11), succumbed to a bout of dejection. There has only been one perfect Servant of God, who, even in the face of bitterest opposition, never gave way to gloom and despair. It is the Saviour of whom Isaiah prophesied, "He shall not fail nor be discouraged" (42:4). This was the One who, facing His dejected disciples, could say, "Be of good cheer; I have overcome the world." Our victory over all forms of depression is found in meditating on Him whose blessed life was a joyous one throughout—"For consider him that endured such contradiction of sinners against himself, lest ye be wearied and faint in your minds" (Heb. 12:3). The secret of His freedom from inner disturbed emotions that result in despair was His constant, unbroken fellowship with His Father and the anticipation of the joy set before Him. Therein lies our victory as well. May we covet the blessing the Lord gave to the church at Ephesus, "for my name's sake [thou] hast laboured, and hast not fainted" (Rev. 2:3).

Various Causes of Depression

The saintliest of men often find themselves in the Cave of

100

Despair or the Slough of Despond. It is the common lot of all to sit at some time or other beneath the willow tree. Solomon reminds us that "man is born to trouble, as the sparks fly upward." We serve a God, however, who is never cast down or weary, and who offers Himself as the "lifter up of [our] head." Satan, sin, and circumstances are responsible for dolefulness, but Jesus is able to relieve all who are oppressed, and depressed, of the devil (Acts 10:38). What, then, are some of the reasons for human disquietude and dispirited feelings?

Impaired Health

Paul knew something of this for he had a thorn in the flesh which caused him pain. Whatever this infirmity of the flesh was, the apostle had to endure it constantly, because its removal was denied even though he prayed that it might be. The more longstanding an ailment, the more it makes inroads upon our peace of mind. Countless numbers of God's children are subject to physical disabilities which He does not remove—a fact to bear in mind in these days of professed healers of all diseases. Strong, healthy, vigorous men often fail to understand the depressing influence of feeble health and how the spirit droops under the weight of such a burden, and of how lack of physical vitality produces a melancholy frame of mind.

If we are hale and hearty we should strive to help by our sincere sympathy those weighted down by suffering. "We then that are strong ought to bear the infirmities of the weak." If we are carefree and able to sing for joy, let us not forget the moan of the afflicted. But if bodily aches and pains are yours and shadow your spirit somewhat, take heart from the counsel of God, and hope in God, who is the health of your countenance. May we ever remember those who, because of their infirmities, are not able to travel to God's house, and may we visit them in their affliction!

Morbid Desire for Sorrow

While it may sound somewhat paradoxical, yet it would seem as if some people are not happy unless they are unhappy. The psalmist sighed, "my soul refused to be comforted" (Ps. 77:2). Although, in the day of his trouble, he sought the God of Comfort, yet he did not receive comfort because he did not desire it. He preferred his discomfort, sorrow, and despondency to the peace of God. Doubtless you have met those who are not content unless they are miserable and depressed. They somehow hug their grief, and glory in their sorrow, and attract to the windows the birds with the black wings and feed them instead of starving the doleful creatures. Like Rachel of old they refuse to be comforted. They have the unhappy knack of looking on the dark side and of living in the shadows. When you urge them to look on the bright side, they lament that there is not a bright side. Well, grace can be theirs to polish up the dark side they seem to prefer.

It is inevitable that all of us will have sorrow of some sort or other, but let us not sin against the divine Comforter by refusing His consolations. We speak about "getting over" sorrow. Somehow we dislike the term. What is better is "getting into" the trials of life to find right in the heart of them the dearest of all friends—the Man of Sorrows Himself. It is only thus that we are preserved from the despondent aspect of grief, and learn that—

> Not a shaft can hit,
> Till the God of love sees fit.

When dear ones are removed there is the tendency to nurse our sorrow, and linger in the valley of weeping until we become pathetic and burdensome. Tears continue to be our meat day and night, and the clouds never vanish from our heart. We sigh and moan, as if no one else had ever lost a loved one. Our gloom is never alleviated. Are we not guilty of

102

the sin of selfishness when we weep and wail as if we were alone in our sorrow?

A Complaining Spirit

The more we complain, the more cause we have for complaining, and a disgruntled heart is never a glad one. The psalmist said, "I complained, and my spirit was overwhelmed" (Ps. 77:3). The prophet anticipates the time when there will be "no complaining in our streets." Alas! today our streets are full of grousers and grumblers. Nothing others can do ever pleases them. They complain about their food, or the weather, or their circumstances. How such mournful murmurers need the spirit of the old lady who had only two teeth, but who was grateful that one tooth was opposite the other, so that she was able to bite! The squid is a kind of cuttle fish that blackens the water about it so that it can hide itself in it. Not only does it shut out its own vision, it obscures the vision of others as well. Just so, the complaining spirit darkens the life and robs the heart of sunshine around.

Insomnia, or Sleeplessness

This black-winged bird hovers over many a bed, especially in these days of pressures. Too often we seek relief in drug and drink addiction. "Thou holdest mine eyes waking" (Ps. 77:4). If God prevents sleep, as He did in the case of King Ahasuerus, it is for a beneficial purpose. But unnecessary worry, despondency, and melancholy exact a sad toll in sleepless nights; and loss of "care-charming sleep, thou easer of all woes," makes it difficult for anyone to be cheerful. Tossing and turning, the sleepless one may rise and flood the dark room with light, but there is a darkness of mind that sleeplessness only accentuates. Because the psalmist blamed God for the darkness, inner darkness became denser.

Often the saints of God, who have long waking periods, do

103

not suffer temperamentally or physically because they spend the sleepless hours in meditation, worship, and communion with Him who neither slumbers nor sleeps. Frances Ridley Havergal, a constant sufferer, left it on record that some of the sweetest hours of her life were the nights of sleeplessness when her heart was awake to God, and her thoughts were filled with praise. Yes, God is able to give to His beloved sleep, but happy are those who can turn restlessness into restfulness, and whose heart reposes in God amid the shadows of night. If, through our own sin or folly, sleep deserts us, then despondency continues through the day that follows.

Ours should be the experience of the psalmist when he reminds us, "I call to remembrance my song in the *night:* I commune with my own heart" (Ps. 77:6). Instead of a sigh during sleepless hours there was a song as he remembered God's past goodness. How victorious we are when we are able to sing songs in the night! Is it not true that sorrow's crown of sorrow is the remembrance of happier things? "Son, remember!" was the solemn word given to the rich man in hell, and the memory of what he might have been and done was a flame tormenting him. Further, there are many who were once like nightingales, filling the air with music, but who now screech like owls and are so doleful. The greater the delight, the more intense the depression when the delight vanishes.

Unfaithfulness of Others

If it be true that David wrote Psalms 42 and 43 at the time of the rebellion of his favorite son, Absalom, then we can understand the cause of his darkened soul. The king was an exile on the east of Jordan, fleeing from his head-strong son, and such a sudden, disappointing crisis broke the father's heart. His depth of despair was as a sword in his bones (Ps. 42:10). Paul also was a lonely man, and this loneliness was intensified by friends who acted unfriendly. There are allu-

104

sions in his Letters to unfaithful companions, for instance, Demas who forsook him. The feeling of sadness and gloom these unworthy partners caused him is poignant—"All that are in Asia turned away from me." "All forsake me." "I was left alone in Athens." Is your heart heavy because friends have proved false? Deceived, are you dejected? Well, do not allow your despondency to deepen into contempt. Dispirited and forsaken though you may be, perhaps while you are sighing God is preparing a still better friend for you.

Mysterious Providences

In a remarkable way David personified his sorrow when he said, "My tears have been my meat day and night, while they continually say unto me, Where is thy God?" (42:3). Seeing all His waves and billows had gone over him (42:7), he found himself cast down because of the apparent inactivity of God to help him. Had He, as his Rock, forgotten him in the hour of deep need? At Calvary, we have an echo of the *whys* of this psalm, in the divine *why*—"My God, my God, why hast thou forsaken me?" Often we find ourselves in a state of gloom and despair because of God's seeming indifference not only to some of the glaring sins and injustices in human society but also to personal problems. Yet He is always in the shadows planning and working out His purposes.

Personal Sin

Multitudes are doleful, disconsolate, and despondent because of their iniquitous state. They are not right with God; they are not ready to meet Him in eternity; and they are depressed—and have every cause to be. Would that they would become so distressed and depressed over their sins that the peril of dying would drive them more speedily to their only refuge—the Fountain at Calvary opened for sin and uncleanness! Or, it may be that you have experienced the joy

105

that came with your salvation from sin's penalty and thralldom, but now you have lost that joy, and find yourself sharing the despair of the prodigal son, "When I remember these
things, I pour out my soul in me," and as you think of the
past, and how you basked in the sunshine of His presence,
you pour out your soul in sighs and moans. "Oh, that I were
as in months past" (Job 29:2). What else can you expect but
remorse and unhappiness of heart if you are not walking in
the light as He is in the light? Believe with David, that God is
able to restore unto you the joy of His salvation.

Advancing Age

Many experience that the evening-tide of life brings shadows and heart-grief. Youth is the time of smiles and sunshine,
as it ought to be; but old age is a tragedy to many who live
alone. With time on their hands they have plenty of time to
think, and become disconsolate. The older some become, the
more susceptible they become to the feelings pulsating in the
breast of David when he found himself cast down and so
disquieted in mind. Days are long for the aged, and there is
time to brood and repine. A description of such loneliness
can be found in a private letter Dr. Dinsdale Young sent to a
friend in which he said, "Alone—all alone, no wifely or
daughterly hand to serve me in my old age." Yet although
age is leaving its mark after the storms and billows almost
engulfed your frail bark, tranquility of heart can be yours if
you are resting in Him who said, "To old age I will carry
you." How inspired are the lines of Browning in *Rabbi ben
Ezra*—

> Grow old along with me!
> The best is yet to be.
> The last of life, for which the first was made:
> Our times are in His hand
> Who saith, "A whole life I planned,
> Youth shows but half; trust God;
> See all, nor be afraid."

106

Victory over Persistent Downheartedness

A most vital and practical question many ask is, How can we defeat spiritual gloom and lift ourselves into, and keep ourselves in, the sunnier sky of cheer? As there is enough despair in the world without adding to it, we should strive after a cure for personal melancholy and dejection. John Gay, quaint poet of the seventeenth century, in *The Beggar's Opera* has the couplet—

> If the heart of a man is deprest with cares,
> The mist is dispell'd when a woman appears.

Doubtless the visit of a kind, understanding, and sympathetic friend can exercise a soothing influence over us when we are cast down, but there is a Friend who sticketh closer than a brother who can relieve us as no other. What wise philosophy there is in the verse of one of Sankey's hymns—

> Go bury thy sorrow, the world hath its share;
> Go bury it deeply, go hide it with care:
> Go think of it calmly, when curtained by night,
> Go tell it to Jesus, and all will be right.

There are, at least, three elements in the antidote for spiritual despondency.

First, we must recognize the fact that depression is tragic.

Such an emotion works havoc in our own life and robs those nearest to us of the pleasure and joy they ought to derive from our company and fellowship. Dejection is the worst feeling we can have, because it magnifies trouble, and drags at and prevents our doing our daily work in an acceptable manner. It makes a mountain out of a mole-hill, shadows blessings, makes the hard things of life more prominent than the good things, robs us of God's smile, weakens His promises, cripples our testimony, and arrests our spirituality.

Second, we must bury our sorrow in the thought of others.

A sure avenue of relief when gloom settles on our spirit, is to go out and visit others as dejected as ourselves, or worse, and seek to encourage them. Too often we parade our personal grief to the exclusion of the cares, agonies, heart-grief of others. Doubtless you have read of the man whose moan was loud because he had no hands, but who met another man with no feet, and thus learned the lesson of sympathy. A radical cure, then, for a brooding, repining spirit is to forget our morbid self, and get out into the world broken by its sins and sorrows, and help bear the burdens of others.

Third, we must turn to God.

Here, alone, is perfect relief. If tempted to be low-spirited, we must follow the example of David and tighten our grip on God, then our soul will shine with the light of heaven. Listen to his voice, "Then will I go unto the altar of God, unto God my exceeding joy: Yea, upon the harp will I praise thee, O God my God" (Ps. 43:4). He alone can erase the furrows on the brow, and the tearstains from the cheek, and the burden from our hearts. By His grace we can lift up our head and smile at the storm.

In seasons of undue depression and disquietude the proper remedy is to expostulate with our soul directly. "Why art thou cast down, O my soul?" Chiding ourselves for dolefulness we should say, "Up, fainting heart, look out of the window and think of the never-failing God, and of all the good things in life." We must sweeten the inner chamber of the soul with sprigs of the sweet herb of hope. "Hope thou in God: for I shall yet praise him for the help of his countenance." The aspect of any event depends largely upon the beholder's point of view. If one's hope is in God, then this stimulates and calms the disturbed soul. Trouble in life would be less disturbing if we were more convinced that God is ours and that we are His.

The successful way of gaining and maintaining a fixed temper of tranquility is constant retreat into the deep, hidden chamber, the secret place of the Most High where storms cannot harass, and where we experience perfect peace.

"Be all at rest!" for rest alone becometh
The soul that casts on Him its every care.

How slow we are to imbibe the lesson of casting all our care upon God! Although we cannot expect to be immune from the trials of life, yet like the apostle we can be sorrowful yet always rejoicing, and bid our disquieted spirit to lean upon His bosom who calmed the angry waves. If your harp is hanging on a willow tree, take it down, right now, and strike up a new song unto the Lord for His unfailing grace.

Hidden in the hollow
Of His blessed hand,
Never foe can follow,
Never traitor stand;
Not a surge of worry,
Not a shade of care,
Not a blast of hurry,
Touch the spirit there.

Theme 11
The "North Side"

It may surprise you to know that the north is not only one of the four cardinal points of the horizon—it is also a quarter that is full of symbolic import. This end of the earth's axis is frequently mentioned in the Bible, its first reference being in Genesis 13:14, and the last in Revelation 21:13.

North—the Sacrifice Side

Offerings had to be slain on "the side of the altar northward" (Lev. 1:11; Ezek. 40:46). Sacrifices killed on the southward side were deemed polluted. In the Church of England, the north side is the altar side, and the side on which the word is read.

As the north represents the dark side of the earth, the Scriptures are as a light shining in the world's darkness. The north, as the death-side, is emphasized throughout the Bible.

1. Abraham lived on the north side—"Lift up thine eyes ... northward" (Gen. 13:14). Sojourning in a strange country with its tents and testings, Abraham knew all about the death-side of obedience to God. When he allowed Lot to choose the best of the land, Abraham died to self-choice.

2. David lived on the north side—"Promotion cometh neither from the east, nor from the west, nor from the south" (Ps. 75:6-7). Why is the north omitted, the only quarter true promotion can come from? The only way up is down—in humility.

3. Jesus lived and died on the north side. Jerusalem was built on the north of Mount Zion. Job tells us that God

110

stretched out the north over the empty place (26:7). Jesus died at Golgotha—the place of a skull, a phrase suggesting emptiness and nothingness.

4. Israel knew about the north side. "I will say to the north, give up" (Isa. 43:6). Sacrifice and surrender from which we shrink are associated with the north, the altar side.

North—the Unwelcome Side

Job, another child of the north, wrote of cold coming out from this quarter (37:5). The Arctic regions are spoken of as the Frozen North. The north is never a pleasant side to explore, spiritually as well as geographically. Death to sin and to all carnal and worldly pleasures brings icy treatment from friends, even religious ones, who know not what it is to live without the camp with Christ (Heb. 13:13). You should rejoice if your separation unto God is resulting in the frozen rivers of friendship. As Jesus watched the retreating forms of those who were unwilling to pay the price of full discipleship, He asked, "Will ye also go away?"

North—the Beneficial Side

The Bible says that the north has its bright side as well as its bleak aspect.

1. Golden sunshine is there. "Fair weather cometh out of the north" (Job 37:22). The ancients regarded the northern spheres as the residences of gods. Sacrifice has its golden pleasures and privileges.

2. Beauty and joy are there (Ps. 48:2). Zion, on the north side, was beautiful for situation. A joy, not of earth, is ours as we identify ourselves with the crucified Christ.

3. Fellowship is there. "The table . . . upon the side . . . northward" (Exod. 40:22). Friends may isolate us because of our allegiance to Christ, but He is ever with us (Heb. 13:5).

4. Tranquility is there. Zechariah tells that it is possible to

experience a quiet spirit even in the north country (6:8). Spiritual isolation may be ours, but in Him, there is peace.

North—the Governmental Side

Jeremiah hints that the north symbolizes "evil" and that God will deal with it (1:14). Joshua found a valley of giants in the north (15:8; 17:15). Look up passages like Ezekiel 1:4; 8:3-5; 9:2; Daniel 11:13-15; Joel 2:20 for other implications of the north as the judgment side. "The King of the North" is to play a prominent part in the formation of the Northern Confederacy.

Solomon reminds us that "the north wind driveth away rain" (Prov. 25:23). God's north wind of justice always drives away the rain of hostility and danger. The priests occupied a chamber with a northern prospect (Ezek. 40:46; 46:19). It may not be a bright prospect but it is always a blessed one. "Lift up thine eyes *northward*"—God is there (Ps. 89:12)!

Theme 12
The Repetition of Surnames

Does it surprise you to learn that the Bible has a good deal to say about surnames? In His commission to Cyrus, the Gentile king, God declared that He had "surnamed" him (Isa. 45:4).

The word *surname* means "an additional name." It represents the family name of a person. Archbishop Trench reminds us that something may be learned from knowing that the "surname," as distinguished from the "Christian" name, is the name over and above; not "sire" name—a name received from the father, but "sur" name (super-name).

It is reckoned that in England alone there are over forty thousand different surnames, or one to every five persons. Surnames were introduced into England by the Normans, and were adopted by the nobility in A.D. 1100.

An Honorary and Symbolic Title

As the custom of bestowing family names was unknown among the Jews, the Old Testament usage of "surname" simply means a flattering or honoring title. Gentiles were so envious of the riches of the Jews that they were anxious to be surnamed Israel, that is, enrolled as members of the Jewish nation (Isa. 44:5).

God surnamed Cyrus "my shepherd," appointing him, thereby, as His instrument of restoration (Isa. 44:28).

Elihu declared that he would not give "flattering titles" or "surnames" unto men. He himself was not overawed by Job's social position (Job 32:21).

113

In the New Testament we have many instances of the use of a surname. Simon surnamed Peter (Acts 10:5, 32); James and John surnamed Boanerges (Mark 3:17); Judas surnamed Iscariot (Luke 22:3); Barsabas surnamed Justus (Acts 1:23); Joses surnamed Barnabas (Acts 4:36); John surnamed Mark (Acts 12:12, 25); Judas surnamed Barsabas (Acts 15:22).

A Label Denoting the Bearer's Life and Labors

There are those whose surnames remind them of what they were or should strive to be. Nobility of task is associated with surnames like Elijah the Tishbite; Nehemiah the king's cup-bearer; John the Baptist; James the Lord's brother; Luke the beloved physician; Zena the lawyer.

In some cases we find the retention of an old name after the reason for it has passed away. An example of this is found in I Samuel 27:3; 30:5; II Samuel 3:3, where Abigail is called the wife of Nabal, even though her husband was dead.

Let us now group together those who are particularly labeled, and who are always identified by their label.

Rahab the Harlot (James 2:25). Why is this appendage carried over into the New Testament? Why not call her Rahab of the Scarlet Thread, or Rahab the Woman of Faith (Heb. 11:31)? Why is she branded forever as a woman of shame? *Matthew the Publican* (Matt. 10:3; Luke 5:27). Is this not another unkind reminder? Why not forget those unjust days? Did he not become one of the evangelists? Then why carry the stigma of a disreputable occupation? *Simon the Leper* (Matt. 26:6; Mark 14:3). Was he not cleansed of his foul disease? Then why not let the reminder of his leprous past fade away? *Mary Magdalene, out of whom went seven devils* (Luke 8:2). If it is against the principle of the gospel to rake up a person's past once they have been forgiven, is it not unchristian to remind a once devil-driven soul of a once polluted body? *Nicodemus, the same who came to Jesus by night* (John 3:1-2; 7:50; 19:39). Why always speak of the

114

fear and cowardice of the ruler who came to befriend Jesus? *Paul the persecutor* (I Tim. 1:13; Acts 22:4). Why is he not always spoken of as "Paul the apostle"?

Perhaps the old labels are carried to remind them of what they once were, and to keep them humble before God. The pit from which they were digged must not be forgotten (Isa. 51:1; I Cor. 6:9-11). Gypsy Smith used to keep his old rusty knife with which he made clothes-pegs to remind him of what he once was. It is blessed to know that all who reach heaven are to lose their old names and possess new ones (Rev. 19:12, 16).

Theme 13
The Divine Tenderness

The direct interpretation of the passage "even as God" (Eph. 4:32), concerns the infinite tenderness of God, expressed in His willingness to forgive the sinner for Christ's sake. And here we have a somewhat significant phrase, *"for Christ's sake."* Christ is always the medium of divine supply, as well as the one Mediator between God and man. Laban confessed to Jacob that he had learned that the Lord had blessed him for *his* sake. In like manner we are always and only blessed by God for Christ's sake.

The Being and attributes of God remain a profound study. The Almighty is incomprehensible, yet the most single-hearted can accept the revelation concerning Him. And in our study of the divine character, we must be careful to maintain a full-orbed vision of God, seeing there is a tendency in some quarters to dwell upon one attribute to the belittlement of another. For example, often His mercy is magnified at the expense of His majesty.

One of the most beautiful and comforting among God's transcendent attributes is that of His tenderness. This part of His nature brings Him near, making Him so real and dear. And not only so, but "tenderness" is sadly needed in these harsh, loveless days when it is a scarce commodity among men.

Dictatorships crucify tender feelings and outrage that which is noble in life. Communism, Nazism, Fascism, yes, and even Materialism, dry up the sweet, the loving, the gracious, and the gentle. Look at the hard, repulsive, unlovely faces of some of the would-be dictators! Such proud men may have greatness, but it is a greatness born of brute force, not of gentleness.

Well, here is the apostle Paul, the once-arch persecutor, urging the Ephesians to emulate the tenderness of God. Do our lives reflect this attractive attribute? Or do we find ourselves hard, bitter, unfeeling, loveless, and unsympathetic? Are we characterized by a lack of gentleness, even of God's gentleness with its power to make us great? Contact with the tenderness of God can soften and refine character. John, the Son of Thunder, was transformed into the Apostle of Love. It is still true that Christ is able to make the rebel a king and a priest. The dying thief was perhaps a murderer, a desperado equivalent to a modern gangster, a stranger to all that was delicate. Yet, at the sight of Jesus who, as He died, exhibited the tenderness of God in praying for His enemies, the repentant thief was so broken up and transformed that, as Robert Browning puts it, " 'Twas a thief who said the last kind words to Christ."

And, if we have lost the tenderer feelings of human nature, it is for us to repair to the source of all gentleness, even the tenderhearted God Himself. "Gentleness," Paul reminds us, is a "fruit of the Holy Spirit." He it is, the blessed Holy Spirit, who alone can enable us to manifest such a Godlike quality.

As the Scriptures present us with several aspects of divine tenderness, it is helpful to faith to combine the pictures so beautifully drawn.

The Eagle that Fluttereth

"As an eagle stirreth up her nest, fluttereth over her young, spreadeth abroad her wings, taketh them, beareth them on her wings: so the Lord alone did lead him" (Deut. 32:11-12).

Three aspects of the eagle's purpose are here indicated by Moses.

First of all the eagle stirs up her nest, compelling the eaglets to fly. Wings grown in the nest on the crag must learn to fly, so out go the young. Destroying the nest, twig by twig, the old eagle's desire is to make the nest too uncomfortable for the eaglets. And it is thus that God sometimes acts toward His own. The nest has to be torn to pieces, especially when the soul becomes too settled among the things of the world.

In the next place, the mother eagle flutters over her young in order to teach by example how to fly. It might well seem as if the eaglets are falling down into a bottomless abyss. The mother, however, is determined to induce her brood to use their wings. She, of course, is near and ready to swoop down to the help of her own. And thus it is with God. He stirs up our nests and makes us use our wings. We become too earthbound. Yet we were made to fly. May we spread our wings and trust ourselves to God.

Then we notice that the eagle spreads abroad her wings. In this way she protects, defends, hides her own in case of attack. With her wings the mother bird can drive off assailants, carry her young on her wings or back, and soar away. At a considerable altitude she will drop the eaglets, compelling them to find their wings, and then, if through any cause they cannot use their wings, she rapidly darts down and places her body beneath her young that they may alight and rest upon it. And what a beautiful glimpse of the tenderness of God this presents as He shelters us with His strong wings! If He cuts us loose from something to which we have clung, He is near to preserve us from falling.

The Father Who Pitieth

"Like as a father pitieth his children, so the Lord pitieth them that fear him. For he knoweth our frame; he remembereth that we are dust" (Ps. 103:13-14).

118

The Fatherhood of God is indeed a sublime truth, but it is efficacious only as it rests upon the kindred truth of the Saviourhood of Christ. Of course, there is a sense in which God is the Father of all. It is He who is responsible for our creation (Mal. 2:10). But in a spiritual sense He is the Father only of those who are reconciled to Him by God the Son. He also declares Himself to be a Father of the fatherless.

There is always a lack in life if one has never had a father's benign and beneficial influence. Are you living with God as your Father? A father's compassion belongs in an eminent degree to God. He displayed it in the gift of His beloved Son and in His sufferings for a sinful race. "In his love and in his pity, he redeemed them" (Isa. 63:9).

Human fathers know how to pity their children when they are in distress. And the tenderness of a father will carry him to great lengths in order to extricate his child from trouble. His tenderness is also expressed in strength, wisdom, and provision. A mother's tenderness is manifested in love, patience, and comfort. Faith is thrice happy when it can sing:

I know my heavenly Father knows
The storms that would my way oppose.

The Bridegroom Who Rejoiceth

"As a bridegroom rejoiceth over the bride, so shall thy God rejoice over thee" (Isa. 62:5).

Here we have another sacred glimpse into the tender heart of God. How does a bridegroom rejoice over his bride? Watch him as he slowly moves toward the altar to claim his bride. What holy joy and deep satisfaction are his as he awaits the union which will indicate the climax of love!

Believers are spiritually joined in marriage to Christ. The Bride is His church (Rev. 21:9), and He is coming to claim His own. Once a bridegroom takes his bride he is supposed to possess her till death do them part. He endows her with all his worldly goods and they become each other's. Thus it is with ourselves. The figures of bride and bridegroom typify the union and communion existing between Christ and His own. As the Bride, the church has been married to the Bridegroom forever. He has endowed her with all He has; and ere long, beloved, He will return to claim His Bride.

The Mother Who Comforteth

"As one whom his mother comforteth, so will I comfort you" (Isa. 66:13).

As a good mother is the "holiest thing alive," we here have another precious insight into the heart of God. It is to the mother that the child usually runs when there are tears to be kissed away. And God calls Himself *El Shaddai*, the Breasted One. This is a delicate and sacred expression. A mother's breasts impart sustenance to her child. And in the perplexed, troubled hours of life it is blessed to know that we can lean upon the heavenly bosom for comfort and relief.

A child, still fretful in spite of a father's efforts to calm and soothe, is soon asleep upon the soft pillow of a mother's breast. Of course, the wonder of God is that He is able to function as father and mother, seeing He made them both. He combines all the qualities of noble-hearted fatherhood and gentle motherhood. As the Father He can inspire courage and fortitude, while in the troubled hours of life God's mother-side is sufficient for comfort and peace.

The Shepherd Who Seeketh

"As a shepherd seeketh out his flock . . . scattered abroad . . . in the cloudy and dark day" (Ezek. 34:12).

The metaphor of a shepherd is a favorite one of the Lord's (Ps. 23:1; 80:1). The prophets exhibited the compassion of Christ under the same figure, "He shall feed his flock like a shepherd" (Isa. 40:11), and Christ Himself used it, "I am the good shepherd" (John 10:11), while the apostles represented Him in the same way (Acts 20:28; Heb. 13:20; I Peter 5:4). In Luke 15 the tenderness of the Shepherd is revealed in His willingness to give His life in order that straying sheep might be found. Are you a lost sheep? Have you strayed? Then the seeking Shepherd, who is the Saviour, is waiting to place you tenderly upon His shoulder and bring you home to God.

The Refiner Who Sitteth

"He shall sit as a refiner and purifier of silver" (Mal. 3:3).

A refiner deals with the molten mass as if it were a child. His precious ore requires careful and delicate handling. Here, then, are depicted the sanctifying influences and graces of Christ. The refiner *sits*. He must sit, seeing that his eye is steadily fixed upon the furnace. If the silver remains too long in the heated crucible, it will be injured. So he sits. He is in no hurry for the purification of his metal. And it is needful for us to go into the furnace of trial and affliction. But Christ is constantly at the side of His own. His eye is steadily intent upon His work of purifying us in love and wisdom. The refiner knows that his silver is ready when he can see his own image reflected in the heated metal. Thus is it with the heavenly Refiner. He knows that His work of purification is completed in His own when He can see His own face reflected.

> Work on then, Lord, till on my soul
> Eternal light shall break;
> And in the presence glorified
> I satisfied shall wake.

121

The Hen that Gathereth

" . . . as a hen gathereth her chickens . . . " (Matt:
23:37).

Here Christ compares His saving, preserving mercy to a hen
covering her brood with her wings in time of danger. He
knew that the Roman Eagle was about to desolate Jerusalem;
thus He pleaded with the inhabitants to seek the shelter He
so willingly offered. Doubtless the Master had often watched
the mother bird calling her young beneath her sheltering wing
(and how they would rush for protection!), but here were
defenseless souls who refused His protection. And of what
folly sinners are guilty when they reject their only possible
avenue of escape from sin and eternal darkness!

Further, the figure of the hen reveals the tenderness the
Lord Jesus exhibited in the days of His flesh. He went about
continually doing good. We see Him saving men and soothing,
calming the troubled minds of the distressed. Always in
touch with a world of familiar objects, such as the hen, Christ
exhibits Himself as the all-compassionate Lord.

The Nurse Who Cherisheth

"We were gentle among you as when a nurse cherish-
eth her own children" (I Thess. 2:7).

The gentleness of the apostle Paul was born in the tenderness of God. This is why meekness, love, and compassion
characterize his writings. He lived near to the heart of his
Lord. This portion, where he speaks of himself as a gentle
nurse, is one of the most affecting in all his Epistles. The
reference, of course, is to a nursing mother, seeing that to
"cherish" means to support or nourish. And Paul was able
not only to bring souls to spiritual birth, but to nourish them
thereafter with the sincere milk of the Word.

122

The nursing profession is a most noble and sacrificial one. Surgeons and physicians are certainly valuable, yet they themselves readily confess that after an operation a great deal depends upon the kind of nursing their patients receive. And new-born souls require a great deal of care. If they are to become strong and robust, then they must be constantly nursed. As a nurse, God offers to make our bed in sickness, which means that He yearns to make us the recipients of His tender care. Alas, we are too often spiritually weak. Our low condition requires constant attention. Yet so great is His grace that He deals kindly with our erring hearts, nursing us back to robust health.

This meditation on divine tenderness, however, would be incomplete if we failed to say that if the forgiveness of God's tender heart is spurned, then another side of His divine nature is seen. Justice, unbending and unchanging, divine justice which was satisfied on Calvary's cross for all who believe, must operate upon the individual if love is finally rejected. For if a soul dies without Christ, for whose sake God is willing to forgive, then the righteous judgment of God is caused to fall upon the guilty sinner. Therefore let us urge sinners to be wise and respond to the tenderness of God, so gracious in its invitation to flee from the wrath to come.

Theme 14
The Divine Guidance

There is no aspect of life about which we have to be so careful as that of "guidance." No matter in what realm we dwell, there is nothing so solemn and necessary as the knowledge of the mind of God.

Some good folks there are who positively assert that they are being guided by the Lord, when subsequent events prove that they simply are following their own inclinations and interpret this to be the will of God. It is little short of sacrilegious to hear the casual way some Christians talk about being "led." Their guidance, we fear, does not come from a heavenly source.

True and unmistakable guidance, however, is promised us in the Scriptures. "I will instruct thee, and teach thee in the way which thou shalt go; I will guide thee with mine eye" (Ps. 32:8). Of course, if this guidance is to be ours, our eyes must be constantly turned toward the Lord. Wandering vision will mean that we shall stumble and lose the pathway of His purpose. It is unfailingly safe to believe that "where God's finger points, God's hand will lead the way." Let us give ourselves, then, to some attempt at an understanding of what the Bible has to say about this all-important matter of guidance.

The Guide

When journeying through unknown regions, it is important to have an efficient guide. Who is He, then, who is offering Himself as our guide? What are His qualifications to act in

124

such a capacity? Well, the prophet Isaiah leaves us in no doubt as to His wisdom and ability: "The Lord shall guide thee continually" (Isa. 58:11).

There are two things that beget confidence in the Lord's guidance. First, there is the perfection of His character, He is all-wise and, as the omniscient One, He knows all things and can therefore lead us aright. Then there is the perfection of His love. A loving heart directs His guiding hand. And He always gives the very best to those who leave the choice with Him. There are times when we are puzzled, as though He errs; but after the mists roll away, we shall bless the hand that guided and the heart that planned.

One must hasten to say that the continual guidance of the perfect Guide rests upon the basis of our acceptance of Jesus Christ as Saviour and Lord. It is true that James says: "If any of you lack wisdom, let him ask of God," but divine help is offered only to "any of you" who are previously referred to as "my brethren." A person lacking in faith or unstable has no right to expect anything from the Lord (James 1:2-8).

The guidance of God, which is the sure portion of those who know the Lord, is not promised to those who live their lives outside the domain of His grace. If we know Him as Saviour then we have every right to seek and expect divine guidance. And once we are His the Holy Spirit begets spiritual sensitiveness as to divine requirements. We become instinctively aware of the mind of the Lord. Abandoning ourselves to Him, and trusting ourselves to His wisdom, we find that life becomes profoundly blessed.

> And now I have flung myself fearlessly out
> Like a ship on the stream of the Infinite Will;
> I pass the rough rocks with a smile and a shout,
> And I just let my Lord His dear purpose fulfill.

The Guided

When Isaiah declares that the Lord guides continually, he

125

makes it very clear that those who are guided are a special class: God's people (Isa. 58:1-11). And for those redeemed and regenerated there are certain features about the matter of guidance essential to be observed. If these phases are recognized, there need be no doubt or uncertainty about the knowledge of God's will.

We must realize our utter inability to decide for ourselves what we ought to do.

We must confess our lack of wisdom, for the promise of help is not for those who are wise in their own conceits or puffed up with their own knowledge and ability. If we have no deep sense of the need of divine guidance, then, of course, we shall not know what it is to throw ourselves upon God. Self-evolved plans will be ours, and self-choice is grievous to Him who has promised to guide us with His eye. Friction and failure are ours when we scheme our own way through life. One step prompted by self can impoverish a whole career. Setting out upon a false track, we find ourselves away from the center of God's will. Misinterpreting our own desires as the will of God, we often embark upon hazardous enterprises which end in catastrophe. To come to the end of ourselves and accept the Lord's plan for life may cut clean across our own self-conceived plans, but "the Lord's choice is always a choice one."

There must be an inherent desire to know the will of God, and then the willingness to accomplish that will when it is fully known.

Years ago the late S. D. Gordon wrote in my autograph album: "The greatest passion that can burn in the human heart is to know the will of God and get it done." We must have no bias. Our own will and desire must be set aside. With the Saviour we must pray: "Not my will, but thine be done."

126

Often there is the temptation to make circumstances fit in with what we imagine to be the will of God for us. Sometimes we declare that the Lord told us to do a certain thing or to go to a certain place when such an action was simply the creation of our own mind.

We must definitely pray and wait for guidance.

Asking God, we must wait for His direction. And what sad mistakes we could avoid if only we prayed more! There are no short-cuts or royal roads to guidance. In response to prayerful waiting upon God, guidance can be ours in all affairs, whether personal, domestic, business, or spiritual. Furthermore, as we wait we come to learn that the *stops* as well as the *steps* of a good man or woman are ordered of the Lord.

We must have a positive expectation that God will grant our petition for guidance.

We must ask "nothing doubting" as James expresses it. For those who pray, wait, and believe, guidance is sure and certain. Expecting the Lord to lead, we quickly discern His voice as He says: "This is the way, walk ye in it." *Isaiah 30:21*

Alas, this is where we so often fail! We pray, and then begin at once to wonder whether God *will* guide. Doubt and impatience assert themselves. If guidance is delayed, we take matters into our own hands. Contrariwise, when we trust ourselves absolutely to the wisdom and hands of our Guide, He never fails to lead us aright.

We must follow a step at a time.

"Take step by step by the Spirit" (Gal. 5:25, Bishop Moule's rendering). God always leads step by step.

127

> O'er each step of the onward way
> He makes new scenes to arise.

Taking the present step, we must leave all further steps until the time comes to take them. Peace and contentment are ours as we proceed to take the next step that God reveals to us in answer to prayer.

> I do not ask to see the distant scene,
> One step enough for me.

We are tempted to regard *one* step of little consequence, yet subsequent steps are vitally affected by the movements of the moment. Eternity alone will reveal the value of single steps. It will then be discovered that God builds a life, not in a moment, but moment by moment. All the great achievements of our modern age represent slow and steady growth. Mushrooms may spring up in a night to wither just as quickly; the oak takes hundreds of years to grow and is rendered impervious thereby to the ravages of storm and time. Therefore, let the unchanging determination of Job be ours. "My foot hath held his steps, his way have I kept, and not declined" (Job 23:11). Let us lay hold of the promise: "As thou goest step by step the way shall open up before thee." And let us never forget to take each step with the feet of prayer and obedience.

Divine guidance is always direct guidance.

There is no uncertainty about the leading of the Spirit. God is light and casts no shadows. If we follow our own impulses or the wishes of others, then we shall move in a mist. It is here that we can detect the weakness of "guidance" as taught by the Oxford Group Movement. A quiet time is urged upon the "grouper" at the beginning of the day, when with a mind blank and a pencil in hand, he must wait for "leading." Yet a moment's thought will suggest the fact that a blank or static mind is an easy prey for Satan as, alas, so many "groupers" have discovered. All mental impressions are not of God. Nothing is more clearly taught in the Scriptures than that there are evil spirits which have access to the human mind. To act contrary to the Scriptures is an evidence that that guidance is not of God, for He will never lead us to speak or act in a way that is antagonistic to His revealed will and written Word.

The Guidance

Divine guidance, like the Guide, is perfect, good, and gracious. Enoch, we are told, walked with God. "It became his life's ambition and the sovereign aspiration of his soul to company with the Eternal, and by such an act he put himself in alignment with the divine purpose and plan and received sure and certain guidance."

The guidance of God is certain.

Isaiah declares: "The Lord shall guide thee continually" (Isa. 58:11). But the paramount question is: How does He guide? Here we reach the heart of our study.

First of all, God guides by His Word, and guidance from this source is certain. There is nothing hazy about the leading of the Scriptures, for as a lamp to our feet and a light unto our path, they show us where and how to walk. Quite often all the guidance one needs is the plain unadorned Word. In special circumstances, it is surprising how the Holy Spirit will cause certain passages to become luminous. For example, if one is troubled about separation from unworthy and unspiritual associations, a passage like II Corinthians 6:14-18 offers immediate and unmistakable guidance.

Again, God guides by the Holy Spirit. It was the Spirit who guided Philip to the chariot of the eunuch (Acts 8:27). Paul was likewise subject to the leading of the Spirit (Acts

129

16:6-7). The Holy Spirit is an unerring guide. Knowing the mind of God concerning every phase of our lives, the Spirit can prompt us to do those things well-pleasing to the Father. And such an infallible Guide will never lead us to do anything contrary to the will of God as revealed in the Scriptures. Is it not blessed to know that we can habitually learn to discern the voice of the Spirit and secure thereby a life devoid of bitter mistakes and wrong turnings?

Of old God sometimes guided His people by dreams and visions. After receiving the prompting of the Spirit Paul was led into Macedonia (Acts 16:9-10). Dreams, however, are a very uncertain method of guidance and do not form part of God's usual procedure, especially now that God's full revelation is given us in the completed Scriptures.

There are times, also, when God guides by circumstances both ordinary and extraordinary. Abraham's servant could say: "I being in the way the Lord led me"; and, time and again, guidance comes as we exercise sanctified common sense amid surrounding circumstances. The position that we are in sometimes interprets God's will. For example, here is a young man who has a desire to be a missionary but is doubtful whether he is being led out to the regions beyond. He has aged parents who are not fit to be left alone and who, if his provision were withdrawn, would inevitably suffer. In such a case, home circumstances offer sufficient guidance. Until conditions change, this young man should see that his duty is to care for his own.

F. B. Meyer often recalled an experience he had crossing the Irish Channel on a dark, starless night. "I stood on the deck by the captain," he says, "and asked him, 'How do you know Holyhead Harbour on a night like this?'

" 'Do you see those three lights?' he replied. 'Well, those three must line up behind each other, and when we see them so aligned, we know the exact position of the mouth of the harbor.' " And Meyer made the following application:

When we want to know God's will there are three things

130

which always occur: God in the heart impelling you forward; God in His Book corroborating whatever He says to the heart; God in circumstances which are always indicative of His will. It is nothing short of folly to set out upon any course until all these three agree.

The guidance of God is personal.

Let us look at Isaiah's pronouncement again: "The Lord shall guide thee continually." *Thee!*—yes, you, my friend, no matter how humble and lonely you may be. God's eye is on the sparrow, and He watches you, too. He loves and cares for *you,* and is willing to guide you as if you were the only one in His universe requiring guidance.

Perhaps some of you have been tempted to think that you are far too insignificant for God to notice. "How can it be possible," you ask, "for a God so great to condescend to guide me in the common, ordinary, everyday affairs of life?" Well, He has promised to guide me, yes, even me. Therefore, let us trust Him to lead us over life's rugged pathway. Say to Him: "Hold Thou my hand, I am so weak and helpless I dare not take one step, without Thy aid," and unerring guidance will be yours.

The guidance of God is continual.

Surely we ought to underline the word "continually" in Isaiah's promise of divine guidance! For the majority of us, guidance is fitful and spasmodic. At times, we are truly led of God; at other times, we choose our own will and way. But guidance is offered not only for the great problems of life, but for all the little matters which demand a knowledge of the will of God as well. He promises to guide us, not sometimes but always; not only in the crises of life but all the way and all the time. And this continual guidance can be relied upon until we reach the end of our earthly pilgrimage. Then, the loving hand of the Guide having led us thus far, He will lead us from the dusty lanes of earth to the golden streets of heaven.

If we are uncertain of the way to take for any earthly journey, it is helpful to have written directions, but what freedom from anxiety is ours if we have the leadership and personal companionship of a friend who knows the way. Guideposts are one thing; guides, another. And blessed be His name, we have the Lord as our Guide to the country whither we are journeying!

The guidance of God is satisfying.

If we enjoy the certain, personal, continual, guidance of God, then we shall know what it is to have our souls satisfied even in times of parching drouth, and to have our bones made fat; we shall be like a watered garden, and like a spring of water whose waters fail not (Isa. 58:11). Others may lose their way, but we are led aright. Others may be barren, but we are fruitful. Drouth may overtake us, straitened circumstances and testings may come, yet with the good hand of our God upon us we can have a source of refreshment unknown to those who have only a self-planned life.

Beloved, let us "cease meddling with God's plans and will." Touch anything of His and you mar His work. You may move the hands of a clock to suit you but you do not change the time; in like manner you may hurry the unfolding of God's will, but you harm and do not help the work. You can open a rosebud, but by so doing you spoil the flower. Leave all to Him. Hands off! "Thy will, not mine. . . ."

Conscious of our proneness to stray when left to ourselves, let us lovingly depend on our heavenly Guide to lead us "o'er moor and fen, o'er crag and torrent 'til the night is gone." Let us follow His way, which is always the best way.

132

God bade me go when I would stay
    ('Twas cool within the wood);
I did not know the reason why.
I heard a boulder crashing by
    Across the path whereon I stood.

He bade me stand when I would go.
    "Thy will be done," I said;
They found one day at early dawn,
Across the way I would have gone,
    A serpent with a mangled head.

No more I ask the reason why.
    Although I may not see
The path ahead, His way I go;
For though I know not, He doth know,
    And He will choose safe paths for me.

Theme 15
The Number of Probation—Forty

A good deal of nonsense, as well as wisdom, has been written on the subject of life's beginning at forty. Life begins at forty! True life can begin long before forty is reached if only one is willing to begin with God. Life as He means it to be lived can only commence when the Spirit of Life enters to regenerate the soul.

Not so long ago I read of one who discredited the idea that life began at forty. John W. Deering was executed in the Utah State Prison for killing a man. Deering reached his fortieth birthday less than two months before his capital punishment. He is reported to have said as he was about to suffer for his crime, "Those . . . who talk about life beginning at forty—I'll prove they are lying. . . . Death is death and that's the end of everything. That's all there is to it." Well, this murderer knows now the reality of the unseen and the eternal. At forty either damnation or eternal bliss commenced for him.

The purpose of this study, however, is to prove that God begins at forty; that the number as employed in the Bible has more than an arithmetical value. From earliest years the figure has enshrined a deep symbolism. Doubtless many superstitions associated with the number arise from the Scripture's use of it.

Of course, in the interpretation of the science of numbers all straining and fanciful interpretations must be avoided. Alas, some have been guilty of subtle trifling with the arithmetic of the Bible, thereby bringing such a theme into disrepute.

Calmly and sanely, then, let us examine the special and

134

sacred number of forty, and discover some of its symbolical associations, admitted from ancient times in many realms of thought.

The Symbolism of the Number

That the figure suggests a marked stage usually related to some great event, period, or experience, can be proved from many of its connections. For instance, it is held that forty years constitutes a generation or epoch, the end of which witnesses maturity. And then, from time immemorial the number has been universally recognized as important both because of its frequency of occurrence in the Bible and the uniformity of its association with a period of probation, trial, separation, chastisement, and humiliation.

The Rabbis regarded forty years as the age of understanding, the age when man reveals and reaches his intellectual prime. The mischievous cry of our age is, "Too old at forty." Yet this is the period of fullest energy and highest achievement. Macaulay in his *Essays* remarks: "No great work of imagination has ever been produced under the age of thirty to thirty-five years, and the instances are few in which any have been produced under the age of forty. Taking the writings of authors generally, the best and most valuable of their works have been produced within the last seventeen years of their lives."

The Koran, the bible of Moslem, says that man attains his strength when he comes to forty, as it was at this age that Mohammed, after leading a life of meditation, took to himself the title of "The Prophet of Mecca."

Tiberius is credited with the saying that "man is a fool or physician at forty." It was at forty that Moses went into the solitude of Midian to learn that he was nobody. Isaac was forty years old when he took Rebekah to wife (Gen. 25:20) and Esau was the same age when he married Judith (Gen. 26:34).

135

Perhaps the wisest of all things said about the age of forty is in Cowley's essay, "The Danger of Procrastination": "There is no fooling with life when once it turns beyond forty."

Other associations of the number are interesting to observe. Forty days represented the usual period required by the Egyptians for embalming. Ancient physicians were wont to ascribe many strange changes to the period of forty. Saint Swithin's Day betokens forty days rain or sunshine. The alchemists looked on forty days as the charmed period when the philosophers' stone and elixir of life were to appear. Quarantine for certain infectious diseases used to extend to forty days. A tranquil rest or nap after dinner is spoken of as "forty winks," implying, of course, an indefinite number.

The Scriptural Significance of the Number

Jerome, who was one of the first to note the importance of forty, declared that this number is always one of affliction and punishment. But that it is not always associated with chastisement will be evident as we proceed. Without doubt the number plays a large part in the sacred Word, and is one of the most conspicuous employed.

At times forty is a round figure. The use of a definite numerical expression in an indefinite sense, that is, a round number, is prevalent in many languages. For example, we say, "a hundred and one" or "a thousand and one" things. Now, we do not mean the exact figures we quote, but use them in an indefinite sense, implying that we are not sure of the quantity. The Persians spoke of "forty years" when they really meant many years. It would seem as if the lax use of numbers was frequent among Israel and their neighbors (cf. Acts 4:22). There are occurrences suggesting a conventional use of the figure when "forty" is not exactly meant. The forty days of Jonah (3:4), read "three days" in the Septuagint. In Acts 13:18 we have "about the time of forty years."

136

Coming to the typical significance of the figure, a safe guide in the study of the symbolism of numbers reminds us that forty is the product of five and eight and points to the action of grace (5) leading to and ending in revival and renewal (8). This double truth is evident when the number is related to a period of probation and testing. When associated with enlarged dominion or extended rule, this is so in virtue of its factors four and ten and in harmony with their signification, namely, material completion (4) and perfection of divine order (10).

Classifying the figure, it will be found that it falls into five groups, all of which are related to probation.

Probation by Trial

To receive the Law, Moses was in the Mount for forty days and forty nights (Exod. 24:18; 34:28; Deut. 9:9-11). Dr. Joseph Parker's apt comment on Moses' somewhat long absence from the people is worth reciting. "The few commandments which we once called the Law could be written in less than a minute each; it was not the handwriting but the heartwriting that required the time."

After the sin of the golden calf Moses was before the Lord forty days and forty nights (Deut. 9:18-25). It may be that the leader of Israel remembered the forty years he had to spend in Midian after his own sin in slaying the Egyptian and burying him in the sand. That the period of forty years spent in the wilderness was one of grief to God and yet one of gracious discipline can be proved by comparing such passages as Deuteronomy 8:2-4; Psalm 95:10; Nehemiah 9:21; Hebrews 3:9, 17. During those forty years, old Israel died out and a new Israel took its place (Num. 32:13).

The forty days' search of Canaan resulted in a penal sentence of forty years (Num. 13:25; 14:33-34; Ps. 95:10): "Each day for a year shall ye bear your iniquities, even forty years."

In the strength of the "angel's food" he received, Elijah was empowered to witness for forty days and forty nights (I Kings 19:8). It was in the same way that the Lord Jesus was nourished.

Nineveh experienced that judgment is always mixed with mercy: "Yet forty days, and Nineveh shall be overthrown" (Jonah 3:4). During this period of probation, the prophet warned the people of coming doom. God in His goodness, however, gave the Ninevites time to repent.

Great preparations have great issues. Thus in compliance with the type and example of Moses, the great law-giver, and Elijah, the reformer, our Lord fasted for forty days and forty nights, during which period He was tempted of the devil (Matt. 4:2; Luke 4:2). The testing of the Lord Jesus differed from that of Moses and Elijah, seeing that they were not subjected to such onslaught on the part of the satanic hosts as our Lord endured during His dark period.

Probation by Humiliation and Punishment

In the record of the Flood, forty is characterized as a number sanctified by judgment and mercy. "I will cause it to rain upon the earth forty days and forty nights" (Gen. 7:4; cf. 7:17). This period was likewise a time of trial for the faith of Noah. Forty days had to expire before Noah opened the window of the ark.

Under alien rule, servitude was permitted in order to chastise Israel for her sins, and bring her back to God. "The Lord delivered them into the hands of the Philistines forty years" (Judg. 13:1).

Ezekiel has to remain on his right side for forty days to symbolize the forty years of Judah's transgression, a day for a year, which with the three hundred and ninety days on his left side make the four hundred and thirty years of Israel's sojourning in the land of Egypt (Exod. 12:40-41; Gal. 3:17; Ezek. 4:5-6).

A fitting type of atonement in which Christ can be seen bearing and putting away our iniquity can be discovered in the forty sockets of silver (Exod. 26:19, 21).

The "forty stripes save one" (Acts 25:2; II Cor. 11:24) bring us to an interesting Jewish requirement. Jews were forbidden under Mosaic law to inflict more than forty stripes on an offender, so for fear of breaking the law they stopped short of the number. If a scourge contained three lashes, then thirteen strokes would equal thirty-nine (Deut. 25:3).

Probation by Prosperity in Deliverance and Rest

Israel under Othniel had rest for forty years (Judg. 3:11); under Barak had rest for a similar period (Judg. 5:3, 31); under Gideon had quietness for another forty years (Judg. 8:28); and under Eli had a beneficial rule for forty years.

Probation by Prosperity in Enlarged Dominion

This aspect has been pointed out by another: Israel was under Saul "by the space of forty years" (Acts 13:21) (apostasy is typified by this period); Israel enjoyed David's reign for forty years (II Sam. 5:4) (militancy characterized this era); Israel enlarged her dominion under Solomon's forty years' rule (I Kings 11:42) (prosperity as a type of the millennium is herewith seen, when Christ as the Prince of Peace will reign for a thousand years)—that is, twenty-five forties.

Lesser kings reigned for a similar period. Jeroboam reigned forty-one years (II Kings 14:23); Jehoash reigned forty years in Jerusalem (II Kings 12:1).

Probation by Waiting

Under this aspect, several associations of the number are drawn together to prove the thought of preparation.

Goliath exhibited himself with pride for forty days. Such a

139

period meant an anxious wait for Israel. But as the days slipped by, the giant gathered greater courage and confidence. "The Philistine drew near morning and evening and presented himself forty days" (I Sam. 17:16). Is this not a typical presentation of Satan's temptation of Christ in the wilderness?

Forty played a large part in the life of Moses, who lived for one hundred and twenty years, that is, three forties. We find him forty years in Egypt learning to be *somebody;* forty years in Midian discovering that he was *nobody;* forty years in the wilderness realizing that God was *Everybody.* "When he was full forty years old it came into his heart to visit his brethren. . . . When forty years were expired" (Acts 7:23, 30). The first two forty year periods fitted Moses for his mission as Israel's deliverer.

Then there came those forty days of lingering upon the mount which, being a time full of testing, approved Moses as a fit person for his prophetical and mediatorial office. Dr. Joseph Parker asks, "What is the meaning of all this withdrawal? The meaning is reception. There must be a time of intaking, there must be periods when we are not giving out but when we are receiving in. Sometimes we do everything by doing nothing." But what a hard lesson this is to learn!

Under this section we can likewise place the great forty days between the resurrection and ascension of our Lord (Acts 1:3): "Being seen of them forty days." What wonderful days of fellowship and instruction they must have been for the disciples!

This period, however, was a somewhat strange one since it belonged neither to the life of Christ on earth nor to the history of His church. Those forty days formed a mysterious borderline between the preresurrection and the postresurrection of the church. It was, of course, a period necessary to confirm the faith of Christ's disciples, and to strengthen the proofs of the resurrection. The forty days He was seen of His own bore witness to the reality of His work and the genuineness of His mission. They were also days of special instruction, for they gave the Master time to impart the full commission for the future government of His church. And in the life of our Lord, the period had its counterpart in the temptation of the wilderness (Luke 4:2) which was symbolic of Christ's perpetual triumph in times of conflict.

What Christ actually did during the forty days He tarried among men as the risen Lord is a matter of conjecture. As with the forty days in the wilderness, so this period was one of solitude and of communion with the Father. Christ, however, was no longer tried and tempted by contact with Satan. Death and resurrection had given Him complete immunity from satanic approach. Doubtless those waiting days were days of intercession in the desert places and heights of Galilee (Luke 4:42; 6:12).

Dr. Parker reminds us that "this is the period of testimony, the period of revelation, the period of true preaching of the Kingdom of God, and it may be that we require forty days and forty nights, representing an indefinite space of time, in which to prove our own resurrection with the Lord." But the beauty of *this* dispensation is that we have the risen Lord with us not only for forty days but "every day" and "all the days" (Matt. 28:20). He is the abiding Friend, Saviour, and Lord throughout our days and nights. One need not be forty years of age before receiving Him as Saviour; rather, receive Him early in life if you would know constant peace and would be *sure* of your eternal destiny before it is too late. Neither need one wait for forty years to pass before going forth to witness in His name. No—nor forty days, but now, today. For God is ready to begin to work in every heart the very moment that heart is ready to receive and yield to Him.

141

Theme 16
The Blessed Trinity

Let us consider in this summary the mode of God's existence. As His mode of Being and operation is of a threefold character, we are compelled, at the outset, to face the mystery of what is called "The Trinity."

Doubtless there are those who have been perplexed by this entrancing theme, asking themselves the question: "Have we one God, or three?" If we are not clear in our explanation of the Trinity, we shall open the door to serious errors. At the very beginning of our meditations, it is needful to observe the following facts:

The Trinity is a mystery.

No perfect knowledge of this wonderful theme is possible to man in his present, finite state. The modes of the existence and operation of the divine Being can never be fully apprehended by human beings. The sacred mystery of the Trinity is one which the light within man could never have discovered. That this truth is infinitely beyond the comprehension of the creature is readily granted.

The Trinity is not fully explainable.

We must further realize that we cannot supply a perfect meaning or definition of the word, person, distinction, or subsistence as used to distinguish between the Father, the Son, and the Holy Ghost. Just as the divine and human natures in Christ who is yet but one Person is inexplicable, so

142

three Persons who are yet but one Godhead cannot be perfectly defined.

The Trinity is a fact.

Although we cannot attain a complete understanding of the manner in which the three personal distinctions of the Godhead subsist, yet the fact is clearly affirmed that in the unsearchable nature of Deity, the threefold distinction exists without distinction or confusion. Here is great depth—the Father-God, the Son-God, the Holy-Ghost-God, yet not three Gods but one God, the three Persons in essence. This is a divine riddle that defies arithmetic, where one makes three and three makes one. Our narrow thoughts can no more comprehend the Trinity in unity than a nutshell will hold all the water in the sea. A man once asked Daniel Webster: "How can you reconcile the doctrine of the Trinity with reason?" The statesman of giant intellect replied: "Do *you* expect to understand the arithmetic of heaven?"

The Trinity is a comforting truth.

When devoutly pondered and reverently believed, the doctrine of the Trinity becomes at once a rock of defense and a spring of comfort and inspiration. The Father is seen as associated with gracious designs toward a sinful world; the Son, as carrying out the divine plan of salvation for sinners; the Spirit, as exercising a sanctifying and transfiguring influence upon the hearts of those who respond to the claims of Christ.

If, as one has said: "We cannot be good Christians without the firm belief of the Trinity," then, by inference, the stronger our faith in the fact of the Trinity, the better our Christianity.

The Trinity is a Scriptural revelation.

This doctrine is taught exclusively by revelation, as neither

natural conviction nor material creation could have enlightened us in the matter. A basis for it has often been
sought and thought to be found in independent speculation
concerning the nature of things in the laws of being and
thought, but it is at least safer to those who accept the Scripture and the revealed will and purpose of God to make them
the whole basis.

It is from the Scriptures alone, as we shall presently discover, that we learn that the Godhead consists of three Persons: The Father, the great Upholder and Purpose of all
things; the Son, the one and only Redeemer of mankind; the
Holy Spirit, the indispensable Sanctifier and Enlightener.
Each of these having His own distinct sphere of operation is
yet found acting together in perfect unison with the Others.

The Trinity is an object of faith.

The Trinity is purely an object of faith; the plumb line of
reason is too short to fathom this mystery, but where reason
cannot wade, there faith may swim. There are some truths in
religion that may be demonstrated by reason: namely, that
there is a God; but the Trinity of Persons in the unity of
essence is wholly supernatural and must be received by faith.

This sacred doctrine is not against reason, however, but
above it. Those erudite philosophers who could find out the
causes of things and discourse on the magnitude of the stars,
the nature of minerals, and so forth could never, by their
deepest search, find out the mystery of the Trinity. It is of
divine revelation and must be adored by those who humbly
and believingly accept it.

The Trinity is a subject that has engaged the greatest minds
during the centuries of the Christian era, but, philosophy
(even Christian philosophy) has failed utterly to explore its
profound depths and explain its full significance. Augustine
gave the study of this mystery the best powers of his mind,
and it is related of him that walking along the seashore on

144

one occasion, absorbed in deep contemplation, he found a little lad digging a trench. When asked what he meant to do, the boy replied that he wanted to empty the sea into his dipper, whereupon Augustine asked himself: "Am I not trying to do the same thing as this child in seeking to exhaust with my reason the infinity of God and to collect it within the limits of my own mind?"

While, however, the Trinity defies the powers of the most gigantic minds, yet in another sense the doctrine is as simple and plain as the fact itself, especially when it is received as revealed truth and not as the result of logical deduction but as a doctrine having Scriptural authority as its basis. The doctrine of the Trinity is a profound and vital subject. Without it Christianity could have no existence.

The Term

The word *Trinity,* is not found in the Bible. It was first formally used at the Synod held at Alexandria, A.D. 317, and said to have taken its place in the language of Christian theology for the first time in a Biblical work of Theophilus, Bishop of Antioch in Syria from A.D. 168-183. The holy mystery, however, was long before this a common article of Christian confession, as is seen by the passage in Lucian, greatest Greek writer of the Christian era and the Voltaire of antiquity, about A.D. 160. In his *Philopatris,* he makes the Christian confess: "The exalted God . . . Son of the Father, Spirit proceeding from the Father, One of Three, and Three of One."

Doubtless the term arose from the need for a word to express the doctrine tersely. It properly means "threefoldness," that is, God's threefold manifestation, and it is not, as it is sometimes said to be, an abbreviation of "tri-unity," which is a term belonging to the realm of metaphysics. The word *trinity* is derived from the Latin word *trinitas* and the adjective *trinus,* meaning "threefold" or "three-in-one."

145

The Truth Itself

It is only when one really sets oneself the task of analyzing all that can be known of this august theme that he realizes how stupendous a task it is. Perhaps it may be as well to proceed along the following lines:

Definitions

Many definitions of the Trinity have been formed by councils and theologians. Possibly a perusal of a few selections may help us to understand more clearly the doctrine. The term itself means "the union of three in one," and is generally applied to the ineffable mystery of three persons in one God—Father, Son, and Holy Spirit.

Irenaeus

One of the earliest confessions is that of Irenaeus who, in his treatise against heresies, demands "complete faith in one God Almighty, of whom are all things; and in the Son of God, Jesus Christ our Lord, by whom are all things and His dispensation by which the Son of God became man; also a firm trust in the Spirit of God who hath set forth the dispensations of the Father and the Son, dealing with each successive race of men as the Father willed."

The Church of England

Article Number 1 of the Church of England affirms: "In the unity of this Godhead there be three Persons, of one substance, power, and eternity; the Father, the Son, and the Holy Ghost."

R. Watson

This eminent theologian defines the doctrine thus: "The

146

Divine Nature exists under the personal distinctions of the Father, the Son, and the Holy Ghost."

W. B. Pope

Dr. Pope says: "One Divine Essence exists in a Trinity of co-equal, personal subsistences, related as the Father, the Eternal Son of the Father, and the Holy Ghost, eternally proceeding from the Father."

When, however, we speak of three persons and one God, we must never entertain the idea of a confederacy of gods, each possessed of distinct individuality wholly apart from the others (as, say, three persons taken from an audience) but, rather, a Trinity in unity. There is one God, without division in a Trinity of Persons, and three Persons without confusion in a unity of essence. Let us express it thus:

The Unity in Trinity

We must not infer that because the three are always mentioned in the same consecutive order, thus—the Father, the Son, and the Holy Spirit—that one is subordinate or superior to the other. This unity of the Persons in the Godhead consists of two things.

The Identity of Essence

In the Trinity there is a oneness in essence. The three Persons are of the same divine nature and substance. Thus there are no degrees in the Godhead; one Person is not more God than another. The Holy Ghost is equal to the Father and Son, and the Son is equal to the Father and Spirit.

The Mutual "In-Being"

The unity of the Persons in the Godhead consists in the

147

mutual "in-being" of them, or their being in one together: "Thou, Father, art in me, and I in thee" (John 17:21). A unity in Trinity means, then, that all three are the same.

The Trinity in Unity

If we were to take three persons from a group and put them together by themselves, it would be almost impossible for them, because of their natural make-up, to agree in everything. Little differences of thought or action would inevitably be seen, sooner or later. But there is about the Trinity a most wonderful, beautiful harmony and unity. Not for one moment has one Person crossed the wishes of Another or acted adversely or independently of Another. The Father, Son, and Holy Spirit are all one in thought, holiness, action, love, grace, and so forth. The Trinity is unity. Each does the same.

The First Person

The First Person in the Trinity is God the Father. He is called the First Person in respect to order, not dignity; for God the Father has no essential perfection which the other Persons of the Godhead have not. He is not more wise, more holy, more powerful than the other Persons are. There is certainly priority, but not superiority. God is always mentioned first, then, owing to the order of His manifestation and work.

The Second Person

The Second Person in the Trinity is God the Son, who was begotten of the Father before all time. See Proverbs 8:23-25, where Christ is described as wisdom personified.

148

The Third Person

The Third Person in the Trinity is God the Holy Ghost, who proceeds from the Father and the Son, and whose work is to illuminate the soul and enkindle the sacred emotions. The essence of the Spirit is everywhere, but more particularly in the heart of the believer. Thus, these Three are one in holiness, love, wisdom, eternal nature, and unity of personality. We can express this most perfect unity thus:

(1) *The Father is the Original Source of all things.*
Genesis 1:1 suggests it: "In the beginning God. . . ."

(2) *The Son is the Medium of all things.*
" . . . hath committed all judgment unto the Son" (John 5:22).

(3) *The Spirit is the Agent of all things, the One whom the Son uses to bestow the blessings of God.*
Ephesians 2:18 is a verse that combines this remarkable Trinity in unity.

Thus the order of divine performance is *from* the Father, *through* the Son, *by* the Holy Spirit. To illustrate this divine unity one might use the demonstration of the power-station, cable, and electric lamp or machine. Concerning Trinitarian unity Dr. Handley Moule has this very comprehensive statement:

The oneness of Godhead is altogether unique and implies a unity of the Eternal Content ineffable, absolute, so that nothing can be more truly one; and necessary, that is to say, such that Its eternal reason for so being is in Itself. . . . In one respect, One; It is in another aspect Three; three eternally harmonious Wills, Agents, Persons, inasmuch as there is between Them knowledge, will, and love. Each has as His nature the entire Divine Nature which is quality, not quantity; Each is truly God; Each is necessarily and eternally One in Being with the Others; there are not Three Gods. Each is not the Other; there are Three Persons.

Heresies

In our thinking concerning the Trinity we need to be aware of at least five errors.

Arianism

This teaching contends that the Godhead consists of one eternal Person who, in the beginning before all worlds, created in His own image a super-angelic being, the only begotten Son, the beginning of the creation of God. The first and greatest Creature evolving through the created Son was the Holy Ghost.

Semi-Arianism

This teaching holds that the Son was a divine Person of glorious essence, like to, but not identical with, that of the Father, and from eternity begotten by the Father by a free exercise of will and power; and therefore subordinate to, and dependent upon him.

Socinianism

This system regards God the Father as the only God, one in Person as well as essence; and Jesus Christ as a mere man, though an inspired Prophet and called Son of God only on account of His miraculous conception in the womb of the virgin; and the term Holy Spirit only as another name for the one God, the Father. The more common, modern, and significant title of this system is Unitarianism.

150

Christadelphianism

This heresy says that God is one Power, the increate Father, by whom all things have been created. Jesus Christ, born of the virgin Mary through the begettal of the Holy Spirit, became Son of God. The Holy Spirit is considered to be simply an energy or power from God. This system makes Christ a created being, and denies the personality of the Holy Spirit.

Millennial Dawnism, now Jehovah's Witnesses

This teaching makes Christ, before His earth life, a created and superior angelic being, and during His earthly life, God. This system is practically silent on the Person of the Holy Spirit.

Illustrations of the Trinity

Up to a certain point illustration is lawful and helpful, but the Trinity in unity being the mode of existence of the Eternal is a thing essentially unique and is therefore lifted far above the possibility of complete comparison or illustration. The student and teacher, therefore, will do wisely to deal very sparingly with such treatment of this doctrine. He will always guard what he does in the way of illustration with a remembrance of the unique nature of the subject and that we have no *perfect* analogy of the Trinity.

Perhaps some of the most striking analogies of this profound truth are:

The Human Constitution

Man is a tripartite being, having spirit, soul, and body—three parts yet one person. There is also a trinity in the Scripture of the self-life—heart, mind, and will.

151

The Sun

In the sun's light we have triple rays giving light, heat, and chemical effects. In the body of the sun there are the substance of the sun, the beams, and the heat; the beams are begotten of the sun, the heat proceeds both from the sun and the beams; but these three, though different, are not divided; they all three make one sun. So is the blessed Trinity—the Son is begotten of the Father, the Holy Ghost proceeds from both; yet though They are three distinct Persons They are but one God. In the atmosphere we also have three in one—light, heat, and air.

Material substance

Matter, we know, exists in solids, liquids, and gases.

Nature

Saint Patrick, the Irish saint, found his Irish audiences utterly unable to take in the idea of the Trinity till he presented a shamrock leaf to them, which, with its three green leaves on one stem, gave them their first intelligent conception of the Godhead—three Persons but one God: One in purpose, and in operation, abiding in and with us. We come adoringly to the Father, through the Son, and by the Holy Spirit.

Another natural illustration of this divine truth is that of the plant with its threefold section of root, stem, and fruit or flower, the last being the revealed part of the whole. Thus we close this aspect of our study by returning to a thought already expressed, namely, the primacy of order. God is first. The Spirit is last because He is the last Person of the Godhead to be fully revealed, and also because it is He who brings to fruition the purposes of the Father and the Son. "He is called the Third Person, not in order of time or dignity of nature but in order and manner of subsisting."

152

So God, the Father, God the Son,
And God the Spirit we adore,
A sea of life and love unknown,
Without a bottom or a shore.

Scriptural Evidence

Coming to the unfolding of the doctrine of the Trinity in the Word of God, one must accept the candid statement that our only authority on this mysterious subject is the Bible; therefore, let us carefully weigh its teaching. An unbiased study reveals the trinitarian view as a view transcending reason but in no way contradicting it.

Old Testament Gleams

This doctrine has been of necessity unfolded gradually in the Scriptures, for each step in the development of the truth had to be made clear before another could be taken. Hence we find in the Old Testament one God who is Creator and Lord. In the New Testament the incarnation reveals Jesus as God who was with God, the Saviour of men. After the event of Pentecost, the Holy Spirit is revealed as God and Indweller of the church.

In the Old Testament, then, there are no dogmatic announcements of this truth, but hints, strong gleams or foreshadowings of it, which gather more definiteness as time rolls on, until revelation is complete. Among the strong gleams the following can be cited:

    (1) The History of Creation (Gen. 1:26): "Let *us* make man in *our* image, after *our* likeness."

    (2) The Fall of Man. After the fall, the same plural form is used (Gen. 3:22): " . . . the man is become as one of *us.*"

    (3) The *Confusion* of Tongues. At Babel, God said,

153

"Let *us* go down, and . . . confound their language" (Gen. 11:7).

(4) The Priestly Benediction. The threefold benediction of the High Priest (Num. 6:24-26) is held by the Jews of old to teach their doctrine.

(5) The Call of Isaiah. In Isaiah the threefold ascription of praise offered to God teaches the Trinity (6:3). Also, the same plural form is seen (6:8)—"who will go for *us*?"

(6) The Commission of the Messiah. In the commission of the Messiah, as announced by Himself (Isa. 48:16), we have another strong gleam of the Trinity: "The Lord God, and his Spirit, hath sent me."

(7) Divine Titles. One illustration of how divine titles are used of all the three Persons of the Trinity can be found by comparing Exodus 20:2, "the Lord thy God," John 20:28, "My Lord and my God," and Acts 6:3-4.

(8) *Elohim*. This plural noun used some five hundred times by Moses (and in another form some five thousand times in the New Testament), accompanied continually by a verb in the singular, reveals the oneness of Deity and the plurality of Persons.

(9) Manifestations of God. There are, in the Old Testament, several manifestations of God which are described as being at once Himself and His Messenger or Angel. Thus God is at once Sender and Sent—God and God's Angel, and these can only be understood as signifying a plurality of Persons in the Godhead, that is, in the account of Jacob's wrestling (Gen. 32), where we read: "Jacob was left alone; and there wrestled a man with him" (v. 24). "And Jacob called the name of the place Peniel: for I have seen God face to

154

face" (v. 30). "He had power over the angel, and prevailed" (Hos. 12:3-4).

Other instances of this can be found in Genesis 16:10; 18:3, 30; 20:11; Exodus 3:2; 23:20-21; Numbers 22:32; Joshua 5:14; 6:1; Judges 2:12; etc. From these passages it is clear that plurality in the Godhead was taught from the beginning. How otherwise can these passages be explained, where God uses the plural pronouns as if speaking of others acting in harmony with Him, or in which the same Person is called Jehovah and the Captain, Angel, or Messenger of Jehovah, or where God is said to be sending the Messiah, to whom divine honors and titles are ascribed (see Jer. 23:6; Isa. 7:14; 9:6; Mal. 3:1).

The New Testament Unfolding

It is the special care of the New Testament to unfold what the Old Testament conceals in respect to the Trinity, and thus it teaches with more distinctness this doctrine, inasmuch as the names, Father, Son, and Spirit, both separately and jointly, are used; and, further, that the Father is God, the Son is God, and the Spirit is God.

In the New Testament, where the references to three Persons are clear and explicit, the doctrine is assumed rather than taught. New Testament writers display a simplicity and assurance, when speaking of the Trinity, proving that it was no novelty to them.

Thus the whole teaching of the New Testament is built upon the assumption of the Trinity and its allusions to the Trinity are frequent, cursory, easy, and confident. The New Testament is trinitarian to the core. Let us quote a few evidences:

155

1. Our Lord's Baptism (Matt. 3:16-17): The Father's voice from heaven; and Spirit's descent, the anointing received; the Son at Jordan, object of the Father's testimony, subject of the Spirit's anointing.
2. The Baptismal Formula (Matt. 28:19): Here we have one name, indicating Trinity in unity, but three Persons.
3. Gifts and Administrations Within the Church. I Corinthians 12:4-6 acribes such to Father, Son, and Spirit respectively.
4. The Apostolic Benediction (II Cor. 13:14). A deeply taught servant of God has said:

It is a comforting and observable fact, that the three Persons of the Trinity are never brought together in the Bible without a result of blessing. We have instances in which each Person, standing by Himself, is an aspect of fear. The Father we see clothed with thunders on Sinai; the Son as the falling stone that grinds to powder; and the sin against the Holy Ghost shall never be forgiven. But there is not an instance upon record in which the three Persons stand together without an intention of grace. And it is a magnificent thought, that the completeness of the Deity in all His essence and in all His operation, is never mentioned but for mercy. The whole doctrine of the Trinity is a subject, not of understanding but of faith. We must come to Him in such a spirit as that which fills the mind of the angels when they cry: "Holy, Holy, Holy, Lord God Almighty, which was, and is, and is to come." This is to rise from prayer to worship, from supplication to adoration.

5. The Guide to Prayer (Eph. 2:18): This passage

156

gives not only the clearest possible declaration of the Trinity but also marks the sole ground of prevailing prayer.

6. The Development of the Church (Eph. 4:4-6): Here such upbuilding is ascribed to the cooperation of the three Persons in the Godhead.

7. The Appeal of Love (Rom. 15:30): This is a silent assertion of the Trinity giving additional beauty to Paul's writing. See also Philippians 2:1, where "consolation of love" refers to the Father, with II Thessalonians 3:5, where "the Lord" means the Holy Ghost. Another exhortation combining the Trinity is in Romans 8:9.

8. The Doxology of Revelation (Rev. 1:4-6).

9. The Worship of Heaven (Rev. 4:6), where we have the triple ascription of praise.

10. The Work of Salvation. Luke 15 shows us the Father, Son, and Holy Spirit at work. The threefold "verily" of John 3 brings the Trinity together: "verily" of the kingdom of God (v. 3); "verily" of the birth of Christ (v. 5); "verily" of the Spirit's witness (v. 11). (See II Thess. 2:13-14; Titus 3:4-6; I Peter 1:2.)

Bearing in mind all that we have gathered from the Old and New Testaments on the subject of the Trinity, we can say that the general trend of teaching can be stated thus:

(1) *In Creation* we witness the cooperation of the Father; the Word; the Spirit.

(2) *In Redemption* God is the Father in the source of grace—He *sends;* Jesus is the grace—He *comes and administrates;* the Holy Spirit is the medium of grace—He *communicates, applies, and seals.*

The practical conclusion of our meditation is evident. This great doctrine of the Trinity avails nothing if locked in the

157

brain—"What shall it profit thee?" Of what value is it to study the Trinity if we ourselves are displeasing to the Trinity? If there be one God subsisting in three Persons, then let us give equal reverence, love, and obedience to all Three. Let us—

1. *Obey God the Father,* even as Christ Himself did (Deut. 27:10; John 4:34; Acts 5:29, 32; II Cor. 10:5).

2. *Obey God the Son* (Ps. 2:12), Kiss of Obedience. What He commands is for our interest and benefit.

3. *Obey God the Holy Ghost.* As He is God, let us render unto Him the tribute of homage and obedience due unto His name (Acts 26:19; I Peter 1:2).

Man himself is a trinity—body, soul, and spirit.

Man is assailed by a trinity—the world around, the flesh within, and the devil beneath.

Man is guilty of a trinity—the lust of the flesh, the lust of the eyes, and the pride of life.

Man is saved by a Trinity—the Father, the Son, and the Holy Spirit.

Theme 17
The Antagonism of Satan

If there is one passage more than any other which summarizes the subtle working of Satan to overcome the child of God, it is the phrase Daniel gives us, "He shall wear out the saints of the Most High" (7:25). "Saint" was a favorite term of the prophet in speaking of the believer. His sevenfold use of it forms a profitable study. It is the saint, more than the sinner, that Satan concentrates on. Because he already possesses the sinner, he does not give him much thought; but because of the holy calling and character of the saint, Satan waits for every unguarded moment to wear down resistance to his power.

The direct application of Daniel 7 concerns the period of Great Tribulation. The ten horns represent the ten-kingdom empire John refers to (Rev. 17), which is a period marked by the hostility of the Antichrist towards the Tribulation saints, ended only by the return of the Ancient of Days to deliver them. The chapter as a whole describes the diabolical plan burning in the savage heart of Satan since he was deposed as Lucifer before the creation of man. For well-nigh six millenniums now, he has been at war with the saints, and he knows that his time is short, so he is manifesting greater wrath for those redeemed by the blood of the Lamb.

There are two aspects of satanic antagonism mentioned by Daniel, "war with the saints" (7:21), and "wear out the saints" (7:25). The first implies a more open, a more active antagonism; while the second suggests a more subtle, insidious and crafty method of thwarting the purpose of God concerning the saints. We speak of a "wearing out process." Job

159

refers to water wearing away the stones (14:19), and this is the method to be most feared by the child of God, namely, the gradual, silent, yet effective force of the enemy. Many saints stand firm in the day of battle against his mighty attacks and assaults, and emerge victorious from his war against them, but who, alas! are ultimately conquered by the imperceptible, unconscious forces of the foe. They are not overthrown in open conflict, but are slowly robbed of their spiritual vitality. Let us try to diagnose the wearing-out process Satan employs. How does he sometimes succeed in wearing out the saints of the Most High?

Through Prolonged Trials

If ever a saint was subject to the process we are considering, it was Job who was forced to cry, "My soul is weary of my life" (10:1). The psalmist also became weary of his groaning (Ps. 6:6; 69:3). A saint who is subjected to continuous bodily suffering and trial, and has a load that never seems to lift, is apt to become worn out. Constant pain confuses the mind, and in many cases leads to depression, or a heavy feeling of exhaustion. Such a condition sometimes leads to negligence of the spiritual means of grace and religious exercises which help to keep the soul in repair. If suffering is not relieved or removed, the spirit becomes burdened, faith is gradually weakened, melancholy sets in—a frame of mind Satan can work upon to great advantage.

This morbid spirit unfits one.

It causes the wheels of the chariot to come off. If the strings of a lute are wet, they can produce no sweet music. And if we are unnecessarily sad and cast down, then the spiritual lute is wet and cannot make the saint joyful, even in tribulation.

This morbid spirit sides with Satan against God.

It opens the floodgate of doubt regarding God's love and care. Faith is silently yet surely worn out, and the brightest saint ends his days in darkness.

This morbid spirit breeds discontent, and ends in death.

We have known most earnest saints to find relief in self-murder. Despair set in, and deepened until utterly worn out by this satanic method, they ended their existence. How we need to pray for spiritual discernment enabling us to detect the ambush of the evil one and overcome him by the blood of the Lamb!

Through Providential Dealings

There are at least two verses which indicate how Satan employs other tactics in his wearing-out process. Solomon exhorts us, "Neither be weary of his correction" (Prov. 3:11). Isaiah expressed the feelings of God in this condemnation, "Thou hast been weary of me, O Israel" (43:22). How true these verses are to experience! The constant chastenings of the Almighty either wear out or nerve up the believer. There are those who permitted providential dealings to make them more virile, strong, and active for God. They are used as steps to climb closer to Him. But the sad story is that too often they wear out those saints who fail to understand the sanctifying purpose God has in permitting untoward experiences to befall them (see Gen. 45:5).

Satan is constantly active, employing all his gathered wisdom and experience in soul-destruction, to disturb the faith in a child of God, and to stop its actings. He knows only too well that if faith in God is not operative, all other graces suffer, just as a watch does if its mainspring is out of order. In these hard-pressed days we meet too many derelict saints who are worn out and useless because they strive against the divine Potter who seeks to mold them into His image. They fought and resisted the divine will and plan for their life until they became exhausted, and are now laid aside, useless, like a worn-out vessel.

Through the Greatness of Life's Tasks

We can never be too watchful against the craftiness and duplicity of Satan. The first and last glimpses we have of him in Scripture is as a "deceiver," and perfection of deceit and subtlety is his. There are two further passages that enlighten us as to the cunning methods he employs to destroy the power of saints, and succeed where others fail. "Thou art wearied in the greatness of thy way" (Isa. 57:10). "Be not weary in welldoing" (Gal. 6:9). If we think that our high and holy calling as saints is impossible of realization, and that no matter how we strive and struggle to be like Christ, failure will dog our footsteps, then after a series of sinnings and repentings we will end up by saying, "I'm giving up. It's no use trying to be a Christian."

Because of the great cleavage between the ideal and the actual we become disappointed, and life is robbed of joy and hope and confidence. God has far too many saints who were once strong, robust, and alert in His cause, but who are now worn out, spiritually crippled. They resemble an institution full of worn-out men and women incapacitated for life's duties and for further service. May grace be ours to wear well, and to emulate the example of Paul who could say, "By the grace of God, I continue." There are two ways by which we can prevent the weariness that life's responsibilities sometimes brings.

Substituting Submission for Suppression

A constant striving in the battle against sin is the error of

162

saint and sinner alike, for holiness, like salvation, comes as a gift. It is one of the stratagems of Satan to wear out the saints, exhaust them through multitudinous efforts to sanctify themselves. They must learn to submit, to cease struggling and wearying themselves. Victory is not to be found in our own efforts but in yieldedness to heaven's will—in trusting, not trying. We must cast our daily doings down at Jesus' feet.

Substituting the Holy Spirit for Human Energy

Nothing can wear out a Christian worker like self-energy, or fleshly efforts. How necessary it is to remember that it is not what we are able to do, but what the Holy Spirit is able to accomplish through us! Many are rushed off their feet not by God, but by Satan, and they become worn out. Others become worn out from doing nothing. Idleness in Christian service is also detrimental to one's spiritual health. Experience leads us to confess to being more tired on holiday than when working. Yet some appear to enjoy one long, spiritual holiday, and little relish service for God and souls.

Through Domestic Difficulties

Esau's choice of wives from another nation was a grief of mind to his parents. It caused Rebekah to say that she was "weary of my life because of the daughters of Heth," and that if Jacob made a similar choice then, "what good shall my life be to me?" (Gen. 26:34; 27:46). Hannah was another who experienced great sorrow of heart because of trying conditions at home (I Sam. 1:5-23). Satan is ceaselessly active in our homes, wearing out, silently yet gradually, many who would be saintly in such a narrow circle. Through constant cares, difficulties, trials, and domestic affairs, there comes an imperceptible weakening of spiritual force and character. It would seem as if Satan is busiest here producing in those who

163

were once so bright in the Master's service, spiritual inertia.

Within the home there are those who, like the earthly brothers and sisters of Jesus, do not believe in His claims. Possibly there is a son or daughter, so ungrateful and unfeeling, like Absalom who tried to rob his father David of his throne. There may be unsaved ones like the sons of Eli the high priest, who know not the Lord, and the daily conflict becomes a wearying load for Christian parents.

Here, then, is the real test if one's home life is not to be broken up. Constant intercession and appropriation of grace to live for God untouched, unmoved amid all the perplexities, vicissitudes, and burdens of the family circle; and to never wear out, spiritually, but to maintain a deep unruffled calm and peace of mind in spite of a surge of care and blast of duties. If Jesus is the Head of the home and all within it love and obey Him, then such a home will be a foretaste of heaven.

> O happy house! where Thou art not forgot,
>   Where joy is flowing full and free;
> O happy house! where every wound is brought,
>   Physician, Comforter, to Thee.
> Until at last, earth's day's work ended,
>   All meet Thee in that home above,
> From whence Thou comest, where Thou hast ascended,
>   Thy heaven of glory and of love!

Through the Daily Routine

Not only do clothes and articles wear out through constant usage. In nature, too, there is a gradual deterioration of the material. "Change and decay in all around we see." As with the wear and tear of life, so is it with the daily round and common task. Sameness and lack of change can produce inertia. When Jethro saw how Moses bowed down under his very heavy daily load, he said, "Thou wilt surely wear away" (Exod. 18:18). Even Jesus was "weary with his journey," and sat on a well where He found both physical and spiritual refreshment (John 4:6). And we are exhorted to "consider him, lest ye be wearied and faint in your minds" (Heb. 12:3).

Is it not amid the responsibilities of everyday life that we can detect the insidious efforts of Satan to weaken our spiritual strength? We have the same old duties to face, floors to scrub, tables to serve, clothes to mend, and mouths to feed, and if one is not careful the day's charge becomes a dread. Yet if all is done for God's glory we can say, "Blessed be drudgery!" We are never worn out by the monotony of life's duties, although they are commonplace, if we lift them up to a higher plane. True, we shall be often weary *in* our work, but never weary *of* it. We often say that it is "better to wear out than rust out." It is better still to reach God's ideal and *last out*. Edward Thring, one of the greatest of English schoolmasters, wrote the following prayer when a student at Cambridge, "Oh, God, give me work till the end of my life, and life till the end of my work for Christ's sake, Amen!"

How apt and full of spiritual suggestion is the appealing question of Jeremiah to those who failed by the way—"If thou hast run with the footmen, and they have wearied thee, then how canst thou contend with horses? And if in the land of peace, wherein thou trustedst, they wearied thee, then how wilt thou do in the swelling of Jordan?" (Jer. 12:5).

Since there is no discharge in the war against the rulers of the darkness of this world, how imperative it is to learn the secret of victory and freshness, and the laws of spiritual health, endurance, and sustenance whereby we can stand the strain of such a conflict. As life becomes more tense, and society more corrupt, people appear to be more devil-driven, and even the saintliest find it increasingly harder to live the divine life. The Scripture presents a twofold secret for our comfort.

First, there is a waiting upon Him who is never weary.

How precious is the promise Isaiah has for our hearts, "They that wait upon the Lord shall renew their strength, They shall mount up with wings as eagles; they shall run, and not be weary; and they shall walk, and not faint" (40:28-31). The word the prophet uses for "renew" can be translated "exchange." No matter how worn out we may be, weariness can be exchanged for divine strength enabling us to face life's responsibilities with gladness and unflagging zeal. May grace be ours to maintain spiritual freshness no matter how we have to run or walk!

Second, there is the constant infilling of the Holy Spirit.

Whether it be in the home, or where we labor for our daily bread, or in the work of the church, an unfailing source of freshness and alacrity, will enable us to resist the wearing out process of Satan—we will be "strengthened with might by His Spirit in the inner man" (Eph. 3:16). When He is at the center of our life then all that would disturb us at its circumference is successfully dealt with, and we become more than conquerors over satanic antagonism. The mighty Spirit is more than a match for those hellish forces that seek to weaken our spiritual life. The healthier a person is, the more he is able to resist germs that would weaken his physical power. If the Holy Spirit keeps our inner life buoyant, strong, fertile, and fresh, then the wearing-out tactics of Satan are nullified, and we are triumphant. How assuring are those lines of Wordsworth—

> Dive through the stormy surface of the flood
> To the great current flowing underneath;
> Explore the countless springs of silent good;
> So shall the truth be better understood,
> And thy grieved spirit brighten, strong in faith.

Theme 18
Romance and Redemption in Ruth

The love story of Ruth is one of the most wonderful, perfect, and touching narratives in Scripture. Easily read in twenty minutes, it is a book that all classes and conditions of people can read with pleasure and profit, seeing that it combines many traits of human life and character. The charming Book of Ruth provides us with the history of a nation, the history of a family, and the history of a soul. Without doubt, it is one of the rarest gems in the realm of literature.

The Book of Ruth is a book that every family ought to read when gathered together, for the story of a wrong step, taken by a Jewish family long ago, will serve to save family life from disaster. Elimelech and Naomi went down to Moab and met sorrow and tragedy. We have no right to move even from one house to another, as well as from one community to another, without the clear guidance of God's Spirit. If we acknowledge Him in *all* our ways, He will direct our paths.

The Book of Ruth is a book that every young woman should read, for it emphasizes the fact that in religious matters, there is no escape from a personal decision. One cannot just *drift* into grace with a companion or a church. Within this Hebrew idyl we have Ruth's decision which leads to nobility and royalty, and also the decision of Orpah, which results in obscurity and oblivion.

The Book of Ruth is a book that all sorrowing hearts can profitably meditate upon. A common grief bound three weeping widows together. "Fellow feeling makes us wondrous kind."

The Book of Ruth is also a book that all true lovers can

167

learn a great deal from, for it reveals the grief of mixed marriages on the one hand, and on the other, the blessedness of the sacred union when two marry in the Lord. An unequal yoke is forbidden in Scripture. What sorrows must be faced when a Christian marries a non-Christian; or a Protestant a Catholic!

The Book of Ruth is a book that all disappointed souls should read. It is one of the best books in the Bible for backsliders to peruse. Naomi, down in Moab, felt the misery of her separation from her own people in Bethlehem. How could she be happy in Moab after having lived in Bethlehem? How can a backslider find pleasure in the world after having tasted the joy of salvation? When, ultimately, Naomi returned to her native land, it was the beginning of the barley harvest. It is always barley-harvest when a backslider cries: "Restore unto me the joy of thy salvation" (Ps. 51:12).

The Book of Ruth is a book that we should persuade all masters and servants to read, knowing that, from one of its underlying principles, the solution of industrial problems in labor circles may be discovered. The delightful relationship existing between master and servants in a dark, chaotic period of Israel's history is one of the superb episodes of the Bible. As Boaz walked through his fields and met his servants, he smiled upon them and said: "The Lord be with thee." And they replied: "The Lord bless thee." In these days of selfishness and greed, we sadly need the revival of the mutual understanding seen in Ruth.

The Book of Ruth is a book that all Bible students should read, since it is rich in typical teaching. Within it there are types of Christ, of Israel, of the church, and of the believer. Here is a favorite book for Bible teachers to expound.

In Boaz, we have a type of Christ. Think of how he is described in the Book of Ruth—as lord of the harvest; dispenser of bread; kinsman-redeemer; man of wealth; advocate; bridegroom; life-giver—titles to which our Lord lays claim.

In Ruth, we have a type of the church. Bought with a

168

price, the Moabitess yet became the bride of the one who purchased her. In this connection, read Ephesians 5:21, 23.

In the union of Boaz and Ruth, we have a type of the composition of the church. Boaz was a Jew; Ruth, a Gentile. Yet both became one. Within the true church regenerated Jews and Gentiles become one. In Christ, there is neither Jew nor Gentile.

Bethlehem means "house of bread" and represents our fullness of supply in God.

Moab means "waste," or "emptiness," and typifies the emptiness, disappointment, disillusionment of worldly pleasures and pursuits.

Outstanding, attractive characters make up a good story. Without them a tale has no appeal. Let us, therefore, try to portray the conspicuous characters making up the Book of Ruth. In Old Testament days, names were associated with the experiences and circumstances of the people. This is why so many given names are rich in spiritual significance. An illustration of this is to be found in I Samuel 25. Abigail, pleading before David for her worthless, churlish husband said: "As his name is, so is he. Nabal is his name, and folly is with him." In effect, Abigail said: "Pay no attention to my husband; he is a fool by name and a fool by nature." Let us seek, then, to gather the story of the Book of Ruth around the outstanding characters the book contains.

Elimelech

The father of the Jewish family, prominent in the Book of Ruth, has a most suggestive name. *Elimelech* means "My mighty God is King." Doubtless it was given him by godly parents when Israel wholly followed the Lord. Such a name was an evidence of their faith in the sovereignty of Jehovah. Elimelech, however, belied the name he bore. It is one thing to possess a good name, but a different matter to have a life correspondingly as good as the name. Elimelech had the best

169

of names, but he did not act as if God was his King. Had he believed in the sovereignty of God, he would have stayed in Bethlehem, and that in spite of famine. But one may argue that there was only one right thing for Elimelech to do; rather than see his family perish from starvation as famine gripped the land, he went down to Moab where there was plenty of bread. Elimelech, however, was a Jew and, as such, he had the promise that in the days of famine he would be satisfied. Had he truly believed that God was his King, he would have remained in Bethlehem, knowing that need could never throttle God. God used the ravens to feed Elijah; He can spread a table in the wilderness.

Are we true Elimelechs? Do we live and act as if God is All-Sovereign, and able to do exceeding abundantly above all we could ask or think? Let us rest in the present tense of such a significant name, "My God *is* King." While His sovereignty is yet to be displayed, He is presently high over all. "The Lord God omnipotent *reigneth.*"

Further, if we bear a good name, one full of spiritual significance, may grace be ours to live the life corresponding to such a name.

Naomi

Having taken her husband "for better or for worse," what else could Naomi do but take her two children and follow Elimelech into Moab? She was a prey to circumstances over which she had no control. It was she, however, who had to bear the brunt of the wrong step her husband took. Hers was the greater loss in that emigration into a heathen land.

Naomi means "pleasant, agreeable, attractive," and suggests all that is charming. And she must have had an unusual personality to have drawn to her heart a lovely girl like Ruth, and held her close with the cords of love. Evidently Ruth the Moabitess had no difficulty in living with her mother-in-law.

The tragedy of Naomi, however, was the fact that ten

170

years in Moab, away from God and His people, dried up her finer feelings—so much so that when she ultimately returned to Bethlehem, her old friends met her with the salutation: "Why, here comes Naomi!" But her disposition had so changed that she replied: "Call me not Naomi, call me Mara." Bitterness had taken the place of beauty. Naomi could not bear the contradiction between the name she bore and the thing she had become. No longer was she delightful to know. Disobedience and grief had coarsened the one-time attractive woman.

Can this be the tragedy of someone reading these lines? You, too, look back and think of the days you were easy to live with. You had a winsomeness of character that drew others to your side. A spiritual or natural charm was yours that made you a channel of influence; but things are different now. You stepped out of God's will, became disobedient to the heavenly vision and, consequently, courted grief and adversity like Naomi of old. And today you are hard, cynical, disagreeable, and irritable. All sweetness of disposition has vanished. Spurgeon used to speak of "sweet sinners" and "sour saints." Have you become a sour saint? Well, the old-time charm can be restored if only you will return to your charming Lord. He alone can restore the years the cankerworm has eaten, and once again make you "lovely and pleasant" in your life.

Mahlon and Chilion

Into that Jewish home in Bethlehem two boys were born, with somewhat strange names: *Mahlon,* meaning "sickly," or "invalid"; *Chilion,* meaning "pining one," or "wasting away." It may be these two were twins and from their birth were frail and weak. Naomi had to guard them from a rigorous life. They required much attention and constant care. This much is evident—that all the while they remained in Bethlehem, their strength could be guarded, but by going down into Moab and

171

marrying heathen women, they only hastened their end. The fast, idolatrous life of Moab was too much for their none-too-robust constitutions, so they found graves in foreign soil. Their sin in marrying Moabitish women may have been the cause of their premature deaths (see Deut. 7:3; 23:3).

The curse of church life and work today is the presence of far too many Mahlons and Chilions—professing Christians who have been sickly since the day of their spiritual birth. How frail and puny they are! Spiritual anemics! Theirs is not robust health. They are akin to those Corinthians whom Paul expected to be full grown so that he could feed them with strong meat. Alas, their spiritual stomachs could not take it, so he had to resort to the milk bottle! We are persuaded that what many church members require is not a pastor but a nursemaid constantly to carry and coddle them. They are so carnal and, therefore, so easily displeased and peeved. Unless stroked the right way, and given full recognition they turn up their noses, and quit at the slightest provocation. Babies are lovely to look at but, if they remain babies, they become abnormalities. God save us from spiritual babyhood.

Orpah

Scholars are divided as to the exact significance of the name, *Orpah*. Some say it means "stiff-necked"; others affirm her name signifies "duplicity," or "doublemindedness." The latter seems to fit in with her character, seeing that her actions prove her to have been somewhat double-minded. While under the roof of Naomi, Orpah was obliged to yield temporary, external allegiance to the God of Chilion, her husband. A crisis on the Bethlehem-Judah road, however, revealed her unwillingness to pay the price of complete surrender.

Orpah knew what to expect if she went all the way into Bethlehem, so she went back to her own people, her own land, and her own gods (1:15-16). Naomi had promised her

172

daughters-in-law no easy road. Orpah knew that the Jews hated the Moabites. She doubtless left Moab under an emotional impulse, but her heart was divided. She left Moab as a place but carried Moab in her heart. The psalmist speaks of his heart as being fixed. Orpah's difficulty was that of a heart that was mixed. She wanted Bethlehem but loved Moab, and being double-minded, was unstable in all her ways.

Ruth

Ruth has always been the writer's favorite female Bible character. Several interpretations have been given of her name. "Fullness" and "satisfaction" have been suggested and are in keeping with her experience. Although she left Moab empty, how full she became! Ruth went all the way in surrender and was crowned with riches, honor, and an imperishable memory. When Orpah left Naomi and Ruth, she went out into oblivion. This was not the experience of Ruth! In Bethlehem, her own life was full, and she filled the lives of others. To Naomi she was better than seven sons.

The meaning of *Ruth* that we like most is that of "a closely drawn friend." Truly she stands out as the personification of true friendship. Why, there is no episode in all literature comparable to that on the Bethlehem-Judah road, when Naomi pled with Orpah and Ruth to go back to Moab. She knew what it would mean for these young widows to cross the dividing line. Orpah planted a cold, loveless kiss upon Naomi's brow, and went back to her heathen ways. Ruth, however, clave unto her mother-in-law and cried: "Intreat me not to leave thee, or to return from following after thee: for whither thou goest, I will go; and where thou lodgest, I will lodge; thy people shall be my people, and thy God my God. Where thou diest, will I die, and there will I be buried: the Lord do so to me, and more also, if ought but death part thee and me" (1:16-17).

Steadfastly minded to go with Naomi every step of the

173

way into the unknown, she stands out in contrast to the fickle-minded Orpah. Remember that, at that time, Naomi was a bitter woman, and it takes grace to befriend an embittered person. Thus Ruth's exhibition of undying friendship is a classic. God knows that we have so-called friends who leave us like Orpah. There are others, however (and the Lord bless them!), who cling to us like Ruth clung to Naomi.

Have you ever been impressed with the fact that Calvary was also enacted on that road back to Bethlehem? *From* Naomi, one woman went out into obscurity, whereas another went *with* Naomi to honor and joy. From the side of the crucified Son of God, one thief went into perdition, the other went into paradise.

Boaz

In a true love story, the heroine meets a good man, marries, and they live happily ever after. So it is in this classic account. The unfolding story can be briefly told. Back in Bethlehem, Naomi was too old to work, yet she must live. Ruth, then, with characteristic kindness and thoughtfulness, went out and labored in the fields of Boaz, where it was her "hap" to come under the notice of her master.

It is evident that the somewhat elderly bachelor evinced more than a passing interest in the beautiful Moabitess. Naomi, who proved herself to be a good matchmaker, brought about the meeting of Ruth and Boaz in the latter's threshingfloor. There it came about that Ruth's property by marriage was redeemed by Boaz, and in turn she became the bride of the man who redeemed her possessions.

Of the Biblical meaning of *Boaz* there is no question. It has been said that his name represents "fleetness, alacrity." Without doubt Boaz acted promptly in the protection, redemption, and marriage of Ruth. All who love the Lord should be "alive and quick to hear each murmur of His voice." Promptly the Word and will must be obeyed. In the description of

174

the temple, however, we are told that the name of its left pillar was Boaz, for in it is strength (I Kings 7:21). Boaz was true to his name. He was strong in love, grace, courage, and integrity. Between the lines of the story he stands out as a strong, reliable man, dependable in every way. May we covet all that his name implies! In this age of apostasy, we are apt to be too weak and vacillating. We need to be strengthened with all might in the inner man. We must "be strong *in the Lord.*"

Obed

Ruth's complete surrender to the God of Israel was rewarded with complete satisfaction and joy. Although a Gentile, she became the bride of a Jew and the mother of one from whom the Messiah was to spring. God blessed Ruth with a son, Obed by name, a name which, although the neighbors had a share in choosing, must have been Ruth's personal choice.

Obed means "a servant who worships." It illustrates Ruth's experience. She started life in Bethlehem as a servant, laboring in the fields of Boaz, but she was a servant who worshiped. "Thy God," she said to Naomi, "shall be my God."

Can we say that we are among God's Obeds? Are we servants who worship? Two classes to be distinguished in our churches are those who serve but seldom worship, and those who worship but fail to serve. We have met preachers who are so busy doing Christian work that they have little time to pray, meditate, and cultivate spiritual aspirations. Somehow they forget that, while the seraphim have six wings, four are used for worship, and only two for service.

The art of worship has been sadly neglected in Protestant circles. We hold no brief for the Roman Catholic Church. We love some Roman Catholics but abominate the system they represent. This much, however, must be said for Catholic churches and cathedrals—they are notable for the atmosphere

175

of worship. Silence, even though it is the silence of death, pervades the buildings. You never see Roman Catholic worshipers indifferent, chattering to each other, or gazing around. Catholic churches have no need of a notice in the vestibule reading: "Please observe silence." Such a notice is found, however, in some Protestant churches. Why, the first moments in some of our church services suggest the rabble of a marketplace rather than the house of God where the Lord waits to meet His people. Church members need to hear more sermons on worship. "Oh, *worship* the Lord!" But Catholicism does not preserve the right balance. It teaches people to worship but not to go out and serve a world of sin and need. Ruth worshiped. She also knew how to toil and glean for herself and others.

As a servant who worshiped, Ruth was amply rewarded. She became the mother of Obed. Obed became the father of Jesse. Jesse became the father of David. David became the ancestor of Jesus Christ. It is thus that Ruth finds honorable mention in the human genealogy of our Lord Jesus (Matt. 1:5).

As our heavenly Boaz, Christ is the One who has the right to reign as King. As the mighty God, He is King. He is also the One whose grace makes us pleasant and attractive. His matchless love begets true friendship. His gentleness makes us great and strong to obey. His holiness calls forth the worship of our hearts and the service of our lives.

Thus we have the sweet, charming love story of Ruth, the letters of whose name spell out the truth of each chapter, making up the book bearing her name.

R stands for *resolve,* which characteristic summarizes chapter 1. Ruth was determined in her resolve to decide for God and His people: "Thy people shall be my people, and thy God, my God." Many children of Christian parents need to make a similar resolve.

U can represent *unselfishness,* a trait which is so prominent in chapter 2. Ruth's chief concern was for Naomi, an aging widow who was not able to glean in the fields. Without hesitation, Ruth left the land of her nativity and, among unknown people, labored to support Naomi and herself in her adopted land.

T brings us to *trust,* and this is the virtue emphasized in chapter 3. Ruth began to reap a rich reward from Him under whose wings she had come to trust. When the matter between Boaz and herself was developing, Naomi urged Ruth to "sit still" until Boaz had finished the thing concerning Ruth and himself. Ruth, as a trusting soul, could afford to sit still. If we know what it is to trust in the Lord with all our heart, then our strength is to sit still.

H indicates *honor,* so prominent in chapter 4, where Ruth learns that they who honor the Lord are honored by Him. As we have already seen, Ruth became the ancestress of our blessed Lord. Hers is an imperishable memory. The Book of Ruth is a commentary on the divine declaration: "They who honor me, will I honor, saith the Lord."

One cannot close this meditation without drawing attention to a most unusual tract by S. Fox, a missionary in India, written many years ago. Its title is "Ruth, Chapter 5, Verse 17." And this is what he says in the tract:

It was in the town of Guntur, about two years ago, that I was asked to address a large meeting one evening in the church building. I suppose there were between five and six hundred people present. The meeting was addressed in Telugu, and the elderly Indian pastor was chairman. I was led to speak on Ruth and Boaz. I pointed out that Ruth was a twice-married woman. Her first marriage to Mahlon being fruitless, she was later married to Boaz. And at once God blessed this union and she became the happy mother of a child, who was the progenitor of David and of Christ Himself. I joined this with the passage in Romans 7 wherein we are told that we

177

have died to the law that we might be married to another, even to Christ. The purpose of the union being that we might bring forth fruit to God. I brought before my audience many points and sought to force them home:

1. Barrenness can give place to fruitfulness.
2. Weakness can be changed to strength.
3. Sorrow changes to joy when we find our Boaz, the Rich Man and the Strong One of Bethlehem—a true type of Jesus Christ. He was born of a woman, born in the same place, born under the law, to bring us eventually to the place of sonship and adoption; delivering us from the curse of the law.

Then further, at the close of the address I said, "Now turn, if you can, to Ruth, chapter 5 and verse 17, and read, if you are able to find it, the story of how Ruth, grown tired of Boaz, after a time leaves him and goes back to Moab; digs up her old husband, hangs the dead bones of Mahlon around her neck, and says, 'This is the one for me.' " Sad to say, many, not knowing their Bible, began at once to search for this strange passage, for it does sound strange, doesn't it? Even the old pastor, right before his congregation, began to fumble to find Ruth 5:17. I waited. A few, at once sensing something wrong, looked into my face to find out if I was serious, for they knew there were only four chapters in the Book of Ruth. Then I drove home the point as follows:

"Friends, you will not find that verse, and please God, may you never find the experience either, for both are out of bounds."

Yes, what an awful thing for the Christian to leave grace and return to law! Or to leave the place of blessing, and backslide into the world. It is like

178

opening up the grave of the dead, and mixing with dry bones, or worse, with that which is putrid and corrupting. What a picture of a backslider, with a dead body around his or her neck! No, the body of sin is for us destroyed, that is, it has no power over us, and is, in the plan of God, removed, crucified, and buried. May we, by the help of this New Husband and Lord, live the risen and glorified life.

Theme 19
The Twelve Gates in Nehemiah

The prophet Isaiah exhorts us to "go through, go through the gates" (Isa. 62:10) which is what we have to do as we study Nehemiah's restorative work. Jerusalem of old was beautiful for its situation, a city compact together and surrounded by walls. Entrance into the city was effected by twelve gates, corresponding in turn to the twelve gates of the New Jerusalem (Rev. 21:21).

The gates of a city were places of greatest concourse for business and judicial proceedings, also for idling. They were centers of public life. Markets were held around them. The special commodities traded in gave the gates their distinctive names. Legal tribunals were also held at these gates. Prophets and teachers went to them with divine messages.

On the other hand, the gates were noted as the rendezvous for gossip. While the maidens and married women of the city went to the wells for conversation, the men found their way to the gates to exchange their tales and confidences.

Through the disobedience of His people, God suffered the city, its walls and gates, and the temple to be destroyed, and the people themselves brought into bondage. After their deliverance from captivity, Ezra was commissioned to rebuild the temple, and Nehemiah's task was to repair the walls and gates of the city. Thus we come to glean a few spiritual lessons from Nehemiah's circuit of the walls and the work he accomplished. Let us follow the patriot as he went from gate to gate.

180

The Sheep Gate

Doubtless this first gate received its name from the fact that sacrificial lambs were led through it (3:1). Beyond this gate was an adjoining pool where the sheep were washed before being slain (see John 5:2).

In the spiritual pilgrimage, all must start at this gate, suggesting as it does a constant witness to the fact that without the shedding of blood there is no remission of sins, no cleansing. Christ was led as a lamb to the slaughter. He was both the Lamb and the Shepherd, and His Person and work form the starting place of all true restoration and redemption. After making the circuit, Nehemiah finished up where he had started, namely, the sheep gate (3:32). So Christ and Him crucified is the commencement and the consummation of all things. D. L. Moody used to say that "souls were always saved in the church where the blood of Jesus is preached." Thus we start with Him, and when we see Him in glory, it will be as the Lamb, slain from the foundation of the world.

The sheep gate is also a reminder of our need as sheep who have gone astray. Here is the wicket gate all must pass through if they would reach the Celestial City. It may be humiliating to confess that we are silly sheep, yet we must begin where God does. One can pass through the church-gate but not through the sheep-gate.

We are told that the priests sanctified this gate. Thus the sacred character of Nehemiah's task was impressed on his workers at the earliest possible moment. God localized His presence in the temple and, girded with divine strength, the people had to repair all avenues leading to His sacred courts.

The Fish Gate

This was the gate that fish from the Jordan River and the Sea of Galilee were brought to. Fishmongers would gather at this gate to market the harvest of the waters (3:3). The fish

181

gate always follows the sheep gate. We are saved to serve—forgiven to fetch others—won to win. Andrew, as a true fisher of men, first found his own brother. Not all, however, who pass through the sheep gate enter the fish gate. They fail in their responsibility to bring others to Christ. They forget the royal commission of going into their little piece of the world to preach the gospel by lip and life. The "fish gate" is one that needs constantly to be kept in a state of repair.

In the Scriptures, fish have most interesting associations. Zephaniah cried from the fish gate (1:10). Do we? Peter learned a lesson on divine provision when he caught that fish with the silver piece in its mouth. Peter, ever impulsive, said "I go a fishing," and he caught 153 fish in his net, symbolic, perhaps, of the haul he landed at Pentecost. The fish Jesus cooked for His disciples' breakfast taught them something of His divine solicitude. The early martyrs used the sign of the fish to represent Jesus as they suffered for Him in their catacomb cells.

The Old Gate

Some authorities feel that this gate received its name because it belonged to ancient Salem, which was said to have been built originally by Melchizedek. "The Old Gate" is identified with three other gates:

The College Gate (II Kings 22:14)

It was here that Huldah the prophetess lived and taught. What do we know of the tuition to be received at "The College of the Feet" where Mary studied?

The Corner Gate (II Chron. 26:9)

The margin has it, "The gate of it that looketh." This gate

182

reminds us of Him who is the chief corner stone (I Peter 2:6). Christ is the Cornerstone of all things.

The First Gate (Zech. 14:10)

As the gate of the old city it suggests Him whose goings forth are of old. He came as the Ancient of Days.

Too many in these apostate days no longer tarry at the old gate. The old paths have been forsaken (Jer. 6:16). The fundamentals of the faith have been forsaken. The old gate of the gospel of redeeming grace is now deemed antiquated and unnecessary. Solomon in his wisdom said, "Remove not the ancient landmarks" (Prov. 22:28). Those of us who believe the Scriptures must needs mend and mind this old gate. We must arise and build. There are those among us who have never left such a gate. It has no need of repair in our experience. The old, old story of Jesus and His love is still our message and our hope.

The Valley Gate

This fourth gate (3:13), opening before the Valley of Hinnon, was repaired by the inhabitants of Zanoah, a name which means "broken." In the experience of the saints of God it typifies the humility needed in the service of the Master. Too often we are proud of our gifts, position, and achievements. We are guilty of a pride of race, or face, or grace, or lace, or pace. We sing about going down into the valley with Jesus, but we know nothing of that brokenness of spirit which results in blessing (Ps. 51:10). The valley is a sign of death (Ps. 23:5). Are we dying daily to pride, haughtiness, and self-glorification? We talk about being "up and doing." We might accomplish more if we were down and dying. Christ humbled Himself. Are we living in the Valley of Humility? Do we wear the apron of humility that Peter spoke of (I Peter 5:6)?

The Dung Gate

One commentator tells us that outside of this gate lay piles of sweepings and offscourings of the streets. The refuse and filth of the city was doubtless carried through this gate to be burned nearby (3:14). Such a gate symbolizes rejection and reproach for Christ's sake. "Thou hast made us as the off-scouring and refuse in the midst of the people" (Lam. 3:45). Nehemiah went through this gate. He was scorned, despised, ostracized, treated with contempt (2:19).

Paul passed through the dung gate. He was counted as the filth of the world, and the off-scouring of all things (I Cor. 4:13). The best the world could offer was but dung in his sight. Christ stooped to this unwelcome gate. He was spat upon, despised, and made to endure all manner of shameful indignities, and the reproach broke His heart.

Martin Luther, commenting upon Matthew 5:10-12, pictures the disciples of the Lord arriving at the gates of heaven and being met there by the Master Himself. One of the questions He asks each one who arrives is, "Wert thou an abomination to the whole world as Mine have been from the foundation of the world?" What kind of reply could we give to such an interrogation? All who welcome the dung gate are in for a rich reward.

The Fountain Gate

Near to the pool of Siloam, this gate is now known as "The Virgin's Fount" (3:15). It was next to the dung gate, where it always is in man's spiritual experience. "Thou hast saved and cleansed and filled me." The fountain ever flowing is a type of the Holy Spirit's ministry in and through the believer (John 4:14; 7:37-39). Out from within the believer, rivers of living water flow to refresh the dry, arid wilderness around. Once cleansed and thoroughly identified with Christ in His reproach, the Spirit flows through us unchecked.

The Fountain Gate was over against the sepulchre, which is also true to type. Calvary and Pentecost are adjacent. It is only as we lay in dust life's glory dead that from the ground there can blossom red a life of fruitfulness. The Spirit-controlled life is ever a channel of spiritual refreshment. We cannot be Pentecost Christians unless we are prepared to become Calvary Christians. Out of the smitten rock the water flowed. Death leads to life. The cross results in a crown. Water from the Spirit-possessed life causes everything to live, whithersoever it flows. Is "the fountain gate" fully operating in your life and service?

The Water Gate

It was from this part of the wall that superfluous water from the temple reservoirs was carried off, and possibly used to irrigate surrounding land (3:26). Water is a figure of the cleansing, irrigating power of the Word of God. (See John 3:5; 13:1-16; 15:3; Eph. 5:26.) Our Lord could say of His disciples, "Now ye are clean through the word which I have spoken unto you." The psalmist also speaks of the cleansing efficacy of the Word: "Wherewithal shall a young man cleanse his way? by taking heed thereto according to thy word" (Ps. 119:9).

Praise God, this gate is in no need of repair. The infallible Word needs no building up or improving. The Scriptures cannot be broken. In the estimation of the modernist, the water gate is very much in need of repair, and he tries to patch it up. But how mutilated the Bible is, once he has finished with it! Because of its perfection, the Word of God is able to repair and restore broken lives. "The law of the Lord is perfect, converting the soul" (Ps. 19:7). If it were not perfect, it would never be able to convert a soul. Everyone born of the Spirit, then, is a fresh evidence of the veracity and divine inspiration of Scripture.

185

The Horse Gate

Through this particular gate on the eastern wall, horses entered the city (3:28). Horses, in Nehemiah's day, were principally used for warfare—"as the horse rusheth into the battle" (Jer. 8:6). We are told, however, that the Lord delighteth not in the strength of the horse. He takes pleasure in those who fear Him (Ps. 147:10-11).

We now come to the warfare of the believer. Because we live in a world of evil and of satanic delusion, our life is one of conflict, and the conflict is becoming more intense. The wrestling is fierce. As good soldiers of Jesus Christ, we have to be tough.

The blessed truth to remember, however, is that we are marching, not *on to* victory, but *from* victory. By His death and resurrection Christ secured a glorious victory for His saints, which they must daily appropriate if they would be more than conquerors. Now they overcome the enemy by the blood of the Lamb. Principalities and powers may muster their unseen array, but resting in Christ's victory, we are more than conquerors. If we would triumph over all our foes, trials, and adversities, we must bring the cross to bear upon them all. When Christ cried, "It is finished," He secured for men not only a perfect redemption, but a full victory over all the powers of hell.

The East Gate

This gate was so named because it was on the east of the temple and was connected with it. It also faced the rising sun (3:29). The Shekinal glory left the east gate, and returned again to it (Ezek. 43:1-2)—"Afterward he brought me to the gate, even the gate that looketh toward the east: And, behold, the glory of the God of Israel came from the way of the east: and his voice was like a noise of many waters: and the earth shined with his glory."

For the believer, the east gate represents the coming of Christ in glory.

> "Upheld by hope" in darkest day
> Faith can the light descry;
> The deepening glory in the East
> Proclaims deliverance nigh.

The dawn is purpling in the east. The Sun of Righteousness is about to rise. Are our faces toward the sunrise? Are we living at the east gate? Through this gate we are to enter the City of God. Some writers identify this gate as "The Gate Beautiful" at which the beggar sat pleading for alms. Made of Corinthian brass, it is said that this magnificent, massive gate required twenty men to close it. Of this we are confident, there is no gate so beautiful to the believer as "the east gate" which will bring him to the "glorious daybreak" (Mal. 4:2).

The Prison Gate

The Revised Version translates "the prison gate" as "the gate of the guard" (3:25; 12:39; II Kings 11:6). It is assumed that the court of prison was at this gate. Prisoners would be pilloried at it, or led to jail through it.

In a sense, we are all prisoners. Though regenerated, we yet are confined in this body of death. We are prisoners of hope. Our captive spirit longs to soar to heights above. How many there are who live in a body crippled by pain and disease! What a happy release awaits them!

Alas, too many of us are prisoners in another way! We are bound with the fetters of indulgence, carnality, formality, prejudice. We do not stand fast in the liberty wherewith Christ has made us free. We are entangled with the yoke of bondage. Yet Christ is able to loose all such prisoners. "If the Son therefore shall make you free, ye shall be free indeed" (John 8:32, 36). It is possible for one to have life but not liberty. Lazarus enjoyed both when Jesus said, "Loose him and let him go."

> Make me a captive, Lord,
>   And then I shall be free;
> Force me to render up my sword
>   And I shall conqueror be.

The Gate of Ephraim

This northern gate (8:16; 12:39), was also as "the gate of Benjamin" (Jer. 37:13). Originally it was named after Joseph's son, Ephraim, a name meaning "double fruit." It was given by Joseph as a tribute to God for His goodness. "God hath caused me to be fruitful in the land of my affliction." So affliction, as well as adversities, can bear fruit to the glory of God.

"The Ephraim gate" fittingly follows "the prison gate," for if we are fully delivered from the prison house of sin and self, we can bear double fruit. "Being made free . . . ye have fruit." How can we bear more fruit and much fruit if we are bound with the fetters of doubt, fear, and pride? What does it mean to be God's Ephraim? Well, double fruit consists of the fruit of holiness in life, and the fruit of souls in service. The one phase of fruit is dependent upon the other.

Further, it is not by strain or effort that we become doubly fruitful. We do not *produce* fruit, we only bear it. Fruit is not the fruit of the Christian, but the fruit of the Holy Spirit. Neither is this double fruit the result of imitation; it is rather *manifestation*. It is the outcome of the One who dwells unhindered within us.

The Gate of Miphkad

Professor Sayce, the renowned archeologist, located this gate at the north-eastern corner of the temple hill (3:31). It was also known as "the registry gate," implying that it was the place of visitation, the appointed place of meeting. Probably it was the gate where the judges sat to register and review, and then settle all disputes and controversies.

For the believer, the Miphkad gate can typify the Bema, the Judgment Seat of Christ, where all differences and disputes between believers will be adjusted. How grateful we are that the Judgment is to be a private one. The Lord and His own will be together. He will not expose our dirty linen to the gaze of the world. As we linger amid the shadows, we are apt to criticize one another. But let us strive to judge nothing before the time.

Two classes are referred to as being occupied with the repair of the gate of Miphkad, namely, the goldsmiths and the merchants. Christ offered Himself as Goldsmith—"Buy of me, gold tried in the fire." He likewise spoke of Himself as a Merchant offering "white raiment" and "eyesalve." If we know Him in this dual capacity, then we need have no fear when we meet Him at His "gate of Miphkad."

Nehemiah completed his circuit where he began, at "the sheep gate." Christ, who was led as a sheep to the slaughter, is the center and the circumference of all. His cross is the *summun bonum* in life.

The gates, being twelve in number, suggest the perfection of government, and these twelve gates we have considered are His gates. If we enter them in penitence and praise, with the government of every part of our life upon His shoulders, then, when the pearly gates open for us, ours will be an abundant entrance into His presence.

189

Theme 20
Divine Providence in Esther

The Book of Esther, which is placed last in the ancient *Megilloth,* shares with the Song of Solomon the distinction of not mentioning God or any divine name. It is thus that we call Esther, "The Book Without God." Yet, as we are to see, God is present everywhere in Esther. Verily, He is a God who delights to hide Himself!

Because of the lack of God's name there were those who questioned the fitness of including Esther in the Sacred Canon. But think of what we would have missed if Esther had been excluded! The book contains an historical account of tremendous importance in the annals of Jewish history. Throughout the centuries God had carefully nurtured His people in order to preserve the royal seed from which the Saviour was to come. The Assyrians and Babylonians had done much to destroy the Jews as a nation, but if Haman's wicked plot to completely exterminate the Jews had succeeded, God's plans and the destiny of man would have been considerably altered.

Connection

Approaching the book as a whole, there is a significant feature to be noted in the use of the "now" or "and" commencing the book. In the ancient Hebrew order of Old Testament books, Esther follows Ecclesiastes, a book with which it has no possible connection whatever. This tell-tale "and," then, is like a body mark on a lost child, proving that Esther has strayed from its original connection.

190

In our English Bible, Esther follows Nehemiah but, as one scholar suggests, it should be placed between chapters 6 and 7 of Ezra, seeing that there is a gap there of some sixty years. "Chronologically, though the book comes after Nehemiah, the events of the book antedate Nehemiah by about thirty years. Esther made possible Nehemiah." Esther, then, can be placed within the interregnum between Ezra 6 and 7 seeing it describes the position of those Jews who were contented to stay in Babylon.

Author

What Origen said of Hebrews can be applied to Esther, "God alone knows who wrote it." Augustine and other Early Fathers ascribed the book to Ezra. The Talmud declares that Esther was composed by "the great men of the synagogue." Several students suggest that Mordecai wrote the book. And the phrase "Mordecai wrote these things" (9:20), proves him to be a penman. The record of his acts, however, suggests that the book was not written until Mordecai had passed away (10:2). Doubtless Mordecai left written material of the events of his day from which Esther was compiled.

From exact information given of secret and delicate matters it would seem as if the book had been written by a Jew, long resident in Persia, who was closely acquainted with court life at Shushan.

Many wise Jews affirmed that Esther was dictated by the Holy Spirit and add, "All the books of the Prophets and all the Writings shall cease in the days of the Messiah, except the Volume of Esther, and lo, that shall be as stable as the Pentateuch and as the constitution of the oral law which shall never cease."

Title

The book we are considering received its name, not because Esther was the authoress of it, but because she is the principal person mentioned within it. Here is the entrancing record of a Jewish orphan girl whose name was changed as she became the queen of a Persian king.

Scope

The period covered by Esther is around sixty years, and falls in between the going up of Zerubbabel from Babylon to Jerusalem and that of Ezra's restorative ministry, and, as we have already observed, can be placed after the sixth chapter of Ezra.

Purpose

A fourfold purpose can be traced in the writing of this book, and of its inclusion within God's Word:
1. To show the condition of the Jews who remained at Babylon.
2. To set forth the overruling providence of God.
3. To manifest God's unchanging love for His covenant people.
4. To declare God's power to overthrow the devices of the wicked.

Authenticity

It may come as a matter of surprise to many to learn that this wonderful little book has been the object of fierce opposition and has received much ill treatment at the hands of many enemies.

One destructive critic, for example, says that the narrative of Esther "consists of a long string of historical difficulties and improbabilities, and contains a number of errors in regard to Persian customs."

192

Another modernistic writer calls it "a poem" based upon a very slight foundation of fact.

Yet another scholar reserves his opinion as to Esther's authenticity and "waits to see whether any documents are hereafter discovered which will confirm and elucidate this isolated court story, with all its various details, and if so, to what extent."

Well, archaeology has silenced this critic. The palace where the scenes of this book were enacted has been excavated, and the various places mentioned have been identified and many events verified.

There is another who writes of Esther as "a story which, in fact, is a tissue of improbabilities and impossibilities."

Still others affirm that the book is the work of pure imagination, and establishes the pride and arrogance of the Jews.

Martin Luther, under whose cloak many of the opponents of Esther hide, was a hostile foe of the book. In his *Table-Talk* he says, "As to the Book of Esther, I would it did not exist, for it Judaizes too much, and has in it a great deal of heathenish naughtiness."

The Jews themselves, however, have always regarded Esther as true history, uniting it with Daniel, Ezra, and Nehemiah. In fact, they hold it in such peculiar esteem as to declare it to be more precious than the Prophets or Proverbs, or the Psalms, and destined to outlast all the Hebrew Scriptures, excepting the Pentateuch.

The strongest proof of the book's authenticity is the continuance of the Feast of Purim, which was instituted to celebrate the deliverance of the Jews from Haman's cruel clutches, and which was observed as we know from II Maccabees 15:36, at no greater distance than the time when the events occurred. The unbroken observance of this feast is the most powerful evidence of Esther's reliability, for the Jews would hardly observe for ages such a solemn festival if the incidents recorded around it were only a fable or a romance.

Key Verses

In the study of any book within the "Divine Library" one should be on the lookout for a key verse, crystallizing the teaching of the book in question. There are two such verses in Esther. The first indicates the inscrutable providence of God. "For if thou altogether holdest thy peace at this time, then shall there enlargement and deliverance arise to the Jews from another place; but thou and thy father's house shall be destroyed: and who knoweth whether thou art come to the kingdom for such a time as this?" (4:14). Mark the phrase "who knoweth." May ours be the hope and trust in God, and in His overruling grace evidenced in Esther's rise to power.

Then there is the truth regarding the certain retribution of the wicked as found in 7:10: "So they hanged Haman on the gallows that he had prepared for Mordecai. Then was the king's wrath pacified." The New Testament commentary on this passage is in Paul's word about reaping what we sow. "Be not deceived; God is not mocked: for whatsoever a man soweth, that shall he also reap. For he that soweth to his flesh shall of the flesh reap corruption; but he that soweth to the Spirit shall of the Spirit reap life everlasting" (Gal. 6:7-8).

Key Thought

Without doubt Esther is the book of the Bible that conspicuously sets forth the providence of God in human affairs. Here we have what Dr. A. T. Pierson calls "the romance of providence." In his introduction, Dr. C. I. Scofield says of Esther, "The significance of the Book of Esther is that it testifies to the secret watch-care of Jehovah over dispersed Israel. The name of God does not occur, but in no other book of the Bible is His providence more conspicuous. A mere remnant returned to Jerusalem. The mass of the nation preferred the easy and lucrative life under Persian rule. But God did not forsake them. What He here does for Judah, He is surely doing for all the covenant people." As a whole, the book illustrates the truth—He knows! He Loves! He Cares!

Key Phrases

Five times over Haman is referred to as "the Jews' enemy" (3:10; 7:6; 8:1; 9:10-24), a designation applied to no one else in Scripture. In his desire to destroy the Jews, Haman stands out as a fitting type of the Antichrist.

Esther is also a book of feasts. "The great feast" to which Vashti refused to come, it has been discovered from unearthed inscriptions, was held to consider the expedition against Greece for which Xerxes spent four years in preparation. He fought the famous battles of Thermopylae and Salamis two years before he married Esther. Esther remained his queen for about thirteen years.

The "feasts" in order are:

Ahasuerus's Feasts	(1:3; 1:5)
Vashti's Feast	(1:9)
Esther's Feast	(2:18)
Esther's Banquet	(5:4, 12, 14; 6:14; 7)
Jews' Feast	(8:17; 9:17-19)
Purim Feast Established	(9:20-32)

Characteristics

In the teaching of this dramatic book attention will be drawn to several unique features. For example, some of the longest verses in the Bible are to be found in Esther. There are seventy-five words in 3:12 and ninety words form 8:9.

Chapter 10, made up of only three verses, is one of the shortest chapters in Scripture. Compare Psalms 133 and 134.

The action of Haman in seeking to exterminate all the Jews (3:6), marks another assault of Satan against the nation from which the Seed of the woman was to come. The two unseen and unnamed actors in the book are God and Satan. Satan was the instigator of the hatred and antagonism of Haman. With Genesis 3:15 before him, the devil, foiled again and again in attempts to destroy the "seed royal," now endeavors to put an end to God's redemptive purpose by slaughtering all the Jews. God, however, defeated the evil designs of Satan at every turn, and made the wrath of man to praise Him. As the Preserver, He saw to it that "the seed" was kept intact.

Another interesting feature of the book is that of the existence of a postal service. It may be that the inauguration of our present-day efficient postal system goes back to the time of Esther. Away back in those ancient times there were postmen who were runners on foot (3:13-15; Jer. 51:31). There were also couriers on horseback (8:10).

Evidently the Persian system for the delivery of letters was perfect. Stables, we are told, could be found along the various routes, at such distances as a horse could accomplish in a day. All the stables were provided with a number of horses and grooms. A postmaster, presiding over each stable, would receive the dispatches along with the tired men and weary horses, and then send on the messages by fresh riders. Sometimes there was no delay in the conveyance of an urgent message, even at night, for night carriers would take up the work of day carriers and thus continue and complete the route. One surmises that there must have been many a weary wait for the postman in those days when there were no trains or airplanes.

Another characteristic feature of Esther is that of "casting the lot" (3:7; 9:24). It has been pointed out that the Persian word for *pur* is "lot." There may be a reference here to the "monthly prognosticators" Isaiah mentions (47:13). Haman sought the counsel of those who professed to know the lucky and unlucky days of the calendar, when he determined upon the wholesale massacre of the Jews. The lot fell upon the twelfth Hebrew month, Adar, which is equivalent to our

March, and on the thirteenth day of that month. One wonders whether this is one of the origins of the superstition regarding thirteen as being an unlucky number. Certainly that thirteenth day of Adar was a very unlucky day for Haman.

The main point in the story of Esther, however, is that of the overruling providence of God. Haman's wicked purpose was circumvented. And to celebrate their deliverance, the Jews instituted the Feast of Purim, which is called "The Feast of Lots" (9:20, 32). Such a feast became a national institution by the general consent of Jews everywhere (9:27), and has remained a solemn Jewish festival throughout the ages. One of the Jewish proverbs is "The temple may fail, but the Purim never." This feast falls in early spring, a month before the Passover, and occupies two days as fixed by Mordecai and Esther, the thirteen and fourteenth of Adar. The day preceding Purim is observed as a fast day in commemoration of Esther's fast before going in, uninvited, to the king (4:16). And at the feast the Book of Esther is read as part of the celebration. We are told that at the mention of Haman's name the Jews hiss and spit as a sign of their contempt for such an enemy. At the conclusion of the book as it is now read by the Jews, there is an appropriate benediction, possibly added by the Greek translators. It reads, "Blessed art Thou, O Lord our God, King of the universe, Who hast contended our contest, judged our cause, avenged our wrongs, requited all the enemies of our souls, and hast delivered us from our oppressors. Blessed art Thou, Who hast delivered Thy people from all their oppressors, Thou Lord of Salvation."

A prophetic note is sounded in the words "should not fail" (9:28), for the feast has never ceased—a testimony, surely, to the inspiration of the book.

The change of names is another noticeable feature of Esther. Evidently it was customary for Eastern monarchs to change the names of those whom they honored. *Joseph,* meaning "increase," was changed to Zaphnath-paaneah, signi-

197

fying "A revealer of secret things" (Gen. 41:45). Esther's Jewish name was Hadassah, meaning "myrtle" (2:7). Her Persian name, *Esther,* means "a star." May ours be the passion to grow fragrantly as the myrtle, and shine as brightly as a star! Some of the ancient rabbis, however, declared that *Esther* meant "to hide," seeing that she was hidden in the house of Mordecai, her guardian; and because her nationality was concealed until the crucial moment (2:10). The greatest of all Monarchs is found to have changed Jacob to Israel, and Saul to Paul. As for ourselves, a new name awaits us in glory.

It will also be found that there is a striking absence of any reference to prayer, praise, Palestine, Jerusalem, or the temple in the book. The Law is likewise unmentioned, unless we take 3:8 as a possible exception. The nearest approach to religion is in the care of Mordecai for Esther (2:7, 15).

The most conspicuous feature of Esther is, of course, the entire absence of God's name. Such an omission, accountable by the fact that it was taken from Persian records, was offensive to the Jews. Probably it was on this ground that it was the last book to be admitted into the Hebrew Canon, and why the Greek translators inserted prayers and various religious expressions.

Various reasons have been assigned for the peculiar omission of any divine name:

1. It has been suggested that the absence of the name of God from the book arose from the increasing scruple against using divine names during the period between Malachi and John the Baptist.

2. Other scholars attribute such an absence out of deference to the fashion of the Persian court, or to a shrinking from irreverence on the part of the writer, who may have viewed it as irreverent to introduce God without necessity into a history which was addressed as much to Persians as to Jews. The book, it would seem, was not so much intended for sacred history as for secular.

3. Perhaps the true reason is to be found in Deuteronomy

31:16-18 where God declares that if His people forsake Him, He would hide His face from them. The Talmud says, "Where do we get Esther in the Law?" and the answer is, "In Deuteronomy 31:18, 'And I will surely hide my face.' " Often *face, name, presence,* are synonymous terms.

4. Another writer has this interesting suggestion to make. More than sixty years had passed since Cyrus had given the Jews permission to return. The vast majority of the people nevertheless remained where they were. Some, like Nehemiah, were restrained by official and other ties. The rest were indifferent, or declined to make the necessary sacrifices of property and of time. God, in His providence, will watch over and deliver the last class, but He will not permit their names and His to be bound together in the record.

It is impossible to read Esther without realizing that although God is not directly referred to, He is the chief actor behind the scenes. As Matthew Henry observes, "If the name of God is not here, His finger is." While we have nothing but history recorded here, all history is *"his-story."* As one writer expresses it, "His is a secret control of the affairs of His people: a hidden hand shifts the scenes. Only the eye of faith sees the divine factor in human history, but to the attentive observer all history is a burning bush aflame with the mysterious Presence."

The absence of God's name, then, need cause no alarm, for "it is that there should be one book which omits the name of God altogether to prevent us from attaching to a mere name a reverence which belongs only to the reality."

A gifted Bible expositor has sought to prove that God is in Esther in a secret way. His name is like buried treasure in the book. The four letters J.H.V.H. represent the Hebrew for *Jehovah.* Here are four passages in which, it is affirmed, God has deposited His name.

The English paraphrase of "all the wives shall give" (1:20) would be "*D*ue *R*espect *O*ur *L*adies shall give to their husbands." Here we have LORD backwards.

199

The command, "Let the king and Haman come this day (5:4), can be expressed, "*L*et *O*ur *R*oyal *D*inner this day be graced by the king and Haman."

The lament, "Yet this availeth me nothing" (5:13), is given as "Sa*D*, fo*R* n*O* avai*L* is all this to me."

Further, "Evil was determined against him by the king" is translated, "For he saw that there was evi*L* t*O* fea*R* determine*D* against him by the king."

By the same reasoning the divine title, I AM represented thus E.H.Y.H. is found in 7:5, "Wher*E* dwellet*H* the enem*Y* that dwellet*H*."

When the name is put forward, it suggests that God is ruling and causing another to act. When the name is put backward it signifies that He is overruling the counsels of others for the accomplishments of His own purpose. To our way of thinking, such an interpretation seems to be somewhat strained but we state it for what it is worth.

Chief Characters of the Book

What a portrait gallery Esther presents! Here are characters widely diverse in nature and purpose.

Ahasuerus

King Ahasuerus was Xerxes of secular history, famous Persian monarch, 485-465 B.C. "The points of moral resemblance in the character of Xerxes, as represented by Grecian history, coincide with the character of Ahasuerus in this book." In this monarch we have a man of uncertain judgment, of wild passion, weak mind, and cruel disposition. His name means "victorious" but he belied the name he bore insofar as the conquest of his baser instincts were concerned. Ahasuerus married Esther 478 B.C. He died thirteen years later. It is said that he was murdered by night by his chamberlain, the captain of the guard. Esther lived far into the

200

following reign of Artaxerxes, her stepson, son of Xerxes. It was under Artaxerxes that Nehemiah rebuilt Jerusalem.

Vashti

The first queen of Ahasuerus has often been misrepresented because of her failure to obey her husband. But she stands out in the story of Esther as a woman of excellent modesty, chaste dignity, and of strong determination.

There was a rule in Oriental society that no woman might appear in public without having her face veiled. Thus had she obeyed the request of her drunken husband, Vashti would have lost her modesty and the respect due to her. Her name, meaning "beautiful," was exemplified by her character. As Dr. Alexander Whyte expressed it: "Her beauty was her own and her husband's and not for open show among hundreds of half drunken men." We, therefore, commend Vashti for her courageous refusal to cast her pearls before swine. "Who will come into this picture gallery of God and admire the divine portrait of Vashti the Queen, Vashti the Veiled, Vashti the Sacrifice, Vashti the Silent?"

Esther

This young, beautiful, patriotic Jewess who gave her name to the book we are considering passes before us as a woman of clear judgment, of magnificent self-control, and capable of the noblest self-sacrifice. Esther is a type of the Messiah of Israel in that she was willing to die for her people.

Haman

A descendant of the Amalekite kings (Num. 24:7; I Sam. 15:8, 32) Haman was seven devils rolled into one. He sold himself to Satan for the destruction of God's covenant people. He has been described as "a man of utmost vanity, blindest prejudices, and capable of the deadliest enmity; a time-serving, selfish, implacable, swaggering bully; a man whose mind was covered over at the top, so as to shut out all lofty aspirations; and close in at the sides, so as to shut out all kindness; and open only at the bottom, for the incoming of base passions, pride, haughtiness, and hate."

Mordecai

This faithful Jew was a Benjamite, a descendant of Saul (2:5). Thus, part of his task was to end the war against Amalek (Exod. 17:16) which was a work entrusted to Saul, another Benjamite (I Sam. 15:2-23). In this connection compare 3:1 with 7:10 and 9:10.

Mordecai is one of the chief actors in the story. With a love so deep for his own people, he was a constant and faithful guardian of their interests. There was no trace of vanity or worldly ambition in his make-up. He was unmoved by success and prosperity. Neither money nor honor could buy him. Amid varied and trying circumstances, Mordecai loyally played his part. He consistently refused to give any man the worship due only to God.

In one of the apocryphal chapters Mordecai is found appealing to God in the following manner, "Thou knowest, Lord, that it was neither contempt nor pride, nor for any desire of glory, that I did not bow down to proud Haman, for I would have been content with good will for the salvation of Israel to kiss the soles of his feet: but I did this that I might not prefer the glory of man above the glory of God, neither will I worship any but Thee." His name signifies "worshipful" or "dedicated," and his life fully illustrated his devotion to God.

Lessons

It is evident to the casual reader of Esther that it abounds in conspicuous lessons. Possibly the best way to glean these lessons, is to gather them around the characters the book portrays.

```
                V   E   H   M   S   N   G   C   R   P
                A   S   A   O   C   O   A   O   E   E
        T       S   T   M   R   E   O   L   U   V   A
        H       H   H   A   D   P   S   L   N   E   C
        E       T   E   N   E   T   L   O   T   N   E
                I   R       C   R   E   W   E   G
                        C   A   E   E   S   R   E           GOD
        B       C   C   H   I       P               C
        O       H   H   A       C       C   D   C   H
        O       A   A   P   C   H   C   H   E   H   A   AMID
        K       P   P   T   H   A   H   A   C   A   P
                T   T   E   A   P   A   P   R   P   T
        O       E   E   R   P   T   P   T   E   T   E   THE
        F       R   R       T   E   T   E   E   E   R
                            E   R   E   R       R
        E                   R       R       C           SHADOWS
        S                                   H
        T                                   A
        H                                   P
        E                                   T
        R                                   E
                                            R

Chapter   1   2   3   4   5   6   7   8   9   10   Key Text:
                                                       4:14
```

Key Thought: **THE REALITY OF THE DIVINE PROVIDENCE**

Chronologically, the book comes in between chapters 6 and 7 of Ezra.

Principal Characters

Ahasuerus . . . . The Vainglorious King
Vashti . . . . .The Veiled Queen
Esther . . . . The Valorous Heroine
Mordecai . . . . The Virtuous Patriot
Haman . . . . The Vaunted Favorite

203

What we learn from Ahasuerus

The record of this sensuous, tyrannical monarch supplies us with several striking lessons. For example, we have:

The Curse of Drink (3:5; 7:10).

What shame and sorrow drink creates wherever it flows! Its hellish influence is not confined to any class. It is here found entering the palace of Shushan, destroying the nobility of a king and bringing grief to the heart of a gracious queen. It was drink that so controlled Xerxes that he was willing to expose Queen Vashti to the gaze of a crowd of coarse revelers. Ahasuerus's action was an outrage on all the customs and privileges and proprieties of his age. He would never have acted in this manner if he had not been flushed with wine.

The tragic story of drink is that in every walk of life, woman is sure to suffer when man becomes intemperate. Where drunkenness reigns she is treated coarsely, her feelings are outraged, her delicacy is wounded, her rights are denied. Often her health and very life are endangered when men drink.

Ahasuerus was a threefold slave. He was—

A Slave of His Appetite (1:10)

As a king, Ahasuerus ought to have set a pattern of dignified demeanor. How quickly strong drink degrades!

A Slave of His Passions (1:12)

Drink aroused the demon within the king. But as Solomon reminds us, "He that is slow to anger is better than the mighty."

A Slave of His Pride (1:15-22)

While perhaps Xerxes loved Vashti, pride would not permit him to revoke an unjust decree. Later in Scripture, Herod, another drunken monarch, was sorry over what he decreed concerning John the Baptist.

But there is another way in which we can treat the autocratic Xerxes. In these ten chapters made up of 167 verses the word "king" occurs over one hundred times, "his kingdom," twenty-six times; and his own name, twenty-nine times. Seven features of the royal monarch can be applied to Christ as King:

(1) Universal dominion (1:1; 10:1)
(2) Made feasts (1:3, 5, etc.)
(3) Showed riches (1:4)
(4) Vessels diverse (1:7)
(5) Rewards service (3:1; 6:1; 10:2-3)
(6) Holds out sceptre (5:2; 8:4)
(7) Punishes the wicked (7:9-10)

Another lesson one can gather as he thinks of Ahasuerus is that of the reproach of ingratitude emphasized in 6:1-14.

Then there is the use of little things. "That night the king could not sleep" (6:1). Why? The simple answer given by a boy was, "Because God wouldn't let him!" Upon that sleepless night turned the whole history and fortune of the Jews. How true it is that "little is much if God is in it." But while there was a sleepless monarch, there was also a wakeful Providence. And the Bible is eloquent with the truth that God uses small things to accomplish His purposes. Therefore, the day of small things must not be despised. We have:

(1) A left-handed man (Judg. 3:21; Ehud)
(2) An ox-goad (Judg. 3:31, Shamgar)
(3) A tent-peg (Judg. 4:4, 21, Jael)
(4) A millstone (Judg. 9:53, Abimelech)
(5) Pitchers and trumpets (Judg. 7:20, Gideon)
(6) Jawbone of an ass (Judg. 15:16, Samson)
(7) Loaves and fishes (John 6:9, a lad)
(8) A sleepless night (Esther 6:1, Ahasuerus)

And that no flesh might glory in His presence (I Cor. 1:20, 27; II Cor. 12:9), God has used the most unlikely people. It was a miner's son, Martin Luther, who, under God, shook the world. It was a cooper's son, John Calvin, whom God used to build up the church in faith. It was a shepherd's son, Zwingli, who established the Reformation in Switzerland. It was the son of a plain burgess, John Knox, who turned Scotland upside down. It was the daughter of a drunken father, Mary Slessor, who became the uncrowned queen of Calabar. It was a shoe salesman, D. L. Moody, who rocked two continents for God.

What we learn from Vashti

From the disposition of this courageous queen we observe:

(1) A violation of a national custom
(2) An outrage upon her womanly modesty
(3) A derogation from her wifely dignity
(4) A slur upon her royal station

The twofold lesson to be learned from Vashti's unwillingness to satisfy a drunkard's desire is the emancipation of womanhood and the cost of a noble stand.

What we learn from Esther

Many lessons can be gleaned from this queen. It was a pity that such a fine woman had to succeed just as fine a woman as Vashti. In Esther's waiting for audience with the king, we have an illustration of prayer. We do not have to wait, however, for the waving of a golden sceptre. In Esther, also, we have the growth of a soul. Note her progress:

(1) Hadassah the orphan
(2) Hadassah the captive in Babylon
(3) Hadassah the beautiful maiden
(4) Esther the queen

Points of resemblance in soul-winning are also present in Esther's passion for others:

(1) Esther was bowed down with a crushing load of sorrow.
(2) Esther felt that no one besides the king had power to help her.
(3) Esther was willing to stake all upon one bold appeal.

Esther can also be taken as a type of the composition of the church, in which Jew and Gentile are merged. Ruth, as a Gentile woman, had a Hebrew husband. Esther, as a Hebrew woman, had a Gentile husband.

In dealing with young girls, the story of Esther can be used with telling effect. The necessity of obedience and the results of good training are evident in Esther's career.

As to the fact of Esther's revenge upon Haman, Dr. H. H. Halley says, "The book does not say nor intimate she did right in that particular. It merely states the fact, a fact common in the history of every nation. If you will accept the Book of Esther as a simple, historical statement, and not be overmuch exercised to find a moral in it, you can see that it is an important link in the chain of events that led to the re-establishment of the Hebrew nation in their own land preparatory to fulfilling their Messianic mission of bringing Christ into the world."

What we learn from Haman

If one were an artist, what material he could find for several striking pictures in the Book of Esther! For example, think of the morning when Haman entered the palace and met the king and, learning that he wanted to honor someone, made the bestowment as high as possible, thinking that Ahasuerus had him in mind. Pride, however, goes before a fall. Haman was called to pay honor to the Jew he hated, Mordecai. From this dramatic reverse we can learn the folly of selfish ambition.

Remembering that Haman was a descendant of Amalekite kings (Num. 24:7; I Sam. 15:8, 32), and that Mordecai was a Benjamite, we are taken back to the sorrow of partial obedience. The work entrusted to Saul is completed. God's war against Amalek is over (Exod. 17:16).

And when we come to the hanging of Haman upon the gallows reared for Mordecai, we have a grim illustration of the certainty of retribution. "His own iniquities shall take the wicked himself" (Prov. 5:22). Other instances of the principle of retribution are before us in Agag (I Sam. 15:33); Adoni-bezek (Judg. 1:7); Judas (Matt. 27:3-5); (see also Num. 32:23; Gal. 6:7-8).

What we learn from Mordecai

The varied circumstances of this noble man and true guardian of Jewish interests are suggestive of many lessons. Carried away as a captive by Nebuchadnezzar, Mordecai's name, which means "bitter bruising," is most apt. But he rose from obscurity to a position of great honor. From Mordecai we learn "the grace of patience," "the goodness of God," "the power of godliness," and "the reward of godliness."

Here was a man who refused to bow to man, and Haman knew that with all his growing power, position was of no avail so long as Mordecai failed to bend the knee.

What we learn from the book as a whole

The danger of material prosperity is one lesson we glean from Esther. There were indulgent Jews who preferred the glamorous life of Babylon to the worship of God in Jerusalem.

Shushan offers a fitting type. Purity is evidenced by the name, which means "A city of the lily." Shushan was the

208

palace of the king. The church is our Lord's Shushan. Shushan was perplexed, and the church is experiencing perplexing times. She has enemies both within and without, eager to overthrow her. Shushan rejoiced, and the church has had her periods of joyous revivals.

Thinking of the Jews, it is interesting to use seven characteristic features given us being typical of believers: Light, joy, gladness, usefulness, honor, and safety are aspects we can trace as we follow the fortunes of God's ancient people in this book.

The postal service mentioned in Esther can also be used in many profitable ways. Preachers, for example, should be diligent, as hastened by the King's commandment. They should also be faithful whether their message is one of life or of death.

Points to be noted in the two postal deliveries are these: First, a message of death was carried to the people (3:13). Such a somber message was universal and brought trouble, bitterness, humility, weeping (3:13; 4:1-3). Second, a message of life had to be sent out in haste. And this word was universal and produced light, gladness, joy, feasting, good days (8:11, 16-17).

Coming to the overruling providence of God, one realizes that although there is no trace of His name in the book, yet He is everywhere. His absence is only apparent. What happened to Israel proves that God reigns. Summarizing the lessons in this connection, we can say:

1. There is an unseen hand behind our human affairs.

> There's a divinity that shapes our end,
> Rough hew it as we will.

2. Both evil and good have their ultimate rewards.

3. The prosperity of the wicked is unsafe and unsatisfying, and it ends in adversity.

4. The adversity of the good is a trial of faith, issuing in prosperity.

5. Retribution is administered with poetic exactness.

6. The most minute events are woven into God's plan.

7. Providence is not fate, but consists of wise and loving benevolence. Freedom and responsibility go together.

Thus, as we take leave of this "Book Without God," we close with the lines—

> Careless seems the great Avenger,
>   History's pages but record
> One death-grapple in the darkness
>   'Twixt old systems and the Word.
> Truth forever on the scaffold,
>   Wrong forever on the throne,
> But that scaffold sways the future,
>   And behind the dim Unknown
> Standeth God, within the shadow,
>   Keeping watch above His own.

Theme 21
Wisdom in Proverbs

"He that would be holy, let him read the Psalms; he that would be wise, let him read Proverbs." So said Dwight L. Moody in speaking of the Bible book we are now considering.

The Psalms speak of the necessity of a clean heart before God; the Proverbs, of a right spirit in our dealings with each other. In the Psalms, we have devotion; in Proverbs, duty. And this is as it should be, for holiness, devotion, and spirituality, such as we gather from the holy Psalms, are meant, in the purpose of God, to fit and equip us for the ordinary duties and common relationships of life, such as the Book of Proverbs bids us face.

This interesting development has been referred to in many different ways. For example:

> After the teaching of devotion in the Psalms, this book [Proverbs] comes in well for admonition and guidance in practical life. . . . The Psalms are to thrill and animate the heart, the Proverbs to direct the way that we should take. . . . David was not more thoroughly trained to be the psalmist of Israel than Solomon was qualified to be the master of practical admonition (Fraser).

> What the Psalms are to devotional life, the Proverbs are to practical life (Pierson).

> From the throne-room of the Psalms, we pass into the business-house of the Proverbs (Anon.).

Men of all branches of life have recognized in Proverbs a book of excellent worth. Its practical wisdom and potent

211

influence for righteousness in all matters relating to home, business, and commerce have placed it in a premier position among the greatest books in wisdom literature. If there are any who fail to see anything wonderfully wise and yet sublimely simple in Proverbs, let him remember what Carlyle said to a young man who declared that there was nothing in the Book of Proverbs: "Make a few proverbs," said Carlyle, "and you will think differently of the book."

Therefore, if we desire to be wise, let us give ourselves more diligently to the study of this treasure house of wisdom.

The Title

The Hebrew word for "Proverbs" is *Mashal*. This word has a twofold significance.

The primitive sense of the word is taken from a root meaning "likeness" or "comparison," as if the first sense of it was that of the principle of analogy underlying it, e.g., Proverbs 25:19: "Confidence in an unfaithful man in time of trouble is like a broken tooth, and a foot out of joint." It is therefore akin to the word "parable" or authoritative saying, and hints that moral truths are taught by comparison or contrast.

It is now connected with the verb "to rule," "to master," "to govern"; hence the word is applied to words which are to rule and govern the life (e.g., Gen. 1:18; 3:16; Exod. 21:8). Thus, the Book of Proverbs is not merely a collection of human wisdom but of divine rules for earth from heaven.

Matthew Henry's comment is apt at this point: "The word *Mashal* here used for a proverb, comes from a word that signifies *to rule* or *have dominion,* because of the commanding power and influence which wise and weighty sayings have upon the children of men. . . ."

This particular word, *Mashal,* is used of: (1) an allegory (Ezek. 17:2); (2) a discourse (Num. 23:7-8); (3) a taunt (Isa.

212

14:4); (4) an argument (Job 29:1); (5) a byword (Jer. 24:9); and (6) a lament (Mic. 2:4).

Ere we leave this point, it may be fitting to understand what a proverb is, and then carry this meaning with us through the rest of our study. Perhaps the best way of stating the matter is the following: "Proverbs are wise sayings, contained in short sentences, which can easily be remembered, and the Book of Proverbs is a collection of wise sayings, given by divine inspiration, and written in poetic style."

Our English word *proverb* means "a brief saying in the stead of many words" *(pro-verba),* and implies pithiness in parallelism. Proverbs have been mottoes that mold life and history. Is it not somewhat strange that a very expressive thing about our own language is the use of proverbs? For instance, think of the condensed wisdom that we have in proverbs that we daily use, such as: "There's many a slip betwixt cup and lip"; "Kill two birds with one stone"; and, "A bird in the hand is worth two in the bush."

The power of proverbs such as these lies in their form; they are short, sharp, incisive, impressive. They assume truth, attract attention, and imprint themselves on the memory and are, therefore, easily remembered.

Turning to the preface of the Book of Proverbs, we find mention of three terms which describe the special aspect of a "proverb," repeated illustrations of which we find through the book.

To understand a proverb (1:6)

Here the word *proverb* indicates, as we have suggested, "a similitude," that is, an illustration of life and truth drawn from material things, e.g., "As cold water to a thirsty soul, so is good news from a far country."

Figure or dark saying ("interpretation," 1:6)

Knotty saying or riddle ("dark sayings," 1:6)

213

Such meanings suggest intricate sayings, like Samson's riddle of Judges 15:12. To our Lord, a proverb was equivalent to an obscure saying (John 16:29).

Besides the form of a simple proverb, the thought may take the form of (1) a fable (Judg. 9:7; II Kings 14:9); (2) a riddle (Judg. 14:12; I Kings 10:1-2); (3) a satire (Isa. 14:4; Hab. 2:6); and (4) a parable (Isa. 5:1-2).

The Authors

The current opinion is that Solomon was responsible for all the sayings that compose the Book of Proverbs. Although he was not the composer of the entire collection, he was certainly the compiler.

During King Solomon's reign, in a special degree, the people awoke to the life, industry, intercourse, and wealth of the world around them and, with such awareness, there came a literary development as well, when the value of the proverb as a vehicle of instruction came to be recognized. The king himself was versatile and had distinct literary tastes, speaking "three thousand proverbs" and of "songs . . . a thousand and five" (I Kings 4:29-34).

While Solomon was the principal author or compiler of the Book of Proverbs, yet a close examination of the book reveals it to be a series of compilations made at different times, confessedly also, to a considerable extent, the work of a number, perhaps a whole guild, of writers. It would appear that there are six sources from which these proverbs have been gathered, and then, under the guidance of the Holy Spirit, placed together into one perfect whole, thus forming a complete book of practical wisdom.

"The proverbs of Solomon the son of David, king of Israel" (1:1)

This title is apparently intended to cover the whole book,

which may bear out the thought that possibly Solomon grouped all the proverbs together as we have them. Some old Jewish writers affirm that Solomon wrote The Song of Solomon when he was young; Proverbs in the midst of his days; and Ecclesiastes when he was old.

Another interesting feature about this title is that it differs from Ecclesiastes. Here it is "Solomon the son of David, king of Israel" because he ruled over all Israel. But in Ecclesiastes, it is "Preacher, son of David, king in Jerusalem," because then, as Matthew Henry observes, his influence had grown less upon the distant tribes, and he confined himself very much to Jerusalem.

"The proverbs of Solomon" (10:1)

These words are repeated, as if in some special sense the collection, commencing here, deserved it. Possibly those set forth in this section were of his own composition.

"These are also proverbs of Solomon, which the men of Hezekiah, king of Judah, copied out" (25:1).

Some think that these proverbs were culled out of the three thousand proverbs which Solomon spoke (I Kings 4:32), leaving out those that were physical and that pertained to natural philosophy, and preserving such as were divine and moral. In this collection, some have noticed that special regard was given to those observations which concern kings and their administration.

"The words of Agur, the Son of Jakeh" (30:1)

Although some have tried to connect this announcement with Solomon, asserting that it was a kind of *nom de plume* that he used, yet it is evident that this person, whoever he was, was not Solomon. He is connected by many scholars

215

with the Massa mentioned in Genesis 25:14 as a son of Ishmael. His home would therefore be somewhere in north Arabia.

"The words of King Lemuel" (31:1)

Here again many have sought to connect this man and ruler with Solomon, affirming that he is expressing the wonderful love and regard that existed between his mother, Bathsheba, and himself. It would appear, however, that the wise, unknown monarch referred to was, like Agur, a descendant of Ishmael, and therefore, like Agur, a king of the same tribe.

"The words of the wise" (24:23; see 1:6; 22:17)

The proverbs bearing this title apparently are ascribed to sages in general, thus indicating that in this time of peace and prosperity, a class of men had arisen differing alike from the priest and prophet, men who studied the practical questions of life in their bearing upon individual conduct, and who cultivated beauty of style in their imagination.

The Scope

Perhaps no better statement of the scope or design of this book can be given than the inspired words found in 1:2-4:

> To know wisdom and instruction,
>> To perceive the words of understanding;
> To receive the instruction of wisdom, justice, and
>> judgment, and equity;
> To give subtilty to the simple,
>> To the young man, knowledge and discretion.

Such words seem to indicate that the general idea of the book is to instruct the young at their entrance into public and active life. But have we not, in Proverbs, rules for the

216

guidance of all, whether young or old? Can we not all find in this book that which will "inspire deep reverence for God, a fear of His judgments, and an ardent love for wisdom and virtue"?

Dr. Arnot has a series of expositions dealing with many of the Proverbs, and the title of his book denotes the true scope of Proverbs, *Laws from Heaven for Life on Earth*. He writes:

> Proverbs is a book of wisdom for the path of us all; and it is God going over the path with us. In Ecclesiastes you have King Solomon going over the path alone in his own experience; but in Proverbs, you have God going over the path with us, pointing out the dangers, the need of care in this direction or in the other. And he who will be a wise man in the one who has his mind and heart and conscience fully equipped with the wondrous truth in this Book of Proverbs.

Ridout observes that there are thirty-one chapters in the book, one chapter a day, for a month. Says he:

> If you will take it, and read a chapter every day for a month, carefully and prayerfully, and note the words of wisdom that are in it, I need not assure you of what value it will be to you. If you will do this again and again your profit will be greater, for it is not a book that you can close and put away, but one that you can live by as a guidebook, through the world.

Characteristics

One peculiarity of the book is that it seems to stand alone. If it was taken out of the Bible altogether, it would still be complete and whole as a book of wisdom. "We are not," says Bishop Hopkins, "to expect generally any connection, either of sense or sentences, in this Book of Proverbs. Other parts of

217

Scripture are like a rich mine, where the precious ore runs along in one continued vein; but this is like a heap of pearls, which, though they are loose and unstrung, are not therefore the less excellent and valuable."

Another characteristic is its literary style. The wonderful poetic beauty of this book is a marked feature. Dr. James M. Gray takes the following illustrations from *The Literary Study of the Bible* as an example of its poetic worth. In 4:10-19 (RV), we have a poem on "The Two Paths," appearing thus:

Hear, O my Son, and receive my sayings;
And the years of thy life shall be many.
I have taught thee in the way of wisdom,
I have led thee in paths of uprightness;
When thou goest, thy steps shall not be straitened;
And if thou runnest, thou shalt not stumble.
Take fast hold of instruction;
Let her not go;
Keep her;
For she is thy life.
Enter not into the path of the wicked,
And walk not in the way of evil men;
Avoid it,
Pass not by it,
Turn from it
And pass on.
For they sleep not, except they have done mischief,
And their sleep is taken away, unless they cause some
    to fall;
For they eat the bread of wickedness,
And drink the wine of violence.
But the path of the righteous is as the shining light,
That shineth more and more unto the perfect day.
The way of the wicked is as darkness,
They know not at what they stumble.

There is yet another characteristic of the book that one may refer to. Proverbs is an anthology of sayings or lessons of the sages—on life, character, and conduct; and it embodies the distinctively educative strain of Hebrew literature. Professor Plumtree remarks that "for the most part it seems to stand, like the proverbs of other nations, on the ground of a prudential, practical morality. Men are warned against sensuality, drunkenness, slander, indebtedness, on the ground that they will find themselves involved in disaster, or shame, or inconvenience. The rewards and punishments of the life to come are hardly mentioned."

Key Verse

This is found in the prologue and is never lost sight of throughout the book. In fact, the rest of the book is a development or expansion of the theme it embodies: "The fear of the Lord is the beginning of knowledge" (1:7).

It is interesting to notice that the word "beginning" may be translated "chief part." And so it is, for no matter what wisdom a man may have, if he lacks the true reverence of the Lord, and holiness, then what true knowledge has he?

Key Words

By gathering the key words together, one is quickly guided as to the teaching of the book: "wisdom" occurs fifty-two times; "wisely," three times; "wise," sixty-five times; and "fools," "foolishness," and equivalents occur seventy-nine times. From this one can see that the central thought of the book is that goodness is wisdom, and wickedness is folly.

"Righteousness" also finds a prominent place in the book, occurring (with the word "righteous") seventy-five times.

Key Thought

The phrase in the key verse that we have mentioned, "the

fear of the Lord," occurs thirteen times throughout the book. Combining this with the key words referred to, we come to understand that there can be no virtue in our dealing with others unless this is based on religious motives. Practical wisdom, resting on and arising out of religious character, is the leading thought of the inspired volume of Proverbs.

Keynotes of Doctrine

Wisdom, which stands for goodness
Foolishness, which stands for wickedness
Righteousness, which stands for life.

Value

One cannot overestimate the supreme value of Proverbs, both as a book to stimulate our faith in God and as a standard of practical morality. First of all, the religious value is important in that its teachings are peculiarly clear and spiritual. Jehovah is set forth as:

The Creator and Governor of the universe and the Disposer of human destinies (3:17; 8:22-29).
Incomprehensible alike in His nature and His works (25:2; 30:3-4).
Active in universal providence (5:21; 15:3; 25:2; 30:3-4).
Controller of outward fortunes and the minds of men (10:22; 21:1).
Declared to be holy, just, and loving; to command and reward piety and virtue, and to abhor and punish all sin, not only here but also in eternity (3:33; 10:3-29; 12:2; 14:32).

Regarding its practical value, Matthew Henry tells us that Proverbs is a book that helps us "to form right notions of things, and to possess our minds with clear and distinct ideas

220

of them; to distinguish between truth and falsehood, good and evil; and to order our conversation aright in every thing."

Analysis

Owing to the miscellaneous character of the book, a detailed outline of it is impossible. However, this brief outline may be followed:

1. Preface, introducing the subject of wisdom (1:1-6)

2. In praise of wisdom (1:7-9)

A Father's counsel to his son. The frequent repetition of the phrase "my son" implies the tone of a father or a sage bringing stores of wisdom and experience to the young.

Another outstanding feature of this section is the personification of wisdom in chapter 8. Such a description of wisdom is interpreted as declaratory of Christ. Proverbs 8:22-26, with John 1:1-3 and Colossians 1:17, can only refer to the eternal Son of God.

3. Maxims bearing on the nature, value and fruits of good and bad conduct in various relations to life (10:22–16:33)

All the proverbs in this section, the longest section of the book, are molded strictly to the couplet form (one triplet only [19:7] being an apparent exception, due probably to the loss of a line), each proverb a parallelism in condensed phrasing, in which the second line gives either some contrast to or some amplification of the first.

4. *Some words of the wise (22:17-24:22)*

In this short section the proverb literature seems for the first time to have become, as it were, self-conscious, to regard itself as a strain of wise counsel to be reckoned with for its educative value.

5. *Further words of the wise (24:23-34)*

The wise sayings under this section refer to wise intercourse and ordered industry.

6. *More proverbs of Solomon (25-29)*

Here there is a tendency to group numbers of proverbs on like subjects (25:2-7). The proverbs in this portion are chiefly antithetic and comparative.

7. *The sayings of Agur (30)*

The form of Agur's proverbs is peculiar, verging indeed on the artificial. He deals mostly in so-called numerical proverbs ("three things . . . yea, four"), a style of utterance paralleled elsewhere only in 6:16-19.

8. *The words of Lemuel (31)*

The words of Lemuel are a mother's plea to her royal son for chastity, temperance, and justice—the kingly virtues. The form used here is the simple Hebrew parallelism, not detached couplets, but continuous.

The last twenty-two verses constitute a single poem in praise of a worthy woman, extolling especially her household virtues. In form, these verses begin in the original with the successive twenty-two letters of the Hebrew alphabet, a favorite form of Hebrew verse. Matthew Henry calls this section "a looking glass for ladies."

Much, much more could be said about this unrivaled compendium of wisdom and counsel, the Book of Proverbs, but space does not permit. Read this condensation of the wisdom of the ages. Read it again and compare your life with it. It is as practical for the daily walk as is the Book of Psalms for the daily worship.

Theme 22
The Church in Solomon's Song

Among the many allegorical interpretations of this love song from the pen of King Solomon, the one stating that it pictures "Christ and His church" is the most prominent. Many spiritual writers, like Robert Murray McCheyne, maintain that these two lines are evident: The Lord, the Beloved One in union with His church, His Bride. The book can be divided and treated thus. Six beautiful similes are employed to describe the various aspects of the Beloved and the Bride. The direct application of the book, especially its sixth chapter, is Solomon's fascination for the Shulamite and her loyalty to her shepherd-lover. What an expression of gratitude for her unique character this chapter contains! But the language of the book is symbolic of the Christian church, as well as the individual believer's association with the Lord. There are some writers who discern in verses 4 and 10 of chapter 6, a gradual unfolding of the truth of the church.

The Church Supernal

"Beautiful . . . as Tirzah, comely as Jerusalem" (6:4). This suggests her position in the heavenlies. In the purpose and plan of God she is to be without spot. "He hath chosen us in him before the foundation of the world, that we should be holy and without blame before him in love" (Eph. 1:4). What an ideal He has for the church!

The Church Patriarchal

"Looketh forth as the morning" (6:10). Abraham is

224

spoken of as "the father of all believers." Jesus said of him, that he "rejoiced to see my day" (John 8:56). In the patriarch we have the first dawn of the character of a called-out body—the promise of the Messiah made known to a dark world.

The Church Levitical

"Fair as the moon" (6:10). While Old Testament saints had light it was but dim and imperfect. Theirs was a partial revelation of God's redemptive purpose. So many of the ceremonies of the tabernacle were shadows of the coming Sun of Righteousness who did not arise until He took upon Himself frail flesh to die. Ancient types and emblems were as a looking through the lattice.

The Church Evangelical

"Clear as the sun" (6:10). The birth of Christ who came as a light to lighten the world was the bursting forth of the Sun upon its darkness. With His coming, and also the advent of the Spirit, there came the spread of the gospel, with its radiant beams being scattered abroad.

The Church Triumphal

"Terrible as an army with banners" (6:10). This aspect can apply to the completion of the church and her translation at the Second Coming of her Head, when He will lead in triumph the innumerable host of the redeemed with all the dazzling splendor of an exceedingly great army. We now come to examine more closely the precious truths associated with the Beloved's expressive designations of the one He loved.

225

The Beauty of Pleasantness

"Thou art beautiful, O my love, as Tirzah." The name *Tirzah* means "pleasantness," and was so called because it was pleasantly situated and of proverbial beauty. The Septuagint translates the phrase as "fair as pleasure," while an old Bible version puts it as, "Thou art pleasant even as loveliness itself." Tirzah was an old, lovely royal city, which had been the royal residence for the kings of Israel from Jeroboam to Umri before the capital was removed to Samaria.

Nothing is so attractive as pleasantness, as David's eulogy of Saul and Jonathan illustrates when he spoke of them as being "lovely and pleasant in their lives, and in their death . . . not divided" (II Sam. 1:23). There are those who seem to delight in saying and doing unpleasant things. But God loves all that is beautiful and pleasing. It is profitable to trace the stream of pleasantness as it quietly flows through Scripture.

> Think of the pleasure God gave to man—"The Lord God made to grow every tree that is pleasant to the sight" (Gen. 2:9).
> Think of the pleasure man can give God—"The offering of Judah and Jerusalem shall be pleasant unto the Lord" (Mal. 3:4).
> Think of the pleasure we can give each other—"Behold, how good and how pleasant it is for brethren to dwell together in unity" (Ps. 133:1).

Did not God create the church to be a beautiful and pleasant sight in the midst of all the ugliness and wretchedness of sin? Tirzah was the ten tribes that revolted after the death of Solomon. But the day is coming when all Israel will be united, and her Beloved will say of her, "Israel My Glory!" As for His church, the blemishes of divisions and of worldliness may mar her beauty, but the time is fast drawing near when the beauty of her Lord will be upon her, and she will

be His spotless Bride. Our personal responsibility as members
of His Body is to reflect His beauty and pleasantness.

> Let me show forth Thy beauty, Lord Jesus,
> Like sunshine on the hills;
> Oh, let my lips pour forth Thy sweetness
> In joyous sparkling rills.

The Comeliness of Peace

"As comely as Jerusalem." The name *Jerusalem* itself
means, "the dwelling of peace," and throughout Scripture
the city is emblematic of peace, although it belied the name
it bore. Within it was the temple, and it was known as "the
city of the living God . . . the joy of the whole earth," having
protecting mountains round about her. What is more comely
than peace? Think of Jesus asleep on a pillow in that boat
tossed about on the water by a fierce storm! Is this not a
type of His church as she witnesses in an agitated world? "In
the world ye shall have tribulation . . . in me . . . peace." How
can this heavenly, God-glorifying peace become ours?

By resting, continually in the Lord

"Thou wilt keep him in perfect peace, whose mind
is stayed on thee, because he trusteth in thee" (Isa.
26:3).

By loving His Word

"Great peace have they which love thy law, and
nothing shall offend them" (Ps. 119:165).

Must we not confess the absence of this comely peace in the
corporate life of the church today? John reminds us that the
world recognizes us as Christ's disciples if we love one
another. Although we lustily sing, "We are not divided, all

one body we"—the sentiment is far from a common experience, for too often instead of fighting together against one common foe, we are found fighting one another. Surely, if we claim to be at peace with God, it is incumbent upon us to be at peace among ourselves, and as a whole, as "comely as Jerusalem."

The Hope of Faith

"Who is she that looketh forth as the morning?" This arresting figure of speech suggests several precious thoughts. For instance, it speaks of—

Freshness

"Looketh forth as the dawn." Dawn is the time of day associated with exhilaration due to the bracing morning air. The shadows of night have vanished, and we open the windows to let the fresh air in. As those who profess to be members of His church we should always present the blush and bloom of spiritual health. The emblem before us can represent the dawning of grace within the soul—our first love, thereafter shining more and more till the perfect day.

Morning Watch

The word "looketh" is used of the Lord—"looking down from heaven," and of man "looking down on earth as through a window." Our life can only be holy, and our testimony effective as we "look forth every morning." Commencing each day with the upward look results in all necessary strength for what the day may hold for it. Anointed with fresh oil we are able to go out into the world confident that the chariot wheels will not drag heavily. Grace will be ours to walk, and not faint.

228

Advent Hope

All who love the thought of the Lord's appearing "look forth every morning" for Him to redeem His promise to return. With the beginning of another day, we look up and ask, "Will it be today, Lord?" For His true church, the dreary night will soon be past, and meridian splendor will be hers—a morning without clouds. Many who looked forth every day for redemption in Israel rejoiced when they saw the Babe. The long, weary night of sorrow and rejection for God's ancient people will vanish and their glorious morning will dawn when they look upon Him whom they pierced and mourn.

The Purity of Witness

"Fair as the moon." Solomon, a master in the use of poetic imagery, implies "whiteness" by the moon, and "heat" for the sun. With the moon there is the thought of brilliance and purity, so we speak about "the silvery moon." While the moon fulfills many functions, there are two that can be distinguished and applied to our hearts.

It shines at night during the sun's absence.

Before the Sun of Righteousness appears, it is the privilege and responsibility of the church to witness during His absence amid the gathering darkness of a condemned world. As the night is far spent, we must redouble our efforts to shine as lights in a world lost in darkness and sin.

The moon has no inherent light.

Instead, it reflects what it receives from the sun. It sends forth borrowed light and illuminates the dark places of earth. In like manner, we have nothing of our own to give the world. In our testimony for the Lord we simply restore a borrowed ray. "We give thee of thine own." We must never forget the question, "What hast thou, that thou didst not receive?"

229

The Energy of Love

"Clear as the sun." The sun is noted, not only for its light and clarity, but also for its burning heat and energizing properties and mighty strength. "Let them that love him be as the sun when he goeth forth in his might" (Judg. 5:31). John saw the countenance of the Lord he dearly loved as "the sun shining in his strength" (Rev. 1:16). The sun is the mightiest factor in the life of earth for everything man and beast require are dependent upon it. Two functions can be stressed:

The sun scatters disease.

What a boon to physical health sunshine is! The sure way to kill spiritual diseases is to live under the life-giving beams of Him who is our Sun. "The Lord God is a sun." The church, likewise, should be as "clear as the sun," putting forth all spiritual energy as she wars against all that is dark and sinful in the world.

The sun gives warmth.

How we all love to bask in it! Travel agents entice us to follow the sun as holidays are contemplated. The world is a cold place to live in and the function of the church is to glow and shed forth that warmth of love toward those living in the winter of their sin. A children's hymn says, "Jesus wants me for a sunbeam," and it is His purpose that all of us who are truly His should be as sunbeams scattering the warmth of divine love wherever we go. It would seem that the church today is more like an iceberg than a sunbeam.

The Influence of Unity

"Terrible as an army with banners." The term *terrible* means "awe-inspiring," or "dazzling." Twice over Solomon

230

uses this descriptive simile (6:4, 10), and its underlying thought is that of bannered hosts, mighty in strength, from whom foes flee. The Shulamite is portrayed as having powerful eyes, and the Beloved found himself conquered, awed, dazzled by her personal charms (6:5). Can we not see in the language Solomon uses here, the church as a militant force? We sing, "Like a mighty army moves the church of God," and all the various conservative denominations can be looked upon as different regiments forming one army and serving one Sovereign. But is the world being charmed, conquered by the witness of the church? Must we not confess that because of her comprise and pursuit of worldly policies and methods she has lost her power to win the world for God?

Terrible! We may shrink in adopting this term to describe the power of the church, but the question must be faced, "Has she the voice of authority, striking terror in the hearts of the godless, and commanding respect?" During World War I, politicians declared that if the church had been the voice of national conscience, fearful carnage would have been prevented. The church ought to be a force, not a farce; active, not artistic; courageous as well as comely; powerful as well as pure; God's battle-axe and weapon of war.

The church should have power to make the ungodly tremble and bring them to their knees. Describing the power of the early church, Paul spoke of those who fell down on their faces to worship God, and reported that God was indeed in His valiant witnesses (I Cor. 14:23, 25).

The church should have power to overcome the world. John, known as "The Apostle of Love," could yet thunder out divine condemnation. He wrote that all who are "begotten of God overcometh the world" (I John 5:4). Hear him as he challenges the church, "This is the victory that overcometh the world, even our faith!"

The church should have power to master Satan, the terrible foe of mankind. God-begotten, she should know how to resist the devil in his efforts to damn mankind. Alas! how-

231

ever, overcome by the world, the church is destitute of the power she once had to turn the world upside down.

Banners! In times of war, regimental banners or colors have proved a great inspiration to those who fought for the country they represented. The banner of the church is a blood-stained one—it is the cross. "It was God's good pleasure through the foolishness of preaching [a crucified Saviour] to save them that believe" (I Cor. 1:21, RV). At Calvary Christ destroyed the works of darkness, and 'neath the banner of the cross, the church is ever terrible. Thrilling stories are told of banners being the symbol of courage, unity, and confidence during raging battles. It should be so with the church militant—

> Rouse then, soldiers,
> Rally round the banner!

The weapons to use are not carnal, but mighty through God for the pulling down of satanic strongholds (II Cor. 10:5). Further, the church has, as an army with banners, a most invincible Captain, or "Leader-in-Chief," as the Dutch version of Hebrews 12:2 puts it. And because He is the unconquered Leader, the church should be found sharing His victory. The church's living Head is her glorious Victor, her Prince divine, her dauntless King, the One who destroyed the works of the devil. Hear His shout of triumph—"I have overcome the world!" His church's obligation is to reap the fruits of His grim conflict with hell, and serve Him in a hostile world as "terrible as His army with banners."

Theme 23
The Reputation of Christ

The Bible is a book of questions, some of which are asked but not answered, like the solemn one we should hear more sermons on—"How shall we escape if we neglect so great salvation?" (Heb. 2:3). The majority of the questions asked are answered in some part or other of the sacred volume.

The First Question in the Bible Is From Satan to Man About God

"Yea, hath God said, Ye shall not eat of every tree of the garden?" (Gen. 3:1). Satan became Satan by questioning the authority of God, and since the creation of man has sought to sow the seed of doubt in the human mind. But this question is answered in the declaration of the character of God who "cannot lie" (Titus 1:2). What God said in the garden to Adam and Eve He meant and, true to His word, condemnation overtook those who listened to Satan's word of doubt.

The Second Question Was From God to Man About His Sin

Conscious that they had treated God as a man capable of lying, our first parents tried to hide from Him. Doubt led to desertion so there came the question, "Adam, where art thou?" (Gen. 3:9). Now a sinner, he required a Saviour, so "Where art thou?" leads to "Where is the Lamb?" (Gen. 22:7). When made conscious of his guilt before a thrice holy God, the sinner hears the voice calling, "Where art thou?" and, upon finding out where he is, he cries, "Where is He?"—

233

the Lamb able to bear away my sin (Matt. 2:2; John 1:29).

The Third Question Is from God to Man About His Fellowman

The first-born of the world's first sinners, became the world's first murderer. This brings us to God's question to Cain, "Where is Abel thy brother?" Conscience-stricken, he shirked the divine question by asking another, "Am I my brother's keeper?" (Gen. 4:9). Our Lord answered this question when He said, "Thou shalt love thy neighbor as thyself" (Matt. 22:39). Andrew believed that he was his own brother's keeper, so after he found the Lord he "first findeth his own brother" (John 1:41).

The Fourth (and most pertinent) Question Is the One from Christ to Man About Himself

The Pharisees had asked Him, "What thinkest thou?" and then He played their game and asked, "What think ye of Christ?" (Matt. 22:17, 42). No wonder we read that "from that day forth" they asked no more questions!

We are all agreed on the point that it is easier to ask questions than to answer them, but the one we are to consider has been fully answered. We learn much in life by asking questions, and this greatest of all questions has much to teach us. All the pressing questions and problems of today are secondary to the pointed question, "What think ye of Christ?" Answer this, and you find the answers to other questions. It will be noted that He asked, "What *think* ye of Christ?" He respects the power of the mind He gave man to face and answer questions. His appeal is not merely to man's emotional feelings. This is why His reputation stands the closest scrutiny and minutest inspection of the clearest and cleverest mind. Let us discover how the New Testament faces the question "What think ye of Christ?"

The Answer of Heaven

The best way to arrive at a right estimation of the character of a person is to approach it from every angle, discovering what his family, his friends, his foes think, and then compare their answers with our own personal observation of the one in question. This saves us from the one-sided opinion or bias we sometimes are guilty of in assessing character. In our consideration of Christ, therefore, let us ask those who loved Him, and those who hated Him what they thought of His character and claims.

God the Father

Reverently, we want to ask what the Father thought of His Son. Usually in a family, the father's thought of his child is the highest and best. Further, he sees what the outside world never discerns, namely, the real person within his offspring. Parents may be somewhat biased and overlook little faults, for they say that "love is blind." But with God the Father it is different, for He has perfect justice as well as perfect love. Had there been any flaw in the character of His Son in a past eternity, He would have deposed Him as He did Lucifer, who perhaps was next to Christ in honor and dignity before he was cast out of heaven and became Satan.

Shall we ask the Father, then, "What think ye of Christ?" Such a question was answered when Jesus commenced His public ministry after living for thirty years as Mary's first-born Son—"This is my beloved Son, in whom I am well pleased" (Matt. 3:17). Could an answer be more explicit than that? Before time commenced, He was His Father's constant delight (Prov. 8:30) and throughout His earthly sojourn His Father found perfect satisfaction in His Son's ways, works, and words. He always sought to do those things that pleased His Father, and thus He gave His Father pleasure. This is why we must hear Him, seeing He was God's perfect man, and man's perfect God.

235

God the Spirit

He is the author of Scripture, and, therefore, ultimately responsible for everything holy men recorded of the Lord Jesus Christ, and was also closely identified with Him in the days of His flesh. What did the Holy Spirit think of Christ? At Pentecost "the Spirit gave them [the disciples] utterance" (Acts 2:4) and what they uttered about Christ was divinely inspired: " . . . hear these words: Jesus of Nazareth, a man approved of God among you by miracles and wonders and signs" (Acts 2:22). Then came the Spirit-prompted declaration, "God hath made this same Jesus, whom ye have crucified, both Lord and Christ" (2:36). From His own teaching we learn how the Holy Spirit loves to glorify the Lord, testify of Him, and unfold to saints the truth concerning Him (John 14-16).

Can we say that we have made Him our "Lord and Christ"? When He has the Lordship of every part of our life, all questioning about Him ceases. Love obeys, and does not ask questions. Once questions regarding His Lordship were answered we read that "no man was able to answer him a word, neither durst any man ask him from that day forth any more questions" (Matt. 22:46).

God the Son

To ask an ordinary person what he thinks of himself might produce an answer of self-adulation and reservation of any faults in his character. Christ asked others what they thought of Him, but in all humility we can ask the question, "What didst Thou think of Thyself, O Christ?" The answer is given in His august claims. He never thought of Himself more highly than He ought; neither was there any trace of self-assumption in His estimation of Himself, as there may be in ourselves when we tell others what we think about ourselves. When a man thinks himself to be something when he is nothing, he is a fool, deceiving himself.

But with God's beloved Son it was totally different, for He was all He claimed to be. David Strauss said of Him that He had "a conscience unclouded by the memory of any sins," and this was His own estimation of His character: "The prince of this world cometh and hath nothing in me" (John 14:30); "Which of you convinceth me of sin?" (John 8:46). It was because He was "holy, harmless, undefiled, separate from sinners" that His death for sinners is so efficacious. Had there been the least stain upon His character, He would have forfeited the right to die as the Saviour from sin. Utterly devoted to the will and work of His Father, He could declare without fear of contradiction, "I do always the things that please him" (John 8:29). He, more than the best man who ever breathed, is the "selfless Man and stainless Gentleman." Thomas Dekker, of the sixteenth century said of Him—

> The best of men
> That e'er wore earth about Him, was a sufferer,
> A soft, meek, patient, humble, tranquil spirit,
> The first true Gentleman that ever breath'd.

The Angelic Host

Having beheld the glory of their Lord from the eternal past, the angels surely knew how to value Him aright, and thus we are right to ask them what they think of Him who for our redemption was made a little lower than the angels. The Scriptures abound with angelic praises for the One who laid aside His robe of eternal glory and was made in likeness of sinful flesh. It was an angel who said, "Thou shalt call his name *Jesus:* for he shall save his people from their sins" (Matt. 1:21). It was an angel who announced, "Unto you is born . . . a Saviour which is Christ the Lord" (Luke 2:11). It was an angel who cried to another, "Holy, holy, holy, is the Lord of Hosts: the whole earth is full of his glory" (Isa. 6:3; John 12:38-39). It was an angel who, with a loud voice pro-

237

claimed, "Worthy is the Lamb, that was slain to receive power, and riches, and wisdom, and strength, and honour, and glory, and blessing" (Rev. 5:12).

Angels, in the height adore Him:
Ye behold Him face to face.

Among the angels, the Lamb has all the glory, for they are ceaseless in their praise of Him who is in heaven as the glorified Son of Man, and now higher than the angels. Having never sinned the angelic host requires no redemption. Therefore, although they magnify Him for all He accomplished as the Lamb for our salvation, they cannot praise Him as can sinners who were emancipated from the thralldom of sin by His sacrifice.

The Glorified

By this vast host we mean those who, while on earth, repented of their sin and received Jesus as their Saviour, and who are now, according to His desire, with Him in glory (John 17:24). If they could come back to earth, what a testimony they would give as to the wonders of their glorified Lord! Having seen the King in His beauty, they would confess that, while on earth, they were not told the half of all His might and majesty.

Yet John in The Revelation tells us what the ravished hearts of all those who form the Church Triumphant in glory, think of Christ. "Thou art worthy, O Lord, to receive glory and honour and power" (4:11). "Thou was slain, and hast redeemed us to God" (5:9). "Blessing, and honour, and glory, and power be unto him that sitteth upon the throne" (5:13).

Thus all heaven is emphatic in its answer to the question, "What think ye of Christ?" They see His face, and gaze upon His wounds, and behold Him as the Father's constant joy, the center of all attraction, the constant admiration of seraphim and cherubim, and the object of the ceaseless adoration of

238

angels. Not until we see Him as He is will we be able to praise Him as we ought. We can, however, prepare for such a glorious sphere by living for His honor as we await our transition.

> 'Tis the Church Triumphant singing
>   Worthy the Lamb;
> Heaven throughout with praises ringing,
>   Worthy the Lamb.
> Thrones and pow'rs before Him bending,
> Odours sweet with voice ascending
> Swell the chorus never ending,
>   Worthy the Lamb.

The Answer of Hell

Very often our foes can give as true a verdict of our reputation as our friends. Because of all He was in Himself as the One in whom was no sin, and hating, therefore, all that was alien to His holy mind and will, Jesus had many foes. Shall we ask, then, all the dark and devilish inhabitants of hell the same question, "What think ye of Christ?"

Ask the Devil

It has been suggested that it was his jealousy of Christ in the past eternity that made Lucifer, as he was then known, the devil he became. Doubtless he knew all about the plan of redemption, conceived by the Father and His Son, and gave himself to the destruction of such a plan. Close to Christ before time began, the devil witnessed His perfect rectitude, and knew Him to be the well-beloved Son in whom the Father was pleased. After his fall and the fall of man that he was responsible for, and the announcement of the coming of Christ as the Seed of the woman, he set about in every possible way to thwart the appearance of Christ as the Saviour of the world. When his plans failed, the devil sought in many

239

ways to destroy Christ before His death on the cross, which was to be God's remedy for sin.

Cognizant of our Lord's inherent holiness, the devil strove to make Him sin, hence the temptations in the wilderness. Had you asked him what he thought of Christ after that fierce conflict, he would have said, "He is different from sinners. He does not yield to temptation. He is the spotless Lord." When Peter tried to dissuade the Master from going to the cross, He said to him, "Get thee behind me, Satan!" He did not reply directly to Peter, but spoke to the subtle one who had prompted Peter to urge his Lord to take an easier way than the way of His cross. Reluctantly, the devil must have recognized that Christ was beyond his power to destroy His character and purpose.

Ask the Demons

The myriads of demons, who were once angels but who rebelled with the devil and left their first estate, knew all about Christ's preexistence. They possess full knowledge of all that He was and all that He became at His incarnation, and the Gospels recall His encounters with these denizens of hell. Dare we ask them the question, "What think ye of Christ?" The Master, we read, "suffered not the demons to speak, because they knew him" (Mark 1:34). But one did speak when dealt with by the Lord, "I know thee who thou art, the Holy One of God." Why, there are some professed theologians who cannot acknowledge His deity as that demon did! James had in mind the demoniac estimation of the authority and power of Deity, when he wrote, "The devils also believe, and tremble" (2:19). But while the satanic host may tremble at the thought of Him because they know all about Him, very few among men tremble as they remember Him. Can it be that sinners do not fear God as they should because the pulpit has failed to present Him in all His justice and hatred of sin, as well as in all His love and mercy?

Ask the Pharisees

We put these constant foes of Christ under this section because He called them, "the children of the devil." In their antagonism to His claims, these religious hypocrites were actuated by the devil, hence our Lord's scathing denunciation of them as his puppets. Yet, strange though it seems, these Pharisees gave utterance to some of the sweetest truths concerning His grace, love, and wisdom. What did they think of Christ? They uttered a blessed truth about Him when they said, "This man receiveth sinners" (Luke 15:2). How hopeless we would have been had He not! Then listen to this Pharisaic estimation, "Master, we know that thou art true, and teachest the way of God in truth, neither carest thou for any man: for thou regardest not the person of man" (Matt. 22:16). What a remarkable confession this was! Those wily Pharisees certainly knew that Jesus did not care a hoot for their opinion of Him. Confounded by His wisdom, we read that "when they heard these words they marvelled, and left him, and went their way" (Matt. 22:22).

Ask the Lost in Hell

It might be deemed impossible to glean what the doomed in perdition think of Christ. Yet He Himself gives us a glimpse of their attitude toward Him. Answering the questions of the Pharisees He related the episode of the Rich Man and Lazarus, and indicated in this dramatic portrayal of life beyond the grave that those in hell are now conscious not only of their eternal loss but that all they heard about the saving power of Jesus while on earth is true. Tormented in the flame of the remembrance of slighted opportunities, they recognize Christ's power as the risen One. "If one went unto them from the dead, they will repent" (Luke 16:30). But He knew better and affirmed that sin-blinded souls on earth are not so easily persuaded, hence His reply to the request from

241

hell, "If they hear not Moses and the prophets, neither will they be persuaded though one rose from the dead" (Luke 16:19-31).

There is no doubt about the reality of Jesus and His saving gospel among those who are eternally restless in the caverns of hell. Why, there are those residing there who can tell others the plan of salvation, but for them there is no relief from their perpetual misery! On earth, they were surrounded with Christian influences. Perhaps born in a Christian home and in and out of church all their days, they were familiar with the saving truths of the gospel. They said prayers, read the Bible, engaged in religious activities—yet they lived and died without Christ as their personal Saviour. Such glorious truth, never to be realized by the lost, only accentuates their misery in hell. In their lifetime on earth they received many good things from God, but they failed to acknowledge the Giver.

The Answer of Earth

Countless volumes have already been written to describe the greatest figure of all ages, but as John puts it at the conclusion of his Gospel regarding the life and works of Jesus, "If they should be written every one, I suppose that even the world itself could not contain the books that should be written" (21:25). There is much food for faith in the meditation upon all that saintly minds have written about Him. The more we read works about His magnificent Person and mighty influence, the more we feel like saying with dear old Samuel Rutherford who was deeply in love with Christ, "My ever-running over, Lord Jesus." But great testimonies as to His worth and work have come also from those who were not His committed followers. The testimony of opponents is often the best evidence we can obtain of the reality of a man or a movement. Napoleon the Great, for instance, said that Alexander, Caesar, Charlemagne, and himself founded em-

242

pires upon force, while Jesus founded one on love, with the result that millions would die for Him. Here is another reputed witness Napoleon gave to the transcendent majesty of our blessed Lord—

> Everything in Christ astonishes me. His spirit overawes me, and His will confounds me. His ideas and His sentiments, the truths He announces, His manner of convincing, are not explained either by human observation or the nature of things. His birth and the history of His life, the profundity of His doctrine, which grapples the mightiest difficulties, and which ask of those difficulties, the most admirable solution. His gospel, His apparition, His empire, His march across the ages and the realm— everything for me a prodigy, a mystery insoluble, which plunges me into a reverie which I cannot escape—a mystery which is there before my eyes, a mystery which I can neither deny nor explain. Here I see nothing human. The nearer I approach, the more carefully I examine everything that is above me. Everything remains grand, of a grandeur which overpowers. His religion is a revelation from an intelligence which certainly is not that of a man.

Then what did Renan, the renowned French skeptic think of Christ? Why, he declared Him to be the greatest genius that ever lived, or will live; that His beauty is eternal; and His reign, endless. "Jesus is in every respect unique, and nothing can be compared with Him. Be the unlooked phenomena of the future what they may, Jesus will never be surpassed." Further, testifying to His early influence upon Rome, Renan said, "Jesus Christ created a paradise out of the hell of Rome." We could go on, *ad infinitum,* quoting the admiration of both friends and foes for Him who is "the fairest of all the earth beside." But let us confine ourselves to what various Bible characters had to say about the Son of God who became the Son of Man that He might make the sons of men the sons of God.

What Did the Prophets Think of Christ?

It was to Him that all the prophets gave witness (Acts 10:43)—and what sublime truths they prophesied concerning Him! The Holy Spirit revealed to these holy men much of the grief and glory of the Messiah who was to appear (I Peter 1:11).

Abraham had a preview of His redemption and reign for Jesus Himself affirmed that the patriarch rejoiced to see his day and he saw it and was glad (John 8:56).

Moses, too, was given a glimpse of Him whom he was to see in the flesh, as he did on the Mount of Transfiguration. Scripture tells us that Moses esteemed "the reproach of Christ greater riches than the treasures of Egypt" (Heb. 11:26).

Isaiah, more than any other prophet, received a divine insight into all that the coming Messiah was to accomplish, earning him the title of "The Evangelical Prophet." What did he think of Christ? "Wonderful, Counsellor, The mighty God, The everlasting Father, The Prince of Peace" (9:6).

What Did the Kings Think of Christ?

Among the kings who testified beforehand the glories of Him who was born a King and will yet reign as the King of kings, there was David, of whom Jesus said that David in spirit called Him (Christ Himself) Lord (see Matt. 22:43). To the psalmist, the One to be born of his house and lineage was "fairer than the children of men" (Ps. 45:2). King Solomon, who knew all about the Calvary Psalm that his father wrote (Ps. 22), likewise believed that Christ would come as the perfect expression of the wisdom of God (Prov. 8:30-32). Whether he had the Messiah at the back of his mind when he wrote his renowned Song, we cannot say. Anyhow, much of what he wrote of the Beloved is symbolic of the beauty and worth of Christ: "My beloved is white and ruddy, the chiefest among ten thousand. . . . His mouth is most sweet, yea, he is altogether lovely" (Song of Sol. 5:10-16).

What Did His Contemporaries Think of Christ?

We can divide those who lived at the same time as Christ into two classes. Those who knew Him from within and those who knew Him from without. What impression did He make upon those who surrounded Him in the days of His flesh?

First, let us take the testimony of those within, or who were more closely associated with Him than others who knew Him. It is most profitable to gather together all their written tributes to Him who came as the Lord of Glory. This fact is evident—that the influence He had upon the lives of many around Him enabled them to go out and do exploits for Him.

Take Mary

The privileged mother who bore Him surely knew Him as no other did. As her Child, Mary gave Him love, thought, and tenderness; and if He bore the facial resemblance of any, it would be that of His mother, seeing He had her flesh. What did she think of the Christ she brought into the world? "My spirit hath rejoiced in God my Saviour" (Luke 1:47). Then she knew Him to be not only the one who came as the promised Redeemer, but as the One worthy of implicit obedience, "Whatsoever he saith unto you, do it" (John 2:5).

Take the Disciples

Jesus could say of those He chose to follow Him, "These have continued with me in my trials." They walked, talked, slept, ate, and wept together. They had countless oppor-

245

tunities of watching Him under all circumstances, and knew Him more intimately than the common people who heard Him gladly. They looked at Him from different angles, yet their testimonies concerning Him concur.

John the Baptist was His cousin, and they must have played together as lads. But John knew that he was the one to prepare the way for Him as the coming King, and confessed that he was unworthy to unloose His sandals. After John's initiation of Christ into His public ministry, he exclaimed, "Behold the Lamb of God, which taketh away the sin of the world" (John 1:29).

Peter was another who had close and intimate contact with Christ, but who, every time he heard a cock crow, remembered how shamefully he had deserted Him in a time of trial. Ask this rugged disciple the question, "What think ye of Christ?" and what answers have you? By divine inspiration he said of Him, "Thou art the Christ, the Son of the living God" (Matt. 16:15-16). In afteryears, when Peter came to write his Epistles, looking back on those three years he spent with Christ when he watched Him under all circumstances, he wrote, "Who did no sin, neither was guile found in his mouth" (I Peter 2:22).

John was also one of the chosen Twelve who knew the Master. In fact, whenever he is mentioned, it is always as "the disciple whom Jesus loved." It was John who leaned on the bosom of Jesus, and knew His secrets as no other disciple did. This is why his Gospel, Epistles, and Revelation tell us so much of Him who came as God's beloved Son to die for a lost world. What did John think of Christ? "We beheld his glory, the glory as of the only begotten of the Father, full of grace and truth" (John 1:14). "The blood of Jesus Christ his Son cleanseth us from all sin" (I John 1:7).

Thomas was the disciple who wanted tangible proof that his Master had risen from the dead and who, when he finally saw the wound-prints in His hands, cried, "My Lord and my God" (John 20:28).

246

James, one of the pillars in the early church, who insisted on faith producing works of mercy, and who proclaimed himself to be "a servant of the Lord Jesus Christ tells us in no uncertain terms what he thought of his Master: "The Lord Jesus Christ, the Lord of glory" (2:1).

Paul never hesitated to tell men wherever he traveled what he thought of Christ. To him, "to live was Christ"; and to die meant to be "with Christ." No disciple has ever surpassed the apostle in his superb estimation of Him he lived to preach and teach about. "I count all things . . . but dung that I may win Christ" (Phil. 3:8). "God also hath highly exalted him" (Phil. 2:9-11)—so did Paul highly exalt the Saviour he suffered so much for in his life and labors.

Having considered appreciations of some of those belonging to the inner circle of Christ's contemporaries, let us now select a few from others in the wider circle of those who knew Him, and allow them to give us their answer to the question "What think ye of Christ?" It may surprise us to learn that some of the greatest evidences of our Lord's unique character and sinlessness came from those who were brought into contact with His sublime personality.

Judas. Although this betrayer was called a "friend" by the One he sold for thirty pieces of silver, and was among those chosen as "disciples," he was never Christ's at heart and proved to be a traitor to his solemn trust. Ask this man of whom Jesus said it would have been better for him had he never been born, "What think ye of the One you betrayed?" Here is the answer, "I have sinned in that I have betrayed . . . innocent blood" (Matt. 27:4).

Pilate, who had Christ before him as a prisoner, had the opportunity of studying Him at firsthand. Impressed with His air of sincerity and courageous demeanor, he asked Christ, "What is truth?" not knowing that *The Truth* stood before him. What did he actually think of Christ? After examining the charges brought against Him he repeated, "I find no fault in this man" (Luke 23:4, 14, 22). When forced to yield to

247

the mob demanding the death of Christ, his protest was, "I am innocent of the blood of this just person" (Matt. 27:24).

Lady Pilate had a troubled night after that unjust trial and could not get the sight of that suffering Man out of her mind. Going off to sleep and dreaming, her conscience was stirred, and in the morning she said to her husband, "Have thou nothing to do with this just man: for I have suffered many things this day in a dream because of him" (Matt. 27:19). Pilate had Christ on his hands, and Pilate's wife had Him on her conscience, and both testified to the innocence of Christ. At His trial, no two witnesses agreed together. Each found something about which to praise Him.

Herod, who had heard all about the reputation of Christ, was a man of keen intellect. He requested to see the prisoner, because he thought Him to be a kind of magician able to produce miracles at will, but Christ did not oblige. He was "exceeding glad" when he saw Him, but his gladness was not of faith, only of curiosity. Pilate and he had been at enmity, but became friends again through their meeting with Christ. Well, Herod, "What think ye of Christ?" After his cross-examination, he could only confirm Pilate's verdict. Herod said, " . . . nothing worthy of death hath been done by him" (Luke 23:15, RV).

The Dying Thief, Christ's fellow-sufferer and companion in death, knew that although he was dying for the sins he had committed that the Man on the middle cross was dying for sin, not His own. "This man hath done nothing amiss. . . ." "Lord, remember me when thou comest into thy kingdom" (Luke 23:41, 42).

The Centurion responsible for the details of the cruci-fixion, had the grim task of seeing that the cruel sentence was carried out. It was his responsibility to stay to the bitter end and pronounce the victim dead. He watched Jesus die, and was overwhelmed by His manner and by the messages He uttered. What was his verdict on Christ? "Certainly this was a righteous man" (Luke 23:47).

248

What has history to say in reply to the self-addressed question: "What think ye of Christ?" Testimony to His worth is not less real among ourselves than it was in the past. In his *Gesta Christi*, C. L. Brace says,

> In the case of all the other great names of the world's history, the inevitable and invariable experience has been that the particular man was a power, then only a name, and last of all a memory. Of Jesus Christ the exact opposite is true. He died on a cross of shame, His name gradually became more and more powerful, and He is the greatest influence in the world today. There is, as it has been well said, a fifth *Gospel* being written—the work of Jesus Christ in the hearts and lives of men and nations.

It is most fascinating to follow succeeding generations and select those from every walk of life, whether sympathetic or hostile to the claims of Christ. Ask and discover from them their estimation of Jesus of Nazareth. In some measure the writer has attempted this task in his two-volumed work on *The Man Who Changed the World*.

The question before us, however, resolves itself into a personal testimony, "What think ye [or you and me] of Christ?" It is not what others, above, around, below, think of Him, although their tributes as we have seen, are valuable. The only Christ worth anything to *you*, is the One you know for yourself. So, what do *you* think of Christ? Can you confess with Peter His preciousness? (I Peter 2:7). Or is He not much more than a name to you? You can evade or ignore the question "What think ye of Christ?" You alone can decide what to do with Him who is called Christ. If you try to avoid Him, then even the attempt to ignore Him is in reality a confession of an opinion about Him.

If you want to be certain of His reality, then you must answer the fourfold call He uttered while among men—

"Come unto me"—as the *Redeemer* (Acts 4:12; Heb. 9:25)

249

"Learn of me"—as the *Teacher* (John 7:46)

"Follow me"—as the *Master* (John 13:13)

"Abide in me"—as the *Life* (John 15:4). We must abide in Him for peace (John 16:33; Eph. 2:14); for direction (Mark 7:37); for friendship (Prov. 18:24). The personal question is, What is Jesus worth to me? Do I consider His price to be above rubies? Can I apply to Him what a multitude of Israelites thought of David?—"Thou art worth ten thousand of us" (II Sam. 18:3). Is He not worth ten thousand times ten thousand of us? Who can we liken unto Him who is incomparable? He is holier than the holiest, mightier than the mightiest, kinder than the kindest. A remarkable fact is that the more we think about Him, the closer our resemblance to Him becomes. By every act of trust and self-surrender to His claims, we receive ever larger measures of His life, so that all the while we are being changed into His image from glory to glory, as by His Spirit. Do you ask *me* what I think of Christ? I have only one answer—He is the center and circumstance of my being, the One I cannot live without, and dare not die without. He is my all and in all!

> Infinite excellence is Thine,
> Thou lovely Prince of Grace!
> Thy uncreated beauties shine
> With never-failing rays.

Theme 24
The Gifts and Glory in John 17

The atmosphere of prayer pervades Scripture. God made men capable of having recourse to Him by prayer, and thus we are provided with an abundance of saints and sinners seeking Him in this way. Scripture also confirms the privilege and power of waiting upon God, and likewise sets forth the conditions upon which God answers prayer. That it is a profitable exercise to gather together the prayers and intercessions of Scripture, as well as divine teaching regarding the right approach to "the mercy seat where Jesus answers prayer," can be found in the writer's volume titled *All the Prayers of the Bible*.

Among all the recorded prayers, none is so sublime and sacred as the one complete prayer Jesus offered and preserved for our enlightenment and edification by John in chapter 17 of his Gospel. "In the days of his flesh, . . . He . . . offered up prayers and supplications with strong crying and tears . . . and was heard in that he feared" (Heb. 5:7). What a remarkable spiritual classic it would be if all of those tear-saturated prayers could have been recorded in a volume! The one we do have, however, is, without doubt, the most remarkable prayer ever prayed—the Prayer Perfect! As we approach a meditation of it, we bow in reverence, for the place whereon we stand is holy ground. This intense intercessory prayer has been described as "the noblest and purest pearl of devotion in the New Testament." Looking at it in the light of its context we see that after having spoken to His disciples about the Father, He turns to speak to the Father about His disciples.

251

Without doubt, John 17 is a simple, filial prayer, containing the outpouring of the Son's heart in the presence of His Father. In fact, Christ uses the filial term, *Father,* six times in the prayer. "Father" was His favorite expression, and this speaks of a holy intimacy between Father and Son. Once He calls God, "Holy Father" (v. 11)—the only time in Scripture He is so named. This term is used in the section of the prayer where Jesus prays for the sanctification of His own. Then we have the phrase "Righteous Father" (v. 25), implying that the basis of any appeal to God is His righteousness.

We look upon this priceless intercession of Christ as a model prayer in that it reveals a methodical presentation of accomplishments and pleas. Too often our prayer-life is ineffective because we lack a plan. When we come before God we ramble, give utterance to any thought that troops into our mind, and wander all over the world without arriving anywhere. When the disciples saw Jesus at prayer, they came to Him and asked, "Lord, teach us to pray" (Luke 11:1). Then He gave them a truly model prayer, the one we call "The Lord's Prayer." We ought, however, to describe it as "The prayer Jesus taught His disciples to pray," because it was not a prayer He, Himself, could use, being the sinless One.

The plan of this favorite prayer is clearly evident, being made up of invocation, supplication, and adoration—a division we should always have before us as we come to commune with God. Too often we come before Him as beggars, beseeching Him to give us this, that, and the other thing. Jesus taught His own to come, first of all, as worshipers, blessing God for all that He is in Himself, then to present their needs, and last of all, to magnify God for His power to answer their petitions. A similar method can be traced in the marvelous prayer before us in John 17, in the twenty-six verses which fall into three clearly defined areas.

The first section is personal. Lifting up His eyes to heaven, Jesus talks to the Father about His aspirations and accomplishments (1-8).

252

The second section is particular. Here Jesus concentrates upon His own—those given Him of the Father. The exclusion will be noted, "I pray for them: *I pray not for the world*" (vv. 9-19, emphasis added).

The third section is general. This part of the prayer is focused on all who throughout the ages will receive Christ through the witness of His disciples. The divine Word they believed (vv. 8, 14) in turn became "their word" (v. 20)—so effective is their testimony (vv. 20-26).

Further, this is the great High Priestly Prayer, a forecast of Christ's entry into His perpetual ministry as the great High Priest, to make intercession for His redeemed ones (Heb. 7:25). Four times over we have the term, "pray," by which is meant intercessory prayer (vv. 9, 15, 20). Enthroned in glory, the Redeemer is our Advocate, pleading the efficacy of His shed blood on our behalf—

> There for sinners Thou art pleading,
>   Then Thou dost our place prepare,
> Ever for us interceding,
>   Till in glory we appear.

Among the fascinating features of this true Lord's Prayer—the prayer He uttered with eyes uplifted—mention can be made of the following three:

1. The phrase, "I have," occurs ten times and represents the authoritative assertion of accomplishment. The fourfold declarations in the first part of the prayer is full of spiritual significance: "I have glorified thee on the earth: I have finished the work thou gavest me to do. . . . I have manifested thy name. . . . I have given them the words which thou gavest me" (vv. 4, 6, 8).

2. Gifts are prominent in the prayer. *Give* and its cognates occur fifteen times. Christ refers to several gifts the Father had bestowed upon Him which, in turn, He gave to His own. Christ Himself was the love-gift of the Father to the world

253

(John 3:16); and believers are the Father's love-gift to Christ. Some seven gifts appear in the prayer:

The gift of saints. Seven times over they are represented as being given to the Son by the Father (vv. 2, 6, 9, 11-12, 24).

The gift of the name. The life of Christ manifested God's name. As *name* means "nature" or "being," this assertion implies that He, by His character and works, revealed what God is like—and continues to do so: "I have"; "I will" (vv. 6, 24).

The gift of power. What an arresting phrase this is about the Father having given His Son "power over all flesh" so that authority could be His to "give eternal life" to believing sinners (v. 2). After His resurrection, He assured His disciples that all power was His in heaven and on earth, and that this all-embracing power was at their disposal as they went forth preaching eternal life to all who would repent and believe (Matt. 28:18-20).

The gift of service. At the outset of His ministry, Jesus made it clear what He came into the world for. "My meat is to do the will of him that sent me, and to finish his work" (John 4:34). Here, in His prayer, anticipating the cry of the cross—"It is finished!"—He says to the Father, "I have finished the work which thou gavest me to do" (v. 4). Work, then, for Him was a gift, not a grind, for He delighted in the accomplishment of a God-given task.

The gift of a message. How striking is the phrase, "The words thou gavest me"! He did not originate the truth He taught. The message Jesus expounded was not conceived in His own mind but received from God, as the repetition affirms: "I have given unto them the words which thou gavest me" (v. 8). "I have given them thy word" (v. 14). Our Lord was God's Messenger in God's Message (Hag. 1:13).

The gift of joy. This bequest was realized by His disciples after Pentecost, when they experienced what it was to be filled with the Holy Spirit and with joy. What do we know about the possession and fulfillment of His joy (v. 13)?

254

The gift of glory. An old promise reads, "The Lord will give grace and glory." Here Christ prays that the glory given Him by the Father might be shared by His disciples (v. 22). Such glory reveals the unity of the Godhead, and the unity of the church as a body. *Glory* as well as *gifts* dominate this most precious prayer. Glory and its cognates occur eight times in it. Paul reminds us that God-given glory could be seen in the face of Jesus Christ (II Cor. 4:6), and the Master prayed that this glory might be given to His followers.

1. The Glory of Sonship. John could declare as to His relationship to the Father, "We beheld his glory" (1:14), and He glorified the Father by His works, ways, and words. Listen to His assertion, "I have glorified thee on the earth" (v. 4). Now He asks the Father to glorify Him, which He did when He highly exalted Him at the time of ascension (v. 1; Phil. 2:9-10).

2. The Glory of Union. One purpose of God-given glory is to authenticate the unity of the Godhead, and the spiritual unity of believers (vv. 11, 22). We are not able to add anything to this divine attribute.

3. The Glory of Identification (vv. 10, 22). Because we belong to the Father and the Son, Christ is glorified in us. No longer here in the flesh to manifest His glory, yet in and through His own Jesus continues to be glorified. Every child of His is—or should be—a cabinet displaying His glory. Paul could say of the saints in Judaea, "They glorified God in me" (Gal. 1:24). Peter would have us so live and act that "God in all things may be glorified through Jesus Christ" (I Peter 4:11). The Scottish Catechism states that "man's chief end is to glorify God, and to enjoy Him for ever."

There is yet another way of expounding our Lord's intercessory prayer, namely, by dealing with its seven distinct petitions. *Petition,* which means "asking," is an aspect of

255

prayer. "Ask and ye shall receive," and Jesus asked seven petitions of His Father.

First Petition (v. 1). He asked the Father to glorify Him, which He did at His entrance into heaven (see Phil. 2:9-10). There was the glory Jesus won as the Son obedient to the Father. But He asks for the return of a past eternal glory that the limitations of His humanity withheld. His is now a special glory through the security of redemption for us.

Second Petition (v. 5). Here we have an emphatic plea for the restoration of His ancient glory "before the world was." Having glorified the Father here on earth, the Son besought Him with His own self to continue the glory He had had with Him in the past and which He now has with added glory.

Third Petition (v. 11). Jesus goes on to ask the Father for the security and safety of those given Him. While He was here below He kept His own (v. 12), now He commits them into His Father's hands (see John 10:28-29, for the double grip). Jesus never lost Judas. This son of perdition lost himself. Our eternal security rests upon the Father's faithfulness to His Son.

Fourth Petition (vv. 15-17). Although Jesus was about to leave the world, He asked that His own might remain *in* it, but not *of* it. "Keep them from the evil." He sought for the sanctification of His own through the sanctifying Word. He clearly states the identification of those He prayed for when He interceded that they might be holy as God is holy (vv. 6-7, 11).

Fifth Petition (vv. 11, 21). Twice over Jesus asks that the unity of the Godhead might be reflected in the one body. "That they may be one, as we are." "That they also may be one in us." Such an organic, spiritual unity is a testimony to the world of the reality of our Lord's incarnation. It is the out-working of this unity that we so sadly need. We may know much about the Bible, its doctrines, and prophecies, but not about how to get on among ourselves.

Sixth Petition (v. 20). Our Lord interceded not only for

256

those God had given Him while here among men; He looked away down the vista of the ages and thought of all who would believe on Him through the life and witness of His own, and asks for them security and unity. In heaven He continues to intercede for them.

Seventh Petition (vv. 22, 24). The glory God gave His Son has been given to us. Now Jesus expresses the wish that we might share heaven with Him and behold His glory. Note "I *will*," not "I *pray*." He does not request the Father to have us with Him, but asserts His authority, "I will that they also whom thou hast given me, be with me where I am." Redeemed by His blood, it is His right to have them with Him. As the shadows lengthen, let us cling to the double desire of the Master: "That they may be with me where I am. . . . That they may behold my glory."

O Jesus, Thou hast promised
   To all who follow Thee,
That where Thou art in glory,
   There shall Thy servant be;
And, Jesus, I have promised
   To serve Thee to the end;
Oh, give me grace to follow
   My Master and my Friend.

Theme 25
Acts: The Atmosphere of Prayer

Attributed to Napoleon is the dictum that "an army marches on its stomach." A contemporary writer, Robert J. Yeatman, says, "Napoleon's armies always used to march on their stomachs, shouting: *'Vive l'Intérieux!'* " Plentiful food not only made the soldiers think well of their leader, but enabled them to follow him in his military adventures. One cannot read the fifth book of the New Testament, sometimes called "The Fifth Gospel," without realizing how it shows us the church marching to glorious victories, not on her stomach but on her knees. Prayer, importunate prayer, pervades The Acts, and is the secret of the church's power to turn the world upside down. Being wrong side up as it was, it was the dynamic intercession and witness of the apostles that reversed it to its right position.

Used as an acrostic, the term *ACTS* suggests the different aspects of prayer, all of which the book illustrates—

*A*doration
*C*onfession
*T*hanksgiving
*S*upplication

The opening words of The Acts, like those of the Gospel of Luke, are addressed to Theophilus. This proves the identity of the author, namely, Luke, the beloved physician. He deemed his historical account of the church's activities as the result of the promised Pentecostal effusion of the Holy Spirit to be a natural sequel to the human Gospel he had penned. Ellicott, who wrote of Luke's Gospel as "The Gospel of the

258

Saintly Life," says that "the natural sequel to such a Gospel was a record of the work of the Holy Spirit, the Sanctifier. Looking to the prominence given to the work of the Spirit, from the Day of Pentecost onwards, as guiding both the church collectively and its individual members, it would hardly be overbold to say that The Acts might well be called, 'The Gospel of the Holy Spirit.' "

There are, of course, various approaches one could make to this most dramatic book of the Bible. Concentrating upon its references to the Holy Spirit, we could show how that at every stage of the church's mighty advance the Spirit's action is emphatically recognized—a fact which prompted A. T. Pierson to suggest that the title of the book should be "The Acts of the Holy Spirit Through the Apostles."

Then because The Acts is a record of the history of the growth of the church of Christ among Jews and Gentiles from the church's inception at Jerusalem and ending at Rome, the book is most valuable as a guide to the organization, mission-work, and worship of the church Jesus said He would build. All of the apostles believed that it was their solemn responsibility to work with the divine Builder in the introduction of a new society which, built of "living stones," was to be the temple of the living God.

What presently interests us about The Acts is its prayer emphasis, and how this was a potent factor in the remarkable evangelistic activities of the apostles, as well as in their lives as individuals. A careful study of this prayer element convinces the reader that

> More things are wrought by prayer,
> Than this world dreams of.

Whenever or wherever those saints in the early church prayed, something happened, for their prayers were no vain repetitions but heart-expressions inspired by the Holy Spirit who was very closely related to those who are found praying, as the following analysis proves:

259

Prayer of Preparation

"These all continued with one accord in prayer and supplication" (1:14).

Several thoughts emerge from a consideration of this first reference to prayer in The Acts. It was a daily, united prayer meeting. The word *accord* is akin to "symphony," suggesting the harmony of differing instruments in an orchestra. Those disciples were not only in one place but also in one mind and actuated by one purpose. Prayer and unity are vitally connected. As to those who formed that first prayer meeting of the church, in addition to the eleven apostles, were the "devout women" that Luke mentions in his Gospel as having ministered to Jesus (8:1-3; 23:49), and "Mary the mother of Jesus." As to "his brethren," these were our Lord's brothers according to the flesh who, although unbelieving while their Brother was alive (John 7:5), were doubtless converted through the raising of Lazarus and through the death and resurrection of their mother's first-born Son. As about 120 formed that communal prayer meeting, which number probably included the seventy Jesus had sent forth (Luke 10:1), a mighty volume of earnest prayer must have gone up from that upper chamber.

The prayer group had not been told how long those daily gatherings for prayer were to go on. "Not many days hence," was the indefinite amount of time the Master had spoken of. They were told that the fulfillment of the promise would not be long, lest faith and patience should fail. The uncertainty as to the exact period they were to wait was a discipline to their faith and patience. Whereas the Authorized Version combines "prayer" with "supplication," ancient versions mention only "prayer." How they prayed, whether publicly or silently, we are not told, but pray they did in respect to "the promise of the Father" (1:4). What must be borne in mind is that they did not focus prayer on the coming of the Holy Spirit. To ask God to do something He has already promised to do, is a

260

travesty of the true function of prayer. Faith accepts the promise, and prayer prepares the heart for the fulfillment of that promise. Those 120 or so disciples waited for God to redeem His promise, which He did on the Day of Pentecost, but the daily prayers of those saints prepared a fitting atmosphere within their hearts for the reception of the promised gift.

It is to be regretted that in our modern times, church prayer meetings are passing out of fashion. The church no longer lives on her knees, but on her schemes and wits, for survival. And, with her efficient businesslike methods of raising money to keep her machinery running, she has little need of communal prayer for support. Deny it as we may, the fact remains that the church was born in a prayer meeting, and her life can only exist in the same atmosphere. Any church, believing that prayer changes things—and persons—and giving prayer priority in its program, is an irresistible spiritual force in the community it represents. This is the witness of The Acts where we have startling results from the church at prayer. As those disciples commenced they continued (2:42), and mighty things happened: "When they had prayed, the place was shaken where they were assembled together; and they were all filled with the Holy Ghost, and they spake the word of God with boldness" (4:31). What a distance the church has traveled from this form of Spirit-inspired intercession with its wonderful spiritual accompaniments! It was only when Zion travailed that she brought forth children.

Prayer for a Successor

"And they prayed and said, Thou, Lord, which knowest the hearts of all men, show whether of these two thou hast chosen" (1:24).

Through his dark betrayal, Judas Iscariot had lost his bishopric, and at a church meeting prayer was offered for a suc-

261

cessor who was qualified to fill the gap. Two disciples, who had companied all the time that the Lord Jesus went in and out among His own, namely, Barnabas and Matthias, were brought before the church. Although heaven's choice was sought, the successor was chosen by lot, or casting votes for each presented candidate. Thus the question arises, was Matthias the Lord's man, or were the voters biased in his favor? While Luke included him in the recognized Twelve when it came to the election of the first deacons (Acts 6:2), and the appointment of Matthias was an honest transaction, there is not sufficient reason to believe that Peter and the rest were divinely directed in their action, which, perhaps, was somewhat premature.

Did not Jesus constantly affirm that disciples were His choice, and His alone—"*I* have chosen you"? Did those in the upper chamber, then, undertake to do what their Lord had kept in His own power? Knowing of David's prediction of another filling the place of Judas, and desiring to have an apostolate of twelve in being again before Pentecost, the resolve to appoint a successor was taken. As Peter was spokesman for the church, he took it for granted that God would approve of the choice made, without asking whether His choice was between two. Are we not guilty of this same fault of going to God not *before* a course of action, but *after* we have decided upon it? As if to say, "Well, Lord, here's our plan, approve it, please!"

After his election by lot, Matthias does not appear again in sacred history. Doubtless he proved to be a most loyal follower of the Lord. Tradition has it that like Stephen he was stoned, and then beheaded because of his allegiance to his Lord. Our conviction is that the vacant place in the apostolate was filled by the Lord Himself when He personally chose Saul of Tarsus (Acts 9:15), who could later write that he was an apostle "not of men, neither by man, but by Jesus Christ" (Gal. 1:1). Although at the time of the election of Matthias, Paul was a fierce persecutor of the church, through grace he became an "apostle of Jesus Christ through the will of God," and not by human lot (I Cor. 1:1). The reader will find a fuller discussion of this matter in the writer's work, *All the Apostles of the Bible.*

When vacancies occur in church circles how necessary it is for united prayer to be focused on evident divine tokens of successors. Too often a pastorless church knows what kind of a man it wants, and although formal prayers are offered for guidance, behind the scenes a good deal of wire-pulling and influence secure the preacher they desire. Spirit-inspired, united intercession, without human bias, never fails to produce the man after God's own heart, whether for the vacant pulpit or for any office in a church's ministry. Somehow in church circles it has been forgotten that when God's work is done in God's way for God's glory, it never lacks God's vindication.

Prayer in the Temple

"Now Peter and John went up together into the temple at the hour of prayer, being the ninth hour" (Acts 3:1).

It is interesting to observe how Luke combines these two co-apostles, Peter and John, for theirs was a striking mutual relationship. In spite of the marked difference in character and conduct, after their joint mission to prepare for the Last Passover they seem to have been inseparable (Luke 22:8). Peter alone denied his Master; John alone continued with Him to the last (John 18:15; 19:26). Yet such was John's magnanimity that although he witnessed Peter's denial, he says nothing about it in his Gospel. You find the two of them together at the sepulcher and in Galilee after the resurrection (John 20:2; 21:7). Here we have them together in the hour of prayer. The word *together* implies not a mere coincidence of place, but unity of purpose. The hour of prayer Peter and John observed together was the third stated hour of prayer

263

according to Jewish custom. Corresponding to our 3 o'clock in the afternoon, probably this was the hour of evening sacrifice (see Ps. 55:17). For a while after Pentecost, the disciples "continued daily with one accord in the temple" (Acts 2:46), and on this day, which was to witness a miracle of intrinsic magnitude, Peter and John visited the temple not only for private devotions, but participation in the ceremonial service of the sanctuary.

It seems, however, that the joint purpose of the two apostles to pray and worship was not fulfilled that day, for as they were about to go into the temple, a beggar, lame from birth, was stretched out at the gate pleading for money. These two partners as fishermen, sharers in looking for the consolation of Israel, companions at the gate of prayer, were now to become joint channels of miracle power, with Peter preaching a most remarkable sermon which resulted in John and he being imprisoned. On that never-to-be-forgotten day when these two came to the temple to pray, God took the will for the deed and magnified His power through them.

The temple, then, had its *daily* hour for prayer, but there are any amount of churches today without a *weekly* hour for prayer. Prayer meetings, once a mighty factor in church life, are gradually being abandoned. The Peters and Johns going together to the church, *just* to pray, are becoming scarcer. Prayerless churches have no power to say to our poor, lame world, "In the name of Jesus Christ of Nazareth rise up and walk." A church may have no silver and gold to give, but if she lives on its knees she has far greater wealth to distribute to a bankrupt world.

Prayer and Ministry

"But we will give ourselves continually to prayer, and to the ministry of the word" (Acts 6:4).

Because of the dynamic witness of the early church, there

was an almost daily increase of men and women becoming disciples. This resulted in an ever-increasing burden of responsibility on the part of the leaders. The charitable side of the church's life, namely, the care of widows and their children out of an organized administration of a common fund for relief, was consuming more and more of the time of those who felt called to preach and teach. So the Twelve brought the church together and explained that the serving of tables was taking up too much of their time, and suggested that seven deacons should be appointed to deal with all matters related to alms-giving. Such men had to have an "honest report" and be "full of the Holy Spirit and wisdom" for a service just as spiritual as preaching the Word.

As for the apostles, such an appointment would set them free for continual prayer and the ministry of the Word. By "prayer" we understand all the public worship of the church in all its various developments, as well as private prayer and intercession. "Ministry of the Word" implies all forms of preaching and teaching. The promise was given that they would give themselves continually to this dual ministry—the word *continually* meaning "to persevere in, or adhere to with single purpose." This plan pleased the church; the seven were appointed and the apostles commended them to God and laid hands on them (6:6). Mentioned here first in the New Testament, the ritual of hand-laying did not imply the transmission of the gifts the chosen seven were to exercise as deacons, but the recognition that they already possessed the requisite qualification for the office, namely, the testimony of others as to their character, the fullness of the Spirit, and wisdom, the latter implying not only practical skill, but a heavenly prudence that taught them how to act in all emergencies. That God set His seal upon this arrangement is seen in what followed (6:7-8).

Apostolic recognition of the preeminence of prayer is seen in that the apostles named it first. The effective ministry of

265

the Word is dependent upon prayer, as the history of The Acts proves. If churches could be persuaded to give more time to intercession than to the preaching and teaching of the Word, greater things would happen through the presentation of truth. The Grecian Jews "were not able to resist the wisdom and the spirit by which he [Stephen] spake" because of a deep prayer-life behind his public utterance (6:10).

Later on, when it came to the setting apart of Barnabas and Paul for their God-given task, prayer of ordination is again seen. This time, however, the leaders not only prayed and laid hands on the two being separated, but they fasted, as they likewise did at the ordination of elders (Acts 13:3; 14:23). In each case, the fasting indicated that the new command called for that intensity of spiritual life of which fasting was more or less the normal condition. Paul, a mighty intercessor, made a practice of fasting (II Cor. 6:5; 11:27). The mind is more alert to and aware of the divine presence and one prays more effectively when the stomach is not overloaded with food. Prayer warriors are those who have learned to spend more time on their knees than sitting at a table.

Prayer of Resignation and for Forgiveness

"As they stoned Stephen, [he called] upon God, . . . saying, Lord Jesus, receive my spirit. And he kneeled down, and cried with a loud voice, Lord, lay not this sin to their charge. And when he had said this, he fell asleep" (Acts 7:59-60).

Here we see a noble martyr at prayer. What a wonderful way to die, whether brutally or naturally! Ellicott reminds us that "these words are memorable as an instance of direct prayer addressed, to use the words of Pliny in reporting what he had learned of the worship of Christians, 'to Christ as God.' Stephen could not think of Him whom he saw at the right hand of God, but as of One sharing the glory of the Father, hearing and answering prayer."

266

Perhaps Stephen had been present at Calvary, and his dying prayer echoed the one he heard Jesus use, "Father, into thy hands I commend my spirit" (Luke 23:46). It will be noted that the term *God* in the sentence is in italics, and was only inserted to complete the sense. "Unto God" was introduced by the Authorized Version. Tyndale has it, "calling on and saying. . . ." The designation "Lord Jesus" involves a recognition of Him in the twofold character of a Sovereign and a Saviour. Stephen addressed Him as a divine Person, asking of the Son precisely what the Son on the cross asked of His Father. Elijah and Jonah petitioned that the Lord would take away their lives or suffer them to die, but the church's first martyr prayed that Christ would receive him when separated from his battered, blood-stained body.

Prostrate on the ground because of the cruel stoning he suffered, Stephen, although exhausted, lifted himself to a kneeling posture, and reechoed another Calvary prayer (Luke 23:34). As the dying Saviour prayed for divine forgiveness for those who had crucified Him, Stephen prayed for his murderers, "Lord, lay not this sin to their charge." Certainly he had the mind of Christ. Augustine in one of his sermons suggested that we owe the conversion of Saul to the prayers of Stephen, which we can accept as the expression of a great spiritual fact. John Wesley said that his "preachers died well." Stephen the martyred deacon died well, for he died praying. No wonder "he fell asleep." While "sleep" is used as a figure of speech in connection with the death of a believer (I Cor. 15:18; I Thess. 4:14), it can also imply that Stephen died a peaceful death in spite of the fury of his murderers and the brutal, violent means by which he lost his life. (See Psalm 37:37.) "When good men die, it is not death, but sleep."

> Prayer is the Christian's vital breath,
> The Christian's native air,
> His watchword at the gates of death;
> He enters heaven with prayer.

267

Prayer for the Holy Spirit

"When they [Peter and John] were come down, [they] prayed for them. that they [the Samaritans] might receive the Holy Spirit" (Acts 8:15).

In this chapter we have Philip the Evangelist fulfilling the part of the Royal Commission about witnessing in Samaria— the bridge between Jerusalem and the world. Hearing and seeing the miracles Philip performed, the people eagerly listened to his message, and there was great joy in the city over his presence and ministry in it. While in Jerusalem, Peter and John heard of the fruitful evangelistic efforts of Philip, and visited Samaria as representatives of the church. Meeting a group of the Samaritans who had believed, the apostles prayed for them that they might receive the Holy Spirit.

As these converts had been baptized in the name of the Lord Jesus, this presupposes that they had received "the renewing of the Holy Spirit" (Titus 3:5-7: I Cor. 12:13). Thus regenerated they already had the Spirit within: "If any man have not the Spirit of Christ, he is none of his." But, "as yet, he was fallen upon none of them," meaning that they had not experienced their share of the Pentecostal gift. When, therefore, the apostles prayed for those saved Samaritans, they received a superaddition of the Spirit's unction manifesting itself in His extraordinary influences, either in the way of inspiration or in that of miraculous endowments or of both combined, as in the case of the apostles themselves (see 10:14; 19:1-7).

Doubtless Philip had prayed that his converts might have the installment of Pentecost, for his prayers were no less effectual than those of Peter and John; but as the latter were in Samaria to inspect and report the mission of Philip to the church and to instruct the converts, being there as the divinely appointed founders of the church, they prayed for them, and their prayers were answered. The Holy Spirit's power was not bestowed through the imposition of the laying

268

on of hands. Such an act simply testified to the fact that the Spirit had fallen upon the believing, baptized Samaritans.

It is vain to pray for a blessing to be emptied out on other believers, blessings we ourselves have not experienced. How certain, then, we must be that we have entered into the fullness of the blessing of the gospel of Christ. But if we have discovered the secret of spiritual wealth, then we dare not hold our peace but must pray that others may come to share the secret. At Pentecost, the Holy Spirit fell upon Peter and John; thus it was with deep feeling that they prayed for the Samaritans that they might be mantled with His power for service.

Prayers for Preservation

> *"Simon . . . said, Pray ye to the Lord for me, that none of these things which ye have spoken come upon me" (Acts 8:24).*

Simon the sorcerer, witnessing the effect of the prayers and the laying-on-of-hands on the Samaritans, offered Peter money to bestow on him the same authority. The key to this wretched man's character was *spiritual ambition,* and so Peter said, "Thy money perish with thee." The sin of Simon is seen in the term *simony,* which denotes trafficking in sacred things, chiefly in the purchase of ecclesiastical offices and preferments. Peter impressed upon Simon the greatness of his sin and urged him to repent lest he became a captive of iniquitous ambition. Alarmed at the thought of such dread punishment, he begged Peter to pray for him, not that his wickedness might be forgiven him, but only that the evils threatened might be averted.

Peter had told Simon to pray for himself, "Pray God, if perhaps the thought of thine heart may be forgiven thee" (8:22), but he asked the apostles to pray for him. Evidently he had no confidence in the prayer of faith, but thought that

269

they possessed some peculiar power with heaven. He turned, not to the Lord who was ready to forgive, but to a human mediator. Peter must pray for him who has not faith to pray for himself. Whether Peter did accede to such a request we are not told. Simon disappears from the history of The Acts. Tradition says that he became "the hero of the romance of heresy." Among the many legends attached to his name is the one of how he tried to prove his unusual power by flying in the air, trusting that the demons whom he employed would support him, but, through the power of the prayers of Peter, he fell down and had his bones broken and then committed suicide.

Prayer of a Convert

"Saul, of Tarsus . . . behold, he prayeth" (9:11).

Ananias, who had been instructed of the Lord where to find the remarkable trophy of His grace, was a little afraid to go to a man who had so severely persecuted the saints. However, when the Lord assured him that he had nothing to fear because he would find Saul on his knees praying, Ananias went on his mission in a different frame of mind. The persecutor was no longer "breathing out threatenings and slaughter," but pouring out his heart to the One he had persecuted. What a change Jesus had wrought in the heart of Saul! Instead of persecuting, he is found praying. Ellicott comments on, "Behold, he prayeth":

> Estimating that prayer by that which came as the answer to it, we may think of it as including pardon for the past, light and wisdom for the future, strength to do the work to which he was now called, intercession for those whom he had before persecuted unto death.

Saul, who became Paul the Apostle, started his Christian

career in prayer, went on to become mighty in prayer, and wrote much on this holy exercise and privilege. Young converts should be encouraged to give themselves to prayer. At first their prayers may be short, simple, and perhaps not altogether correct as to Scriptural conditions of prayer; but the more they pray, the better they pray, discovering that prayer is a gift that increases with its use. As they journey on, the newly saved come to realize that

> Prayer is the Christian's native breath,
> The Christian's native air.

Prayer for Resurrection

> *"Peter . . . kneeled down, and prayed; and turning . . . said, Tabitha, arise" (9:40).*

The power of prayer of faith calls for the silence and solitude of communion with God. Therefore Peter asked all the people gathered in the death chamber to retire and leave him alone to stand between the living God and the dead girl. No doubt Peter recalled how Jesus acted in the case of the raising of the daughter of Jairus (Matt. 9:23-24). Peter "kneeled down, and prayed," we are told. Such "kneeling became the lowly servant, but not the Lord Himself, of whom it is never once recorded that He knelt in the performance of a miracle." Peter was only the instrument in the miracle of the resurrection of Tabitha, but Jesus was the miracle worker Himself in the raising of Jairus's daughter.

How graphic, yet how simple and natural is the narrative! Peter had the inward assurance that his prayer would be answered so he said, "Tabitha, arise!" The girl opened her eyes and sat up and Peter presented her alive—evidence of the completeness of the miracle. There is about this incident an air of charming reality. Power to raise the dead was an apostolic gift, which has been in abeyance since the end of the

Apostolic Age. What the church calls "Prayers for the Dead" are not related to their present physical resurrection from the grave. As for praying for them after they are dead, they remain dead as far as their bodies are concerned and are beyond the realm of prayer. Our prayers can only be for the living. For those sick unto death, we may pray that if it is the divine will they may not die, but live to declare the glory of God. We can, however, intercede with tears that those who are *spiritually* dead will arise from their grave of sin and lust into the newness of life forevermore.

Prayer of a Soldier

> *"Cornelius . . . one that feared God . . . and prayed to God alway" (Acts 10:1-2).*

This devout soldier must have been conspicuous among the Roman officers in Nero's legions. With this chapter we enter on an entirely new phase of the Christian church, in that it describes "the opening of the door of faith to the Gentiles." To Peter, "the Apostle of the Circumcision," and very much a Jew, was conferred the honor of initiating the entrance of Gentiles into the church without circumcision. Cornelius was the first Gentile to be received by baptism without the rite of circumcision (see Eph. 3:6, RV). Peter, of course, required a vision from God to persuade him to take this critical step. Afterwards he was not very consistent in his conduct about this matter (Gal. 2:11-12).

Cornelius, the man chosen by God to be the first Gentile to be received into Christian fellowship, was held in high repute for his virtues. But with all his admirable qualities he needed to be saved and receive the salvation Christ alone can give (Acts 4:12; 11:14). Famous and good though he was, Cornelius was not exempted from the use of what the Shorter Catechism calls those "outward and ordinary means, the Word, sacraments, and prayer, whereby Christ communi-

272

cates to us the benefits of salvation." Perhaps we can briefly summarize the recorded facts of this renowned praying soldier in this way—

He lived in Caesarea, a Roman town and the residence of the Roman governor. It was the most markedly Gentile town in the whole of Judaea.

He held the rank of centurion, an officer who had command of a legion which was made up of one hundred soldiers. A centurion could not rise to a higher rank, save through exceptional circumstances.

He was wealthy, as his large household of servants and slaves, his liberal alms-giving, and his love for the Jews indicates. The size of his household mark him out as a man of superior social position. This name connects him with the *gens Cornelia,* one of Rome's old aristocratic families.

His high personal character is presented to us in seven features—"devout," meaning he was sincerely religious, and indicating a special type of devotion belonging to a Gentile convert to Judaism. He "feared God," which implies that he had forsaken his native paganism as a Roman, and had come to believe in and serve with reverence and godly fear the God of Israel. The addition "with all his house" is interesting to observe. He was not content with having found the living and true God for himself, but sought to impart the knowledge of his new faith to those near and dear to him as well as to his soldiers and slaves, all of whom loved to serve such a master (10:7).

> When Jesus has found you,
> Tell others the story.

He was kind to the Jewish people, giving them "much alms." By "the people" we are to understand the Jews of Caesarea as distinct from Gentiles (see 26:17, 23; 28:17). With Paul (Rom. 1:16), the centurion felt he was a debtor to the Jews. This almsgiving was seen by the eye of God (Acts 10:36).

273

He was a man given to prayer. He looked beyond the people of God to the God of the people. He "prayed to God always," and, as Peter assured him, his prayer was heard (10:31). On the day of his momentous vision, Cornelius continued in prayer until the tenth hour—about 3 P.M.

He was visited by an angel and an apostle. In response to his prayers and alms, God sent an angel to Cornelius, one of those blessed spirits sent forth to minister to the heirs of salvation. Angels are usually viewless, but this one came in visible form and the soldier was frightened. But the angel reassured him. Then he replied, "What is it, Lord?" He was told to send to Joppa for an apostle who would tell him all about God's comprehensive redemptive purpose. Thus Peter, and not an angel, was the appointed preacher of the good news of salvation for Gentiles and of their union with saved Jews in the church of the living God. As Peter proclaimed the message of Christian liberty, a second Pentecost was experienced by those first Gentile believers. Cornelius was not required to be circumcised, but he was obliged to be baptized.

Prayer is prominent in the record of Cornelius, for it was as Peter was praying that he received the vision of God's purpose to be no respecter of persons, and to welcome Jews and Gentiles alike into Christ's kingdom (11:5; see 22:16). Cornelius is presented as a man of unceasing prayer. Although a soldier in the Roman army, he was not ashamed to be seen praying. He saw no contradiction between serving his emperor and the God he had come to fear. He was a "devout soldier," and down the ages there have been many like him in the fighting forces.

One of the most notable among British soldiers was General C. Gordon, who was not only a brave and fearless officer, but a sincere Christian. When in a campaign, his fellow officers knew that when they saw a white handkerchief outside Gordon's tent, he was at prayer and was not to be disturbed. Sir William Dobbie, the gallant soldier associated with the siege of Malta in World War II, wrote of prayer,

It is the means by which we establish living contact with Almighty God, our Heavenly Father, a contact through which His Spirit and His vitalizing power flow from Him to us, and by which His strength is imparted to us and our life is renewed. As we read the Gospels we cannot but be struck by the immensely important part prayer played in our Lord's life. He was constantly in touch with His Father through prayer, and devoted long periods to its exercise.

Prayer for Deliverance

"Peter therefore was kept in prison: but prayer was made without ceasing of the church unto God for him" (Acts 12:5).

What a fervent church prayer meeting that must have been! It was held in the home of "Mary the mother of John, whose surname was Mark: where many were gathered together praying" (12:12). This was an emergency calling for instant and earnest intercession, not only for Peter's liberation but for a happy outcome of his trial, both for the sake of the apostle and of the cause for which he was suffering. This was a crisis prayer meeting, such as we find in the Book of Nehemiah.

Those heartfelt petitions were heard, and God sent an angel to deliver Peter from prison and safely conduct him till he was out on the street. Conscious of what the angel had done (10:9, 11), Peter made his way to the home where he knew the saints were praying, knocked on the door, and the young maid Rhoda came and asked who was there. When Peter replied, the girl immediately recognized his voice, but became so excited she left Peter standing outside and ran back to tell the prayer-partners that their prayer had been answered and that Peter was outside the door.

275

What was the reaction of those who were unceasing in their intercession for Peter's release? This fact is evident, those dear saints did not mix faith with their prayers. They failed to remember the word of the Lord Jesus, "Whatsoever ye shall ask in prayer, *believing,* ye shall receive" (Matt. 21:22). Think of their exclamations when the maid said Peter was at the door. "Thou art mad!" This is a reaction a person can scarcely resist when he hears what seems far "too good to be true." "It is his angel." No, it can't be Peter himself. Perhaps it is his disembodied spirit. How exquisite is the touch of nature here! Though Peter's release had been the burden of their fervent prayers during the time they spent together in communal intercession, they, despite themselves, thought of the answer to their prayers as a thing incredible. Theirs was the same unbelief displayed by the disciples who "believed not *for joy* and wondered" at the tidings of their Lord's resurrection.

How true to pattern was their unbelief! Often we pray for what we can hardly credit the bestowment of when it comes in answer to our prayers. "This, however, argues not so much hard belief as that kind of it incident to the best in the land of shadows," says the *Commentary on the Whole Bible,* "which perceives not so clearly as it might how very near Heaven and Earth, the Lord and His praying people are to each other." Doubtful though the praying saints were when Rhoda asserted that it was Peter knocking at the door, she kept steadfastly affirming that it was he. How shamefaced the rest must have been when finally they discovered that Rhoda's testimony was true!

> Faith is a living power from heaven
> Which grasps the promise God has given.
>
> Such faith in us, O God, implant,
> And to our prayers Thy favor grant.
> In Jesus Christ, Thy saving Son,
> Who is our fount of health alone.

Prayer at a Riverside

". . . a river side, where prayer was wont to be made" (Acts 16:13).

In this stirring, momentous chapter we have three wonderful conversions associated with prayer. The bank of a river became a "house of prayer" for godly women who had no synagogue to gather in. How grateful they must have been when Paul and Silas joined them for prayer and to minister the Word. Gathered at this prayer meeting alongside a small stream were the first fruits of Europe unto Christ, and note that they were of the female sex, of whose accession and services honorable mention is made (Acts 16:14). Lydia, the prominent businesswoman of Thyatira, attended the open-air Bible conference which Paul conducted and her heart became responsive to the deep, spiritual teaching the apostle presented. No earthquake was necessary to save her, as in the case of the jailor later on. Her heart opened to the Lord as silently as a bud opening to the morning sun. "The scene is one which might call for the master touches of a great painter. The river flowing calmly by, the preacher sitting and talking familiarly, quietly, but earnestly to the group of women, one, at least, among them listening with looks and tears that told of deep emotions, and the consciousness of a new life."

A day or two after Paul and Silas had rested up in the hospitable home of Lydia, they made their way to the usual place of prayer by the riverside, and another female came under the sound and spell of the gospel. Demon-possessed, this damsel was totally different in character from Lydia. The one was at the top of the social ladder, the other at the bottom; but the God who saved the one was able to save the other. "They went to prayer," but it would seem that they never reached the prayer meeting. There came an interruption which resulted in a marvelous trophy of God's saving grace. How would we react if, on the way to the weekly

277

prayer meeting in our church, God thrust a lost, degraded sinner in our pathway?

It is more than likely that this slave girl had found her way to the riverside sanctuary, and had heard Paul expound the Scripture, for she said of Silas and him, "These men are the servants of the most high God, which show unto us the way of salvation" (16:17). Through Paul's exorcism of the evil spirit possessing her, she came to experience the power of that salvation in her own life. Her continued cries for deliverance from her thralldom were heard. Grace restored her to her true self, and in all likelihood she became one of the women who labored with the apostle, repaying them to some degree for the suffering she had unwillingly brought upon both Paul and Silas. For as the result of her conversion, the apostles were beaten with many stripes and cast into prison through the instigation of those men who had controlled the girl and made money on her supposed inspiration.

Prayer in a Prison

"At midnight Paul and Silas prayed, and sang praises unto God" (Acts 16:25).

These faithful evangelists, wonderfully used of God, entered into the fellowship of their Master's suffering. Taken prisoners, they first endured punishment of unusual severity, for the many stripes would leave their backs lacerated and bleeding. Paul wrote afterwards of being "shamefully treated" at Philippi (I Thess. 2:2). Then they were cast into "the inner prison," a dark cavernlike cell below the ground, dark and damp and foul, where the vilest outcasts were imprisoned. To add to their torture and indignity, their feet were made fast in stocks. Further, the jailor was commanded to exercise more than usual fidelity and strictness in the execution of his treatment of these two prisoners.

But tribulation could not silence Paul and Silas—"at midnight they prayed, and sang praises unto God." Habitually they had prayed and sung hymns, and they were not going to let a dirty dungeon close their mouths, even though they could not kneel, fastened as their feet were in the stocks. Their prayerful psalmody revealed their confidence in God and their superiority to human spite and violence. How apt are the words of Tertullian to the martyrs of his time, "The leg feels not the stocks when the mind is in heaven. Though the body is held fast, all things lie open to the spirit." From the sufferers came "songs in the night." "They prayed, and sang praises."

> Prayer and praises go in pairs,
> He hath praises who hath prayers.

What a delightful touch Luke gives us—"And the prisoners heard them." It was midnight, but they could not sleep. Instead they listened eagerly to the two unusual prisoners in the filthy den. Ordinarily the vile vaults echoed with wild curses and foul jests. Never before had the outcasts and criminals heard prayers and praises in such a place. Perhaps some of those prisoners were won over to Christ as the result of the joyous and victorious example of the two men who were suffering unjustly.

Suddenly, at that midnight hour as Paul and Silas prayed and praised, there was a great earthquake. Was there any connection between the indifferent attitude of the apostles to their suffering and the convulsion of nature? As a young believer I had the privilege of hearing the late General William Booth, founder of The Salvation Army, preach on the conversion of the jailor, and this sentence has remained with me for well over sixty years: "God was so well pleased with the prayers and praises of Paul and Silas that He said 'Amen!' with a mighty earthquake."

Well, it took an earthquake to save a coarse, brutal, hardhearted man like that jailor. When he saw the supernatural calmness and courage of these evangelists and realized how they had saved him from suicide, trembling and conscience-stricken he cried, "Sirs, what must I do to be saved?" Immediately his question was answered, and he believed, as did all his family and servants.

That restitution is one evidence of conversion is seen in the striking action of the saved jailor: "He took Paul and Silas the same hour of the night, and washed their stripes"—the cruel stripes he himself had inflicted on those innocent men. He sought to alleviate the suffering he had caused. There were the two washings. The jailor washed their stripes, as a sign of repentance toward God and his reverence for the godly prisoners. Then he yielded to baptism, symbol of the washing of regeneration. He washed the blood off the backs of Paul and Silas. Now through the blood of the Lord Jesus Christ, the jailor was cleansed from wounds worse than those he had inflicted on others. What a happy ending to that apostolic prayer-and-praise session in a prison cell! The saved, rejoicing jailor could sing,

> His blood can make the vilest clean,
> His blood avails for me.

Like Lydia and the demon-possessed girl, the prison keeper came to know "the way of salvation" these men declared.

Prayer of Farewell

"When he [Paul] had thus spoken, he kneeled down, and prayed with them all" (Acts 20:36).

There is no recorded speech in the entire realm of literature comparable to Paul's farewell. This moving message to the elders of Ephesus which Luke the historian recorded word for word is full of living personal interest. Ellicott's comment of the address of Paul, bearing as it does the internal marks of genuineness, offers a most fitting summary—

No writer of a history adorned with fictitious

280

speeches could have written a discourse so essentially Pauline in all its turns and touches of thought and phraseology, in its tenderness and sympathy, its tremulous anxieties, its frank assertions of the fulness of his teaching and the self-denying labours of his life, its sense of the infinite responsibility of the ministerial office for himself and others, its apprehension of coming dangers from without and within the church. The words present a striking parallel to the appeal of Samuel to the people (I Sam. 12:3).

The parting scene at Miletus is most heart-moving. Those elders, feeling they would never again see the much-loved face of Paul, kissed it in the last embrace before embarkation. Nothing can be more touching than the three last verses in the chapter containing Paul's farewell message. They leave an indelible impression of rare ministerial fidelity and affection on Paul's part, and of warm admiration and attachment on the part of those Ephesian elders. A passing reference to another parting scene of perhaps even tenderer emotion can be found in Paul's letter to young Timothy (II Tim. 1:4). Would that such scenes were frequent in the church today! Prayers, tears, kisses were associated with that sad farewell.

The next chapter records another farewell not so sorrowful as this one. Before Paul took ship to Ptolemais he kneeled down on the shore and prayed for and with the disciples, their wives and children, who had assembled to bid the apostle bon voyage (21:5). The preacher will find a good deal of sermonic material in the farewells or partings in the Bible record. Alas! not all of them are associated with sincere, heartfelt prayer.

Prayer of Gratitude

"When he [Paul] had thus spoken, he took bread, and gave thanks to God in presence of them all" (Acts 27:35).

281

Luke's account of Paul's voyage to Italy and all the perils of the sea which all the prisoners endured is surely a literary classic. J. S. Alexander in his valuable *Commentary on The Acts,* says that this chapter, containing Paul's last recorded voyage with its shipwreck, "is chiefly remarkable for the fulness and exactness of its nautical details, which the latest and most critical investigations have only served to render more surprising in themselves, and more conclusive as internal proof of authenticity and genuineness."

The divine word of encouragement, "Fear not, Paul!" may have been an answer to his prayer "prompted by the fear, not of death or danger in itself, but lest the cherished purpose of his heart should be frustrated when it seemed on the very verge of attainment." Although the narrative carries no actual prayer the apostle prayed during that disastrous storm, yet had he not prayed the visit of the angel of God would probably not have occurred. He assured him that while the ship would be lost, there would be no loss of life, all being saved (27:22-25). Believing this message of divine protection, Paul became the source of calm strength to crew and prisoners, with the presence of mind to act aright in such a state of emergency.

Too often in times of physical danger, people panic, become terror-stricken, and desperately cry to God for deliverance. Misery and dejection grip their hearts. But here was one man whose looks and tone, suggesting a brave, calm confidence in the God to whom he belonged and whom he served, steadied the nerves of the rest on that doomed ship. Soldiers and sailors under such adverse circumstances might have become sullen and unwilling to help. They were, in fact, prepared to seek self-preservation, and let the ship sink, but the prompt vigor, clear discernment, and the declared faith in God which Paul manifested, kept all on board together until the worst was past and "they escaped all safe to land."

Paul urged the hungry men, who had battled with the elements for so long without food, to eat what rations they

282

had to keep soul and body together until they landed at Melita. The apostle's practical insight and human sympathy must have endeared him to the rest on board. He assured them that not a hair from the head of any of them would fall. As they all sat down to eat, Paul prayed and "gave thanks to God in the presence of them all," not only for the food before them, but for the way He had preserved them from death. No wonder those 276 souls were all of good cheer! The faith and influence of one brave and godly man had banished their despair. "The hearty cheerfulness of the apostle had communicated itself, as by a kind of electric sympathy, to his companions. They looked to him as their friend and leader, and had spirits to eat once more" (27:25, 36).

Paul's prayer of gratitude was a most impressive act in such circumstances, and planted a testimony for the God he so faithfully served in the breasts of all who sailed with him. Do we display the faith and courage that sustains us in the adverse circumstances of life? And do we by word and action recommend the God we serve to those, similarly tossed about by the billows of trial and suffering, but who hitherto did not know Him as "the Master of ocean, earth and sky"?

Prayer for Healing

"Paul . . . prayed, and laid his hands on him, and healed him" (Acts 28:8-9).

The shipwrecked voyagers found hospitable people on the island of Melita. By *barbarians* we are not to understand a savage people. The term was used to describe all races that did not speak Greek (Rom. 1:14; I Cor. 14:11). The travelers to Italy found the natives to be kind and considerate, who "showed no little kindness." Because of the rain and cold, shelter was provided; and, as warmth was necessary, ever-practical Paul gathered a bundle of sticks. Out of this a viper

283

fastened on his hand and the natives judged this an omen that Paul was a murderer and that, although he had escaped the storm, a terrible death would now overtake him as a criminal, "Though he hath escaped the sea, yet vengeance suffereth not to live."

Paul, however, thought nothing of it. He simply shook off the beast into the fire. The people waited to see his hand inflame and the quick poison bring almost sudden death. But Paul felt no harm. We are not to gather from this that the viper was not poisonous and therefore unable to produce a terrible death. Believing that God would continue to preserve him, the apostle rested in the promise of his Master, "They shall take up serpents and . . . [they] shall not hurt them" (Mark 16:18). The natives changed their minds when nothing happened to Paul: they called him a "god" instead of a "murderer."

Publius, the chief, or governor of the island, kindly extended to Paul and one or two of his companions the hospitality of his home for three days. The father of Publius "lay sick of a fever and of a bloody flux"—language Luke the physician uses with professional precision. Paul entered the sick room, prayed for the stricken man, laid his hands on him, and he recovered. Other diseased people around came to the apostle and he healed them in accordance with the same promise of Mark 16:18: recovering of the sick by laying on of hands. Thus, as Jesus rewarded Peter for the use of his boat (Luke 5:3-4) so Paul richly repaid Publius for his gracious hospitality. Laden with many gifts, and also with necessary provisions for the voyage on the ship, *Castor and Pollux,* the whole company, now greatly refreshed by the stay on the island, set sail for Rome. While nothing is said of their three-month stay at Melita, we can be assured that Paul took every opportunity to preach Christ to the islanders. An accredited tradition affirms that the beginning of the Christian church at Malta, the modern term for Melita, sprang out of Paul's memorable visit.

As for "prayers for the sick," James has some pertinent things to say about such particular intercession (5:13-20). Prayer, even though accompanied by faith, does not always heal the sick. Paul himself had a most troublesome physical disability that he prayed to the Lord about three times; but his thorn in the flesh remained, the promise being given that the sufferer would have sufficient grace to live with his "thorn," thus magnifying divine strength in his weakness. Sometimes prayer seems to prevail and the sick are healed. But there are other times when prayer is just as earnest and sincere, but sickness in those prayed for remains. "The will of the Lord be done."

Concluding our coverage of "prayer" in The Acts, we find Paul ultimately settled in his own hired house to which came seekers from far and near to hear him preach and teach the things concerning the Lord Jesus Christ (Acts 28:30-31). What a house of prayer that must have been! As a prisoner, the apostle was not allowed to go out and preach in synagogues, or "churches" in the homes of disciples; but all were allowed free access to him, which turned out to be more favorable for the furtherance of the gospel (Phil. 1:12). The periods of intercession as well as of spiritual instruction in that hired house must have exercised a tremendous influence over those who visited it. Paul wrote of prayer as being an all-sufficient resource for saints in their warfare: "Praying always with all prayer and supplication in the Spirit, watching with all perseverance and supplication for all saints" (Eph. 6:18).

> All earthly things with earth shall fade away:
> Prayer grasps eternity: Pray, always pray.

Theme 26
Romans: The Teaching of Salvation

The apostle Paul is preeminent among New Testament writers as the exponent of the many facets of God's salvation from the penalty and power of sin. His matchless Epistles are saturated with all that is involved when sinners are saved from sin's guilt and government. He is, indeed, "the Evangelist Extraordinary." Terms such as *save, saved, salvation,* and *Saviour* occur almost fifty times in his writings, and the kindred term *deliver,* used in connection with the emancipation of the soul from satanic dominion, is employed some twenty times. The apostle's undying passion was to preach salvation by grace (*grace* is one of his favorite terms) and lead sinners to the Saviour who had delivered him from so great a death.

Doubtless such particular emphasis sprang from his own remarkable experience of God's power to suddenly apprehend a sinner, convict him of his sin, and then just as suddenly snatch him as a brand from the burning. Nothing could be more dramatic than what happened to Paul, when, as Saul of Tarsus on the way to Damascus, he was found breathing out threatening and slaughter against the disciples of the Lord. He had given his consent to the murder of a truly saved soul, Stephen, and waited to witness the brutal slaying of this first martyr of the Christian church. Such a magnificent, victorious, Calvary-like death, with the murdered one praying for the forgiveness of his slayers, must have blistered his conscience; and to drown its voice he redoubled his efforts to hunt down all who claimed to follow the Saviour. While Philip the Evangelist was strenuously saving souls in Samaria, Paul was tireless in his persecution of the saints.

The term "breathing out," or breathing in, inhaling, implies how Paul was living in an atmosphere of rage and murder. Possibly there is an allusion here to the panting or snorting of a wild beast. But in a moment of time the miracle happened—his chains fell off and he rose up and followed the One he had persecuted. The illumination from heaven, which enlightened Saul, who became Paul, was not a flash of lightning, but a supernatural light into which he was translated (Acts 9:1-9). Almost immediately after that transforming vision, Paul preached that Jesus was the Son of God, and wherever he went he "spake boldly in the name of the Lord Jesus." This unique trophy of God's saving grace and power had sought to slay those who followed Christ as "The Way." Now that he is a conspicuous follower himself, the Grecians against whom Paul, the new convert, disputed went about to slay him (Acts 9:29).

From the moment of his deliverance from the shackles of sin and religious bigotry, Paul had no doubt about the reality and depth of his salvation. "I know whom I have believed, and am persuaded that he is able to keep that which I have committed unto him against that day" (II Tim. 1:12). Further, with his dynamic conversion, there came a divine, direct call to serve the One who had saved him, and he went forth to proclaim unceasingly, as a chosen vessel, the amazing grace of God to the Gentiles, to kings, to the Children of Israel. Through his instrumentality, multitudes were brought to the Saviour, and down through the ages myriads more have come to experience that the gospel is the power of God unto salvation through the apostle's Spirit-inspired and grace-saturated writings. The apostolic Apologia will never be superseded: "This is a faithful saying, and worthy of all acceptation that Christ Jesus came into the world to save sinners; of whom I am chief" (I Tim. 1:15).

It would be a most profitable exercise to go through the fourteen Epistles (if we include Hebrews), among his masterly works, which we have no hesitation in doing, and clas-

287

sify Paul's teaching on the doctrine of salvation. But let us confine ourselves to Romans, which Godet, the French theologian, described as "The Cathedral of the Christian Faith." At the outset of our pursuit do we fully understand what is meant by the glorious, evangelical, Biblical term, *salvation*? Too often we limit its implication to initial deliverance from all just guilt as we receive by the faith the Lord Jesus as our personal Saviour. Going out to testify, we thank God that we are saved—saved on a certain day in a stated place.

But if someone should stop you one day and kindly ask you the question, "Are you saved, my friend?" you would be in order to reply, "Do you mean have I *been* saved, or am I *being* saved, or have I yet *to be* saved?" In Romans, Paul emphasizes these three aspects of salvation—past, present, prospective—and his teaching on the subject cannot be understood unless the distinction between these tenses is recognized.

Our *past* salvation became ours the moment we received Jesus as the only One able to save us from all our former sins.

Our *present* salvation concerns our daily deliverance from sin's government and dominion by the power of the indwelling Spirit.

Our *prospective* salvation is yet to be experienced, and will be ours when Jesus returns, as He said He would, to completely deliver us from sin within our hearts and sin around us in the world.

I Have Been Saved

Ever conscious of that instantaneous salvation that came to him on that Damascus road, Paul, who as we know from The Acts related the miracle of his conversion three times over, could write to the Romans—"I am not ashamed of the gospel of Christ, for it is the power of God unto salvation to every one that believeth" (1:16).

Salvation, then, from an evil past is a gift we receive as

288

soon as we open the avenues of our being to the One who died to save us. "If thou . . . shalt believe in thine heart that God hath raised him [the Lord Jesus] from the dead, thou shalt be saved." Being saved, "with the mouth confession is made unto salvation" (10:9-10). Then comes the message God has used for the salvation of countless numbers since Paul penned it, "For whosoever shall call upon the name of the Lord shall be saved" (10:13).

Writing to the Ephesians, Paul could say, "By grace ye *are* saved" (2:5). The apostle also wanted Titus to remember that "according to his mercy he saved us" (Titus 3:5). All of these, and many other passages, emphasize a finished, irrevocable transaction, for what God accomplishes by His Spirit on the basis of Christ's death and resurrection is forever. Regeneration is a divine act in the life of the repentant, believing sinner, and can never be repeated. Thus, in this sense it is true to say, "Once saved, always saved;" and "I am His, and He is mine—forever!"

God sent His Son into the world that the world through Him might be saved. Then comes the authoritative word of the Son Himself, "He that believeth on the Son *hath* everlasting life" (John 3:17, 36). *Hath* means "has it at the present time, never to lose it." If, therefore, we are asked the question, "Are you saved?" and we reply, "I hope so," or "I think so," we reveal a lack of assurance in the positive declaration of both our Lord and Paul. The moment we accept the Saviour we pass from death into life, and become a new creation in Him.

A fact we are apt to forget, however, is that salvation is not "some thing" but Someone, namely, the Saviour Himself. "Behold, God is my salvation" (Isa. 12:2). True, salvation is a gift, but the gift is in the Giver Himself. Does not John make this clear when he says, "This is the record, that God hath given to us eternal life, and this life is *in* His Son. He that *hath the Son* hath life" (I John 5:11-12)? This life, then, that we receive when we accept the Saviour is not only *in*

289

Him, but *is* the Saviour Himself. "*I* am the life." Therefore, when He enters the heart as Saviour, it is to abide (John 14:6; Rev. 3:20).

Paul could not explain the miracle of all that happened on that spiritual birthday of his, but he did know "whom he had believed," and ceaselessly witnessed to the certainty of his salvation from past sin. When some of us look back to the days of our former lusts, we cannot tell how the red blood of Jesus made the black heart of the sinner whiter than the snow; but we know that when He entered our sin-cursed, sin-stained lives, transformation of life and character became evident. How grateful we should be, then, if out of redeemed hearts we can sing,

> 'Tis done, the great transaction's done,
> I am my Lord's, and He is mine.

I Am Being Saved

While it may appear to contradict the point just considered (past, completed salvation), the statement, "I am *being* saved is really complementary to it. In writing to the Philippians, Paul urged them to "work out your own salvation with fear and trembling," but he was careful to add, "It is God which worketh in you" (Phil. 2:12-13). If salvation is not within, then it cannot be worked out. The present aspect of salvation is but the outworking of the inwrought work of grace. Having received Jesus as the Saviour, we set out to walk in Him as such. This brings us to the practical side of our position in Christ, for, as His, we are to show forth His salvation from day to day. Or, because *He* is our salvation, we must allow Him to manifest His life through our victorious living. It is this present tense that brings us to a consideration of Paul's repeated "much more": "Christ died for us. *Much more* then being now justified by his blood [present assurance of a past

290

transaction], we *shall be* [future experience] saved from [coming] wrath through Him." "For if, when we were enemies, we were reconciled to God by the death of his Son, *much more,* being reconciled, we shall be saved by his life" (Rom. 5:9-10).

To have passed through the wicket gate of salvation is indeed something to be eternally grateful for. Bless God we have been saved, or reconciled to God! But let us guard against making the starting place the stopping place, for Paul says there is *much more* for us than being saved when we believed. Our salvation from coming wrath is assured, for "there is, therefore, now no condemnation to them which are in Christ Jesus." The question is, Are we being daily saved from the enticements and dominion of sin? It will be noted that Paul speaks of a double salvation, namely,

A salvation by the death of Christ.
A salvation by the life of Christ.

The first aspect takes us back to that happy day that fixed our choice on Christ as Saviour. We saw Him hanging on a tree for our sins and, receiving Him into our life, we became saved sinners because of His death.

The second aspect is concerned with the present. When we were saved, our sins were dealt with, "I, even I . . . will not remember thy sins" (Isa. 43:25). "Thou hast cast all my sins behind thy back" (Isa. 38:17). Through the blood all past sins were blotted out. But although the *fruit* went, the *root* of sin remains. When God saved us He did not take away our old Adamic, sinning nature, but made us the recipients of a new nature. This accounts for the conflict within: "When I would do good, evil is present with me." Had we been left with only one nature, the newness of life, then we would have been perfectly holy, with no evil bias within for Satan to appeal to. But the *old man* remains, and because the *new man* is diametrically opposed to his habits and ways, there is continued conflict as to which man is to rule.

291

But victory is assured over the root of sin, which was not eradicated in our acceptance of Christ as Saviour. By *His death* He saved us from the fruit of the root; now by *His life* He is able to save us from any sproutings of the root. "Sin shall not have dominion over you." What, exactly, did Paul mean by "His life"? Not Christ's earthly life. There is no salvation through trying to emulate the spotless life He lived among men. No, by "His life" Paul means not the Christ after the flesh, but the Christ alive forevermore. And we are saved from sin's attractions, allurements, and affections by His risen, glorified, throne-life. Because Christ lives, He enables us to live victoriously. He has no place in His program for sinning saints, seeing He has illimitable power to lead us to follow Him in the train of His triumph.

Cleansed from the guilt of the past by His efficacious blood, are we being daily delivered from yielding to sin through the power of the Saviour who ever lives to make intercession for us?

> Be of sin its double cure,
> Cleanse me from its guilt and power.

Can we say that the moment-by-moment salvation from sin's enticements is ours because we obey Him who "liveth, but was dead"? Or, saved, are we yet miserably defeated, limping along with only one-half of the gospel? God has made infinite provision for our *present* as well as our *past*—for our sanctification as well as our salvation. Life from a condition of spiritual death is ours; but are we experiencing the life more abundant?

> Love's resistless current sweeping,
>   All the regions deep within.
> Thought, and wish, and senses keeping
>   *Now,* and *every instant,* clean
>   Full salvation!
> From the guilt and power of sin.

292

I Have Yet to Be Saved

We sometimes sing, "More and more, still there's more to follow," and this is true in respect to the salvation provided for us by God through the death and resurrection and reappearing of His Son who was born a Saviour. While not within the province of our meditation, it can be observed in passing that Paul makes it clear that all Israel will yet be saved (Rom. 11:11, 14, 26; see 9:26). The passage, however, relevant to the future of those who have been saved, and are being saved, is the one Paul has in the portion dealing with Christian life and service. Exhorting the saints to arouse themselves from their spiritual lethargy, seeing "the night is far spent and the day is at hand," the apostle announces, "For now is our salvation nearer than when we believed" (Rom. 13:11). Well, now, what brand of salvation is this? Were we not saved when we first believed? Yes. Are we not kept daily saved, and we keep on believing? Yes. Then what feature of salvation has Paul in mind when he tells us that it is *nearer* than when we believed? As the context reveals, it is associated with the return of the Saviour to gather His saved ones home.

At the time we first believed we received salvation from the penalty of sin. As we keep on believing we experience salvation from the power of sin, but we must also have salvation from the entire presence of sin. We need to be wholly delivered from a sinning nature within us, and from a sinning world around us. We have a redeemed life, but it is in an old body—a prisoner of hope awaiting a redeemed body. This is what Paul calls "the redemption of our body" (Rom. 8:23), which will be ours when Jesus returns and transforms the body of our humiliation into a glorious body like unto His own (Phil. 3:20-21). Then we shall be saved to sin no more, being forever saved from a sinning world (see II Cor. 1:10).

This blessed, final installment of a heaven-provided salvation is certainly nearer than when we first made the acquaintance of Christ as Saviour. We live in momentous days, heavy with prophetic significance, and on every hand there are evidences that the coming of the Lord draweth nigh. "When these things *begin* to come to pass . . . then ye know that the kingdom of God is nigh at hand" (Luke 21:28, 31). Sooner than we expect, He who promised to return for His saved ones may appear. Are we ready to meet Him and receive from Him the completion of our wonderful salvation?

Separated unto Jesus,
   Loos'd from all the world beside,
Blinded by the advent glory,
   Hour by hour would I abide.

So from glory unto glory,
   Gladden'd by the advent ray;
All the path is growing brighter,
   Shining unto perfect day.

Theme 27
Galatians: The Wondrous Cross

In many respects the Epistle to the Galatians, sometimes called "The Magna Charta of Liberty," is one of the greatest writings to come from the gifted pen of the apostle Paul. There are several facets to this brilliant diamond of truth. Approaching the Galatian Letter, we can study the contrast between law and grace, and note Paul's strong emphasis concerning deliverance from legalism. Or we could confine ourselves to the doctrine of the Holy Spirit as unfolded in the Epistle, for Paul's classification of this soul-satisfying theme in this letter is unique. Then we might come to Galatians thinking only of arrested spiritual progress, and develop a message on the cause and cure of "backsliding," for far too many Christians begin in the Spirit and end in the flesh.

What impresses our mind, however, as we study Galatians, is the fact that it stands out in all the writings of Paul as a cross-exalting Epistle. There is no other New Testament book that deals with the cross of Christ in so many ways as this one which left such an impact upon Martin Luther. If we were to give the Epistle a caption, we would write over it, "The Crucified and His Cross." It is essentially "The Epistle of Calvary," relating the cross to life and experience in unmistakable terms.

Paul's purpose in writing this matchless letter was to combat the mutilated gospel and the compromising ministry that the Galatian church had countenanced. In forceful and clear terms the apostle declares that a full understanding of the redemptive work of Christ is the only safeguard against license and legalism of any kind.

295

Take your New Testament, note these allusions to the cross in every chapter of Galatians, and see if Paul is not worthy of being known as "The Apostle of Calvary." Had he been familiar with the hymnology of our time, his favorite spiritual song might well have been:

> In the cross of Christ I glory,
>   Towering o'er the wrecks of time;
> All the light of sacred story
>   Gathers round its head sublime.

Chapter 1: The Cross and Deliverance from an Evil World

"Who gave himself for our sins, that he might deliver us from this present evil world" (1:4). Christ, by His death and resurrection, not only saves us from eternal judgment but also from surrounding wickedness here and now.

Chapter 2: The Cross and Cocrucifixion

"I am crucified with Christ: nevertheless I live; yet not I, but Christ liveth in me" (2:20). The mystic touch of identification with Christ in His death, burial, and resurrection is sadly neglected by church-going people today.

Chapter 3: The Cross and Redemption from the Curse

"Christ hath redeemed us from the curse of the law, being made a curse for us" (3:13). The One always obedient to God, who had never violated His law, was the One who was willing to bear our curse, enduring our penalty.

Chapter 4: The Cross and Adoption into Sonship

"To redeem them that were under the law, that we might receive the adoption of sins" (4:5-7). The Son Himself was

296

willing to die that we might be called the sons of God. All who are born anew by the Spirit of adoption are sons, and if sons, then heirs of God.

Chapter 5: The Cross and Its Continued Offense

"Then is the offense of the cross ceased" (5:11). "Offense" is actually "scandal." What, then, is the scandal of the cross? Cicero wrote: "The cross, it is so shameful it never ought to be mentioned in polite society." It was, of course, a most scandalous thing to die as a felon on a wooden gibbet. What do we know about sharing the shame of the cross?

Chapter 6: The Cross and Its Persecution

"Lest they should suffer persecution for the cross of Christ" (6:12). If we seek to make a fair show in the flesh, we shall miss much of the hostility the preaching of the cross produces. Live the cross, and you will quickly know what it is to have fellowship with His sufferings. Also in this chapter we have the cross and its glory. "But God forbid that I should glory, save in the cross of our Lord Jesus Christ" (6:14). Paul had no other boast. Writing to the Corinthians, he said that he determined to know nothing among men save Christ and Him crucified. This Galatian Letter, as well as all his other Letters, reveals how Paul lived at the heart of Calvary.

Some of the old writers were wont to speak of Calvary as "the divine academy of life." No matter how highly educated we may be, our education is not complete unless we have graduated from such an academy. Paul tarried in such a school of spiritual learning while in the backside of the desert and, in his teaching on the cross, he shares with us the treasures of this divine tuition.

It must not be forgotten that all Paul knew about the meaning and message of Calvary was received directly from

297

the crucified One Himself. Going back to the autobiographical sketch in Galatians 1, Paul, in his emphatic statement as to the authority of the gospel of redeeming love and power which he preached, says: "It is not after man. For I neither received it of man, neither was I taught it, but by the *revelation of Jesus Christ*" (1:11-12, emphasis added).

The One who died on the tree knew, as no other, the full import of such a death, and in turn gave Paul a distinct revelation of the true significance of "the old rugged cross."

What, then, were some of the lessons the apostle learned about the cross from the slain Lamb Himself, leading him to glory in it?

A Law That Had Been Satisfied

This was the initial lesson he had to master in the divine academy, and how overwhelmed Paul must have been as the sinless Substitute for sinners instructed him in the substitutionary aspect of the cross. His mind was not prepared (neither is ours) for the further truth of the cross until this initial aspect is fully comprehended. In the Person of Christ, sin was judged, condemned, and expiated. Thus, without apology, the apostle declares that by "the works of the law shall no flesh be justified" (2:16). Not only did he preach that "Christ died for our sins"; Paul made it personal: "the Son of God, who loved *me* and gave himself for *me*" (2:20).

Combating the legalism that he encountered in Galatia, Paul thunders out a blood-bought emancipation of liberty from the law's curse and condemnation. All who disobey God's ancient law are under a curse. "Cursed is every one who continueth not in the works of the law, to do them" (3:10). In His death, Christ endured this curse. Now by faith we can know what it is to sing: "Free from the law, O happy condition." Because of this curse, the sinner was under condemnation: "The soul that sinneth, it shall die." The Lord Jesus, however, took our death and made it His own. "He

298

tasted death [or *deaths*] for every man." Having no sin of His own, He was yet made sin—*not* a sinner—for us.

A Love That Had Been Manifested

While the apostle came to learn that the heart of the cross was the very heart of God, yet the aspect of divine love exhibited at Calvary was that of Christ's love: "The Son of God, who loved me." And it was because of this sacrificial love of the Saviour that Paul counted himself honored to be known as His love-slave.

A Liberty That Had Been Secured

Passages like Galatians 1:4; 4:9; 5:1, leave no doubt about the blood-bought emancipation that the cross represents. Calvary disposes of all legality. Sin may pursue us right up to the cross, demanding the wages of death, but at Calvary the claim is disallowed. Justice pursued us up to the cross, demanding vindication; it received it in the cry: "It is finished." Liberty from sin and self is the coronation stone of the cross. Paul could join in John's Calvary doxology: "Unto him that loveth us and *loosed* us from our sins by his own blood" (Rev. 1:5, RV; see also I John 1:7).

A Life That Must Be Lived

Many who believe in a crucified Christ are not willing to live a crucified life; yet the two are nailed together. In Galatians 6:14, Paul summarizes for us all that he learned about the cross. He reduces his teaching to three crosses:

Christ on a cross: "God forbid that I should glory, save in the cross of our Lord Jesus Christ."
The world on a cross: " . . . by whom the world is crucified unto me."
The believer on a cross: " . . . and I unto the world."

299

The cross, then, is the divine laboratory where the flesh is cauterized and put to death (2:20; 5:24). The burning caustic of the cross must be applied to the world and the flesh as they arise to laud it over us. The cross is the boundary line or terminus between believers and the world. All legal, carnal elements in the world lost their hold on Paul. Is this experientially true of us? Are we content to let the world go by? Are the shame, scandal, and persecution of the cross our glory? No saint can reach for the old life without crossing Christ's grave, for we died in Him. That blessed cross of His, then, is not only the center of the universe, of Scripture, of history— it must be at the very center of every part of our life. The cross must be known not only as a doctrine but as a dynamic, bringing every phase of life into conformity with His death.

Theme 28
Ephesians: The Unfolding of God

Readers of Paul's Prison Letter to the Ephesian church can profit from various outlines of the Epistle given by different expositors. One of the most serviceable is that which is founded upon the word *heavenly* (1:3). So we have—

> The Heavenly Calling of the Church (1-3)
> The Heavenly Conduct of the Church (4-6:9)
> The Heavenly Conflict of the Church (6:10-24)

The exposition of Ephesians given by Ruth Paxon deals with the "Wealth, Walk, and Warfare of the Christian." My own handling of Paul's Letter, however, may appear to be somewhat unusual. Constant reading of it led the writer to classify the majority of the words forming the Epistle under the letters of the alphabet. For instance, under *A*, "apostle" is used three times—"according," seven times, etc. By this method, the truths Paul set out to emphasize were alphabetically arranged with the number of their appearances, and consequently there evolved several *cameos* made up of the exact phrases found in this "Epistle of the Heavenlies." Shall we let these priceless phrases speak for themselves?

The Will of God (1:1)

The divine will was the basis of Paul's call to the ministry, and the cause and consequence, ground and background of all revelation and manifestation the apostle experienced. The *origin* of the call was the Will of God; the *organ*, the apostle himself; the *object* of the call the edification and enlightenment of the saints and faithful in Christ Jesus.

301

Work out the following cameo of *The Will of God*—
1. Called by His will (1:1)
2. Good pleasure of His will (1:5)
3. Mystery of His will (1:9)
4. Counsel of His will (1:11)
5. Understanding of His will (5:17)
6. Accomplishment of His will (6:6-7)

The Gift of God (2:8)

What a bountiful giver God is! All His gifts are without repentance. In a parenthetic outburst Paul instructed the Ephesians to know that grace, first and last, was the sole source of their salvation of which theirs was a present realization. But what was the exact gift Paul had in mind? Was it salvation or faith? Are not both implied—the gift of salvation and the gift of faith to accept salvation? Saving faith is not natural faith but a bestowed gift enabling the sinner to accept Christ as a personal Saviour.

The Household of God (2:19-20)

No other Pauline Epistle unfolds the spiritual position of the true church as does Ephesians, and this feature makes it of great doctrinal value. Here, the church is viewed as—
The Body (1:22-23)
The Household of God (2:19-20)
The Habitation of God (2:22)
The Temple (2:21-22)
The Center of Divine Wisdom and Glory (3:20-21)
The Bride (5:25, 32)

The Habitation of God (2:22)

As the figure of "the household" is domestic in nature,

302

that of the church as a "habitation" is spiritual. Under the Old Dispensation, God localized His presence in the tabernacle and the temple (John 4:20-21), and the Jew had to journey there in order to worship Him. Then, God had a tabernacle for His people; under grace His people are His tabernacle, or dwelling place. The church is "the mysterious cabinet of the Trinity." The term *dwell* means "to abidingly make one's abode" (John 14:20). What an overpowering thought it is that every believer is "a temple, hallowed by the indwelling Lord" (I Cor. 16:17; see 6:19). What a deterrent against any form of sin the recognition of this fact is!

The Grace of God (3:2, 7)

"Grace" is the first and the last word of this "Epistle of Grace" (1:2; 6:24). Paul deemed it to be an honor to act as a dispensing steward of the undeserved mercy of God. The dual thought dealt with in the passages before us is that "grace" is a gift, and that it is given to the least. The word *dispensation* means "age or period," and since the coming of "the Spirit of Grace" at Pentecost we have had the age of grace. Paul was ever jubilant as he expounded God's elective grace in its richness and sufficiency (I Cor. 9:17).

The Wisdom of God (3:10)

Because divine wisdom is "manifold" it is not confined to one particular sphere, but covers all realms. This "much-varied, many-sided, many-colored" wisdom has been entrusted to the church to display before heaven and earth. The wondrous hues of this divine attribute were all personified in Christ, whom God made unto us Wisdom (I Cor. 1:30). If we would possess the wisdom—"pure, peaceable, gentle, and easy to be entreated," all we have to do is to appropriate it by faith (James 1:5; 3:17).

The Fullness of God (3:19)

Filled even "unto" (RV). Not filled *with* this fullness but *unto* it. The grand goal is to be filled according to capacity even as God is full (Col. 2:2-9). In the Epistle, Paul presents a triad of fullnesses. "The fulness of God" (3:19); "The fulness of Christ" (4:13); "The fulness of the Spirit" (5:18). Although we have such wealth at our disposal, we live like spiritual paupers. An ocean of abundance is ours, yet we content ourselves with a mere trickle of the divine resources at our disposal. May grace and willingness be ours to possess our possessions!

The Son of God (4:13)

This phrase not only declares the deity of Christ, it likewise emphasizes the divine Fatherhood. Christ is the only Son the world has ever known who did not have a human father. He came as the only begotten Son of God (Ps. 2:7); and He sent His only Son to earth as a missionary (Rom. 1:4; Heb. 4:14). The glory of the gospel is that the Son of God became the Son of Man, that He might make the sons of men, the sons of God (John 1:12; Gal. 4:4-7).

The Life of God (4:18)

This unique phrase staggers the mind. Our Lord described the kind of life God imparts. As He is "the eternal God," it is "life eternal" (John 17:3). Salvation is the life of God within the soul and all who are destitute of this kind of life are spiritually dead (I Tim. 5:6).

The Spirit of God (4:30)

Not only is the Holy Spirit from God; He *is* God (Acts 5:3-4)! The Spirit, like the Saviour, came from God, and since His advent has been in the world as the administrator of the affairs of the church—the Lord's body. The Third Person of the Trinity shares the holiness of the First Person. Over one hundred times He is referred to as "the Holy Spirit." Why? Because He is intrinsically holy, came from a holy God, represents the holy Son, and seeks to transform those He indwells into the holiness of God.

The Followers of God (5:1)

This arresting phrase literally means "imitators of God." We are to imitate or copy God, chiefly in His essential attributes of love and forgiveness. It is from the original form of the word "follower"—*mimeomai*—that we have "mimeograph," or a copy. We are to be imitators, not of those who follow God, but of God Himself. This is not mere imitation, trying to live and act in a Godlike way, but involves surrender to God that He might live out His life *in* and *through* our lives.

The Kingdom of God (5:5)

Dual dominion is herewith stated, for what is God's is Christ's who thought it not robbery to be counted equal with God (John 5:18; Phil. 2:6). Paul speaks of the present kingdom into which we have been translated and in which spiritual kingdom the sovereignty of God and of Christ must be recognized (Col. 1:14).

The Wrath of God (5:6)

Arthur May's translation of this passage speaks of this wrath as "ever descending upon the sons of disobedience" who are "children of wrath" (2:2-3; Rom. 2:5). Divine wrath is not inconsistent with divine love. God is holy and righteous and as a pefect moral Governor and Lawgiver He demands obedience and punishes those who transgress His commands.

Divine wrath is never unjust. God cannot be guilty of spite. Divine anger is ever subordinate to divine mercy (Ps. 30:5; 103:8; 145:8).

The Fear of God (5:21)

Some of the best manuscripts read: "the fear of Christ." Either phrase is true, for the Father and He are one. This "fear" is not the kind experienced under the rule of a tyrant. God is not a cruel, merciless dictator. The kind of "fear" we are to exhibit is that of reverential trust, obedience, and worship—a holy fear which hallows every aspect of life. Fear the Lord, ye His saints!

The Armor of God (6:11, 13)

Pauline Epistles are rich in their use of military metaphors. Close and long contact with Roman guards provided the apostle with effective illustrations of Christian conflict. The complete armor of a Roman soldier included shield, sword, lance, helmet, greaves, and breastplate. Paul does not mention a "spear" but he adds girdle and shoes which, although not reckoned as a part of armor, were yet necessary for the soldier. What a magnificent and elaborate description Paul gives us of the full panoply of God! Because of the craftiness, shrewdness, and careful planning of the devil, and also his methodical devices of error, we must have divine protection, and all that is necessary has been provided. But it must be "put on" or appropriated by faith (II Tim. 4:7). It will be noted that no armor is provided for the *back,* for we are meant to face the foe, not retreat from him. The knees also are unprotected, seeing the armor for them is constant, believing prayer—the mightiest weapon of all against every satanic assault. As good soldiers of Jesus Christ we can only be more than conquerors when fully armed.

306

The Word of God (6:17)

This offensive weapon of the Christian is absolutely of God and one which Jesus used most effectively against Satan in the wilderness (Matt. 4:1-11). The infallible Word is the Spirit's two-edged sword (Heb. 4:12). This same phrase, "The Word of God," is used of Christ as He came revealing God to man and reconciling man to God. Thus, the Living Word and the Written Word are mighty weapons to put to flight the powers of evil. Sin and error and heresy cannot exist where Christ and the Scriptures are fully obeyed (I Peter 1:25; Col. 1:25; II Tim. 3:16).

While the designation *God* is used over thirty times in Ephesians, that of *Father* is employed some eight times, and both terms imply that He is the source or spring of any or all blessing. "All my springs are in thee" (Ps. 87:7). Each of the references to divine Fatherhood carries its own significance.

God Our Father (1:2)

As a Father, He is perfect and therefore not subject to the frailties of human fatherhood. As our *Father,* He understands all about the needs of His children, and as our *God,* He can meet those needs.

The Father of Our Lord Jesus Christ (1:3; 3:14)

How near and dear the relationship was between Father and Son! As He died, Jesus surrendered His spirit to His Father. As a Son He never failed in obedience to His Father's will.

The Father of Glory (1:17)

God is always characterized by "glory" (Heb. 9:5; Acts 7:2). This Pauline expression can imply the Father's mani-

307

fested presence (Ps. 108:5). He is not only essentially glorious in Himself, but the source of all true glory.

The Father of All (4:6)

There is a good deal of unbiblical talk about the Fatherhood of God these days. God is certainly the Father of all men in respect to creation, just as He is spoken of as the Father of the rain. But He is not the Father in heaven that our Lord spoke about, unless there is sonship based upon redemption. God is the heavenly Father only of those who have received the Spirit of adoption (Gal. 4:5-7). Access to the Father (4:18) is only through the mediation of His Son (John 14:6).

Thanks to the Father (5:20)

If an earthly father is grieved over the ingratitude of his children, how do we think our heavenly Father feels when so many of His children forget to praise Him at all times for His unfailing goodness?

Peace and Love from the Father (6:23)

Blessings from God come to us with the love of His fatherly heart. There are no prayers in Paul's Epistles surpassing the two in Ephesians in depth and intensity, in spiritual breadth and elevation (1:15-23; 3:14-19).

Theme 29
Ephesians: The Unfolding of Christ

Ephesians is a Christ-magnifying as well as a God-glorifying Epistle. Over sixty times Paul mentioned Christ in the six chapters that form this Letter. Then, of the divine pronouns used, *his* is most prominent. Everything is *His,* and the Holy Spirit delights in taking all that is His and making it ours. The striking phrase common to the Epistle is "in Christ," suggesting its central theme, namely, all things are summed up in Christ. He is the element of the believer's life, the One in whom he lives, moves, and has his being (Acts 17:28). A Christian is one who is in Christ and indwelt by Him. Here, again, let us collate the exact phrases, and note their implication.

The Apostle of Christ (1:1)

Paul's apostleship was not of man (Gal. 1:1). All the apostles were disciples of Christ, but not all disciples were apostles. An apostle was a disciple called and named thus, and one who had seen and heard Christ and had witnessed His resurrection (Matt. 10:2; Acts 1:21-22). Paul both saw and heard the risen Christ on that Damascus road (Acts 9:4-5; I Cor. 15:8).

The Father of Christ (1:3, 17)

"The Father glory-clad" was the only Father Jesus had. Although He came as "The Son of Man," He was not *a* Son of *a* man. When He was but twelve years of age He spoke of

309

God as His Father (Luke 2:49). What love, adoration, obedience, and submission are wrapped up in the tender phrase He often used, "My Father"!

The Blood of Christ (1:7; 2:13; 6:12)

The Bible is a crimson book, and Paul's Epistles drip with the ruby blood of the Redeemer. The modern, cultured mind may reject all reference to blood-shedding and blood-washing as being repugnant, but the fact remains that "without shedding of blood there is no remission [of sins]" (Heb. 9:22; 10:18). Because "the life of the flesh is as the blood," when Christ shed His blood He gave His life on our behalf (Matt. 26:28). The efficacy of His death abides (I John 1:7).

The Prisoner of Christ (3:1; 4:1)

As an ambassador in bonds, Paul looked upon himself not as Nero's prisoner, but as the Lord's. The apostle had committed no crime meriting punishment. He was in prison for "the Gentiles," that is, for preaching to the Gentiles. As Paul recognized that the will of the Lord controlled all events in his life, he knew that it was His permissive will that he should suffer captivity. His bonds made for the furtherance of the gospel, and were used as the ground for an appeal to a closer walk with God in the lives of those to whom he wrote.

The Mystery of Christ (1:9; 3:3-4, 9; 5:32; 6:19)

By the use of this term "mystery," Paul implies not something mysterious or difficult to understand, but rather as a matter previously hidden but now brought to light, a secret revealed. What exactly was the mystery of Christ? In this narrative Paul is dealing with the composition of the church, and reveals that it was the redemptive purpose of Christ to fashion both Jews and Gentiles into one body. It is no mys-

310

tery or secret in Old Testament days that God would save Jews and likewise save Gentiles. The mystery hid from the ages was that both Jews and Gentiles would be woven into the mystic fabric, the church of the living God. This was the mystery revealed to Paul by the Head of the church Himself (Gal. 1:12).

The Riches of Christ (1:7, 18; 2:4, 7; 3:8, 16)

The expressive word Paul uses to describe heavenly riches—"unsearchable," actually means "untraceable." We cannot trace its source completely. We do not fully know "whence it cometh and whither it goeth" (John 3:8; Job 5:9). Grace is like an inexhaustible mine whose treasures can never be completely explored. What wealth is ours! Riches of glory! Richness of mercy! Riches of grace! The question is, Are we appropriating all we have in and through Christ? "All that I have is thine." Then let us live on our bountiful inheritance.

The Love of Christ (3:18-19)

The reader will find it profitable to link together all the *love*-passages in Ephesians (1:4, 15; 2:4; 3:17; 4:2, 16; 5:2, 25; 5:28, 33; 6:23-24). Among the paradoxes of our faith is the ability to know the unknowable, and see the invisible (Heb. 11:27). How comforting are the four dimensions or the rectangular measure of Christ's love! Its proportions are foursquare like the heavenly Jerusalem John wrote about (Rev. 21:16). This eternal, sacrificial, and immeasurable love of Christ can only be measured by "the golden reed" of man's emptiness and weakness, gilded with His glory. There is the *breadth* of love—it is worldwide, including lost souls wherever found—its manifoldness of provision. There is the *length* of love—extending to all ages: from eternity to eternity, and it will endure as long as God Himself. There is the *depth* of love—it cannot be fathomed, and goes down beneath all human need. It is so profound that no creature is able to fully understand it (Rom. 11:33). There is the *height* of love—it is beyond the reach of any foe to deprive us of it. Height can also suggest the exalted position of those whose lives have been claimed by such an embracing love.

> It passeth knowledge, that dear love of Thine,
> My Saviour, Jesus; yet this soul of mine
> Would of Thy love, in all its breadth and length,
> Its height and depths, its everlasting strength,
> Know more and more.

The Gift of Christ (4:7)

Among Paul's favorite words *gift* holds a prominent place, especially in this Epistle in which he used it fourteen times. In the narrative at this point, the apostle is dealing with the manifold gifts the ascended Lord bestowed upon His church. A diversity of graces and offices are given to the members of His body according to the measure of faith (Rom. 12:3). "Unto *every one* of us"—so there is no born-again believer without a regeneration-imparted gift to be used in the Lord's service. The tragedy of the church is nonuse of unrecognized gifts. There is no Christian without a gift. Have you discovered yours? And are you using it to the utmost limit?

The Body of Christ (4:12)

The three figures Paul uses of the church are "the bride"—expressing love, union, and intimacy; "the body"—indicating the ideas of life and interdependence; "the building"—speaking of unity, cohesion, and utility. "The body" was Paul's favorite term for believers (1:23; 2:16; 3:6; 4:4, 12, 16; 5:25, 30). Christ, as the Head of the body, is well able to control all its affairs and direct its actions (1:22; 5:25). A human body is not only a living organism but an organization

312

of many members and functions. It is so with the body which is His church. The apostle makes it clear that the church is a holy temple—not a corrupt one like the temple of the goddess Diana (2:21; 4:4), and a glorious habitation, existing for the glory of her Head who loves her as a bride (5:25, 29).

A profitable division of Ephesians is—

1. The Church Before the Lord (1-3)
2. The Church Before the World (4-6:9)
3. The Church Before Satan (6:10-18)

It must be made clear that a person may be a member of a church as an organized assembly of professed religious people, and yet not be a member of the church which is His body. The only membership the apostle stresses is membership in the body. Thus, the question of paramount importance is, Are we in Christ, as well as in a visible house of worship as members?

The Fullness of Christ (1:10, 23; 3:19; 4:13; 5:18)

Our blessed Lord was, and is, "the fulness of the Godhead bodily" (Col. 2:9). Arthur Way translates the phrase, "the stature of the fulness of Christ" as "the standards of Messiah's own perfection." The word Paul used for "fulness" is *pleroma,* expressing the fullness of the divine nature (Col. 1:19). "He filleth all" implies, "He filleth for himself." As the Creator, Preserver, and Governor of the world, He fills *all* the universe with *all* things. He is our Fullness and we are to be His fullness (Col. 2:10; Eph. 5:18). Is ours the fullness of the blessing of His gospel (Rom. 15:29)?

The Kingdom of Christ (5:5)

Another translation of this verse puts it, "The Kingdom of Christ who is God." As Emmanuel, He is "God with us." The context here contains a solemn warning against indulgence in the sins of idolaters. Works of darkness are incompatible with

313

membership in the kingdom of heaven. The unworthy Christian has indeed an inheritance in the Lord's present spiritual kingdom and in His coming visible kingdom to his own awful responsibility. But if his life is not in harmony with the principles of the kingdom, then, in a spiritual sense, "he is one that hath not, from whom shall be taken away that which he hath" (Matt. 13:12).

The Name of Christ (5:20)

There is more in Paul's admonition than the mere recital of a name. *Name* represents manifested character, the integrity of the one bearing the name. It represents what the person actually is, and not only a label by which he is known. When our "thanksgiving" is offered in the name of Christ, we are really asking God to hear us on the basis of all Christ is in Himself; and on the merits of His accomplishments God hears and answers prayer. As Ellicott suggests, use of the name suggests, "identification, perfect unity with Him, adoption to sonship within the ground of sonship, and a unity which is the ground of perfect confidence in prayer."

Is ours the spirit of habitual thanksgiving? Do we give thanks for *all* things, even the most unpleasant, unwelcome things of life? If we cannot give thanks *for* all things, we can certainly be thankful *in* all things. We may not be able to read the meaning of many of our tears, but we can bless God, even as we weep, that He knows what is best for His children. "Ill that He blesses is our good." If there is nothing within the heart to disturb our fellowship with the Lord, then, no matter what circumstances may prevail, we can live on Thanksgiving Street.

The Servants of Christ (6:6)

The word Paul uses for servants is *bondsmen* or *slaves,* and in the paragraph (vv. 5-9), means the hardest form of subjec-

314

tion, namely that of slaves to masters, still under the same idea that both are "in Christ." "The slave is the servant of Christ in obeying his master—the master is a fellow-servant with his slave in the same divine Lord." To quote Ellicott's most valuable commentary again—

> To be a slave, looking on his master's authority as more power imposed by the cruel laws of man, this "eye-service" is found to be an all but irresistible temptation. It is only when he looks on himself as "the slave of Christ"—who Himself "took on the form of a slave" (Phil. 2:7, Berkeley Version) in order to work out the will of God in a sinful world, and to redeem all men from bondage—that he can possibly serve from the heart.

Paul always practiced what he preached. When he wrote this Epistle he himself was a bondsman or slave, but grace was given him to glory in his bonds. What the world counted ignominy he counted the highest honor, and was thus more proud of his shackles than a king of his diadem. A slave in Christ was actually the Lord's freeman, and entered "a service which is perfect freedom" (I Cor. 7:22).

> He is the freeman whom the truth sets free,
> And all are slaves beside.

We have thus seen how full Ephesians is of Christ's worth and work. How Paul loved to magnify the Lord he so faithfully served! May our lives and lips ever extol the same glorious Lord!

What do we know about spiritual slavery? Do we look upon ourselves as slaves, slaves of Jesus Christ? Who and what is a slave? Over one hundred years ago they practiced slavery in America. Who was a slave then? A slave was a person who had no right to anything he possessed. His body was at the disposal of his master; if he had any talents they also were at the disposal of his master; if he had offspring they also were

315

looked upon as the possession of his master. A slave had no right to anything he possessed. Paul says: "We are slaves of Christ." Are we? When people are urged to be fully yielded to the Lord, they sometimes protest: "Well, I can do as I like with my time; it is no business of yours what I do with my leisure and money." But we cannot do as we like with all we represent if we are His slaves. Our talents are not our own, they are the Lord's. When people are asked to dedicate of their substance, their money, they reply: "That is no business of yours, I can give as I like with what is my own." But they cannot if they are the Lord's. As slaves, we have no right to anything that we possess. All that we are and have has been redeemed by the blood of Christ; we are not our own. Calvary has the prior claim on our life. Nothing we have is ours; all is on trust. This was the truth George Matheson had in mind when he wrote—

Make me a captive, Lord,
  And then I shall be free,
Force me to render up my sword,
  And I shall conqueror be.

Theme 30
Ephesians: The Unfolding of the Spirit

One of the most profitable methods of studying a book or chapter of the Bible is to gather out of it what is recorded on a particular theme. The marvel of the Word is that more than one glorious topic or doctrine can be found in almost every Bible book. Take, for example, the Epistle of Paul to the Ephesians. A. T. Pierson fittingly called it "The Alps of the New Testament," for here we scale heights and span breadths unknown. Talk about variety of truth! Ephesians has it. Some of these days I would like to write a commentary on this matchless Epistle by Paul. What heart-inspiring hours one will have expounding the cameos of God, cameos of Christ, cameos of grace, cameos of the divine will, cameos of saints, and cameos of sinners found in Ephesians! Why, there is no end to the possible approaches to this Epistle. Here, however, we must content ourselves with but one aspect of truth in Ephesians, namely, Cameos of the Spirit. Where have we another book as God-glorifying, Christ-exalting, and Spirit-magnifying as the Epistle to the Ephesians? Altogether it presents some thirteen references to the Spirit.

The Blessings of the Spirit (1:3)

The phrase "blessed with all spiritual blessings" can also be translated "the benediction of all blessings of His Spirit." The verse as a whole offers a proof of the three Persons forming the Godhead. A close study of verses 1-14 reveals many of the blessings of the Spirit. Mark these in your Bible:

1. An unbroken relationship (v. 4)

317

2. An unquestioned acceptance (v. 6)
3. A redemption none can rob us of (v. 7)
4. A union never to be dissolved (v. 10)
5. An unfading inheritance (v. 11)
6. A seal, never to be disowned (v. 13)

Blessings innumerable are ours in and through the Spirit. Let us not, however, be taken up with the blessings to the exclusion of the Blesser Himself. A subtle scheme of Satan is to have us occupied with a gift rather than with the Giver.

Once it was the blessing,
Now it is the Lord.

The Sealing of the Spirit (1:13; 4:30)

Paul's two references to this aspect of the Spirit's ministry are worthy of prayerful meditation. The Spirit is the seal, and the sealer is God. Therefore, because the believer is divinely sealed, no one nor anything can break the seal. Among other things, a seal indicates ownership, and once we are sealed with the Spirit we become the Lord's forever. The sealing is eternal (4:30).

It is also important to realize that the saving and the sealing synchronize. The moment a believing sinner receives Christ as Saviour, the Holy Spirit enters as the evidence of a finished transaction. Being sealed with the Spirit is not some postregenerative experience, as the wording of the Authorized Version would imply: "after that ye believed, ye were sealed." The Revised Version says: "having also believed, ye were sealed with the Holy Spirit of promise."

Attention must also be given to the title Paul uses in this verse of the Spirit: "The Holy Spirit of *promise.*" Why is He named thus? Well, He came as the promise of the Father and as the promise of the Son. He also inspired holy men of old to write all the promises the Scriptures present, and He alone

318

can enable us to understand and appropriate the precious promises of the Word.

The Earnest of the Spirit (1:14; cf. II Cor. 1:22; 5:5)

The Holy Spirit is our foretaste of heaven, the advance portion of a glorious inheritance. The Scotch have a very expressive term for "earnest." It is the word *arle.* A farmer buys a field from a neighbor. Once the transaction is completed, the buyer scoops up a handful of the earth and puts it in a bag. This is the *arle, earnest, pledge,* that he bought the entire field and can possess it when he desires. In like manner the Spirit is our *arle,* the earnest or pledge of all that we shall inherit.

> I have a heritage of joy,
> That yet I must not see,
> The hand that bled to make it mine
> Is keeping it for me.

The Illumination of the Spirit (1:17)

When Paul mentioned the Ephesian believers in his prayers, he interceded for them that they might know what it was to experience the ministry of the Spirit as "the Spirit of wisdom and revelation in the knowledge of Christ." As there is not one useless word in the Bible, there must be a distinction between "wisdom" and "revelation." The terms indicate that God's Spirit operates in a twofold way. As the "Spirit of wisdom" He works in and upon the mind. Comprehension of a divine revelation is impossible apart from Him through a Spirit-possessed and enlightened mental faculty. Christ opened the *understanding* of His disciples (Luke 24:45) as He also opened unto them the *Scriptures* (Luke 24:32). The one opening is necessary to accomplish the other. As the Spirit of revelation, He opens the truth of God; as the Spirit of wis-

319

dom, He opens our minds or understanding to receive the revelation. And all of His ministry in this twofold way is to bring us a deeper knowledge of Christ (John 16:14).

Access by the Spirit (2:18)

The immediate context at this point is the introduction of both Jew and Gentile, as together forming the mystic fabric that we know as the church of God, into His presence. The Spirit, who is responsible for the formation of the church, introduces her to the Father. In this age of grace we approach God through the agency of the Spirit. We worship Christ by the Spirit. God can only be worshiped in the Spirit.

The Building of the Spirit (2:22)

What a master builder the Spirit is, and how effectively Paul assisted Him! But what is the sacred task of the Spirit? Is it not the completion of the church, the Lord's body? Christ is the chief cornerstone of this invisible structure and in Him we are fitly framed together: "In whom ye also are builded together for a habitation of God in the Spirit" (vv. 19-22, RV).

Is the Spirit near the end of His sacred task? Possibly the paucity of results in gospel work is an evidence that He is. Once a builder is almost at the end of building a brick church, he does not require as many bricks for the tower as he did for the walls. The question of paramount importance is: Have you been built into the temple of God? It is sadly possible to be in the church organization and not be a part of the organism, the true and invisible church.

The Inspiration of the Spirit (3:5)

The mystery of Christ, or the mysteries hid from the ages, is the composition of the church. It was no mystery to Old

320

Testament readers that Jews would be saved, or even that some Gentiles would be saved. What was hidden from them was the truth that saved Jews and saved Gentiles would form one mystical body, the church (v. 6). Paul was the one privileged to reveal such a mystery: "By revelation was made known unto me the mystery." And this sublime revelation was given to the apostle by the Spirit.

All truth is revelation. Phases of truth can only be discerned by the Spirit (I Cor. 2:13-15). He it was who inspired the truth (II Tim. 3:16). Peter also affirms that the Holy Spirit is the source of revelation (I Peter 1:11; II Peter 1:21).

The Power of the Spirit (3:16)

In one of his superb prayers, Paul prayed that the saints might be strengthened with power through Christ's Spirit in the inner man. "Strong will power infused by His Spirit into your innermost nature," is how Arthur Way translates this passage. How different such power is to the energy of the flesh! A good deal that passes for spiritual power today is merely fleshly energy.

Let us be careful never to separate the power from the Person. Power is not *something* but *Someone*. Often misguided saints plead for "power" as an intangible force which God can be persuaded to pour out upon them. "Ye shall receive power, after that the Holy Spirit is come upon you," said our Lord (Acts 1:8). The Spirit *is* the power.

What is power? It is the manifestation of the presence and purpose of the Spirit. May ours be the experience of Micah, who was full of power by the Spirit (3:8).

The Unity of the Spirit (4:3-4)

The Spirit as "One" is the only Person who can make possible "one body." In verses 4-6 of this chapter, Paul enumerates seven ways by which the Spirit unifies believers.

It is also our responsibility to "maintain the unity of which the Spirit is the author." Paul urges us to "endeavor to keep the unity." Alas, we are miserably failing in such a commendable endeavor! What divisions, estrangements, bitter feuds, and separations characterize the church today! "We are not divided, all one body we" is one of the lies that we sing on a Sunday. While we have little sympathy with much of the union of denominations, we *must* strive for a spirit of unity among believers.

The Grief of the Spirit (4:30)

This great passage teaches us many things about the Spirit. First of all, it offers a proof of His personality. Grief is possible only by a person. We know, then, that He is not a mere influence or emanation from God, for an influence cannot be grieved. Grief is an element of the heart. Where there is no love, there can be no grief. Because the Spirit, then, can be pained, we know that He is the Spirit of love. In verses 31-32, Paul sets forth those things pleasing or painful to the tender Spirit.

Then the apostle speaks of the Spirit as "holy." Over one hundred times in the Bible is He thus defined. Why is He called "holy"? Because of His inherent holiness: He comes from a holy God, represents the holy Son, inspired the Holy Scriptures, and transforms us into the holiness of God.

> Every thought of holiness
> Is His alone.

All believers are sealed with the Holy Spirit of God unto the day of redemption, which is the day when our bodies will be redeemed. The Spirit is our "perpetual Comforter and our eternal Inhabitant," as Augustine described Him.

322

The Fruit of the Spirit (5:9)

The Revised Version renders this verse: "The fruit of light is in all goodness and righteousness and truth." There is no contradiction, however, between "Spirit" and "Light." Christ came as "the Light of the world." The Holy Spirit is referred to as "the Spirit of Christ." Thus, by deduction, He is "the Spirit of light." Along with Ephesians 5:9, read Galatians 5:22. Sowing the light, we reap a golden harvest: *within* there is goodness; *without,* righteousness and truth.

The fruit of the Light is in all goodness. It is grace embodied. All that is alien to the Holy Spirit is burned out of the soul.

The fruit of the Light is in all righteousness. Here we have the sanctification of the conscience which makes possible unswerving loyalty to God's holy and perfect law. We scorn to stoop to anything crooked or doubtful.

The fruit of the Light is in all truth. Truth is not only in our speech but in our thoughts. Ours is no make-believe faith. We are delivered from sham service and a sham orthodoxy.

Living in blissful harmony with the will of the Spirit, we are enabled to walk day by day with the unseen Saviour who is Light of light.

The Fullness of the Spirit (5:18)

The observant reader will have noticed a threefold fullness in Ephesians: "the fulness of God" (3:19); "the fulness of Christ" (4:13); and here, the fullness of the Spirit: "Be ye filled with the Spirit." As the continuous, present tense is used, the apostle implies that the Spirit-filled life should be the unvarying, perpetual experience of the believer. There is only one baptism with (not *of*) the Spirit, but many infillings. The following verses in the chapter set forth in no

323

unmistakable terms the evidences of the Spirit-filled life. Paul's contrast, "Be not drunk with wine," is expressive. One can have too much of the cursed liquor, running like water in America—but a believer can never have too much of the Spirit, or rather, the Spirit cannot have too much of us. Would that we could be as God-intoxicated as those of whom it was said: "These men are full of new wine."

The Sword of the Spirit (6:17)

How true it is, as Paul reminds us, that the weapons of our warfare are not carnal but mighty through God to the pulling down of strongholds (II Cor. 10:4)! The Word of God is our mightiest weapon in such a spiritual conflict, seeing that it is "the sword of the Spirit." We can say of it what David said of Goliath's sword, with which he consummated his decisive victory over the giant and the Philistine host: "There is none like [it]; give it me" (I Sam. 21:9). The infallible Word of God is the two-edged sword well able to conquer its foes, slay error, and destroy sin.

The Intercession of the Spirit (6:18)

It is in the goodness of God that we have two divine Intercessors—one within (Rom. 8:26-27) and the other above (Heb. 7:25). In verses 10-20, Paul deals with the armor of the believer. The covering for the knees is "all prayer and supplication, praying at all times in the Spirit." If it be true that an army moves on its stomach, it is likewise true that the church lives, or should live, on her knees. An old saint of God spoke of our knees as "heaven's knocker." In the military set-up of the Salvation Army, they have what is known as "knee-drill."

There is, of course, a vast difference between saying prayers and praying. Jude speaks about praying in the Spirit, which coincides with Paul's teaching about the Spirit being the inspirer of true, effectual intercession, (Eph. 6:18; Rom.

324

8:26-27). We do not know how to pray as we ought, but the Spirit makes intercession for the saints according to the will of God. He alone can create the prayers that we should offer to God.

> Pray, always pray,
>> The Holy Spirit pleads
> Within thee all thy daily,
>> Hourly needs.

Theme 31
Ephesians: The Unfolding of Grace

Paul is prominent among the apostles as "The Apostle of Grace." In his Epistles, the term *grace* figures twice as often as in all the rest of the New Testament. Some twenty-two times he speaks of "the grace of God" and of "His grace"; fifteen times of "the grace of Christ" or "the grace of the Lord Jesus Christ"; once conjointly of "the grace of our God and the Lord Jesus Christ" (II Thess. 1:12). "Grace," is the first word of greeting and last word of farewell in the Letters of Paul.

As "the chief of sinners," the apostle gloried in divine grace (I Cor. 15:9; I Tim. 1:13-14). How he reveled in such an evangelical truth, and commended the same grace to a world of sinful men (Acts 20:24)! The Epistle we are considering is full of grace. Because the word is used thirteen times in Ephesians, the Epistle is known as "The Gospel of the Grace of God." *Grace* is a characteristic key word of the book.

The Nature of Grace (1:2; 6:24; Gal. 1:11-12)

To Paul, God's grace included the sum of all blessings that come from God through Christ. What is grace? It means free favor, the sovereign, undeserved, unmerited mercy of God; and is a fearless, comprehensive word which reveals the heart of God and the gospel.

Grace is a direct opposite to sin, works, the law, and all human merit. It is God's way of meeting and conquering man's sin (Rom. 5:20; 6:1, 15). Grace and works can never be mixed. Salvation is all of grace and, once saved, we work for the Saviour. Grace deals with all men upon one common ground, that of being sinners. "All have sinned" (Rom. 3:23). Grace levels their moral condition, and only reaches those who feel their need of it (Luke 5:31-32). "Grace is the un-merited favor of God bestowed upon those who justly merited the judgment of God."

Grace does not imply God's passing by sin, but supposes sin to be so horribly vile in God's sight that He cannot toler-ate it. If man was able, by his own deeds, to patch up his ways so as to be acceptable to God, then there would be no need of grace. Grace, however, reveals the utterly ruined and hopeless state of the sinner, and also God's graciousness in dealing with sin and the sinner. Thus Paul is jubilant as he expounds the richness and suffering of God's grace (1:3-14). How forcibly he reminded the Ephesians that grace, first and last, was the cause of their salvation. Paul also put his charac-ter at the back of his assertion that his gospel of grace was received directly from the Lord Himself (Gal. 1:11-12).

The Source of Grace (1:2)

Grace is God's pitying, forgiving disposition toward men as weak and wretched, guilty and lost. God provided grace, and Christ personified it (John 1:14-17). He came as the expres-sion and vehicle of the grace of God and completely identi-fied with God in unmerited, unrestrained love toward sinners. Although sin was inconceivably repulsive to God's holiness, yet the soul was inconceivably precious to Him, leading Him to provide a way of reconciliation for every sinner.

This first chapter is notable for its "doubles":

1. A Double Blessing—Grace and Peace
2. A Double Source of Blessing—God and Christ
3. A Double Designation of Recipients—Saints and Faith-ful
4. A Double Authority—Apostle and the Will of God

327

The association of grace with peace is interesting to note. Peace is united with grace, like a mother and daughter or twin sisters. These two virtues are the source of all blessings from God, revealed and operative in Christ. Grace is the foundation of peace. Grace is the source; and peace, the consummation. There can be no peace without grace, revealing as it does the divine character.

Used as an acrostic the word *grace* can be profitably developed in this fashion:

G—*God* is its author (Titus 2:11)
R—*Righteousness* is its basis (Rom. 6:13)
A—*Atonement* is its channel (Rom. 3:24)
C—*Christ* is its glorious sum (II Cor. 8:9)
E—*Eternity* is its duration (Eph. 2:7-9)

Some writers have seen in the two expressions "grace" and "peace" the two divisions of Ephesians. Dean Alford says that this Epistle is made up of "God's grace toward us and our faith towards Him." Grace from God—peace for us. Campbell Morgan expressed it well when he wrote: "Grace is the river flowing from the heart of God. Peace is the resulting consciousness of the filling of the heart of the trusting soul. The river and the peace alike come from the Lord Jesus Christ."

The Glory of Grace (1:6)

Paul's love for superlatives is clearly evident in this Letter to the church at Ephesus. Grace is a tremendous word in itself. Wherein consists "the glory" of such grace? The acknowledgement of all God's creatures of the gloriousness of God's grace is the burden of the exhortation before us. God's essential glory is best manifested in His grace. His almighty power is declared chiefly in the revelation of mercy and pity (Exod. 33:18-19; 34:5-7). "God considers His glory best realized in the spectacle of souls redeemed and regenerated by

328

His grace, and to decree that it should be thus realized for our sakes."

Glory is an attribute of grace, and grace grandly displays itself in glory. No wonder Paul uses extravagant language as he meditates upon the plenitude and splendor of redemption. Glowingly he extols the transcendant riches of divine grace. Here is the ultimate aim of foreordination. Praise is called forth from the saints as grace displays itself in glory. Grace is not only a favor or gift, but the revelation of the divine character. Grace designates the active principle in God of man's salvation through the Lord Jesus Christ. Thus God is praised for what He *is* as well as for what He *does. Glory,* another ruling word of Ephesians, is linked on to "riches" and "fullness." Language seems to fail the apostle as he describes the matchless grace of God.

When God glorifies His grace, He glorifies His whole character, and the glory of grace is that human merit does not help it nor demerit hinder it. The brilliance of this grace is also seen in its unlimitedness and perfection. Grace has no limits, no bounds. Neither our joy nor our peace depends upon what we are to God, but on what He is to us, and this is grace. How deep in debt we are to God's unfathomable grace!

The Riches of Grace (1:7)

"Riches of grace and riches of glory are material enough for the sermons of a Methuselah." *Riches* is another thoroughly descriptive Pauline term (2:7; Rom. 2:4; Col. 1:27; 2:2; Phil. 4:19). Ephesians is saturated with the undeserved bounty of redemption, the surpassing riches of His grace. Man is saved not according to his merits, but according to the riches of such grace. "The idea of richness in grace, glory, mercy, is especially frequent in this Epistle," (1:18; 2:7; 3:8, 16).

"In relation to praise," says Ellicott, "stress is laid on the gloriousness of God's grace, so here, in relation to enjoyment of it, on its overflowing richness" (2:7; 3:8, 13; Rom. 3:24; 9:23). We are saved not according to the narrowness of our own hearts (Col. 1:11), but according to His might and the wealth of His grace. God does not promise something He is unable to perform. He is sure of His own resources before bequeathing His wealth to His own. He never runs short when it comes to the deliverance of the soul from sin. He is abundantly able to save. H. A. Ironside used this simple illustration of "according to":

> It does not say "out of" His riches, but "according to" His riches. Here is a millionaire to whom you go on behalf of some worthy cause. He listens to you and says: "Well, I think that I will do a little for you," and takes out his pocket-book and selects a ten-dollar bill. Perhaps you had hoped to receive a thousand from him. He has given you "out of" his riches, but not "according to" his riches. If he gave you a book of signed blank cheques all numbered and said: "Take this, fill in what you need," that would be "according to" his riches.

The pity is that with so much guaranteed wealth at our disposal we yet live as spiritual beggars. God's grace abounds, overflows, has no fixed limit. In His bank there is more than enough for all the destitute of earth.

The Salvation of Grace (2:5)

It is all because of grace that we were saved and kept in a state of salvation. The two phrases, "justification by faith" and "salvation by grace" are popularly identified and substantially identical in meaning. Perhaps the more advanced stage of the process of redemption in Christ is associated with salvation—past, present, and prospective—which is all of grace. Justification is the release of a prisoner on his pronounced pardon—salvation a continuing state of liberty.

The triumph of grace is seen in that man's sin and hatred of God are overcome by His triumphant love and mercy that the cross reveals. The believing sinner is saved by grace alone. This is all his plea. The great mountain peak of Ephesians, then, is that grace is the cause, the spring of salvation. Sin can drag a man down to the lowest depths—grace can raise him to the highest heights.

Because in our natural state we were dead in sin, salvation or a spiritual resurrection is all of grace, which is God's free gift. Human worth and works are unavailing to save, and the unifying of law with grace is "another gospel" (Gal. 1:9).

Until our last breath there will be need of grace and, bless God, there will always be grace for every need. The bestowal of grace never impoverishes God.

Examining the true nature of grace, two basic thoughts emerge which require constant emphasis:

First, behind the conception and initiative of grace is the undeserved mercy or generosity of God. What the sinner could never possibly merit or deserve has been generously and freely provided by God. Grace is everywhere spoken of as something man can never acquire, but only appropriate (3:7; I Cor. 1:4; II Cor. 6:1; 8:1, 9).

Paul contrasts *grace* and *debt* (Rom. 4:4), the latter representing payment, a contract which men are obligated to meet. Grace, however, is something unearned and undeserved. The apostle also contrasts *grace* and *works*. If works could save (Rom. 11:6), then there would be no need of grace. But because grace is all-sufficient, works are rejected (2:5-9).

This brings us to our next basic idea: "Grace needs no supplement." Nothing else is necessary for man's salvation. To add anything destroys the purpose of the cross. Paul learned the great secret that the grace of God requires no human additions to be effective for salvation, and in all his Letters he is enthralled and dominated with the conviction

331

that the sinner can neither earn nor achieve favor with God. He can be saved only by grace, and by grace alone.

The Purpose of Grace (2:7)

The saints of God are to be His display cabinet. The end of grace is not only our salvation, future certainty, and eternal happiness, but also the display of God's glory (3:10-21). Both here and hereafter we are to show forth the surpassing riches of His grace. "The ages to come," can be translated "the ages which are coming on." Time and eternity are looked upon in one great continuity, with the saints conspicuous as monuments of God's exceeding grace. *Exceeding* means "over-shooting the mark." Grace gives us more than we deserve.

The manifestation of the riches of God's grace is looked upon as His special delight, and as His chosen way of manifesting His own self to His creatures. Grace springs from His love, and is displayed in all His benefits.

The Channel of Grace (2:8)

The peerless grace of God avails nothing for the sinner unless all that such grace has provided is appropriated by faith. Grace made salvation possible, but it is only faith that can make this salvation the actual experience of the sinner. We are saved by grace (that is God's part): through faith in Christ (that is our part).

Is grace, or is faith the gift of God? The answer is—both! As Ellicott puts it: "This attribution of all to the gift of God seems to cover the whole idea—both the gift of salvation and the gift of faith to accept it." Salvation is all of grace. God does not save on a fifty-fifty basis, partly grace, partly good works. Salvation is all of grace lest any man should boast, and only by the faith the Spirit inspires and imparts can such

332

salvation be realized. Man is so helpless that of himself he has not even the faith necessary for his salvation.

The Stewardship of Grace (3:1-14)

Having dealt with God's elective grace in the previous chapter, Paul reminds the Ephesians that he was in prison because he proclaimed such a message. The origin of his captivity is traced back to the jealousy of Jewish leaders over the free admission of Gentiles into the church of Jesus Christ. So the apostle declares that his "bonds" were profitable on behalf of the Gentiles (3:13; II Tim. 3:10).

The phrase, "I, Paul," expresses the fact that he was the agent employed by the Spirit to enlighten the Gentiles, after having been first enlightened by the same Spirit (3:3, 5, 9). Having experienced the boundless grace of God, he communicates the good news to others (1:9), and thus becomes a "dispenser" or "steward" (I Peter 4:10). The expression *dispensation* means "the office of dispensing." The admission of Gentiles into the church was a Spirit-given revelation (1:9-10; Gal. 1:12) and one that he had to share. All who are saved by grace should function as dispensers of another's property, meaning, of course, that efforts must be made to bring others to share in the grace of God. "The revelation of salvation to the Gentiles was 'the dispensation,' that is, the peculiar office in the ministration of the grace of God to the world assigned to Paul by God's wisdom" (1:10; I Cor. 1:17-24).

The Preacher of Grace (3:7-8)

Paul deemed it a high privilege to be called to preach the gospel of redeeming grace. How wonderfully he was enabled by the Spirit to extol God's grace! A deep sense of unworthiness overcame Paul as he thought of God's special grace and favor to him. How unworthy a vessel he was to hold such a treasure—(see I Cor. 15:9-10; II Cor. 4:7; 11:30; 12:9-11;

333

I Tim. 1:12-16). Three times over Paul blesses God for the honor of preaching among the Gentiles the inexhaustible wealth of grace (3:2, 7-8).

It is said that D. L. Moody, the renowned American evangelist, once studied the word *grace* in this way. Moved by his subject, he ran into the street and, with characteristic impetuosity, seized the arm of the first passer-by and said:

"Do you know about grace?"

"Grace who?" asked the amazed man.

Then Moody poured out his soul on the subject of God's love.

Such an approach to people would possibly not be appreciated today, but the same sort of bubbling-over enthusiasm would be really effective.

The Recipients of Grace (4:7)

Grace is not for a select few, but for all men. If you take away the *G* from "Grace" you are left with "race" and grace is for the race. In the narrative, however, Paul associates "grace" with "gifts." "To every one of us the grace [the one "grace of the Lord Jesus Christ"] was given." Grace was "given in the divine purpose in the regeneration of the whole body, although it has to be received and made our own, separately in each soul, and gradually in the course of life."

Grace manifests itself in different gifts and the diversity of gifts functions in the one Body (I Cor. 12:4; Rom. 12:4-8). The gift and gifts of grace are all alike connected with Christ's ascension, and these gifts to men must be exercised under the Spirit's direction. In his expression of the universal sweep and power of God in men's lives, Paul urges the recipients of grace to employ their heaven-inspired gifts to the full so that other lives can be enriched.

The Life of Grace (4:29)

It is the solemn obligation of all who are saved by grace to have a life fragrant with such grace. While grace is certainly an act of God, it must become a state in which we live, move, and have our being. As used in this passage *grace* has the meaning of "goodness" or "graciousness." If one's lips are clean, then they can supply what is necessary in the hearer's spiritual condition. When we are right with the Lord, then we can note by the quick insight of love, what each man's need is and, hastening to speak accordingly, "give grace" or blessing to meet that peculiar need (II Cor. 1:15; I Thess. 3:10).

Grace is received not only from God, but is shown to others. When God's grace has been poured into our life and lips (Ps. 45:5), then there will be the manifestation of pleasantness, charm, and winsomeness of bearing and speech. The phrase "a gracious woman retaineth honor" (Prov. 9:16) implies a woman of grace, that is, of attractive appearance and manner. Alas! too many are saved by grace and have gifts of grace but are far from gracious in their actions. The sins of egotism, pride, self-honor and self-aggrandizement, and criticism and belittling of others rob so many of the children of grace of graciousness (Luke 4:22). Are we good to those who do not deserve kindness? Do we give graciously and freely? Are we forgiving, tenderhearted, emulating thereby the God of all grace—and graciousness? It is of little use preaching "grace," if we do not practice it.

The Benediction of Grace (6:24)

The salutation "Grace be with you," in various forms, was Paul's peculiar and favorite signature written with his own hand (II Thess. 3:17). This characteristic "token" closes all of his Epistles. The fact that it is found at the conclusion of Hebrews stamps this Epistle as Pauline. Here the benediction is at once general and conditional—"to all who love our Lord Jesus Christ in sincerity" (see I Cor. 16:22).

The word *sincerity* is given as "incorruptibility" in the margin, a word applied to the immortality of heaven (Rom.

335

2:7; I Cor. 15:42; 15:50, 53-54; II Tim. 1:10) and also to human character on earth (Titus 2:7; Eph. 6:24). As used by Paul, the term means "with a love immortal and imperishable, incapable either of corruption or of decay, a foretaste of the eternal communion in heaven."

God's undiminishing grace embraces the saints of every age, and will endure throughout the eternal ages. Such grace so rich and full and free not only saves from sin but sustains us in the dark and difficult hours of life. No matter what crises may arise, His grace is ever sufficient. Oceans of grace surround us; let us, therefore, plunge deep into such a bountiful provision.

> And a new song is in my mouth
> To long-loved music set;
> Glory to Thee for all the grace
> I have not tasted yet.

All the figures of speech Paul uses of believers convey the truth so prominent in the Epistle, namely, our unity in Christ.

Theme 32
Philippians: The Portrait of Christ

Paul's priceless Epistle to the Philippians was probably written during the period of his two-year imprisonment in Rome (Acts 28:30) around A.D. 61-63. This is why there are allusions in this Epistle to the apostle's strict imprisonment and to the uncertainty of any release. "So occasioned on the one hand by present circumstances," says Bishop Handley Moule, "and on the other guided by the secret working of the Holy Spirit to form a sure oracle of God for the church forever, the letter was dictated, and the greetings of the writer's visitors were added, and the manuscript was given over to Epaphroditus, to be conveyed across Italy, the Adriatic, and Macedonia, to the plain and hill of Philippi."

Philippi was near the head of the archipelago; now the city is a scene of ruins. Wrote Bishop Lightfoot: "The city itself has long been a wilderness. . . . Of the church which stood foremost among all the apostolic communities in faith and love, it may literally be said that not one stone stands upon another. Its whole career is a signal monument of the inscrutable counsels of God. Born into the world with the brightest promise, the church of Philippi has lived without a history and perished without a memorial." Yet the spiritual influences of that church will never pass. To the saints in every age and nation, the letter written by Paul in his Roman dungeon has acted as a cheerful guide along the most rugged paths in life.

Philippi took its name from Philip of Macedon, 359-336 B.C., who made it a town of importance and of military strength. He also worked most vigorously the silver mines in

337

the district. Thus it became "the chief city of that part of Macedonia" (Acts 16:12). Conspicuous in this city of prestige was Lydia, the purple-merchant (Acts 16:14). A vivid account of Paul's work in Philippi is recorded in Acts 16. He maintained intercourse with his Philippian converts. Messages were frequent between them (Phil. 4:16), and reveal an affectionate and untroubled intimacy.

There are various ways by which we can approach this remarkable Epistle that assumes soundness of doctrine and stresses Christian experience. There was little in the Philippian church to set right. The believers there formed a normal New Testament assembly.

The Epistle indicates the position and influence of women in the Christian life of the church. In Acts 16:14-19, two females brought to Christ by Paul are mentioned. Then in Philippians 4:2, two more, who evidently held important influence in the church, are named. Freely Paul speaks of his debt to spiritually minded women. Women were held in reverent regard by Macedonian men.

Another striking feature of the Philippian Epistle is the pecuniary liberality of the Philippians themselves. Paul, always a grateful man, deeply appreciated the material provisions with which his converts supplied him. The majority of those making up the gift were poor. "The poor help the poor." The giving of the comparatively poor to missionary causes is vastly greater than that of the rich. If the wealthy gave to the same degree as the poor working people do, there would be no scarcity of money for the Lord's work.

Many expositors draw attention to the emphasis on "joy" in the Book of Philippians. And it is, indeed, "The Epistle of Rejoicing." There are five references to joy, and twelve references to rejoicing. Paul did not fail to serve the Lord with joyfulness and with gladness of heart (Deut. 28:47). C. I. Scofield groups the teaching of Philippians around joyous triumphs over trials:

1. Christ, the believer's life, rejoicing in suffering (chap. 1)

338

2. Christ, the believer's pattern, rejoicing in lowly service (chap. 2)
3. Christ, the believer's object, rejoicing despite imperfections (chap. 3)
4. Christ, the believer's strength, rejoicing over anxiety (chap. 4)

Our own personal study of the Epistle, however, convinces us of the fact that Paul's object in writing it was to exalt Christ, whom he specifically mentions forty-seven times in the book. Around the apostle were those Judaizers who held "lowered and distorted views" of the Person of our blessed Lord. These views later developed into Ebionite Christology, which Irenaeus identified as heresy during the second century. There were two phases of Ebionism.

The Pharisaic Ebionites held that Jesus was born in the ordinary course of nature but that, at His baptism, He was "anointed by election and became Christ," receiving power to fulfill His mission as Messiah, but still remaining man. He had neither preexistence nor deity, in their view. Modernism is the present form of this phase of Ebionism.

Then there were the Essene Ebionites, who were, in fact, Gnostics who held that Christ was a superangelic, created Spirit, incarnate at many successive periods in various men, for instance, in Adam, and finally in Jesus. At what point in the existence of Jesus, the Christ entered into union with Him, was never defined by the "know-alls."

In his Christ-exalting Epistle, Paul presents the Lord in His preexistence, voluntary humiliation, vicarious death, and victorious triumph over all foes.

The aspects of Christ, and our relationship to Him, emphasized by Paul in this Letter, sparkle like the facets of a diamond. Let us try to summarize the apostle's Christology.

Encircled by Christ

Seven times Paul uses the pregnant phrase "in Christ

339

Jesus," or "in the Lord." An old scholar has reminded us that "every Christian is a Christ-enclosed man," and no New Testament writer understood this truth to the degree that Paul did. A. T. Pierson informs us that the three short words "in Christ Jesus" are the key not only to Paul's Epistles but to the whole New Testament. As a "very small key may open a very complex lock and a very large door, and that door may itself lead into a vast building with priceless stores of wealth and beauty," so this brief phrase, a preposition followed by a proper name, expresses the mutual relation of the believer to Christ.

Paul uses the phrase and its equivalents, "in Christ," "in Christ Jesus," "in Him," and "in whom," almost 150 times in his writings. Such phrases indicate our new life in Christ, declared by Himself in the memorable words: "Abide in me, and I in you" (John 15:4). Christ is the sphere of our being. It is in Him we live, and move, and have our being. Pierson draws a distinction between a *sphere* and a *circle*. A circle surrounds us *but only on one plane*. A sphere encompasses, envelopes, encircles us in every direction and on every plane. "If you draw a circle on the floor and step within its circumference, you are within it only on the level of the floor. But if that circle could become a sphere, and you be within it, it would on every side surround you—above and below, before and behind, on the right hand and on the left."

The sphere surrounding us also separates us from whatever is outside of it. It also protects whatever is within it from all that is without. Furthermore, it supplies what is necessary to those within. How real these facts are when applied to Christ, who is the sphere of our whole life and being! In Him we are surrounded by Him. In Him we are separated from all external foes, secure in any peril that may arise, and supplied with all that we need.

Paul found himself in two spheres. As he wrote, he was "in bonds" (1:13) and yet he was "in Christ." Had he not been in Christ, His adversity would have been unbearable. John

340

was "in the isle called Patmos" but he was likewise "in the Spirit," and the latter encirclement made his prison a palace.

Paul starts his Letter by affirming that all the saints, not some of them, are "in Christ Jesus" (1:1). His benediction ends with a salute to "every saint in Christ Jesus" (4:21). The saints, or devotees of God, are kept saintly, seeing that Christ encircles them. He is between them and sin. Surrounded by the Holy One, all in Him are holy ones.

The characteristic Pauline note appears again in a most unusual fashion. True, Paul was in bonds; but he thought of himself, not as a prisoner of Nero but of Christ: "my bonds in Christ" (1:13). What was manifest about Paul's captivity was that it was "in Christ"; it was due to no political or social crime, but to his union with his Lord. Christ, Paul knew, was between him and his foes. Thus his fetters only made for the furtherance of the gospel. Chained as he was to soldiers of the Praetorian Guard, he witnessed to all who were thus close to him and spread the gospel through the whole praetorian. His indifference to adversity nerved the saints to more courageous endeavor. His brethren "in the Lord" waxed confident by Paul's bonds (1:14). They leaned on a leadership that proved by self-sacrifice to be strong. Out they went to be more lavish in their efforts and ventures. The fearless apostle could preach Christ in spite of his bonds, so why should they not venture all for Him?

As Paul was confident that Christ was His security, he assured his friends that, in spite of his imprisonment, he could abide and continue in his witness and ultimately return to them, which should cause them to abundantly rejoice "in Christ Jesus" (1:26). It is blessed to know that Christ is between us and all that would hinder our supreme joy! He knows how to overrule the forced separations of life. As we await reunion, consolation is ours "in Christ" (2:1).

All who are "in Christ" must manifest His disposition. He died to self-interest. His meat was to do the will of the Father. He "emptied" Himself and "became obedient unto

341

death." This mind, "in Christ Jesus," must also be our mind (Phil. 2:5). Humility, patience, and sacrifice must characterize us. Grace must be ours to "lay in dust life's glory dead."

Several times over Paul reminds us that Christ is the sphere of our perfect joy and satisfaction. "Rejoice in the Lord" (3:1, 3; 4:4, 10). Paul had nothing to rejoice over in his prison cell but he was happy in the consciousness that the Master, for whom he had counted loss as gain, was near at hand. Pierson says of this Epistle, that it is "like one long *song in the night,* a kind of prolonged echo of that midnight prayer and praise which marked Paul's first experience in the city of Philippi. . . . The man who sang and prayed in his inner jail is the man who in this Epistle, a prisoner at Rome, sings 'Rejoice in the Lord alway, and again I say, Rejoice!' (4:4). If this Epistle has any special keynote which is the controlling thought in all these melodies of a holy heart, it is this: 'In Christ Jesus Satisfied.' " Says Bishop Moule: "Self has yielded the inner throne to Christ, and the result is a divine harmony between circumstances and the man, as both are seen equally subject to and usable by Him."

What perfect encirclement is ours! With Christ within us, around us, above us, beneath us, how safe we are! He is between us and all hostile influences; between us and all anxieties and cares; between us and all unholy forces; between us and all discontent; between us and all self-advantage; between us and all possible need.

> Not a shaft can hit
> Till the God of Love sees fit.

Enriched Through Christ

Simple prepositions like *by, through,* and *of,* speak to us of the spiritual wealth that awaits our appropriation. And the repetition and variety of these words must have some intense

342

meaning. Christ is not only our sphere of being but our source of every blessing. Let us examine the links in this chain of truth.

First of all, Christ is the procuring cause of the fruits of our new life. The fruits of righteousness are ours "by Christ Jesus," and these fruits must be borne unto the glory and praise of God (1:11). The righteousness that Paul mentions is the rightness of the regenerate will, regarded as in accord with divine law. Christ, who personified this law, is the true basis of righteousness in our lives.

It is also "by" or "through" Christ that we enter into possession of all we need here, with the riches of glory as our vast reservoir of supply: "My God shall supply all your need according to his riches in glory by Christ Jesus" (4:19). The glory of both grace and providence is lodged "in him" for His people. "By him" all spiritual and material needs can be fully met.

Relief from all unbelieving anxiety can be ours only "through Christ Jesus" (4:7). What a curious threefold cord the narrative presents: anxiety for nothing; thanksgiving for anything; prayerfulness in everything! Our only channel of relief from carping care is Christ. He alone can communicate the peace of God to anxious hearts, seeing that Christ is the representative of the God of peace (4:9). What a blessed life this is! Hearts and minds are garrisoned by Christ Jesus. Bishop Moule says: "Even the details of our mental action, as we plan, reason, judge, and the like, shall be shielded from evil by the peace of God. . . . The Lord is the place of peace."

Further, "through Christ" we find strength for all things. He is between us and all weakness: "I can do all things through Christ, which strengtheneth me" (4:13). We receive ability to do all things through Him who is all-powerful: "in him who enableth me." It is only as we are in vital union with the Head that, as members, we are able to do or to bear. Paul's strength was not only made manifest but made perfect in his weakness. Paul provided the weakness; Christ perfected

343

His strength. "Omnipotence needs impotence for its sphere of working." Man's extremity is God's opportunity. Paul's ability to do all things was not acquired by frequent exercise; it was a disposition which he had by grace. It was "through Christ."

While meditating upon Paul's priceless Letter to the liberal-hearted Philippians, one is impressed with the various cameos of Christ which the apostle displays. Each of these beautiful cameos is worthy of comment, but we simply set them forth for the reader to study. Taken together they demonstrate how Christ is the cause, the channel, and the consummation of all things:

1. The servants [slaves] of Christ (1:1)
2. The day of Christ (1:6, 10; 2:16)
3. The bowels [heart] of Christ (1:8)
4. The spirit of Christ (1:19)
5. The gospel of Christ (1:27)
6. The belief of Christ (1:29)
7. The name of Christ (2:10)
8. The things of Christ (2:21)
9. The work of Christ (2:30)
10. The knowledge of Christ (3:8)
11. The faith of Christ (3:9)
12. The apprehension of Christ (3:12)
13. The cross of Christ (3:18)
14. The grace of Christ (4:23)

Going over the four chapters of the Epistle again, we cannot fail to observe how Paul emphasizes the believer's obligation toward Christ. All He is to the believer is fully stated. But all Christ is to, and has for, His own is balanced by what they must do for Him. Our responsibility is of a ninefold nature.

1. Preach Christ (1:15-16, 18)

Paul mentions two kinds of preachers: those who are

344

prompted by good will and love; and those who are guilty of envy, strife, and contention. Judaistic teachers preached a mixture of law and grace, yet Paul rejoiced because they did convey to pagan hearers the primary fact of salvation—Jesus Christ. The apostle, however, never ceased to warn believers that the teaching of the Judaizers was pregnant with spiritual disaster. Commenting on these verses, Bishop Moule remarks: "It is a sorrowful paradox, but abundantly illustrated, that the true Christ could be emphatically, and in a sense earnestly proclaimed with a wrong motive." May grace be ours to preach Christ by lip and life, in a way pleasing to Him and fruitful in results! Let everyone take to heart these lines of Grace Noll Crowell:

> Preach Christ, O men—His blood, His saving power!
> Never the need was greater in an hour
> Than in this hour! Cry out His blessed name.
> O preachers, teachers, set the world aflame
> For Christ, that those who walk earth's darkened roads
> May feel His hand beneath their heavy loads,
> May come to know Him as their Saviour, Friend,
> Who will walk with them until the journey's end.
> Preach Christ, O men! Their hunger is so great!
> The days are swift—there is no time to wait.
> You hold the Bread of Life within your hands,
> And the Living Water for their thirst. The lands
> Of earth cry out for what you have to give;
> The living Christ—preach Him, that they may live.

2. Magnify Christ (1:20)

Like Count Zinzendorf, Paul's one passion was Christ. He was a Christ-consumed being. Thus life and death to him were a dilemma of blessings "in Christ." Here he desired to manifest Christ so as to have Him praised. Paul wanted to make his Lord bright and beautiful to eyes which otherwise saw nothing attractive about Him to desire Him.

Scarred and imprisoned though his body was, Paul longed to have Christ glorified both in and through it. He knew that his body was "the soul's necessary vehicle for all action on others. Through the body alone could others 'see' how the man had peace and power in his Master, living or dying; through the words of his lips, the looks of his face, the action or patience of his limbs." We cannot but think of John and Betty Stam, and of the influence Paul's courage had on them as they faced brutal martyrdom in China.

3. Live Christ (1:21)

The alternative of life or death is still in the mind of Paul, and his words take on a new luster when we remember that he wrote them at a time of suspense regarding the issue of his trial. Whether it would be life or death he did not know, and apparently did not care. His was an "holy equanimity."

To Paul, *Christ was life:* "I am . . . the life" (John 14:6), and to him, living was completely full of Christ, wholly occupied with and for Him! How a person completes the phrase "For me to live is . . . " shapes his character and determines his destiny. Evidently the apostle had a preference for death. He knew it would be better for himself to depart and be with Christ; but it was more needful for the Philippians and others whom he had won to Christ to live and encourage them by his life and labors. He would have more time for fruitful toil for the Christ he dearly loved, if he continued to live his earthly life.

4. With Christ (1:23)

A born-again believer is one who is *in* Christ, *like* Christ, *for* Christ, and *with* Christ. Once union with Christ is brought about, companionship with Him never ceases. The redeemed are *with* Christ, here and hereafter. Paul endured as seeing Him who is invisible. To fold up his earthly tent, however, and find himself in the actual presence of Christ would be "far better."

5. Confess Christ (2:10)

The apostle's declaration regarding adoration ascending from creation in its totality must be examined in the light of the context (2:5-11). Although equal with God, Christ made Himself of no reputation, humbled Himself, died as a felon on a cross. His humiliation, however, is to be rewarded with exaltation. Animate and inanimate, personal and unconscious creation are said to worship the exalted Christ. Heaven and hell, demons and angels, saved and lost, all alike will recognize the lordship of Jesus.

Paul makes it clear that the Father is to be the ultimate object of adoration. The Christ of God, as the Nicene Creed reminds us, is at once divinely adorable in Himself and the true medium for our adoration of the Father.

The question of present concern is: Are we confessing Christ as we should as we linger amid the shadows? Too many who name His peerless name are guilty of hiding their light under a bushel.

6. Trust Christ (2:19, 24)

A peculiar affection existed between Paul and Timothy. It was young Timothy who sought to keep Paul well informed as to the welfare of the churches the apostle had founded. There was no other like him in natural fitness for such a task. As for Timothy's visit to Philippi, or his own visit, Paul trusted the Lord to guide and direct their steps. Paul would do nothing on his own initiative. He trusted the Lord to make the way clear and to provide all that was necessary for the journey.

7. Win Christ (3:8)

In order to understand what Paul means about "winning Christ," we must follow his thought in the portion covering verses 4 through 9. Much credit and respect had been his because of his Jewish stock, zealous attachment to the law, and to the traditions of the elders; but all prestige and power were counted loss for Christ. Paul came to understand that Christ crucified could alone profit him. Privileges, Jewish or otherwise, yes, all that the apostle counted valuable or gainful, upon which he had depended for favor with God he counted loss for Christ. After enumerating past advantages, he swept everything into the scale which Christ overweighed. All prospects of personal, national, and ecclesiastical distinctions were freely and fully sacrificed for Christ's sake. Paul suffered the loss of all, that Christ might become his gain.

Paul's contempt for past gains is expressed in the phrase: "I count all things but loss . . . do count them but dung." The word he uses for "dung" means the vilest dross or refuse of anything, the worst kind of excrement. It also implies "the leavings of a feast." Bishop Lightfoot says: "The Judaizers spoke of themselves as banqueters . . . at the Father's table, of Gentile Christians as dogs . . . snatching up the refuse meat. . . . Saint Paul has reversed the image." The language used shows how utterly insignificant and unavailing the apostle esteemed everything alongside of the gain of Christ. Would that we could share Paul's contempt for all self-honor, self-glory, self-advantage and advancement, and seek Christ, Christ *only*!

8. Know Christ (3:10)

There are two precious phrases that we can join as we meditate on verses 9 and 10: "found in him" and "know him." In order to know Christ we must be found in Him. Position comes first; then privilege becomes ours. Intimacy

348

and fellowship form fruit from the root. Forsaking his own righteousness, Paul accepted the righteousness which had its origin in God, then passed on to assimilation "in Christ." He went on from the crisis of knowledge to the process of growing knowledge, and became lost in Him whose love passeth knowledge. Spiritual harmony with the sufferings, death, and resurrection became the passion of Paul.

9. Expect Christ (3:20)

Paul, knowing that the seat of his citizenship was in heaven, eagerly anticipated the coming of Christ, so that he could have a redeemed, glorified body to appreciate all the glories of heaven. Time and life were fast sinking away into the shades of death for the apostle, but he was upheld by the "blessed hope." He looked for the Lord who had been the center and circumference of all things in his life to come from heaven. Amid his extreme sufferings, he triumphantly witnessed for Christ, knowing that the effulgence of the dawning glory of the eternal world would soon be his.

Enough has been written to show what a Christ-exalting Epistle Paul sent to the Philippians. It reveals his determination to know nothing among them save Christ and Him crucified. Paul loved and lived Christ. His work and writings were saturated with his passion to glorify his Lord. Paul, like Hudson Taylor, believed that if Christ "is not Lord *of* all, He is not Lord *at* all."

Theme 33
Thessalonians: The Second Advent

Thessalonica, a city of Macedonia now known as Salonica, was previously called Thermae, so named because of its famous hot springs. On account of its marine and geographical position on the Thermae Gulf, it not only commanded a share of the commerce of western Asia and southern Europe but was also a logical starting place for the gospel to reach Europe.

The church in Thessalonica was founded by Paul during his second missionary tour and was the second church established by him. Circumstances regarding this are referred to in Acts 16 and 17. A revival broke out during one of the apostle's evangelistic tours, and so great was the spiritual upheaval that the world seemed to be "turned upside down" (see also Acts 27:2; Phil. 4:16; II Tim. 4:10; I Thess. 1:1; II Thess. 1:1).

The two Epistles that Paul sent to the Thessalonian church mark the beginning of his writing ministry. Many scholars affirm that I Thessalonians was the first New Testament book to be written and is, therefore, the earliest piece of Christian writing in existence. Certainly it was the first of Paul's Letters. It was penned around A.D. 54, some twenty-one years after Calvary and sixteen years after Paul's miraculous conversion.

Some have wondered why, if I Thessalonians was among the first New Testament books to be written, it is not placed earlier in the New Testament. The Holy Spirit, who superintended the arrangement of Scripture, did not follow any chronological order but, rather, gave a progressive revelation.

350

The Epistle to the Romans was written some six years after I Thessalonians; yet it comes first in the order of Paul's Epistles simply because Romans commences with the foundational truths of the faith. The superstructure of Christian living and experience follows and reaches a climax in I Thessalonians, which contains the clearest presentation of Christ's return to be found in the New Testament.

It is interesting to trace the occasion of the Thessalonian Letters. Paul's dynamic presentation of Jesus as Christ resulted in his arraignment on a charge of treason against Caesar (Acts 17:3-8). Driven from the city, which grew to greatness under Rome, Paul left Silas behind to carry on. Later on he sent Timothy to Thessalonica to bring him word as to the condition of the church. Timothy returned to Paul at Corinth and reported on their loyalty under grave persecution. The church became renowned for its doctrinal purity and spiritual power. Timothy also reported concerning the death of some of the faithful believers at Thessalonica, and Paul responded by writing a letter commending the church for its loyalty to the Word and consoling those who mourned. Vividly he depicted the second advent of Christ, assuring the bereaved members that their dead would not be overlooked at His return. The Second Epistle was written a few months later, after Paul's banishment from Thessalonica by unbelieving Jews.

A reading of both Epistles reveals that there are no Old Testament quotations or allusions, seeing that the bulk of the converts were Greeks who had left paganism for Judaism. There were, of course, some Jews among the members of the church in that city (I Thess. 1:9; 2:14). Being addressed to young believers, the Epistles contain no elaborate arguments. Prominence is given to practical exhortations and admonitions as to common duties. Both Letters are personal in tone, proving the close bond between Paul and his spiritual children. He commended them as examples of the highest evidence of Christianity.

351

The two Letters must be studied together, seeing that both of them are taken up with the second advent which is distinctly mentioned twenty times. Thessalonica was noted for its materialism; inscribed upon the tombs of numerous of its citizens were these words: "Death Is an Eternal Sleep." But Paul reassured the saved but sorrowing saints of a glorious resurrection. The style of the Letters is the same, and one letter is bound to the other (cf. I Thess. 3:12 with II Thess. 1:3). The first three chapters of Thessalonians are personal and historical; the last two, didactic and hortatory. The Second Epistle gives consolation under persecution (chap. 1); consummation of evil (2:1-12); and a closing exhortation (2:13–3).

Taking the Epistles separately, we find Paul developing in the first one various doctrines in connection with the second advent. Doctrines such as election (1:4), the Holy Spirit (1:5-6; 4:8; 5:19), assurance (1:5), the Trinity (1:1; 5:6; 5:23), conversion (1:9), the Christian walk (2:12; 4:1), sanctification (4:3; 5:23), man's threefold being (5:23), and resurrection (4:16) are discussed in the light of Christ's return. The *parousia,* or personal presence, is used some twenty-four times, and that as a comfort in death, a motive to patience, a help to purity, the ground of rejoicing, and a separating and sanctifying power. All problems are to be solved in the light of such an expectancy. The saints must abstain from sin and practice holiness, seeing that the Lord Jesus is coming again. The bereaved can bury their dead with joy and hope because of the rapture awaiting them. Christ is coming for His own, which constitutes the first stage of His second advent.

The Second Epistle followed as the result of the First. Some of the members were swept away by fanaticism, believing that Paul had informed them that Christ was coming instantly. Work was abandoned. Many became idlers and visionary. In their unconverted state, these deluded souls had been accustomed to myths and delusions and became an easy prey to their own imaginings. So Paul wrote II Thessalonians to correct the fanatical views erroneously deducted from his First Epistle. He rebuked the idle Thessalonians, exhorting them to continue in the constancy and faithfulness that they had previously manifested. Paul gives a clear view of the man of sin and of events associated with the second stage of Christ's second advent. In I Thessalonians, Christ is seen coming for His church; in II Thessalonians, He is seen coming with His mighty angels and His own to take vengeance upon His foes. The keyword of both Epistles is "waiting" (I Thess. 1:10; II Thess. 3:5).

Let us give ourselves to a fuller consideration of the First Epistle, written as it was with the tenderness of a nursing mother, the authority of a father, the devotion of a friend, and the courage of an apostle (1:2, 5, 7-8, 11). Conduct, we are told, is always affected by conception. If, therefore, we scorn the great truth of the rapture, as set forth in this First Epistle, what else can we have but soiled garments and unlit lamps? If it be true that "the power of any life is in its expectancy," then those expecting Christ to return should live the most powerful and fruitful of lives. It is with these considerations in mind that we now turn to the practical outworking of the second coming of Christ, as given in First Thessalonians.

In this First Epistle, Christ's return is mentioned at the close of each chapter, and these different aspects suggest a fivefold relationship:

In 1:9-10, the blessed hope is connected with our salvation, and the message of patience is prominent.

In 2:19-20, the return of Christ is associated with joy and service, and the rewards of it are here unfolded.

In 3:12-13, Christ's appearing is connected with love, and our conduct Godward and manward is in view.

In 4:13-18, His coming is declared to be the spring of comfort. Here suffering and sorrow resulting from death are uppermost.

In 5:23, the descent of Christ is joined to holiness; for here

Paul outlines, for the guidance and inspiration of the Thessalonians, the true character of a saint.

Now let us examine these five chapters with their fivefold advent relationship more closely.

As a Believer

In 1:9-10, the believer is a *turning one,* and patience is the virtue emphasized. The threefold view of the believer's life is given under three words: *turn, serve, wait,* and he has a full-orbed experience if he is characterized by all three.

Some turn but do not serve. Others turn and serve but do not wait, for they either neglect or reject the extremely practical truth of the second coming.

It is interesting to observe how this threefold phase of the believer's life dominates this first chapter of the book. In verse 3, there is "the work of faith," which is seen in "turning to God from idols"; then there is "the labour of love," as seen in "the serving of the living and true God"; and finally there is "the patience of hope," as expressed in "the waiting for God's Son from heaven."

The past is characterized by salvation; the present, by occupation; and the future, by expectation. Faith rests on the past; love works in the present; and hope endures as seeing the future. And the fact that we serve as we wait goes to prove that the truth of the coming of Christ does not cut the nerve of effort but only serves to strengthen our hands for all legitimate labor.

The order of these old-fashioned conversions is significant; the Thessalonians "turned to God from idols" and not "from their idols to God." The motive in their salvation was not repulsion, occasioned by the grossness of idols, but the attraction of the character of God as presented by Paul. Our great task is not to tamper with idols belonging to unconverted people, but to get the people to God.

Moreover, the preaching of this threefold message would

354

make for the same result today. One reason why the church is flirting with the world is because she has put out of her mind the expectation of God's Son returning from heaven. Activity she has in plenty, but this third attitude is missing.

Michelangelo, because of his prolonged and unremitting toil upon frescoed domes, acquired such an habitual upturn of countenance that, as he walked the streets, strangers, observing his bearing, set him down as a visionary and eccentric. If we profess to be Christians, with our citizenship in heaven, let our faces be set thitherward. Instead of looking at the earth, as the man with the muck-rake did, let us walk the dusty lanes of life with that upward look, keeping ourselves unspotted from the world.

As a Worker

In 2:19-20, the believer is a *serving one,* and the joy that results from service is in view. Thessalonian converts were to be Paul's "crown of rejoicing" at Christ's return.

Someone has translated verse 19 to read: "It is the thought of presenting you to Him that thrills us with hope, joy, and pride—the thought of wearing such a decoration before Him." Paul was to be prouder of these new-born souls than a king of his crown or a champion of his laurels. There are other crowns to earn, but this one is the great incentive to service: that souls will be in glory because of our influence and testimony. Would it not make for a mighty revival if every believer truly lived and labored in the light of this promised reward? Mother: What about your daughters? Father: Your boys? Sunday school teacher: What about your scholars? Will they be with Christ because of your witness? Possibly you have all your heart may wish for here: a comfortable home in which you are unafraid of poverty or loneliness; children rising up in love and loyalty. But what of the future? Will you experience the joy and thrill of the apostle? Will there be any stars in your crown? Is yours to be a joyless

355

meeting with the Saviour, with no rewards from His gracious hand? Or are you among the number who hasten the coming by "gathering in the lost ones for whom our Lord has died"?

As a Brother

In 3:12-13, the believer is a *loving one,* and love in its Godward and manward objects is outlined. "Multiply you in love until you have enough and to spare of it." One is afraid that there is not much love to spare among Christians. "So that you may not only love one another abundantly, but all mankind." In the narrative, Paul illustrates his deep love for the Thessalonians. "Night and day" they were upon his heart, and "as a nurse" he sought to cherish them. And brotherly love, he urges, leads to a life of holiness; for a loveless heart can never succeed in the quest after holiness. True love sanctifies the one who loves.

Paul urges these Thessalonian saints to increase and abound in love or, as Weymouth expresses it, "grow and glow in love." And surely we can never have too much of this fruit of the Spirit! The tragedy is that much sweet fruit is frosted.

Paul prays that his converts might be loving in a superlative degree—overflowing with love. And such a message is needed in these days of spiritual coldness. As we get nearer to the moment of our Lord's return, it would seem that the devil is active, drying up the spring of love; for never was such a loveless feeling prevalent among professing Christians as is apparent today.

We heartily sing: "We shall know each other better when the mists have rolled away"; but why wait until the future for a better understanding of each other? If we are to live together up yonder, let there be more unity here. Let us get put right with each other, and then keep right with each other until the Lord Jesus comes. "Be at peace among yourselves" (5:13). The old-time way of expressing love was by a kiss—greet one another with an holy kiss (5:26). Kicking

356

rather than kissing is our attitude. Why, a revival of love among God's people, in view of Christ's coming, would make for a great ingathering of the lost!

As a Sufferer

In 4:13-18, the believer is a *weeping one,* and comfort in view of death is in mind. Many of these Thessalonians were troubled about their dead. The prevalent, pagan idea is expressed in a heathen inscription discovered at Thessalonica:

> After death, no reviving;
> After the grace, no meeting again.

Ignorance may cause unnecessary sorrow and despair. A mother, not having learned that her little one who fell asleep is safe in the arms of Jesus, will be tormented by unnecessary and unreasonable pain. It was so with the sorrowing believers in Thessalonica who were ignorant concerning the Lord's return and of the condition of their blessed dead. So Paul sends this Letter to comfort the sorrowing in the assembly, stating that both the dead and the living will participate in Christ's coming. He alleviates their sorrow, suffering, and separations, by showing that they are not worthy to be compared with the glory of Christ's return.

The secular life of today is without much hope, as was the pagan life of old. Attention is fixed upon the present world and all discussion as to the future is avoided. People are content to have a good time and risk what is to come. The saints of God, however, can comfort one another with these words written in this chapter, although it may sound strange to the ears of the world when God's servants say that they "love His appearing."

As a Saint

In 5:23, the believer is described as a *holy one,* and the

357

sanctifying influences of the blessed hope are brought before us. What a fitting climax this is!

Moffatt translates the verse: "Now the peace of God consecrate you through and through! Spirit, soul, and body, may you be kept without break or blame till the arrival of Jesus Christ." "Without break"—this is Godward relationship; communion, holiness, and prayer being kept intact "through and through." "Without blame"—this is our manward relationship; fellowship, conduct, and testimony all operating until He comes. Paul urges us to have all parts of our complex being ready against Christ's return.

1. Our Bodies. These, as temples of the Holy Ghost, are to be delivered from all pampering, excess, and neglect, and used only for His service and glory. We are to have holy hands, continually doing good; holy feet, running incessantly upon His errands; and holy lips, pleading His cause afar.

2. Our Souls. All the powers of thought and imagination are to be consecrated. All unholy, wrong thoughts are to be banished. Our consciences and self-life must be disciplined by His Word and Spirit, until they obey His dictates without murmur.

3. Our Spirits. We are to have pure worship and devotion, worthy of God, and worthy reverence and trust. Thus our complex nature, outward, inward, and upward, must be sanctified in view of our Lord's return.

> With such a blessed hope in view
> We would more holy be.

And what He commands, He supplies. He calls us to holiness and supplies it. "Faithful is he who calleth you, who also will do it" (5:24). Augustine expressed it well when he said: "Give what Thou commandeth, then command what Thou wilt."

Theme 34
2 Timothy: The Christian Worker

Special significance is attached to this Second Epistle to Timothy, seeing it was the last letter written by Paul. It is for this reason that it has been called "The Swan Song of Paul." Shortly after writing it the apostle faced martyrdom for Christ's sake, and thus the Epistle bears the stain of the writer's blood. A good deal of sentiment is attached to the last letter from a friend before his home-call, and Paul's last message was to his much-loved son in the faith, his companion, Timothy the Evangelist. How this young man must have treasured it!

It was written from a cold, damp, dark Roman dungeon about A.D. 67, toward the end of Nero's reign. Paul was scheduled to appear before the emperor, and the immediate motive in writing to Timothy was the apostle's intense desire to see him once again before death parted them. This urgent wish is several times expressed in the Epistle (1:4; 4:9, 11, 21). Paul was alone—friendless among foes. Demas, a one-time close follower, had forsaken him and Alexander the coppersmith had been evil-disposed toward him, all of which induced Paul to send this request for his son in the faith to hurry to him to be with him in his last hours. How true and tender was the affection that bound these two valiant hearts together! With no Christian friend near to console him except, probably, Luke, it was to Timothy that Paul turned for sympathy and aid. But whether Timothy reached Rome in time to comfort his devoted friend and spiritual father before his bitter end is not revealed.

One of the objects of this Last Will and Testament was to

359

inform Timothy of the dangers that threatened the writer, and to fortify his courage. He bade Timothy hasten to his aged friend and to bring with him Mark from the east. Evidently Paul had previously appeared before Nero, but his case had been adjourned (4:16-17). He expected to appear again in the winter and wrote Timothy, whose liberty from prison made it possible for him to come at once (Heb. 13:23) to bring with him the necessary articles Paul had left elsewhere (4:9, 11, 13, 21). Expecting a speedy martyrdom (1:8, 16; 4:6), and uncertain whether Timothy would arrive in time, the apostle sends him a farewell warning as to heresies he must combat, and also a parting message encouraging him to zeal, courage, and patience. Not knowing whether he would be spared to give last instructions with his own lips, Paul fills his last letter with fatherly exhortations applicable to Timothy in his continuing witness for the Master.

With a calm resignation, Paul said that he was "ready to be offered." Written under the shadow of death, this Epistle is full of light and shade, shadow and hope. Expressing his affectionate regard for Timothy, and his ardent desire to see him, Paul counsels his beloved son in Christ not to shrink, but to share his spiritual father's shame and suffering for Christ and His truth. By the grace and power of God, Timothy must endeavor to fill the gap and to function as a faithful minister of the Word of God; an opposer of false teachers; a prophet in perilous times; a sufferer in Christ's cause; and a saint eagerly anticipating Christ's return.

Among the matchless Epistles of Paul there are three that are grouped together and known as the Pastoral Epistles, namely I and II Timothy, and Titus. All three belong to his old age, and bear his mature thought. They also carry an imperative stamp, being made up of ministerial imperatives, such as "Guard the deposit"; "Hold fast the form of sound words"; "Preach the Word"; etc. Sound doctrine and practical piety are the prominent interests in these Epistles. Paul's creative days are over; his battles are fought; his course is run.

360

Completing touches remain to be added and a final seal set to the work and teaching of his long and honored life. These three Letters emphasize that purpose.

Taking I and II Timothy together, we observe how one Epistle complements the other. In the First Epistle we have the ideal church every pastor should have. In the Second Epistle the ideal pastor every ideal church should have.

In the First Epistle, Timothy is urged to preach a straight gospel, and to guard the doctrine, which was his message from God. This is the Silver Trumpet.

In the Second Epistle, Timothy is exhorted to live a straight life, and to guard his testimony, which was his life from God. Here is the player behind the Silver Trumpet.

The First Epistle reveals the internal condition of the church at Ephesus over which Timothy was pastor (I Tim. 1:3).

The Second Epistle depicts what kind of pastor Timothy was to be. Paul, in no uncertain terms, describes what pastor and church must be like, both then and now. Pure churches —pure pastors! May they be ours in increasing numbers!

Written especially for young Timothy, the personal element in the Second Epistle is strongly marked. "Timothy, my dearly beloved son" (1:2). This is why there is a moving, paternal touch about this farewell letter of Paul's. Here we have the veteran worker's final advice to a younger fellow laborer. In no other Epistle does the true, loving, undaunted, and trustful heart of the great apostle speak in more consolatory, yet touching accents as in this most human document. Made up of four chapters in II Timothy, we have the suggestion of a fourfold gaze:

In chapter 1, the apostle looks back over the past. There is the remembrance of Timothy's affectionate grief at parting, his faith, his family associations, and of his spiritual gift received at ordination.

In chapter 2, Paul looks at the present and gives directions

361

to Timothy on how to conduct himself amid the manifold difficulties of his position.

In chapter 3, Paul looks forward to the future and forewarns and forearms his friend against the dangers and troubles he foresees in the history of the church.

In chapter 4, the gaze is lifted from earth to heaven, for although as a chained, persecuted, deserted, and suffering warrior, the apostle awaits martyrdom, his sky is bright with the dawn of a coming, glorious day.

Being, however, one of the three Pastoral Epistles, we prefer to see in Paul's "Swan Song" in II Timothy, the fourfold obligation of the Christian pastor, teacher, or worker.

The Minister and His Mission (chap. 1)

Among the descriptions given of those who labor in the gospel none is so expressive as that which Paul uses of Timothy, "A Minister of God" (I Thess. 3:2). Such a title is not to be limited to one who has had a college education, who holds a certain ecclesiastical position as "Reverend," and is distinguished by a certain dress. This appellation applies to all who are saved by grace, and are called and equipped by the Holy Spirit to serve God in some divinely appointed sphere, and by His power to make full proof of this ministry. Further, this is a "calling," not a "profession": "who hath . . . called us with a holy calling." This ninth verse constitutes the key verse of the first chapter—"Who hath saved us, and called us with a holy calling."

Paul is careful to put conversion before calling, salvation before service. God calls none to serve Him who have not been saved according to His purpose. The sons of Eli served Him, but did not know Him, so their professional service was not divinely accepted. We must be born anew by the Spirit as a prerequisite to a divine call to serve God. Saved, we must serve, for we were saved to serve.

Because of the sacredness of their task, all who minister

362

unto the Lord, must guard themselves against the threefold danger of slackness, stagnation, and the fear of man. Associated with making our calling and election sure, are these marked features—

1. The Presence and Power of the Holy Spirit (1:7)
2. The Partaking of Afflictions (1:8; see 3:12; 4:5)
3. The Promise of Eternal Security (1:9); double committal (1:12, 14)
4. The Possession of Fundamental Truths (1:13; see 2:2)

The Minister and His Master (chap. 2)

If the motto of the previous chapter is "Be Brave," the suitable motto of this second chapter is "Be Thorough." As this chapter is prominent in the way it outlines the Christian worker's relationship to his Lord, its opening words constitute the key verse: "Be strong in the grace that is in Christ Jesus" (2:1). He who calls us equips us to serve Him aright. "Faithful is He that calleth you, who also will do it" (I Thess. 5:24). He is the source of strength for service. He never sends us forth to the warfare on our own charger. The phrase "in Christ Jesus" was a favorite one with Paul who used it, in different ways, some 160 times in his Epistles. Whether "in Christ," "in Christ Jesus," "in the Lord," "in whom," or "in him," such expressions convey the truth that He is fountainhead of all the power and patience we need to witness for Him in an apostate age. It will be found that the chapter contains a series of metaphors illustrating our relationship to Him who called us to follow and labor.

1. He is the commander, we are the soldiers (2:3-4, "chosen" or "enlisted")
2. He is the umpire, we are the athletes (2:5; see I Cor. 9:24)
3. He is the husbandman, we are the laborers (2:6; fruit depends upon labor)
4. He is the employer, we are the workmen (2:15)

363

5. He is the owner, we are the vessels (2:20-21, purged, prepared)
6. He is the master, we are the slaves (2:22, 24)

Flee—negative side. *Follow*—positive side. As those, then, called to serve the One who saved us we have—

Strength for the Fight (2:1)
Wisdom for the Work (2:7)
Prospect of a Glorious Reward (2:11-12)

The Minister and His Message (chap. 3)

Over this chapter we can write, "Be Watchful," for the minister of God, having looked to his charge, then to his Lord, must now think of his relationship to the Scriptures. Perilous times and false voices make it imperative for him to abide in, and constantly study, God's Word. Thus the key verse of the chapter reads, "The holy scriptures. . . . All scripture is given by inspiration of God" (3:14-17). In this wonderful portion, Paul declares unequivocably his faith in the Scriptures as being divinely inspired. "All," (or "every") Scripture affirms that the Bible not only contains the Word of God, but is His infallible Word from beginning to end. "Holy men of God spake as they were moved [borne along] by the Holy Spirit." Any worker will be perplexed and badly equipped if he fails to—

Admit the Scriptures to be inspired by God
Submit to the Scriptures in order to be sanctified
Commit the Scriptures to memory to draw upon in need
Transmit the Scriptures to others for their salvation

A perusal of this third chapter reveals these features of Scripture—

As a Source of Comfort and Guidance in Perilous Times (3:1-13)

In these remarkable verses we have an ancient mirror of

364

modern events, a description of the last days preceding the coming of the Lord. What a somber outline the passage is of the deplorable character of man, outstandingly common today. Never in the course of history has life become so evil. Paul was among those William Cowper wrote of in "Winter Walk at Noon":

> The prophets speak of such, and, noting down
> The features of the last degenerate times,
> Exhibit every lineament of these.

The word Paul gives us for "perilous" (II Tim. 3:1) is equivalent to the phrase Jesus used of the conduct of the two demon-possessed men, "exceeding fierce" (Matt. 8:28). Thus, we can freely paraphrase the apostle's opening verse of the chapter before us, "Demonized times shall come." And there is no other way to describe the terrible crimes, bloody revolutionary elements, the abounding iniquity of our times, reflecting as they do, the catalog of infamy and vices Paul gives us. Knowing his time is short, Satan is manifesting great wrath.

Believers, discerning the times, are not perplexed—although they are saddened—by the prevailing features of these last days. They are not side-tracked by false voices for, living near "the more sure word of prophecy," they discern how the condition and character of human society is heavy with prophetic significance. God's inerrant, infallible Word is a light unto their path enabling them to watch and pray amid the gathering clouds. They study the Word and thereby show themselves approved unto God.

As a Source of Salvation of the Lost (II Tim. 3:15)

The only hope the slaves of sin and apostates have of emancipation from their fetters is through the Saviour the Scriptures present. Holy Scripture alone can make them wise

365

unto salvation through faith in Christ Jesus. The gospel of His redeeming grace and power is the sole medium of deliverance from the guilt and thralldom of sin. And, in these iniquitous days, we have need to get back to the preaching of ruin by the fall, repentance for sin, redemption by the blood, regeneration by the Holy Spirit.

At the turn of this century, General William Booth, Founder of the Salvation Army stated, "The chief dangers in the twentieth century will be religion without the Holy Spirit, Christianity without Christ, politics without God, heaven without hell." What a true prophet the old general turned out to be! All the more reason for us to preach his gospel of blood and fire, and to fling the message into the face of a godless world: "Ye must be born again!"

As a Source of Spiritual Knowledge (II Tim. 3:16)

One evidence of Scripture as the divinely inspired Word of God is its profitability in the understanding of doctrine, reproof, correction, and instruction in righteousness. That a person may have a mental knowledge of Scripture without a deep spiritual experience is seen in the case of Nicodemus of whom Jesus asked, "Art thou a master in Israel [a man who was familiar with Old Testament Scripture] and knowest not these things?" (John 3:10). It is sadly possible for one to know the Book of God, yet not know the God of the Book. Because the truth of Holy Writ is spiritually discerned, the Spirit, who inspired holy men to write Scripture, must be within us as the source of our sanctification and illumination: "That which I see not teach thou me: If I have done iniquity, I will do no more" (Job. 34:32).

As a Source of Spiritual Equipment (II Tim. 3:17)

The "minister of God" is likewise a "man of God," or a man God possessed and God controlled; and the more such a

366

man lives in the Scripture given by inspiration of God, the more complete, thoroughly furnished unto all good works, he becomes. No man in the ministry who neglects personal Bible meditation and study is fully furnished for the task he assumes, namely, "A minister of the Word." If he preaches essays on various secular themes instead of proclaiming the blood-red evangel, he will never make full proof of his ministry. His supreme mission in the world is to rescue the perishing by telling them of Jesus who is mighty to save. God never fails to manifest His power through such preaching (Titus 1:3). Therefore, the unceasing, solemn obligation of the man of God is to preach the Word!

The Minister and His Motive (chap. 4)

What a mighty spiritual upheaval the church and the nation would experience if only all ministers lived by this chapter in which Paul portrays the features of a preacher after God's own heart! It is a chapter every preacher should daily read in the solitude of his own study if he would be delivered from mere lip-preaching. Paul preached in the light of eternity, hence the quality and results of his utterances. He never preached to please, but always for the prize—"the crown of righteousness." Confidently and unashamedly, Paul confesses that the constraining motive or incentive in all untiring loyal service for the Master was the prospect of seeing Him, and receiving from Him the "Well done, good and faithful servant." The apostle found stimulus in "the blessed hope." "This one thing I do . . . I press toward the prize." The key phrase of the chapter is "Be Strenuous."

To live and labor in the light of the judgment seat of Christ, with its rewards for dedication and devotion to His cause, enables one to serve Him to the limit. Paul loved the thought of his Lord's appearing, and thus his last Epistle is dominated by such a glorious prospect.

367

He believed that Christ had brought not only life, but immortality to light through His gospel (1:10).

He ever kept before him "that day"—the day of the Lord's return for His own (1:12, 18; 4:8).

He anticipated the privilege through grace of sharing the throne of his reigning Lord (2:13; 4:1).

He had an insight into the portents of his Master's second coming advent signs (3:1-9).

He loved the very mention of Christ's appearing. Not only had his mind grasped all the facets of such a truth, his heart, likewise, was held captive by the hope of seeing Him he dearly loved and sacrificially served (4:8), which is the key verse of this chapter. Untold numbers of preachers have found that there is nothing so revolutionary in their ministry as to live and labor in the light of the judgment seat, before which all saints are to appear (4:18).

The few autobiographical touches Paul gives us as he closes his farewell letter reveal him to be the happy warrior he was. Without doubt, he stands out as the magnificent hero of the faith, and as the Apostle Extraordinary.

He was the *lamb* ready to be offered (4:6). His martyrdom was near but he had no fear. His frail bark was about to be loosed from its moorings.

He was the soldier who had fought, not *a* but *"the* good *fight"* (4:7, RV). He had lived out his exhortation to young Timothy, "Fight the good fight of faith" (I Tim. 6:12).

He was the athlete who had finished the race with great honors. What a remarkable course he had run (2:5; 4:7)!

He was the trustee who had preserved the sacred deposit of the whole body of revealed truth. "I have kept the faith" (4:7, RV; Jude 3).

Truly these assertions describe a noble end to a most noble life! Sealing his remarkable testimony with his blood, Paul entered the presence of his Master to receive the laurel, safely "laid up" for him, from the scarred hands of his Living Lord—

We live in deeds, not fears; in thoughts, not breaths;
In feelings, not in figures on a dial.
We should count time by heartthrobs. He most lives
Who thinks most—feels the noblest—acts the best.

This is how Paul, the greatest Christian in Church History, lived. May grace be ours to follow in his train!

Theme 35
Philemon: Christian Courtesy

Lord Byron, in *Don Juan,* has the expressive lines—

Though modest, on his unembarrassed brow
Nature had written "gentleman."

How true a sentiment of the apostle Paul is Byron's couplet! His modesty is seen in his self-depreciation: "less than the least"; "the chief of sinners." Paul's Epistle to Philemon reveals his gentlemanliness. Without doubt he belonged to heaven's spiritual knighthood. He was one of God's gentlemen. Grace made him gracious in his dealings with others. He never forgot his obligation to adorn the gospel. Tennyson's words fit Paul's manners—"O selfless man and stainless gentleman."

Too many preachers, conservative in their theology, are most ungracious in their behavior. They lack gratitude, unselfishness, kindness, and those finer traits and attractive courtesies commendable in every person and especially in a Christian. Not so, Paul. Whether he dealt with master or slave, rich or poor, Christian or heathen, his approach was kind and thoughtful, considerate and courteous. "He bore without abuse the grand old name of gentleman."

We might well ask the question, "What is a gentleman?" Charles Dickens put this conception of a gentleman on the lips of Oliver Twist, "I shall be a gen'l'm'n myself one of these days, perhaps with a pipe in my mouth, and a summer-house in the back garden." But possessions do not make a gentleman. As the old proverb says, "It is not the coat that makes the gentleman." Edmund Burke claimed, "A king can make a nobleman, but he cannot make a gentleman."

One who is not well-born and lacks a good education and social position can yet be a gentleman after the Bible order. He can have that refinement of manners, attractive behavior, finesse, and courtesy born of the Spirit. He can be like the Master of whom old Thomas Dekker wrote in 1570—

> The best of men
> That e'er wore earth about Him was a sufferer.
> A soft, meek, patient, humble, tranquil spirit,
> The first true Gentleman that ever breathed.

Christ was the "finished Gentleman from tip to toe," Lord Byron speaks of in *Don Juan.* And Christlikeness and gentlemanliness are akin. Courtesy is a trait of a Christ-possessed Christian. The dictionary describes a gentleman as "one who belongs to a stock." The "gens-men" in Roman law were only those who had a family name, were born of free parents, had no slave in the ancestral line, and had never been degraded to a lower rank. Paul had such a pedigree, but it was grace that made him a nobler gentleman. Shakespeare, in *Winter's Tale,* has the line, "We must be gentle, now we are gentlemen." Paul, however, could change the thought and say, "We must be refined, now we are regenerated," and his Epistle to Philemon is a beautiful cameo of knightliness. One of its peculiar features is its aesthetic character. It is a model of delicacy and skill in the effort to reconcile parties at variance. It reveals the triumph of love. "It is a precious relic of a great character." Philemon is unique as a perfect masterpiece of pure politeness. The courtly manners of Paul, the benevolence and hospitality of Philemon himself, illustrate that distinctive character of the early disciples compelling the heathen around to exclaim, "See how these Christians love one another!"

Bishop Handley Moule, comparing this Epistle with the much-admired letter of Pliny to his friend Sabinianus to ask pardon for a young freedman, who had offended Sabinianus, says, "It is a graceful, kindly letter, written by a man whose character is the ideal of his age and class: the cultured and thoughtful Roman gentleman of the mildest period of the Empire. . . . His heart has not the depth of Paul to clasp Onesimus in his arms and to commend him to Philemon as a friend in God for immortality."

Because of its infinite charm, and the fact that it is simple and unartificial in style, the Epistle to Philemon has been called "a little idyll of the progress of Christianity." Other writers, because of its graceful and delicate courtesy, have spoken of it as "The Polite Epistle." Within it there is no insincere compliment. Paul in a manly, straightforward, yet captivatingly persuasive way presents his case to Philemon. The apostle gives us a specimen of the highest wisdom as to the manner in which Christians ought to manage social affairs.

"The incomparable delicacy of this letter of Paul's has often been the theme of eulogium," says Alexander Mac Laren. "I do not know that anywhere else in literature one can find such a gem, so admirably adapted for the purpose on hand. But beyond the wonderful tenderness and ingenuity born of right feeling and inbred courtesy which mark the letter, there is another point of view from which I have been in the habit of looking at it, as if it were a kind of parable of the way in which the Master pleads with us to do the things that He desires. The motive and principle of practical Christianity are all reducible to one—the imitation of Jesus Christ. Therefore it is not fanciful if here we see, shining through the demeanor and conduct of the apostle, some hint of the manner of the Master."

It is the concensus of opinion that Paul wrote Philemon during his first Roman imprisonment, around A.D. 62, the same time he wrote Colossians, both Epistles being delivered by Onesimus. This may account for some of "the undesigned coincidences" between Philemon and Colossians. In both, Paul and Timothy head the Epistle, Archippus is addressed, and Paul appears as a prisoner. In none of his Epistles, how-

372

ever, does Paul reveal his great heart and care for every member of the church as he does in Philemon, which is a personal letter fragrant with a sense of honor and politeness. In many ways this Epistle proves that "gentleman is written legibly on Paul's brow." Let us summarize it in this sevenfold fashion:

1. His Fragrant Remembrance of Others

If "memory is a Paradise from which we need not be driven," then Paul was sublimely happy, for he was rich in his friendships and in his remembrance of them. John Ruskin in *Seven Lamps of Architecture* calls gentlemanliness another name for intense humanity. Well, Paul shared this quality in an unusual degree. He was keenly alive to the value of Christian friendship, and as a prisoner depended on others for personal needs. Onesimus supplied both wants and won the apostle's heart, so that he became much attached to the one-time slave. When, reluctantly, he sent Onesimus back to Philemon, Paul, because of his natural craving for human sympathy, found the parting painful.

It may be worthwhile to form a closer acquaintance with Paul's friends named in this short Epistle, many of whom were, to adapt John Dryden's phrase, "God Almighty's gentlemen." First on the list is—

Philemon (v. 1)

The recipient of the letter bearing his name is tenderly referred to as "our dearly beloved," or "beloved friend" and "fellow-laborer." Many Bible names are full of significance. *Philemon* means "friendly," and this trait is, as we see, one that Paul commends. Philemon's prayers, love, generosity, and hospitality were always in Paul's mind (5, 7, 21-22). As a "fellow-laborer" Philemon had assisted in the cause of Christ in many ways.

All we know of Philemon is in this letter Paul sent him.

Evidently he lived in Colosse, was a believer, possessed considerable wealth (v. 22), and was held in high esteem by Paul. Philemon's house was the rendezvous of believers. "The church" met in his home, and as the head of the Christian congregation in Colosse, Philemon's influence must have been considerable. It has been suggested that Philemon was led to Christ by Paul during the apostle's ministry in Ephesus. Philemon might have visited Paul, seeing the apostle had not visited Colosse up to this time.

Apphia (v. 2)

Because of her association with Philemon, it is felt by many scholars that Apphia was the wife of Philemon. Otherwise she would not have been mentioned on such a domestic matter. As a "beloved sister" Apphia is identified as a sincere believer, since the name means "faithful."

Archippus (v. 2)

While his name signifies "leader of horses," and may be indicative of his employment or pleasure, yet it was in a spiritual warfare that he was a sharer of similar dangers and hardships (II Tim. 2:3). Living amid military sights and sounds in Rome, it was only natural for Paul to employ such terms. There is no Biblical support of the view that Archippus may have been the son of Philemon, even though he may have lived in his home and was an active worker in the church at Colosse; hence Paul's exhortation to Archippus, "Take heed to the ministry which thou hast received in the Lord, that thou fulfil it" (Col. 4:17).

A further word is necessary regarding "the church in the house," in which Archippus had an active part. Originally, believers met in large houses of wealthy Christians. Some would provide plenty of room for the gathering of saints. Not until long after the apostolic age were separate buildings for

374

worship erected. These early assemblies were characterized by unity (Ps. 133) and consisted of—

(1) Messages from the apostles announced or read (Col. 4:16)
(2) Prayers offered for the apostles and all men (I Tim. 2:1)
(3) Singing of psalms and spiritual hymns (Col. 3:16)
(4) Scriptures read and explained (I Tim. 4:13)
(5) Commemoration of the Lord's Supper (Acts 20:11)
(6) Collections taken for pressing needs (I Cor. 16:2)

Onesimus in his unconverted state must have often witnessed these gatherings in Philemon's home, and wondered what they were all about. This we know, the runaway slave's heart was not touched nor won for Christ until he heard the gospel from the lips of prisoner Paul in Rome.

Epaphras (v. 23)

Although *Epaphras* is the same name as *Epaphroditus*, this is not the same person who brought the contribution from Philippi to Rome about this time (Phil. 2:25). Epaphras lived in Colosse (Col. 4:12). Epaphroditus lived in Philippi and held office in the church there. Paul speaks of him as a "fellow prisoner" (Col. 1:7). This does not mean that he had been cast into prison on Roman authority, but that he became a voluntary companion-captive in exile. "To remember the brethren in bonds was accounted the same thing as being bound with them" (Heb. 13:3). Willingly he took up residence with Paul in the lodging where he was guarded by "the soldier that kept him."

Mark (v. 24)

This is the same Mark whose surname was John, the man Paul had disagreed with Barnabas about (Acts 15:37-39; I Peter 5:13). Whatever it was in Mark that made Paul dis-

375

approve of him joining the missionary crusade, he eventually made good and became a valuable helper to Paul in the closing days of his life (Col. 4:10; II Tim. 4:11) and the writer of the Gospel bearing his name.

Aristarchus (v. 24)

From the various references to Aristarchus ("excellent chief") (Acts 19:29; 20:4; 27:2; Col. 4:10) we gather something of his work and worth. He was a fellow laborer, a fellow prisoner, and a fellow traveler of Paul. Tradition has it that he became the bishop of Apamaca.

Demas (v. 24)

Although Demas is mentioned along with Mark and Luke as Paul's fellow laborer (Philem. 24) and a companion during the apostle's first Roman imprisonment (Col. 4:14), Demas was one friend who gave Paul a good deal of heartache at the end of his life. The most poignant words Paul ever penned was, "Demas hath forsaken me, having loved this present world" (II Tim. 4:10). Love of worldly ease and home comforts became his snare—a sad contrast to Paul's lot and to "all them that love his [Christ's] appearing" (II Tim. 4:8). The one love blasts the other.

Luke (v. 24)

The beloved physician was doubtless a great help to the aged Paul. As a loyal companion and fellow laborer, his medical attention must have been deeply appreciated by Paul. Luke was the writer of the Third Gospel and of The Acts (Luke 1:1-4; Acts 1:1; Col. 4:14; II Tim. 4:11). In Paul's last imprisonment, when others forsook him, Luke remained loyal to the end. "Only Luke is with me" (II Tim. 1:14; 4:11). Evidently of Gentile parentage, Luke was the only

376

Gentile among the writers of the Bible. Tradition tells us he suffered death by martyrdom between A.D. 75 and 100. As we look back over these and other friends of Paul, the words of Pollock, the poet, come to mind—

> Some I remember, and will ne'er forget:
> My early friends, friends of my evil day:
> Friends in mirth, friends in my memory, too.
> Friends given by God in mercy and in love,
> My counsellors, my comforters and guides:
> My joy in grief, my second bliss in joy.

2. His Sincere Appraisal of Character

With all the grace of a spiritual knight, Paul knew how to give honor where honor was due. He deeply appreciated kindnesses bestowed upon him, and he was quick to commend those who did so. Yet, lovingly but with justice, he condemned those whose defection from truth and holiness were apparent. The Epistle to Philemon is a striking example of Paul's insight into character, and of his ability rightly to evaluate the true worth of those who surrounded him.

Take, for example, Paul's approach to Philemon in verses 4 through 7. With instinctive kindliness and conscious diplomacy, he praises Philemon for his Christian life and labors. From the lips of Onesimus he had heard so often of Philemon's love, faith, and liberality. The tired hearts of the poor or otherwise distressed, harassed saints had found in Philemon a haven of rest, and Paul, without flattering, extols the one whose life was the fruit of a loving heart.

We can readily see how Paul's recommendation of Philemon prepared his mind for the apostle's request on behalf of Onesimus. Paul purposely puts Philemon's love first, seeing it was an act of love he planned to ask him to demonstrate. "Love and faith" are not the right theological order. Faith has the precedence, then love—the fruit of faith. When Paul

377

asked for the communication of faith (v. 6) he requested liberality from faith—the sharing of what he had (Heb. 13:16).

The same assessment of human worth is seen in Paul's estimation of Onesimus (vv. 10-17). No matter what the runaway slave had been, grace had transformed his life, and Paul extols the virtues supplanting the past vices of Onesimus. Paul was not blind to the fact that Onesimus belied the name he bore. *Onesimus* means "profitable"; but he had been not only unprofitable, but positively injurious—he had wronged his master, possibly by stealing from him. But now Onesimus was highly profitable in spiritual as well as practical things. Skillfully Paul covers a once-hated name with two shields, "my son" and "begotten in bonds." The one-time slave was now a son and a partner. No longer must Onesimus be dealt with as a chattel but as a Christian. Paul plays on the name of Onesimus and in effect he says, "He did not show himself truly as Onesimus, but he is changed now and become worthy, yea, twice worthy, of that expressive name."

3. His Tender Appeal for Forgiveness

The kingly heart of Paul begs forgiveness for Onesimus. How could Philemon spurn such a gracious overture? Paul strengthened his plea in several forceful ways (v. 9). First of all, it was Paul who was presenting the plea—Paul, the well-known apostle, whose praise was in all the churches and who was held in high esteem everywhere. In the second place, he pleads his age. Nearing seventy, his weakness of age aggravated by his prison sufferings, he must therefore be listened to with respect. In the plea of his age there may be a suggestion that Philemon was a good deal younger than Paul. In the third place, the apostle speaks of his bonds. And we can imagine how Paul's hardship would appeal to Philemon's heart. Further, Paul had not long to live. The shadow of martyrdom was over his path. Perhaps the strongest plea for

Philemon's forgiveness of Onesimus was the fact that Philemon owed his own salvation to Paul's faithful witness (v. 19). In urging Philemon to take back Onesimus as if he were Paul, the apostle puts the case as if he himself had been guilty of the wrong done to Philemon. Such an appeal was backed up by the reminder that he was Philemon's father in Christ. He was under obligation to comply with Paul's request, seeing he owed all he had in grace to him. Martin Luther's comment on this plea is, "Paul strips himself of his right and therefore compels Philemon to betake himself to his right."

Paul also wanted Philemon to know that there must be nothing half-hearted. His forgiveness of his former slave had to be warm, full, and free. "Receive him, that is, mine own bowels" (v. 12). Paul counted Onesimus as dear as his own heart. Such language implies the intense affection of a parent for a child. It is more than certain that Paul's fervent plea did not fall upon deaf ears. Paul's recommendation for clemency met with a favorable reception (Col. 4:9). It is said that Philemon liberated Onesimus and became the bishop of Berea, ultimately at Rome.

4. His Lofty Estimation of Suffering

Paul, more than any other man, knew how to glory in his tribulations. He never groaned under his burdens. His shackles could not bind his spirit. True, he was a prisoner—but a prisoner in Jesus Christ (v. 1, 9). Roman fetters bound hands and ankles, but they were the bonds of the gospel (v. 13). It was Christ's cause, and no infringement of Roman laws, that had put him in chains. Paul traced everything to the Master he dearly loved and sacrificially served. Samuel Rutherford used to date his letters from his Scottish prison—"Christ's Palace, Aberdeen." Outwardly, Paul was Nero's prisoner. Inwardly, he was Christ's. Some of the Moravian missionaries sold themselves into slavery that they might preach Christ to the slaves. Paul treated his bondage as a God-given opportunity for the furtherance of the interests of the gospel (Phil. 1:12-13). "Stone walls do not a prison make" (Acts 28:20).

Can we say that although prison walls, tangible or intangible, shut us in, we yet have a heart enfranchised? If in a sick chamber, or in some restricted sphere, there are letters we can write, and a sweet resignation we can maintain—the influence of which can reach far and live long. Bound in some way or another, we can yet be God's freeman.

> Make me a captive, Lord,
> And then I shall be free;
> Force me to render up my sword,
> And I shall conqueror be.

5. His Noble Consideration for Propriety

There was never anything rude or crude about Paul's dealings with those around him. He was never off guard. Everything about his speech and action was proper. True, in a moment of passion, he insulted the high priest by calling him "a whited wall." Learning, however, that it was the high priest he had addressed, he humbly apologized with all graciousness.

Of Paul's approach to Philemon, Bishop Ellicott remarks, "The exquisite tact with which Onesimus' fraudulent treatment of Philemon is alluded to (v. 18)—the absence of anything tending to excuse or palliate the misdeed, yet the use of every expressive sentiment calculated to win the fullest measure of Philemon's forgiveness—have not failed to call forth the reverential admiration of every expositor from the earliest times to our own day."

Martin Luther also wrote of Paul's manners with characteristic human tenderness and Christian insight. "Philemon showeth a right noble lovely example of Christian love. Here we see how Paul layeth himself out for poor Onesimus and with all his means he pleadeth his cause with his master and

380

so setteth himself up as if he were Onesimus and had himself done wrong to Philemon." Would that we could exhibit the same tact, wisdom, and spiritual guile when faced with the problems of others (vv. 8, 10, 14, 19).

C. A. Joyce, the well-known British educationalist and popular broadcaster, has given a fascinating insight into life among prisoners, especially of young offenders in need of corrective training, in his latest book, *Thoughts of a Lifetime*. Possessed of a firm religious faith and a sincere concern for others, in this volume he reveals what a deep understanding of basic human nature he has. Fully convinced that in setting Christian standards, the first rung of the ladder is courtesy, the author firmly states that all he mentions in his book applies not to work among young offenders only but to society in general. He says:

> There is no home, no office, no works that could fail to be improved by this thing called courtesy, and the essence of the whole thing seems to me to be just this: in private life, in industry nationally or internationally, when we really sort it out, everything depends on personal relationships.

And that—in 1971—is as timely a statement as one could expect to hear!

6. His Unceasing Love for Souls

Paul had long practiced the art of watching over the souls of others. His long and loyal witness was an exhibition of his own exhortation to serve the Lord in and out of season. D. L. Moody's determination was, "I must speak to one soul each day about Christ." Paul never waited for opportunities to come his way to win souls—he made them, as Philemon proves (vv. 10, 12, 16).

Without hesitation, Paul speaks of Onesimus as his son whom he had begotten in his bonds. He knew Onesimus had been a slave. His name was that of a common slave. But Paul knew that in the matter of salvation, all men were sinners and had to be treated as such on equal terms. It may be pointed out here that in the latter days of the Roman Empire, slaves of Roman masters were immensely numerous. It was difficult for a Roman to pass muster in society if he had less than ten slaves. None of the apostles sanctioned slavery, neither did they stir up animosity in slaves against their masters. They emphasized the spirit of love toward each other. Thus Alexander MacLaren wrote of Philemon, "By the principles which the Epistle expresses, by the results which it involved, this little letter became the Magna Charta of freedom throughout the world."

Untiring in his labors for the Master, Paul won Onesimus. As Christ on the cross preached to the thief, so the apostle witnessed to the runaway slave who, after his conversion, proved his worth. Paul would have retained Onesimus, for he had implicit trust in him as a "brother beloved." Faithfully Onesimus cared for Paul as a son for his father, and such a bond between the two helped to remove any dislike Philemon might have had in the reception of Onesimus. Now he would be "much more unto thee," as Paul put it. Through grace, master and servant had been brought nearer and into a more lasting relationship. God had overruled past evil for the ultimate good of all.

While Onesimus had actually run away from Philemon, Paul uses the softer term of "departed" and that "only for a season." The word "perhaps" (v. 15) suggests God's overruling providence. God has His own designs—His own secret stairs. An old Scottish saint said, "I thought He would come by the way of the hills, and lo, He came by the way of the valleys." How true it is that there is a divinity shaping our ends, rough hew them though we may! Onesimus absconded of his own accord, yet a higher will was in operation. From the human side, the slave foolishly and fearfully left his master. From the divine side, God was guiding Onesimus to the prison cell to meet one whose love for souls was to change his whole life. Onesimus went back to Philemon who, agreeing to Paul's request, received his one-time slave as a brother in the Lord. All was forgiven. The two were perfectly reconciled. Nothing could divide them again, for now they were bound together in an undying life (Gen. 45:5). While they lived, Philemon and Onesimus would be partners in spiritual interests, partakers of the same faith.

Paul speaks of Philemon as owing him his own life, which is but another way of saying that Philemon owed his salvation to the apostle. So master and slave alike had been won for Christ. Then, Timothy, Paul's companion (v. 1) was also his son in the faith. How very many stars will adorn the apostle's crown! Can we say that we are borne along by the same passion for souls? Irrespective of their position and condition, do we approach men and women as those who are lost in sin, and who can be delivered only by the Saviour's power?

7. His Utter Disregard for Self

Selflessness is a conspicuous trait of true refinement, and such a trait was Paul's to an eminent degree. Shakespeare in *King Lear* says, "The prince of darkness is a gentleman." While he can transform himself into an angel of light, the satanic prince has no innate gentlemanliness. It is only a false veneer—a make-believe. Paul, however, was never guilty of manufactured courtesy to attract attention to himself. His knightliness sprang from his Christlikeness, and colored all his actions.

As an apostle, Paul could have commanded Philemon to take Onesimus back, but because of the love between them, he besought him (v. 10): "For love's sake I rather beseech thee" (v. 9). Paul would not impose his apostolic authority. Philemon must willingly concur in Paul's request (v. 14). Delicately Paul bases his appeal on all that Onesimus had done for him. What Philemon would have done for Paul, in his

383

prison cell, Onesimus had done as a living substitute. Using a softer term for "robbed," Paul said he was willing to make good any "wrong" Onesimus had been guilty of. "I will repay it" (v. 19). Unselfishly Paul is ready to assume all the indebtedness of Onesimus. There is, of course, a significance beyond this application of Paul's words to Philemon. All of us are deep in debt to Christ. There is a sense in which we owe ourselves to those who won us for Christ. There is a bond of tenderness between the two. But it was Christ who paid our debt. A man raised up from some crippling disease owes his life to the doctor. Christ redeemed us at great cost to Himself, and we owe Him all we are and have.

Paul's unselfishness comes out in many ways in this precious letter of emancipation. For instance, he displayed no sense of superiority. He took no advantage of his apostleship. He looked upon others as equals. So we have the terms "fellow prisoner," "fellow laborer," "fellow soldier," "partner," "brother." Too many preachers lack this spiritual attractiveness. They are too much taken up with their own prestige, position, and superiority. It is foreign to them to think of others as being better than themselves.

Paul was also humble enough to confess that he depended on the prayers of others. He, himself, had his prayer list of those he constantly remembered (v. 4), and in turn he wanted to be prayed for (v. 23). He urged Philemon to pray that he might be liberated and then enjoy the loving hospitality of his home (v. 22). We can imagine how the prospect of such a visit to Philemon would secure a kindly reception for Onesimus. Once Paul reached the home, he would see how Onesimus fared after being welcomed back by Philemon. Had he treated him as Paul's other self?

How fitting it is that this Epistle, which illustrates such courtly manners, should end with a benediction of grace! Paul tells us that he wrote Philemon with his own hand (v. 19). Bishop Lightfoot reminds us that "a signature to a deed in ancient or mediaeval times would commonly take the form, 'I, so-and-so.' " Paul meant by his Epistle, then, coming as it did from his own hand, not only to ease the way for the return of Onesimus to his wronged master, but to show us how to act in all graciousness to all men. There is a proverb that condemns us if "you have good manners, but never carry them about with you." Paul, however, shows us how always to carry good manners about with us, and to live and act as those belonging to the aristocracy of heaven.

Theme 36
Hebrews: Better Things

The Epistle to the Hebrews is one of the most important books of the Bible in that it contains the most exalted presentation of Christ to be found anywhere. A prayerful, careful study of the Epistle leads to a greater reverence for the Captain of our salvation, who is the chief subject of this New Testament counterpart of Leviticus. Here we see Jesus magnified above all others as One above and apart from all others. The design of the writer was to prove that Jesus of Nazareth, whom Jewish rulers put to death, was none other than their Messiah, the Son of God, superior to everyone who preceded His incarnation. No one can meditate upon this Epistle without being deeply impressed with the matchless grandeur and superiority of Him who was the express image of the Father.

It is from Hebrews that we discover how Old Testament shadows find their substance in Christ, and that the gospel is the full and final revelation of God to man. The Law given by Moses is shown to be the divinely appointed preparation for Him to whom all the Old Testament gives witness. Leviticus, with its priesthood and offerings, was God's picture book for His ancient people, and in Hebrews the pictures are explained for the spiritual benefit of those He redeemed by grace. The sacrifices and services of old were "figures of the true," or "the shadow of good things to come" (9:8; 10:1).

A striking feature of the Epistle before us is the way it opens—abruptly: there is no name, no introduction, no salutation, no thanks, no prayer, as the other Epistles have. It opens as sublimely and majestically as the first book of the Bible—"In the beginning God." Hebrews begins, "God . . . in

386

times past." Godet, the renowned French theologian, says, "This Epistle without introduction or subscription is like the Great High Priest of whom it treats who was without beginning of days or end of years, abiding as High Priest continually. It is entirely fitting that this book should remain anonymous."

As to its authorship, Origen said, "God alone knows who wrote it." Volumes have been written in the discussion of who penned it. The title giving it to Paul is not found in the oldest manuscripts. Some have assigned the Epistle to Barnabas. Martin Luther favored Apollos as its author. Yet others ascribe it to Luke. G. Campbell Morgan contended that the book has Paul's thinking in Luke's language, which may account for similar terms in Acts and Hebrews. From Early Church days its Pauline authority has been accepted. Whoever wrote it, we like him, because he put God *first*. If, as it has been said, we can trace the anonymous to God, whoever the writer was he was inspired of God for every sentence bears the authorship of the Holy Spirit.

As the title describes, the Epistle was addressed to Hebrews—Hebrew Christians of some definite community (10:25; 13:7, 17), who were in danger of going back to Judaism. The writer proves in every respect that the Christian faith and the church mark a great advance over the Jewish system and so urges the Hebrew professors of Christianity not to go back but to go on. Hence, the Epistle adapts itself especially to those Jewish converts who were exhorted to let go everything and hold fast the faith. *Christian progress* is the consistent appeal of the Epistle as demonstrated by the repeated challenge, "Let us go on!" We never remain static in Christian experience; if we are not going forward, then we are going back.

While there are many features of Hebrews we would like to deal with, our present concern is with its key word, *better*. This word occurs thirteen times in the thirteen chapters which form the Epistle, and it is used to express the contrast

387

between the Old and New Dispensations, stressing the superiority of the latter. Here, "the old is *not* better." The key verse gives us an epitome of the whole Epistle, "God having provided some better thing for us, that they without us should not be made perfect [complete]" (11:40). Let us, then, examine the chain of references where *better* is found.

Better Than Angels (1:4)

The word *better* means "greater, stronger, more powerful." Jesus became greater than angels after He had made "purification of sins." In His past glory He was superior to the highest created angelic being (Eph. 1:21; Phil. 2:9). God had, in ancient times, declared His law through the media of angels (2:2), but grace and truth came in the Person of Jesus. By inheritance He obtained a more excellent name than angels. By essential right He was the Son of God and worthy to receive the worship of angels (1:6) who are not to be worshiped (Rev. 22:8-9). No *angel* ever received the title "Son of God." True, they are spoken of in an inferior sense as "sons of God" (Job 1:6; 38:7), but *Son,* as used of Jesus, is unique. Angels were employed to carry out divine purposes, but the Son of God is the One addressed in the phrase "Thy throne, O God, is for ever and ever."

But the adulation "much better than angels" seems to contradict the assertion "Thou madest him a little lower than angels" (2:7). This quotation is from Psalm 8, and the Hebrew text there reads, "a little less than God." The margin of Hebrews 2:7 has it, "A little while inferior to angels." Ellicott, however, affirms that the true rendering of the Hebrew should be restored. Becoming "God manifest in flesh," Jesus yet, because of the limitations of His human form, appeared to be a little less than God. Jesus, then, is greater than angels in name, in kind, and in degree. He is superior to all His creatures, and angels were a part of His creation. His character and conduct, work and worth, give Him an excellency

388

which transcends and eclipses that of the angels of God who minister to the heirs of salvation.

Better Things (6:9)

This verse is introduced by one of those important, pivotal *buts* of Scripture. The writer had been describing the terrible state of apostates. Then he gives the warning about the peril of those who follow those whose end is "nigh unto a curse" (6:1-8). For those who truly believe there are better things, things accompanying their salvation, to experience. Among these "better things" are our labor of love, our fruitfulness in service, our kindness to fellow saints, our unceasing, full assurance of hope, our inheritance of the promises of God (6:10-12).

Surely it is *better* to be an apostle than an apostate, a possessor than a professor, a redeemed believer than a rejector. If we constantly seek all the blessings arising from our salvation, and which ought to accompany it, there is no fear of us ever putting the glorious Captain of our Salvation to an open shame. The first part of this chapter is a solemn warning to those who have never gone the whole way in surrender to the claims of Christ, and are in danger of becoming willful rejecters of the Crucified One. If they do reject Him, their end is destruction. The "better thing" God foresaw for His own was their being perfected together in perfect consummation and bliss (11:40).

Better Hope (7:19)

Actually, there is no contradiction between the psalmist's declaration "The law of the Lord is perfect" and the statement given in this verse, "The law made nothing perfect." The word *perfect,* carries the idea of "completion," and the Law in itself was not complete. Because of things it could not do it was *weak* (Rom. 8:3) or characterized by "weakness and unprofitableness" (Heb. 7:18). The Law could proclaim, but it could not provide righteousness. Its function was to point us to Christ whose righteousness was applied to us (Gal. 3:24).

The better hope, then, is coming of the Righteous One as "the end of the law for righteousness to every one that believeth" (Rom. 10:4). The Law is now disannulled, and in its place we have a better, or greater hope. This more powerful hope stands connected with the "better covenant," and the "better promises" (7:22; 8:6). It is only through this "better hope" that we can draw nigh to God. Under the Law only anointed priests were allowed to participate in the service of the sanctuary. But now, with a nobler meaning, priesthood belongs to all God's people who are saved by grace. In addition, they have, as the result of this "better hope," the prospect of "the blessed hope."

Better Testament (7:22)

The terms *testament* and *covenant* are more or less akin; thus in chapter 8, verse 6 the phrase "a better covenant" or "testament" is given in the margin. If there is any distinction to be drawn between the two words, a "covenant" is a contract or bond between living persons, while a "testament," or "will," only comes into effect after the death of the testator. For the "better hope" we now read a "better testament"; the new idea is not different in substance, but it is more definite and clear. The very promise of the "other priest" brought with it a "better hope"; the recollection of the divine oath is fitly succeeded by the mention of a *covenant* or *testament.*

What a compelling phrase this is: "By so much was Jesus made a *surety* of a better testament." In English law, a surety is a bondsman, or one bound with and for another who is primarily liable—the *principal,* or one legally liable for the debt, default, or failure of another. At Calvary, Christ made Himself liable for our debts and defaults and paid them

390

in full. He blotted out the bill of default against us. Elsewhere in the Epistle, "surety" is given as "mediator" (8:6; 9:15; 12:24). "As through the Son of Man the covenant becomes established, so in Christ, our Great High Priest, it remains secure; the words addressed by God to Him as Priest and King contain the pledge and the covenant's validity and permanence." The Old Testament ends with the word "curse," but the New with the better word of "grace."

The New Testament is "better" because it is *absolute* not *conditional* as was the Old, and *internal* not *external* as it was. The former days, then, are not better than those under grace (Eccles. 7:10). Under the Better Testament there are no *ifs*, no injunctions we must observe to do. There are only *I wills:* "I will make a new covenant. . . . I will put my laws in their mind. . . . I will be to them a God, and they shall be to me a people. . . . I will be merciful to their unrighteousness. I will remember their iniquities no more" (8:8-13). The former covenant received its dissolution at the cross. It has vanished away. Under grace, we are free from the law—"O happy condition!"

Better Promises (8:6)

The ministry of Jesus as the Mediator of a "better covenant" is more excellent than the imperfect priests of the Old Covenant. His ministry is above all others because His testament excels their law, and it is "better" because it is established upon better, or greater, promises, which are given by God. Being based upon the "better covenant," this, then, becomes the law of His kingdom and the declaration of His procedure. The man who accepts the promises by entering into the conditions laid down is dealt with according to this law.

Israel was God's earthly people, and thus His promises to them, related to their possession of, and life within, an earthly city and kingdom. The promises of the old Law were of an

391

earthly and temporal nature. But the redeemed who form the church of the Living God are a heavenly people, seated with their glorious Head in the heavenlies; and so the promises of the New Covenant, sealed with the blood of the Mediator, are heavenly, spiritual, and eternal. What exceedingly great and precious promises belong to those who have been made partakers of the divine nature (II Peter 1:4)!

Better Sacrifices (9:23)

In the previous part of the chapter the writer contrasts the First Covenant with its ministrations of the tabernacle, with the greater and more perfect Tabernacle not made with hands. The High Priest had to enter the most holy place once every year with the blood of sacrifice to atone for his own sin and the sins of the people. Jesus, the High Priest of good things to come, holy, harmless, and undefiled, shed His own blood to atone for sin and entered into the holy place of heaven, having obtained an eternal redemption for us.

The sacrifices of old were patterns, or parables of "better sacrifices." The use of the plural here need not confuse us. It arises from the studious generality of the terms of the verse. To "these things" the natural antithesis is "better sacrifices." The ministry of Christ, the true High Priest with His presentation of but *one* sacrifice, is clearly emphasized in the context: "Christ was once offered to bear the sins of many" (9:28).

> Not all the blood of beasts
> On Jewish altars slain,
> Could give the guilty conscience peace,
> Or wash away the stain.
>
> But Christ, the heavenly Lamb,
> Takes all our sins away,
> A sacrifice of nobler name,
> And richer blood than they.

392

Better Substance (10:34)

In the references to afflictions, bonds, and recompence of reward, the Pauline touch is evident. The context covering verses 32-39, are certainly reminiscent of many of the sufferings Paul says he endured for Christ's sake. Phillips' translation of the verse before us is helpful: "You knew that you had a much more solid and lasting treasure in Heaven." We can take joyfully the spoiling of our earthly possessions when we have the assurance of a better possession beyond—the one that no man can rob us of.

Patient endurance is to be rewarded when we see Him "that shall come will come, and will not tarry," for He will be our eternal treasure. Earthly riches and reputation may appear to be solid and lasting; but no matter what their nature, they are only temporal. All that awaits us in heaven is eternal.

> Heaven and earth may fade and flee,
> First-born light in gloom decline;
> But, while God and I shall be,
> I am His, and He is mine.

Better Country (11:16)

Their sojourning in the land God brought them into was to the patriarchs of old a constant symbol of their sojourning upon the earth as strangers and pilgrims. But they all died in faith, for they looked for a city without foundation whose Builder and Architect is God. Are *strangers* and *pilgrims* the same? No, for a *stranger* is a man away from home, while a *pilgrim* is one on his way home. And the saints of old, as well as ourselves, if saved by grace, are both. Here below, in this sinful world, we are strangers away from home, for our citizenship is in heaven, but as pilgrims we are on the way home to a better country, in which sin, sickness, sorrow, and Satan cannot enter.

The marvel is that before they desired that heavenly country, it had been provided, for "he prepared for them a city." But because of the lofty desire those ancient saints had, or, rather, because of their faith and love towards God in which the desire was founded, and of which, therefore, the longing for a better, or heavenly country was the expression, God was not ashamed "to be called [literally "surnamed"] their God" (see Gen. 17:7; 26:24; Exod. 3:6).

> I have a heritage of joy
>   That yet I must not see;
> The Hand that bled to make it mine
>   Is keeping it for me.

Better Resurrection (11:35)

Reference is made to "women [who] received their dead raised to life again." The two women so miraculously blessed were the widow whose son Elijah raised from the dead (I Kings 17:22-23) and the Shunammite whose son Elisha brought back from the dead (II Kings 4:35-37). But these two resurrected boys, along with those Christ raised from the dead, did not remain alive forevermore, but died again. Yet all those past heroes of the faith, some of whom died terrible deaths, believed in a better resurrection than those who were raised from the dead. They believed that when raised, at the trumpet sound, they would remain alive forever—that death would no more have dominion over them.

If we are not among those who are alive when Jesus returns for His own and go home to heaven by the way of a grave, then a glorious resurrection will be ours. Then with our Risen Lord, we shall be able to say, "We live, but were dead, and, behold, we are alive for ever more." When the corruptible puts on incorruption, then "death is swallowed up in victory" (I Cor. 15:54-55).

Hear ye the trump of God resounding,
    Saints, arise! saints, arise!
Through death's dark vaults its note rebounding,
    Saints, arise! saints, arise!

Better Blood (12:24)

The whole verse reads, "To Jesus the mediator of the new covenant, and to the blood of sprinkling, that speaketh better things than that of Abel," that is, Abel's blood. The sense here is that the shed or sprinkled blood of Jesus speaks more powerfully than that of the outpoured blood of Abel, which Cain, his brother, was guilty of. Because of the excellent sacrifice Abel offered unto God, although dead he yet speaks or is spoken of (11:4). But his blood cries out for vengeance, whereas Christ's blood pleads for mercy. Abel was a martyr, and his blood cries out from the ground and led to his slayer being branded as a murderer. Christ died as a substitute for sinners, and His blood cries out from heaven for the deliverance from the guilt and penalty of sin in all who repent and believe.

God was the avenger of "righteous Abel," but Jesus Christ the righteous is our advocate with the Father, and He is the propitiation for our sins (I John 2:1-2). The cultured, unregenerated mind may despise the preaching about the blood of Jesus, but without it there is no remission of sins.

    Abel's blood for vengeance
      Pleaded to the skies;
    But the blood of Jesus
      For our pardon cries.

Theme 37
Peter's Epistles: Suffering

Every book in the Bible was written for a purpose. The Holy Spirit, controlling the minds and pens of the forty writers of the sacred Word, saw to it that each writer emphasized a particular phase of divine truth. In the realm of ordinary literature, authors do not always disclose their purposes. Some books are written to preserve history, others for edification of another kind, others for scientific reasons, still others merely as entertainment, and so forth.

The penmen of the Bible, particularly those of the New Testament, state the purpose they have in mind as they set out to record divine truth. John Macbeath wrote that they "put on record the words and works of Christ: to persuade to faith in Christ; to give assurance of eternal life; to stimulate hope and glory and love; to correct opinion and belief; to lead to action and obedience."

When we read Peter's Epistles, we quickly realize that he wrote in such a way as to warm the hearts of his readers. His First Epistle was definitely designed to encourage the saints of God to face a time of suffering and martyrdom with stoutness of heart. And as "one of the martyr fellowship of pain," he was the best man to write such a letter. Written under the shadow of his own cross, Peter was well qualified to use militant language as he urged the believers of his day to meet the hostility of the Roman Empire without fear or retreat. This letter, which F. B. Meyer called "the child of many tears and much sorrow," was written when persecution was already upon the church. The aim of the apostle, feeling the pressure of time, was to fortify the hearts of his readers by

396

sending them a message, not of condolence but of courage. The apostle told them that suffer they would—and must!—for Christ's sake, but he urged them to lift their minds from surrounding trials to the mighty forces of God which operated on their behalf without lapse of time or power, and to the fact that "Christ also suffered."

To those who were to suffer "for his sake," the comforting reference to Christ's suffering altered their outlook on their tribulation. Now, to suffer was no longer a penalty, but a priceless privilege. The act of surveying Christ's wondrous cross transformed complaint to courage. This is why Peter's writings are not set in the minor key. Saints, emulating the example of the Master, must always glory in their griefs, sing in their sufferings, and triumph in their trials!

Time is always on the side of those who suffer for the One to whom one day is as a thousand years and a thousand years as one day (II Peter 3:8). The day of reckoning is ahead, when the righteous Judge will deal with those who ill-treat His little flock. Thus Peter exhorts his readers to keep before them the prospect of the Lord's return and allow the blessed hope to stir them to diligence as they await death (II Peter 3:14). This is why "the theme of the epistle," as E. Schuyler English reminds us in his commentary, *The Life and Letters of St. Peter,* "is the contrast between present suffering and future glory; and its purpose, to strengthen the brethren who are called upon to bear severe testing as the trial of their faith. It is sometimes called, 'The Epistle of the Living Hope.' "

To their faith, the saints must add virtue (II Peter 1:5, RV), and the word Peter uses for *virtue* implies "fearlessness, courage, endurance," or the "Mr. Valiant" whom John Bunyan describes.

Alexander Smellie tells us that there was a moment in the French Revolution when the Republic was ringed round with enemies. The Prussians were on the Rhine, the Piedmontese in the Alps, the English in the Netherlands; La Vendee had rebelled in the west, and Lyons in the east. But Danton cried: "We need audacity, and again audacity, and always audacity." It was a sanctified audacity that the apostle Peter called for in the holy war in which the saints of his day were engaged. They must be willing to dare anything and everything for Christ's sake, and be prepared to die as they dared.

Classifying Peter's teaching on suffering helps us to note its different phases. It is a word he uses somewhat freely, fifteen times, in fact. There are right and wrong kinds of suffering. There are sufferings that are mutual, material, physical, social, personal, beneficial, and vicarious. All of these aspects were dealt with by the apostle in his Epistles. Scofield's notes supply us with the following serviceable outline:

Suffering in the First Epistle of Peter is set in the light of:

1. Assured salvation (1:2-5)
2. The great glory at Christ's appearing (1:7)
3. Christ's sufferings and coming glories (1:11)
4. The believer's association with Him in both (2:20-21; 3:17-18; 4:13-15)
5. The purifying effect of suffering (1:7; 4:1-2; 5:10)
6. Glorification of Christ in the believer's patient suffering (4:15)
7. Disciplinary aspect of suffering (4:17-19; cf. I Cor. 11:31-32; Heb. 12:5-13)

Perhaps a running commentary on the suffering of Christ and those He redeemed may prove helpful.

The Sufferings of Christ

Peter repeatedly refers to the vicarious sufferings of Christ. In fact, each chapter of his First Epistle carries some allusion to the cross. First of all, he reminds us that our Lord's sufferings were foretold by the Holy Spirit in Old Testament Scripture, and that angels, with holy curiosity, sought to know more of the mystery of the cross (I Peter 1:11-12). Then the apostle makes it clear that Christ suffered for us (I Peter

2:21, 24) "who his own self bare our sins in his own body on the tree."

Quintin Hogg, who spent his fortune building the magnificent Polytechnic Institute in London for the spiritual and physical welfare of the young manhood of the city, was once asked what it cost him to erect such a pile of buildings. He replied: "Not much; just the lifeblood of one man." The building of the church—the habitation of God—cost the lifeblood of Him who came as the God-Man.

Then, as we shall presently see, Peter calls upon the saints to reciprocate the sufferings of Christ: "Follow his steps." Christ suffered for us in the flesh, and we must arm ourselves with the same mind (I Peter 4:1). Further, Peter relates the sufferings of Christ to the trials of the saints, and then forewarns his readers of martyrdom and forearms their minds. Our Lord's sufferings were all-sufficient to make atonement. The saints through the ages suffer for His sake, but He "once" suffered for sins, and the word *once* means "once for all." By His death, Christ procured a perfect salvation for a sinning race. His was a swift, quick death; but for His followers there is a continuous martyrdom: "I die daily." Peter speaks of the longsuffering of God (I Peter 3:20; II Peter 3:9), which longsuffering spells salvation (II Peter 3:15). Discipleship implies the willingness to be *long* on *suffering*. Love to the Lord suffers long. The cross is taken up daily.

The apostle then goes on to tell us that he himself was a witness of Christ's suffering (I Peter 5:1). He was present at Calvary when his Lord died. As an apostle, he submits the credential. The Gospels do not record that Peter was at the cross; nevertheless, he was an eye-witness of the crucifixion and never forgot that a similar fate awaited him (II Peter 1:13-14). Isaac Watts has taught us to sing, "When I survey the wondrous cross," but we can do so only by faith. We were not present when our Lord died. Peter's eyes, however, had been fixed upon that cross of shame. The word he uses for "witness" is from the Greek term *martus,* from which we

399

get *martyr,* and its use was limited in Peter's day to those who suffered a violent death in the cause of truth. The term is employed today in a wider and milder sense, in which some speak of a person as being a "martyr" to a certain complaint or physical illness.

The Sufferings of Saints

There are some phases of suffering that we cannot avoid and will never understand here on this earth. The dominant theme of the Book of Job is the problem of pain and suffering. Not until we reach the land where all tears are wiped away shall we be able to penetrate the mystery of so much that our loving God permits. This we do know: a good deal of suffering is our inevitable lot as fallen creatures. The entrance of sin into the world brought with it the multiplication of sorrow. If suffering is not the result of our own sin, then it comes to us as the consequences of another's transgression.

There are times when the saints of God "suffer wrongfully" (I Peter 2:19). Peter's reference is evidently associated with the slavery which was "a universal and unchallenged feature of the social life of the time." Sometimes Christian slaves were harshly treated. So, when Peter urges servants or bondslaves to be obedient to their masters and to endure patiently their unjustified suffering at the hands of men (I Peter 2:18-20), his exhortation takes on a deep significance. Their incentive in the patient endurance of forced suffering is the example of Christ. He threatened not (I Peter 2:23). He never paid His persecutors back in their own coin. Self-vindication was not in His vocabulary. Enduring the contradiction of sinners against Himself, He left Himself in the hands of God "that judgeth righteously" (I Peter 2:23). When we are the innocent recipients of any form of suffering, it is comforting to know that vengeance is God's and that He will repay.

400

Not only are we patiently to endure unjust suffering, but Peter goes on to say that, if we suffer for the sake of righteousness, we should sing over our suffering. Cruel forces should never terrorize us, the apostle courageously declares (I Peter 3:14). And, further, it is far better to suffer for truth than for evil (I Peter 3:17). If, therefore, we are called upon to suffer as Christians, we should not be ashamed of our scars but glorify God in the afflictions (I Peter 4:14, 16). This must have been the valiant spirit of John and Betty Stam, martyred missionaries to China, as they faced the terror of their heartless persecutors and executioners many years ago. Here, again, the incentive to a holy defiance amid imposed suffering is the example of our blessed Lord Himself, who suffered in the flesh. Suffering brings us into a unique fellowship. It makes us "partakers of [or "partners in"] Christ's suffering" (I Peter 4:13). It was Paul's ambition to become a "Fellow of the Order of Suffering"; thus he declared: "That I may know . . . the fellowship of his sufferings" (Phil. 3:10). Both Peter and Paul had caught this truth from their Master's own word and life (Luke 9:23). And let it be noted, the taking up of the cross is not the equivalent to enduring "a thorn in the flesh." Christ made clear that a cross consists in the denial of self, of complete obedience to His will.

The truer we are to the Lord, the greater increase of suffering we can expect. If we are not suffering in some way or other for His dear sake, then it is very likely that there is something wrong with our spiritual experience. Yet care must be taken not to court unnecessary suffering, as Peter shows (I Peter 4:15). How practical the apostle was! Useless suffering is caused when we thrust our noses into other folks' business. There are too many busy bodies in other men's matters these days.

Let us conclude on an inspiring note. If we are partakers of Christ's sufferings now, He will make us "partakers of the glory that shall be revealed" (I Peter 4:13; 5:1). Glory followed the sufferings of Christ (I Peter 1:11) and the same

401

glorious future is to be ours (I Peter 1:3-9). The apostle Peter, facing his own cruel death, knew that after his cross there would be a crown (II Peter 1:11-14). The undying wonder of heaven is the nail prints in the hands of the Saviour, still visible in His glorified body. And it will be so one day in behalf of the noble band of martyrs and sufferers for Christ's sake—theirs will be a luster, grandeur, and reward far beyond that which any angel can anticipate.

Theme 38
1 Peter: The Features of Judgment

As the distinctive note of Peter's First Epistle is preparation for victory over suffering, it is fitting that its key word is *suffer*, which, with its cognates, occurs eighteen times. Our Lord predicted sorrow and suffering for His own (Matt. 24:8-9), and when it overtakes them they are not to be ashamed, but are to glorify God in the fire of persecution. All down the ages the church has had to pass through the deep waters of reproach, suffering, and martyrdom. But the rule of Providence is that when God brings great evil and sore judgments upon the nations, He begins with the purging of His own people: "Lo, I begin to bring evil on the city which is called by my name" (Jer. 25:29); "... begin at my sanctuary" (Ezek. 9:6). And here is Peter saying, "Judgment must begin at the house of God" (I Peter 4:17). There are at least three features of this particular judgment to distinguish.

1. The Season of Judgment

"The time is come ... begin." The phrase "because the time is come" indicates that this particular judgment was about to begin when Peter wrote, and the word "begin" shows that in his mind it would be a long process. The "judgment" in question was the fierce persecution the early Christians were to suffer. Under succeeding Roman emperors countless numbers of saints did perish. Satanic hostility was experienced by Peter's Lord, then by the "Big Fisherman" himself who, like his Lord, was crucified. This torment of the saints will not cease until Satan is cast into the lake of fire (Rev. 20:10).

403

Judgment has not yet touched sinners. Their pleasure and prosperity seem to be uninterrupted here, but Scripture affirms that unless they repent they will be suddenly destroyed, and that without remedy. God suffers His own to pass through tribulation now. They have their hell now, but heaven hereafter. With the sinner it is the reverse. Judgment for the church, then, represents severe trial and adversity, but the trial of her faith is much more precious than gold that perishes. Suffering for Christ's sake shapes character and proves the reality of our profession.

Stormy days were already overtaking the church when Peter wrote his Epistle. Christ had predicted them, and now they were about to break forth in all their terror. But, as F. B. Meyer says in his commentary on First Peter, "Bitter as they were, such times are needed—needed as the North-east wind to break off the dead and useless timber in the Spring: needed as the winnower's fan to separate the chaff from the wheat. Without these searching times of judgment, the Church becomes filled with those who make a profession of godliness, but deny its power; whilst without them even the godly and genuine are apt to become too luxurious and self-indulgent, wrapt in slumber, and indifferent to the needs of the world. So from time to time it is needful for God to set Himself to the work of discrimination, of crisis, of judgment."

Has not the time come for the judgment of God upon the life and conduct of the present day church? Is she not in need of a drastic overhaul, and deep searching of heart, and of the disciplinary work of the Holy Spirit? We can, of course, speak of the church in general terms, forgetting that it only becomes what its members make of it. Therefore, collectively and individually, the sifting of God is necessary.

2. The Nature of Judgment

It is imperative to distinguish between the many judgments

mentioned in Scripture. There are future judgments for nations, saints, sinners, Satan, and apostate angels. There is a present judgment related to the believer. "When we are judged, we are chastened of the Lord" (I Cor. 11:32). The Spirit is the scrutinizer, examiner, and judge who thoroughly searches the heart; and we need more of His ministry as "The Spirit of Judgment" sifting and exposing all that is sinful, carnal, and worldly in our hearts and habits.

This is a divine judgment.

Human judgment is not always just or merciful. It is easy to judge each other, and our conclusions are often wrong. But divine judgment is always right and for our present good. Through the Word, read or preached, the Holy Spirit reveals where correction is necessary in character and conduct.

This is a minute judgment.

God said that He would search Jerusalem with candles (Zeph. 1:12). If something small and precious is lost in a corner of the home, then, like the woman in the parable, we take a candle or similar small handy light to search for it. This is the kind of thorough inspection the psalmist had in mind when he prayed, "Search me, O Lord!" (Ps. 139). Once God takes over the investigation, He leaves no corner unsearched but goes into every nook of our being, exposing things large and small. Such an honest search may prove humiliating, but what His light reveals His blood can cleanse. If deep penitence results from the judicial work of the Spirit, divine mercy operates for our rectification.

This is a gracious judgment.

When judgment begins in your life and mine, it is not condemnatory but corrective. Our present judgment is not

405

for destruction, but for sanctification; not our condemnation, but for consecration. God never afflicts us willingly, or without cause, but judges, penetrates our motives, actions, and relationships for our spiritual good. His chastening is always, if not pleasant, profitable.

This is a constant judgment.

When it begins with the saint it never ends during his earthly pilgrimage. At the close of each day we should check up with God and see where we have come short of His glory. Long accounts are hard to settle. As we walk in the light, it keeps revealing our blemishes, and the blood keeps on cleansing us from them.

3. The Recipients of Judgment

Peter cites the objects of God's judicial work, namely, "the house of God" and "them that obey not the gospel of God." Saints and sinners are both included. The judgment of the church is here and now; the judgment of the lost at the Great White Throne—the most awesome of all judgments. Although the disobedient are often found within the church, Peter distinguishes the saved from the lost.

"The House of God"

This term is equivalent to the church, which Peter describes as a "spiritual house" and singles out for the commencement of divine judgment: "Begin at my sanctuary." Unless the church is living in obedience to the will of God, she cannot influence those outside her borders who do not obey God. As the church, or any local church, is made up of members, we have a personal responsibility to keep right with God. Are we partakers of His holiness? Do we live in accord with His mind and will? Do our afflictions, sorrows, losses, make us less selfish and more fit for His kingdom? God hates sin; and He hates it most in those who are His and will never rest unless He cleanses them from its defiling touch. Sins of saints are more grievous than those who do not know the gospel because the sins saints commit are sins against light and knowledge.

Corporately

Taking the church as a whole, or churches in particular, is it not evident that because of their impotence in a world of need, the time of judgment is overdue? Is it not the responsibility of each church to face up to the necessity of regulating its life by New Testament standards? Are practices condoned contrary to the mind of Him who founded the church? In at least three realms there is need for spiritual readjustment:

1. In the conception of the Church's institution and ministry
2. In the methods of support and maintenance
3. In the presentation of modern doctrines

Individually

As any house or church of God is made up of units, it behooves each member to subject himself to heart-searching tests; to go to his knees and discover what hinders the revival the church so sorely needs. Is it not time that the rod of judgment fell upon many hindrances to the manifestation of the mighty power of God? To list only a few:

Our spiritual impoverishment. We have profession, but no power. We are always confessing our sin, but do nothing about its removal. Thus our church makes no difference to the lost world outside.

Our worldly conformity. The miracle of Pentecost was the placing of the church in the world. The masterpiece of Satan has been the placing of the world in the church. Did not

407

Jesus say that His church would be in the world (as a witness) but not of it? Today, however, she is very much of the world. The marks of separation from worldly policies and pursuits are conspicuous by their absence.

Our carnal-mindedness. Pride and prejudice, criticisms and divisions mar the atmosphere of love in a church. Instead of fighting together against our common satanic foe, we burn up precious time fighting each other.

Our desecration of God's Holy Day. What disregard there is for preserving the one day in the week that God claims for Himself! Multitudes of church members feel that if they give God an hour in the morning, that relieves them of their obligation toward Him, and the rest of the day is theirs to do as they like with.

We live in an age of increasing worldliness, materialism, and iniquity. Unbelief and agnosticism are rife in theological circles so that young men enter the ministry doubting their beliefs, and believing their doubts. If the church is to be as a signpost pointing the way back to God, there will have to come a thorough searching and cleansing of her courts. Christ established His church in the world to honor Him and to bring lost souls to Him. His declared mission was to seek and to save the lost. Is this not His church's preeminent task as well?

"Those that obey not the gospel of God"

This aspect of divine judgment is solemn, sure, and certain. If God deals drastically with those who profess to be saved in order to make them channels of blessing, what will the end be of those who willfully reject the gospel? If saints who depart from the revealed will of God suffer, what terrible perdition must befall those who spurn that will altogether? The believer knows that no matter how grievous present judgment may be, that suffering cannot pass the limit of his mortal life. With the unbeliever, however, it is different, because no matter what tempest may break over his head, he knows that is only the beginning of sorrows for him. For the believer, the best is yet to be. For the unbeliever, the worst is yet to be, seeing that through death he passes into unrelieved misery and outer darkness. For the believer, the sufferings of this present time are nothing in comparison with the seething abyss, or bottomless pit awaiting the unbeliever.

Peter concludes his paragraph about the righteous and the sinner in judgment with the comforting words about the committal of the soul to God. How safe and strong we are in the hands of such a faithful Creator and Redeemer! None can pluck us out of those mighty and merciful hands of His. "Without anxiety or alarm you may look out from them on the wrecks of matter and the crash of worlds. Those hands shall ultimately bear you, as they did your Lord, through all the heavens, and set you down at His own right hand in glory."

Theme 39
John's Epistles: The Rapture

At the outset of this summary it is fitting to ask what we mean when we speak of the Rapture of the church. The actual word itself, although constantly used by all lovers and students of prophetic Scriptures, is not found in them. *Rapture* is associated with "rapt," which means the fact or act of being transported from one place to another, and is found four times—

In the act of the Spirit snatching away Philip (Acts 8:39)

In the experience of Paul caught up to Paradise (II Cor. 12:2-4)

In the snatching away of the man child (Rev. 12:5)

In the disappearance of the saints when Christ returns (I Thess. 4:17)

Rapture, related to *harpago,* meaning "raptured, or snatched away," is from the Latin *Rapio,* a form of which is "rapus," the root of our English words "rapt" and "rapture," a term found in English literature. For instance, writing of one who is carried away by violence, Samuel Daniel says: "Now as the Libyan lions outrushing from his fen rapts all away." Then Edmund Spenser, describing waters carried away, sees, "the circled waters rapt with whirling spray." Matthew Arnold, in "The Scholar Gypsy," has the lines,

> Rapt, twirling in thy hand a wither'd spray
> And waiting for the spark from Heaven to fall.

As the lion outrushing rapts all away, and as the whirling pool rapts with whirling spray, so will the Lion of Judah seize His own from a ruthless world as He took Elijah in a whirl-

410

wind to the skies. Thus, properly, *rapture* is a proper term to employ when speaking of the removal to heaven of the waiting church when Christ returns to the air, and rapts or speedily removes her to heaven, there to be with Him forever (I Thess. 4:13-18).

Another common meaning of the word *rapture* is that of "ecstatic and transporting joy," which, too, will be the experience of the church when rapt aloft to be with Christ. Robert Browning wrote of "the wise thrush," and its "first fine careless rapture." William Wordsworth describes one whose death he had heard of as, "The rapt one of the godlike forehead." Even Robert Burns used the word in the same sense:

> Ev'n ministers, they hae ben kenn'd
>   In holy rapture
> A rousing whid at times to vent
>   And nail't wi Scripture.

But our rapturous joy, when we see Jesus, will far outstrip all forms of ecstatic emotion that men experience here on earth. When transported to the skies ours will be an ecstasy unknown before.

> What an anthem that will be,
> Ringing out our love to Thee,
> Pouring out our rapture sweet
> At Thine own all glorious feet.

As we have already hinted, it is a most profitable exercise to gather out from any given book of the Bible the various aspects of a selected theme, being careful not to build up a doctrine on it. The Bible is a progressive revelation, as well as a complete one, and thus attention must be given to what other books record on such a particular theme, and thereby, view it as a whole. We are now to concentrate on what the apostle John has to say about the second advent of our Lord in his Epistles. The reader can follow out this plan by studying what he had to say in his Gospel and also in his Book of

411

the Revelation. Spoken of as leaning on the bosom of Jesus and as the disciple He loved, John lived near to the heart of his Lord and shared His secrets as, perhaps, no other disciple did while they were together. He, it was, who recorded the memorable promise that Jesus would return to gather His redeemed ones unto Himself (John 14:1-3). Here, then, in his First and Second Epistles are the references to the fact and features of the Rapture. The Third Epistle has no mention of Christ's return, an omission shared by Philemon. (These two Epistles—III John and Philemon—are the only two books out of the twenty-nine that form the New Testament that have no direct reference to the promised return of Christ.)

Sign of the Rapture

John has much to say about the appearance of the antichrist and of antichrists as constituting a very definite sign of the second coming of Christ. Listing the verses, we can see at a glance the characteristics of spurious Christs: "Ye have heard that antichrist shall come, even now are there many antichrists; whereby we know that it is the last time" (I John 2:18). (That those described were once in the church is proved by the next verse, "They went out from us, but they were not of us.") "He is antichrist, that denieth the Father and the Son" (2:22-23). "This is that spirit of antichrist, whereof ye have heard that it should come; and even now already is it in the world" (4:2-3). "Many deceivers are entered into the world, who confess not that Jesus Christ is come in the flesh. This is a deceiver and an antichrist" (II John 7).

Both the plural and singular are used, for antichrists are the forerunners of the dreaded antichrist—a term used only by John. Apostates, like Hymenaeus, Alexander, Philetus, and Diotrephes were caricatures or counterfeits of Christ. Who or what is an *antichrist*? *Anti* means "instead of," or "make-believe, spurious." Paul gives us the description of *the* antichrist he calls "the man of sin . . . the son of perdition" (II Thess. 2:3-4), who is revealed as being in opposition to or antagonistic to the claims of Christ. Not only does he manifest hostility toward Him, but exalts himself as God. Usurping the authority of Christ, he presents himself in place of Christ, or under the guise of Christ. Before the coming of the true Christ as King of kings, this false Christ will ape the Christ of God.

As to the manifest features of an antichrist or any anti-Christian teaching, John says these are the denial of the Fatherhood of God and the eternal Sonship of Christ (I John 2:22-23). Anti-God and anti-Christ are the marks of *the* antichrist that it would seem Christ had in mind when He said that the world would eventually worship one who should "come in his own name" (John 5:43). Our Lord also prophesied of "many false prophets"; and "*the* false prophet" is one of the "many" and becomes head of them all (Rev. 13:16; 19:20). As Seiss, the renowned expositor, puts it, "He will be the consummation of all false prophets, as he is by emphasis *the* false prophet in the same way that the first beast is *the* Antichrist of the 'many anti-Christs.' " Is it not tragic to reflect that we have some of these anti-Christ deceivers in clerical garb today? Openly they declare that God is dead, and that Christ may have been a son of a man, but was certainly not *the* Son of Man, or *the* Son of God. Too many of our theological colleges are riddled with professors and tutors who, by their anti-Christian teaching, are preparing the way for the manifestation of the predicted antichrist.

Shame at the Rapture

To John, the second coming was not merely a doctrine but a dynamic; not only a truth to be accepted by the mind, but a hope influencing every phase of life. In fact, he linked exhortations to practical duties to the majority of his references to Christ's return. Here is the aged apostle's appeal,

"And now, little children, abide in him; that, when he shall appear, we may have confidence, and not be ashamed before him at his coming" (I John 2:28). Phillips, in his New Testament in Modern Speech, expresses it thus, "Little children, remember to live continually in Him. So that if He were suddenly to reveal Himself we should still know exactly where we stand, and should not have to shrink away from His presence."

We are not to be afraid at the thought of His coming, nor ashamed before Him when He appears, or when we stand before Him at the beme, or judgment seat, of Christ. John stresses the opposite to fear and shame in his declaration that "herein is our love made perfect, that we may have boldness in the day of judgment: because as he is, so are we in this world" (I John 4:17). If we are living in the light of the Rapture, then we shall not shrink away with shame because of unconfessed, uncleansed sin, but welcome our entrance into the presence of the Redeemer. If we are ashamed of Him now, then we are a shame to Him, and will be abashed when we ultimately see Him. Such a feeling of disgrace arises from something that has been done contrary to the will and purpose of the Lord (II Cor. 10:8; Phil. 1:20). May we so live as to be ready to meet Him with a joy unspeakable and full of glory! If we allow "the blessed hope" to sanctify us, then no shame will be ours when He comes.

Sharers of the Rapture

John uses two precious filial terms to describe those who will participate in the Rapture, namely, "the sons of God," and "little children." How amazed John is that such a privileged relationship is all because of the love of our heavenly Father (I John 3:1-2). The emphasis is on the *now*— "Beloved, now are we the sons of God." *Now*—not a future anticipation but a present position. "God sent forth his son . . . that we might receive the adoption of sons. And because ye are sons, God hath sent forth the Spirit of his Son into your hearts, crying, Abba, Father" (Gal. 4:4-7). We are His sons, because we were "born of him" (I John 2:29). Actually the phrase here means "born *out of* God." We are part of His own Being, being "born . . . of the Spirit" (John 3:5). In regeneration we were made partakers of the divine nature. "Sons of God," then, is a title that expresses divine life and kinship. Because, through grace, we are His sons, He will bring us to glory (Heb. 2:10). No wonder John said, *"Beloved,"* for this is an amazing truth that because of His love, God calls us His sons (I John 3:1-2)!

"Little children" is another characteristic designation for those who are the Lord's. The word *little* as used here has no connection with age or size. Six times over in his First Epistle, John employs this appellation of tender and caressing love (2:1, 12, 28; 3:18; 4:4; 5:21). Possibly it was a reference to John's advanced age—about ninety years old when he wrote the Epistle—and, being old, he felt a fatherly care for those who were his spiritual family. The affectionate word for "children"—*teknia*—means "born ones," or, as the Scotch would say, *bairns,* and the connections of the term are profitable to observe. C. I. Scofield divides the Epistle in this manner:

The Little Children and Fellowship (1:1 – 2:14)

The Little Children and the Secular and Religious World (2:15-28)

The Little Children Knowing Each Other (2:29 – 3:10)

The Little Children Living Together (3:11-24)

The Little Children and False Teachers (4:1-6)

The Little Children Assured and Warned (4:7 – 5:21)

The thought of shame and misery of sin always melted the loving, holy heart of John, and so he cautioned to his spiritual children that they should "sin not" (2:1). Goder, in his commentary on John, quotes at length the story of Eusebius, one of the Early Fathers, about the apostle calling a lapsed youth, "My child." This young convert of his turned again to

415

"the weak and beggarly elements" of the world and became a thief. John found his way to the robber's haunt, but the young man, on seeing him, took to flight. John, forgetful of his age, ran after him, crying, "O my son, why dost thou fly from me thy father? Thou, an armed man—I, an old and defenseless one? Have pity on me! My son, do not fear! There is still hope of life for thee. I wish myself to take the burden of all before Christ. If it is necessary, I will die for thee, as Christ died for me. Stop! Believe! It is Christ who sends me." How could the backsliding youth resist a passionate appeal like that!

Both terms, "sons of God" and "little children," imply a birth-relationship. Being the human agent of the regeneration of those he addressed, John speaks of them in language associated with a spiritual family. Only those born anew by the Holy Spirit are the sons, or children of God. Those out of Christ may be the creatures of God, but they are not His children. Rather, they are children of disobedience. Jesus told those who resisted His authority and claims that they were children of the devil; that he (the devil) was their father, not the heavenly Father (John 8:41-44). How certain we should be that ours is the spiritual relationship qualifying us to participate in the Rapture!

Surety of the Rapture

Having heard his Lord say, "I will come again, and receive you unto myself" (John 14:3), the apostle was fully persuaded that his beloved Master would redeem His promise and appear the second time. John was also present when the heavenly evangelists announced, "This same Jesus, which is taken up from you into heaven, shall so come in like manner as ye have seen him go into heaven" (Acts 1:11). There is, therefore, the ring of certainty about the apostle's advent declarations. "When he *shall* appear" (I John 2:28; 3:2).

To appear means "to be evident." *To be manifested* im-

416

plies something more than appearance. A person may appear under a false guise or without disclosure of his true identity. But when Jesus comes we are to see Him *as He is.* He will be revealed in His true character. This will be the *Parousia,* the Greek word for "personal presence." Jesus said, *"I* will come again," and John, believing in the personal return of his Lord, could pray, "Even so, come, Lord Jesus." Appearing to His own when He returns, He will not then appear to the world. This final phase of His appearing will take place when He comes back to earth to usher in His millennial reign.

The "when" John used (or "if," as some old texts read: "if he shall appear") does not express any doubt as to the *fact* of Christ's return, but rather uncertainty as to the circumstances. The *fact* is certain because of all Christ is within Himself as "the Truth." He was not a man that He should lie. Having said, therefore, that He would come again, He must appear the second time—and He will. But the *time* of His coming is as uncertain as the *fact* is certain, hence, the necessity to watch as we wait so as to be ready when He suddenly breaks through the clouds saying, "Arise, my love, my fair one, and come away!"

Similarity at the Rapture

Without any fear of contradiction, John affirms, "We know that, when he shall appear, we shall be like him" (I John 3:2). Like Him! It is beyond the human mind to fully comprehend all that is implied by this declaration of similarity between Jesus and ourselves. We are to see Him as He is. What will He be like when He comes again? Why, the very same as He was when He ascended on high after His resurrection! The disciples who saw Him disappear were consoled when the two men from heaven told them that "this *same* Jesus" would return in like manner as He vanished. Thus, physically and morally, we are to resemble Him. Is this not the truth Paul taught the Philippians who looked for the

417

Saviour from heaven?—"Who shall change our vile body [or the body of our humiliation], that it may be fashioned like unto his glorious body" (3:21). *Then* our likeness to Him will be complete.

The certainty of such a transformation and the unknown glory associated with it is implied in the phrase "It doth not yet appear what we shall be." Through matchless love we are *now* the sons of God, but a still greater divine privilege will be ours when we see the Son of God and are changed into His image. The more we see Him as He is reflected in His Word, the greater is our desire to live like Him now, and the more intense is our longing to awake in His likeness. D. L. Moody was greatly blessed by the ministry of Andrew Bonar at Northfield when he preached with great effect. As he came to leave for his native Scotland, Moody asked Bonar to send a photo of himself, which he did. But on the back of the photograph Bonar had written, "This is not very good of me, but I expect a better likeness when Jesus comes, for the Bible says, 'I shall be like him.' "

> "Upheld by hope," that wondrous hope
> That I shall see His face.
> And to His likeness be conformed
> When I have run the race.

Sanctifying Influence of the Rapture

"Hope," it has been said, "is the more of desire." John goes on to say that "every man that hath this hope in him purifieth himself, even as he is pure" (I John 3:3). This is "the blessed hope" Paul wrote about that enables us to live "soberly, righteously, and godly, in this present world" (Titus 2:12-13). Alas, however, the saintliest on earth are not without blame or blemish!

> The highest hopes we cherish here,
>   How fast they tire and faint;
> How many a spot defiles the robe
>   That wraps an earthly saint;
> Oh, for a heart that never sins:
>   Oh, for a soul washed white;
> Oh, for a voice to praise our King,
>   Nor weary day or night!

Such an aspiration will be fulfilled when we see Jesus, the perfection of purity. It is as *sons* of God that we have this hope, and purity is one of the requirements of sonship. We cannot live just any kind of a life if we truly believe that our holy Lord may return at any moment. The phrase "purifies himself" is in the present tense and implies "constantly purifies himself." It is the same thought the apostle has when he tells us that "the blood of Jesus Christ his Son cleanseth [keeps on cleansing] us from all sin" (I John 1:7). As when our spiritual light increases we discover more in our life that is alien to His holy mind and will, so will the experience of this continual cleansing become deeper.

> With such a blessed hope in view,
>   We would more holy be;
> More like our risen, glorious Lord,
>   Whose face we soon shall see.

Service Rewarded at the Rapture

Coming to John's Second Epistle, we find that the key word is "the Truth," that is, the whole body of revealed truth as found in Scripture. The apostle makes it clear that this is our sole authority for doctrine and life, as well as our unfailing resource in our age of spiritual declension and apostacy. Fidelity to doctrine is not only a test of whether we are in reality sons of God, but also an evidence of our readiness for Christ's return (II John 7-10).

"Look to yourselves," or, "Take care of yourselves," is a call to self-examination to discover whether we are abiding in the doctrine of Christ. If we are not, then we are not of His (II John 9).

"Lose not those things which we have wrought." We must be careful not to throw away all the labor that has been spent on us. Paul was always cautious lest, after having preached to others, he should become a castaway, or disapproved, or thrown to one side. If we are truly sons, we must lose many things, but we cannot lose Christ. It is possible (how sad if such should happen!) to lose the graces of the Christian life that recommend Christ to others.

"But . . . we receive a full reward." We are to live and labor, not for *a* reward, but for the "full reward"—"full" implying here "completeness" or "the utmost," as "full corn in the ear"—not able to hold any more. Ellicott comments, "The diminution of the reward would be in proportion to the gravity of the error. The reward would be the peace of God which passeth all understanding, the blessed stability, firmness, and joy which truth and love communicate." (See Gal. 4:2; Col. 3:24.)

Are we to receive the *full* reward that loyalty to Christ, His truth, and His cause merit? A reward, let us remember, must be earned. We do not work for a "gift." It would not be a gift if we had to labor for it. But the degree of our reward at the judgment seat of Christ depends upon our love and loyalty to Him (I Cor. 3:12-15; see Matt. 25:14-30). If we are unfaithful to the Lord and His Word, we do not lose our soul, but we do lose our reward. The tragedy is that many of us will stand before Christ at that day with a saved soul but a lost life—nothing to our credit. We shall be saved—yet so as by fire. May grace be ours to labor for the highest reward the righteous Judge can bestow!

We close with John's appeal, "Little children, it is the last

420

hour" (2:18). As we are living in the period just before the close of this age of grace, it is imperative to make the apostle's three safeguards our very own—

The Lord above, as our Advocate (2:1)

The Spirit within, as the Unction (2:20)

The Word in hand and in heart (2:14)

The recognition and realization of these facts make us more than conquerors, and by knowing and doing the will of God we learn the secret of living forever (2:17).

Toil, workman, toil; thy gracious Lord
Will give thee soon a full reward:
Then toil, obedient to His Word,
Until He come.

Theme 40
Jude: The Apostasy

In these days of deepening apostasy, we need to live in the priceless Letter of Jude. He was no middle-of-the-roader. Conspicuous for his spiritual discernment, Jude exposed the apostates of his day in no uncertain terms.

Made up of only twenty-five verses, a distinction the Epistle shares with the Book of Philemon, this closing Epistle of the Bible depicts the hopeless prospect of all those who abandon a God-given faith and, on the other hand, the blessedness of those who abide faithful to the Lord and His Word. As the last Epistle, it has a pertinent message for these last days. "The Peril of Apostasy and the Profit of Faith" is how C. J. Rolls summarizes this Letter in his masterly synoptical study of Jude. S. Maxwell Coder calls his studies of this Epistle, *The Acts of the Apostates.* Without doubt Jude condenses for us the truth of the previous twenty-five books of the New Testament, and introduces us to The Revelation. Here we have *multum in parvo* (much in little), which feature led Origen, one of the early fathers, to say of Jude: "This is an Epistle of few lines, but one filled full of the strong words of heavenly grace."

Our own study of Jude brought to light the interesting fact that its writer built his brief message on the principle of the triad. Believing with Solomon that a threefold cord is not quickly broken, Jude groups truths together in trinities. Let us now trace some of these trinities in unity.

A Threefold Relationship

The Epistle opens with a suggestive trinity of facts: "Jude the servant of Jesus Christ and brother of James."

1. A National Relationship

The name "Jude" not only relates him to his matchless Letter, stamping him as the writer of it, but also to the Jewish people. *Jude* or *Juda* is related to *Judah,* meaning "praise" or "praise the Lord." It is quite possible that he was a descendant, like the Master Himself, of the tribe of Judah.

2. A Spiritual Relationship

With due humility, Jude speaks of himself as "the servant of Jesus Christ." He could have called himself "the brother of Jesus Christ," for according to the flesh this was his relationship. From Matthew 13:55-56 and Mark 6:3, we discover that, after the marriage of Joseph and Mary, several sons and daughters entered their home in a natural way. The Roman Catholic Church erroneously teaches that Mary never had other children but was a perpetual virgin. The lists given make Jude or Judas (not Iscariot) the fourth son born to Mary, after the birth of Christ.

Jude, however, places the spiritual above the natural, even as the Lord Jesus, his half-brother, had taught. "Whosoever shall do the will of my Father, which is in heaven, the same is my brother, and sister, and mother" (Matt. 12:46-50). Being a servant of Christ, then, was much more important to Jude than being bound to Him by human ties. The lowliest Christian is nearer kin to Christ than those of closest earthly bonds.

3. A Natural Relationship

Jude and James were full brothers in that they came from the same parents. Mary was the mother also of Jesus, but He had no earthly father—He was "conceived of the Holy Ghost." Much discussion centers around the identity of this particular James. This we know, that Jude must have meant the one mentioned among the brothers and sisters of Christ.

A Threefold Position

Jude gives us a threefold portrayal of those to whom he addressed his Epistle: *sanctified, preserved,* and *called.* Some scholars reverse the order of the first verse and make it read: "the called ones, beloved in God the Father, and preserved in Jesus Christ"; and, in grace, this is the right order.

1. Called Ones

As the result of the Spirit's ministry, a believer is a "called one." After hearing the divine call, he called upon the name of the Lord and was saved. Alas, "many are called but few are chosen." Our churches possess many who are *cold,* and some who are *frozen.*

2. Beloved in God the Father

While some of the oldest manuscripts read "beloved of God" instead of "sanctified by God," both designations are true. As the beloved of God we are set apart from sin unto God. As the objects and recipients of His love, we likewise share His holiness. All His called ones are saints. Some, however, are more saintly than others.

3. Preserved in Jesus Christ

Whether we accept "kept for Jesus Christ," or "preserved in Jesus Christ," the thought is the same. We are kept *by* and *for* Him. Preservation is what our Lord prayed for on behalf of His own (John 17:11). As we shall see, "kept" is one of the key words of Jude. How privileged we are to be included among those the Lord preserves!

A Threefold Salutation

The triad is characteristic of salutations in most of the Epistles. Paul expressed himself in similar fashion (Titus 1:4).

1. Mercy

This attribute has reference to the past, in spite of all its record of weakness and failure. We would never have become "called ones" had it not been for divine mercy. And until our last breath, all of us will be deep in debt to such mercy.

2. Peace

This is our Lord's legacy to His beloved ones. "My peace I give unto thee." Having thus peace *with* God through Christ, we have peace *from* God amid all the vexations of life.

3. Love

What preserving love is His! As abiding love, it assures our future both here and hereafter. These three qualities are to be multiplied unto us. We are not to have barely enough to get along with. God is never niggardly in His giving. As Dr. Rolls expresses it: "There is an abundance of all three, namely, lots of mercy to keep our endangered feet, leagues of peace to garrison our enraptured hearts, and loads of love to constrain our ennobled wills."

A Threefold Purpose

In verses 3 and 4, Jude tells us how he came to write his Epistle. He commences this portion with "beloved," an endearing term that he uses three times (vv. 3, 17, 20). He then states that, with all diligence, he set out to write of three things: of the common salvation; of the faith delivered unto the saints; and of certain apostates who had wormed their way into the church.

1. *"To write unto you of the common salvation" (v. 3)*

It would seem as if this was the initial purpose of Jude as he took up his pen, and what a message on salvation he could have written! The word *common* has a twofold meaning: first, "something cheap, inexpensive"; second, "something universal, for all." English parks are called "commons," seeing that anyone can use these facilities. It could not be the first meaning that Jude intended, for there is nothing cheap about our salvation! It cost Jesus Christ His ruby blood to redeem us. No, it was the second thought that Jude had in mind, a salvation for all.

2. *"To write unto you, and exhort you that ye should earnestly contend for the faith" (v. 3)*

The general theme of Jude is the defense of the faith in an age of apostasy. The word Jude uses for "contend" is more accurately translated "agonize." It is the same word we find in Luke 13:24: "Strive to enter in." Too many are hesitant and weak-kneed when it comes to the defense of the faith. Others contend, all right, but are so contentious, so hard, so loveless. The truth must be defended in love. By "the faith," we understand the whole body of revealed truth, and this faith has been delivered once for all to the saints. Therefore "the faith" is unchangeable, irrevocable, and no man dare tamper with it. If he does, dread judgment will overtake him.

3. *"There are certain men crept in unawares" (v. 4)*

In this solemn warning, Jude describes the apostates in no uncertain terms. Three traits distinguish them: they creep in unawares; they turn the grace of God into lasciviousness; and they deny the only Lord God.

These "certain men" are "ungodly men." Six times over, a double triad, Jude uses the term "ungodly." *Crept* means "enter by stealth." In a crafty, unnoticed way, the modernist steals into the life of the church. How suave and subtle he is, but how dangerous his work! How tragic it is that destroyers of the faith have crept into some of our seminaries, colleges, and churches! They are traitors to a sacred trust.

426

Wrong thinking leads to wrong living; liberty leads to license. The grace of God is turned into lasciviousness. What matters, they seem to think, though one be as cruel as Nero, as greedy as Judas, or as worldly as Demas, for "God is love," so why worry? How deceptive it is thus to trade upon the love of God, forgetting His hatred for anything alien to His holy mind and will.

The lowest step on the ladder of apostasy is now reached: "Certain men . . . denying the only Lord God, and our Saviour Jesus Christ" (or "our only Master and Lord, Jesus Christ"). Jude uses the Greek word *despotes,* from which we have the English word *despot* meaning "sovereign master." Thus, "Modernism, pressed to its logical conclusion, is the denial of Christ's sovereignty. The critics of the Word soon become the critics of the Christ, who kept that Word inviolate and constantly upheld its complete authority." Jude says of these apostates that they were ordained to condemnation. What else can they expect but the severest condemnation, in face of their secret and subtle, then open and blatant destruction of the faith?

A Threefold Historical Apostate Reference

As a Jew, Jude was familiar with Old Testament history and, in verses 5-7, he uses his knowledge with telling effect. By the Spirit's unction Jude discerns how wonderfully the Lord has acted in the past with people, angels, and cities, and he skillfully uses his Scripture examples of apostasy as a warning to other apostates. We have in order, as Dr. Rolls expresses it: "Israel's infidels (v. 5), angelic anarchy (v. 6), and Sodom's sensuality (v. 7)."

1. The Unbelief of Israel (v. 5)

Although Israel was a highly privileged nation, signally blessed of God, yet there were those within it who were guilty of hardening their hearts against the Lord. Their inward state did not correspond to their outward standing. Guilty of perversity and disobedience, they perished in the wilderness.

2. The Fallen Angels (v. 6)

Are we not warranted in linking this declension of the angels to Genesis 6? Is there not a connection between the angels leaving their first estate or original abode and function, and cohabiting with the daughters of men? (See more clearly in the writer's booklet, *Are These the Last Days?*) For their terrible apostasy, these angels are reserved unto the appropriate time of their punishment, perhaps at the Great White Throne (II Peter 2:4). The same bonds of darkness await all present-day apostates.

3. Sodom and Gomorrha (v. 7)

This verse should challenge all who deny the faith and the Lord who bought them, seeing the destroyed, sensuous cities are "set forth as an example." Whereas the evil inhabitants of Sodom and Gomorrha were consumed by material fire, the judgment of *eternal* fire awaits them who deny the faith. Our Lord, you will remember, declared that those rejecters around Him would suffer a more fearful catastrophe: "It shall be more tolerable for the land of Sodom in the day of judgment, than for thee" (Matt. 11:24).

One expositor of the Epistle that we are considering says of these three warnings: "The first is the *worldly;* the second, the *satanic;* and the third, the *fleshly* opposition to the divine will."

A Threefold Apostate Sign (vv. 8-10)

A comparison of Jude with II Peter 2 reveals a remarkable

similarity of language describing the work and ways of apostates. The one portion, however, is independent of the other. Think of this unholy trinity; filthy dreamers who defile the flesh, despise dominions, and speak evil of dignities!

1. These Filthy Dreamers Who Defile the Flesh

Man's heart is naturally defiled. It is desperately wicked. But what a designation to use of religious professors! Their dreamings defile the flesh. Distorted visions, couched in the very language of Christianity, are common to Modernism. Apostates are those who reject "the faith" yet retain its outward form (II Tim. 3:5; 4:3-4).

2. Who Despise Dominions

What is known as destructive criticism, or liberalism, is actually spiritual lawlessness. Christ's authority is discredited and denied. It is not, "What saith the Lord?" but, "What saith our own rational mind?"

3. Who Speak Evil of Dignities

In verses 9 and 10, Jude gives us an illustration of treating with contempt those who are vested with authority. Michael, in spite of his high angelic rank, would not dare rebuke the devil. Today, however, there is revolt against all authority. It is an age of lawlessness. The Modernist rebels against the authority of Christ and the Word that reveals Him.

A Threefold Apostate Corruption

In verse 11, Jude gives us a trinity of men whose names stand out as revolters against God and His authority, and upon whom divine judgment fell. Cain, Balaam, and Korah were brought out of the dim past to warn all those of the

Church Age that God's attitude toward rebellion against His authority has not changed.

1. The Way of Cain (Gen. 4)

The son of Adam preferred to offer the fruit of his own labor rather than a sacrificial victim as an offering to God. C. I. Scofield says: "Cain is a type of the religious man, who believes in God and in 'religion,' but after his own will, and who rejects redemption by blood. Compelled as a teacher of religion to explain the atonement, the apostate teacher explains it away." Modernism, the religion of Cain, is *fleshly confidence.*

2. The Error of Balaam (Num. 22 – 25; 31:16)

We must distinguish between the *error* of Balaam (v. 11), the *way* of Balaam (II Peter 2:15), and the *doctrine* of Balaam (Rev. 2:14). Balaam's error was a greedy grasping for material reward. He tried to serve God and mammon. He was a two-faced prophet. Balaam "stood undecided at the crossroads facing the appeal and aspiration for righteousness, and the lure and lust for material renown, and there perished," says Dr. Rolls. Monetary advantages, popularity, and men's praise and approval form a snare. Balaam's error was *love of present gain.*

3. The Gainsaying of Korah (Num. 16)

Korah perished because of his usurpation of spiritual privileges. He sought to rebel against Moses and Aaron, God's representatives. He wanted equality with them. He tried to bring them down to his level. Terrible judgment overtook him for his arrogance. Today the Modernist endeavors to bring Christ down to the level of his own humanity. Christ and God are one; Christ is equal with God and *must* receive equal respect, honor, and dignity.

These three Old Testament characters of ill repute, then, fittingly describe the progressive apostasy of our own day. Would that all who deny "the faith" might be warned by such a trinity of apostasy!

A Threefold Group of Apostate Traits

From verses 12-19, Jude gives us a threefold setting forth of the characteristic features of apostates. His vivid, dramatic, and most expressive appellations fall into three groups, with each group commencing with the expression, "these are" (vv. 12, 16, 19).

The First Group (vv. 12-15)

At least five traits are discernible in this first set. Apostates are "hidden rocks." In verse 4 we read of how "certain men crept in unawares" into assemblies for the purpose of wrecking the faith of the members. The same stealth is emphasized again by Jude. Treacherously they entered the love-feasts under false pretense, feasting with others as if of them, "shepherds that feed themselves without fear" of judgment falling upon them for their hypocrisy. How many there are today who are apostates in heart but who persist in wearing Christian garments! May God expose these wolves in sheep's clothing!

They are "clouds without water." This simile of waterless clouds carried along by winds is most descriptive. Clouds with the appearance of holding refreshing rain for the dry, barren ground, yet empty of water and easily blown away by winds, portray the hypocrisy of those who promise what they cannot perform (Prov. 25:14). Too many are carried about with the changing winds of religious cults (Eph. 4:14). They are not stable but shifty. They have no steadfast convictions. Modernists are empty clouds. Thirsty souls approach them eagerly, but go away unrefreshed.

431

They are "autumn trees without fruit." Religious professors who deny "the faith" may be trees, but they are fruitless, twice dead, uprooted. Israel, though a well-tended vine, brought forth wild grapes (Isa. 5), and eventually became an empty vine (Hos. 10:1). Modernism is barren of spiritual results, and twice dead—dead spiritually within, dead or destitute to influence those without. It is also rootless. Believers are so different: they are ever fruitful, seeing that they are rooted in God (Ps. 1).

They are "raging waves of the sea." Here we have a figure of the ferocity of those who will not brook any opposition to their wills, ideas, and interpretations. Unbelief can become very loud, boisterous, and insistent upon foisting itself upon those who love the truth; and, when fully encountered, unbelief foams out its shame.

They are "wandering stars." Apostates are not like those planets moving in their "regular orbits with mathematical precision and order, subservient to the laws of their Creator, but are like erratic meteors or comets that flash in the heavens for a short time and disappear in darkness forever," as Robert Evans states in his valuable booklet on Jude. The blackness of darkness forever is the inevitable end of apostates.

Jude calls Enoch the prophet as a witness to the judgment that will overtake all those who depart from and deny "the faith." Four times, in verse 15, Jude calls apostates "ungodly." While Enoch's prophecy may be directly associated with the Flood, it covers all those who flout the authoritative revelation of God.

The Second Group (vv. 16-18)

Six further distinguishing features of apostates are given by Jude in this second section.

They are "murmurers." Israel of old was guilty of the sin

of murmuring, earning thereby the judgment of God. When a person murmurs, he is not resigned to, or willing to rejoice in, the will of God. Murmuring inevitably leads to open rebellion against God.

They are "complainers." Finding fault with one's fellow-man is all too common today. Malcontents are a plague to society.

They "walk after their own lusts." Whether the lusts belong to the "good" self or the "bad" self, so-called, the thought is the same, namely, the seeking of one's own will. These first three traits are in direct opposition to the requirements of grace: "soberly" (toward *self*); "righteously" (toward *men*); "godly" (toward *God*) (see Titus 2:12).

They speak "great swelling words." We can translate this phrase "loud-mouthed boasters." Modernism is guilty of loud boasting. In this connection, one remembers the rebellious mouth of the little horn (Dan. 7:8).

They have "men's persons in admiration because of advantage." It is an abominable thing to flatter a denomination leader, for example, in order to gain an advantage! It is possible to have rebellious eyes as well as a rebellious mouth (John 5:44).

They are "mockers." Peter has a word about this conspicuous feature of the last days (II Peter 3:3). When scoffers are numerous, the judgments of God are about to fall. It was so in the days of Noah. Today many religious leaders openly mock at the return of Christ and kindred truths. Divine teachings are scoffed at and discarded as being antiquated and useless. As these traits multiply around us, we realize how near we are to the last times.

Third Group (v. 19)

Jude gives us a further trinity in the distinguishing marks of the apostate in this verse.

"They . . . separate themselves." Assuming superiority of

attainment over others, an unscriptural separation follows. The Pharisees, "separated ones," stood aloof from the rank and file of Jews around. Modernism has developed an exclusive coterie.

They are "sensual." Those who fail to discern the deep things of God (I Cor. 2:14) act upon the impulses of the natural mind. Dependence is upon the senses and not upon the Spirit. Sensual wisdom ends by becoming devilish (James 3:15).

They "have not the Spirit." Blind leaders of the blind are devoid of the Spirit. No matter how cultured, gifted, and religious a person may be, if the heart is destitute of the Spirit, he does not belong to God (Rom. 8:11; Eph. 1:13).

A Threefold Appeal

While the short Epistle of Jude begins like a bright morning, a dark cloud quickly comes over the scene. As we have pointed out, false teachers and spiritual apostasy are mercilessly exposed. Wreckers of the church are fully and faithfully portrayed by Jude. Modernism tries to destroy the body of truth. But as the liberals try to pull down, we ourselves are to increase our activity and keep on building up ourselves in our most holy faith. We cannot *build* "the faith," but we can build our lives and witness *upon* it. Jude goes on to describe how, in a threefold way, we can build effectively.

We must "pray in the Holy Spirit." There is a vast difference between saying prayers and praying with all supplication in the Spirit (Eph. 6:18). Prayer in the Spirit is prayer of the highest order and from the deepest impulse. It is the form of prayer rooted in regeneration and constantly inspired by the Spirit. Such prayer brings us into harmony with our interceding Lord in heaven. Not knowing how to pray as we ought, the Spirit helps us in this infirmity (Rom. 8:26-27). As we build ourselves up in "the faith," the heart responds to the study of the Word and finds expression in prayer.

We must "keep [ourselves] in the love of God." The key word, "keep," occurs six times in Jude. It is as we are kept from falling (v. 24) that we are enabled to keep ourselves in the love of God. Jude does not contemplate the possibility of the believer getting outside the sphere of God's love. That is impossible. The writer is warning us not to lose the enjoyment of that love by waywardness and worldliness.

We must "look for the mercy of our Lord Jesus Christ." Apostates do not have the forward look, for Bible prophecy is discredited. But all who earnestly contend for "the faith" know that a part of that faith is a genuine expectation of the Lord's return for His own, a return completing His mercy toward us. Since we are preserved in Christ Jesus, He must return to possess us fully.

A Threefold Obligation

Building, praying, keeping, and looking result in sanctified activity. Those who fail to cultivate all that belongs to "the faith" separate themselves from others (v. 19). With those who love and look for the Lord, it is different. They go out to "rescue the perishing and care for the dying."

We must "have compassion on some, making a difference." Remembering that Jude is dealing with apostates, we must use every legitimate effort to reclaim them. The margin reads: "convince some, who doubt," or, "on some have mercy, who are in doubt: while they dispute with you." God grant us compassionate hearts, even for those who blatantly deny our precious faith!

We must save others "with fear, pulling them out of the fire." Fiery judgment awaits all who die out of Christ, whether they are religious sinners or conspicuously ungodly. Anyone who rejects the testimony of the Word is lost, no matter how educated he may be. With all godly fear we must warn apostates of their dreadful end.

We must "hate even the garment spotted by the flesh." Sin

435

defiles everything it touches. Christ, however, could touch the leper and yet remain undefiled. We are to love the sinner but hate his sin; but our witness can only be effective as our garments remain unspotted by the world.

A Threefold Benediction

How fittingly Jude concludes his brief but wonderful Epistle! In the midst of apostasy, as we reprove error and contend for the faith, victory is ours as we rest on God's ability. "Him that is able"—this is a blessed phrase with which to introduce a sublime doxology.

He is "able to keep you from falling." God is able to guard His own from the satanic subtleties of apostates in these last days. He can grant us spiritual perception whereby we can detect the slightest deflection from His Word.

He is "able to present you faultless [without blemish]." What a day it will be when, in the presence of His glory, we shall be as holy as the Lord! Exceeding joy will flood our glorified hearts.

"To the only wise God, our Saviour, be glory." He is worthy of the superlative praise of His people. "The only *wise* God." Man's exalted wisdom is paltry alongside His infinite wisdom! The margin adds, "through Jesus Christ our Lord." All external wisdom, glory, majesty, dominion, and power are God's through Christ.

Thus this Epistle which describes a ceaseless struggle against apostate forces ends with the eternal blessedness of those who are presented faultless before Him. What exceeding joy awaits the saints who remain loyal to the Lord and to His Word!

Theme 41
Revelation: The Lamb

The evolution of the lamb in Scripture forms a most profitable meditation. The Levitical and typical significance of the lamb dominates the Bible. Lambs were an integral part of almost every Jewish sacrifice. While the first mention of lambs is in Genesis 21:28,—"Abraham set seven ewe lambs of the flock by themselves"—it is taken for granted that the firstling of the flock that Abel presented to God was a lamb. His was a more excellent sacrifice than Cain's, seeing that it represented the shedding of innocent blood (Heb. 11:4). Christ's offering resulted in better things than that of Abel (Heb. 12:24).

Lambs chosen for an offering had to be faultless males and in keeping with the established estimate of animal perfection (Mal. 1:14). They had to be under one year old, meek, gentle, and have a tractable nature. Lambs for sacrifice had to be kept whole—"a bone of him shall not be broken" (John 19:36; cf. Exod. 12:46; Ps. 34:20)—and must be roasted. The lamb was the symbol of unity: the unity of the family, the unity of the nation, the unity of God with His people whom He had taken into covenant relationship with Himself.

The typical significance of the lamb is not hard to trace. It typifies:

1. Christ, the paschal Lamb, who became a sacrifice for our sins (cf. Exod. 29:38-41; with John 1:29 and Rev. 5:6, 8)
2. True believers, manifesting the lamblike qualities of humility and meekness (Isa. 11:6; Luke 10:3; John 21:15)

437

3. Beneficent teachers, who are not guilty of cruelty or barbarity (Jer. 11:19)
4. Innocency, as personified by a wife (II Sam. 12:3-4)
5. The antichrist, who will ape the power and prerogatives of Christ as the Lamb (Rev. 13:11)

The offering of lambs by sinning Israelites could never grant them redemption from sin. They were accepted by God in virtue of the sacrifice of His Lamb, the Lord Jesus Christ. The question asked by Isaac, as he accompanied his father up Mount Moriah—"Where is the lamb for a burnt offering?" (Gen. 22:17)—is unanswered all through the Old Testament. Multitudinous lambs had been placed upon blood-stained altars, but the cry for *the* Lamb had no response until we come to John's declaration: "Behold the Lamb of God, which taketh away the sin of the world (John 1:29).

Abraham's reply to Isaac's question is significant: "God will provide himself a lamb" (Gen. 22:8). In His love and mercy God did provide Himself as the Lamb. His Son, who was "very God of very God," became the Lamb through whose stripes we are healed.

> Not all the blood of beasts
> On Jewish altars slain
> Could give the guilty conscience peace
> Or wash away the stain.
>
> But Christ the heavenly Lamb,
> Takes all our sins away;
> A sacrifice of nobler name
> And richer blood than they.

Prophets and apostles loved to think of Christ as the sacrificial Lamb. Isaiah wrote of Him as the Lamb led out to slaughter (Isa. 53:7; Acts 8:32). John the Baptist had the distinction of being the forerunner of Christ, the Lamb (John 1:29). John Wesley said that his whole business here was to cry: "Behold the Lamb." It is our solemn business to reecho that cry. Peter extolled the preciousness of Christ's blood, who died as a Lamb without blemish and without spot (I Peter 1:19). The apostle John was also lost in contemplation of Christ as the Lamb, as the last book of the Bible clearly proves.

Let us meditate upon this unique figure of the Lamb, describing as it does the Person and plan of Christ.

Think of His Nature

Emphasis is laid upon the definite article: John tells us that Christ is *the* Lamb. All the lambs of the Old Testament, upon Jewish altars slain, merely typified the offering up of this perfect paschal Lamb. The Lord Jesus is the great and only Lamb whose sacrifice is efficacious to redeem and save lost sinners. Yes, and the Lamb was a fitting figure to use, seeing that Christ completes all the hopes enshrined in the sacrifices, rites, and symbols of Jewish ritual.

Think of His Innocence

A child untried and ignorant of the great and gross sins of life is spoken of as an innocent child. But Christ's innocence was greater. His was innocent holiness, an innocence tested but never lost. His life remained unsoiled. As sunbeams never contract the filth they shine through, so our blessed Lord remained holy, harmless, and undefiled. True, He "became sin"—but *never* a *sinner.* Had He sinned, He would have forfeited the right to be our Saviour; but being sinless, He can save.

Old Testament lambs remained innocent simply because they had no consciousness or knowledge of evil, but God's Lamb was holy. He had a very intimate acquaintance with evil, and yet He refused its seductive charms. Tested as we are, yet He remained victorious.

Think of His Gentleness

Meekness is associated with a lamb, but in God's Lamb meekness was not weakness. A lamb is a docile animal. How astonishing it is, therefore, to read of "the wrath of the Lamb" (Rev. 6:16)! Silent amid suffering is God's Lamb, but His very gentleness makes Him great. The meek inherit the earth, said He; and as God's meek Lamb He will yet see the whole earth filled with His glory.

Think of His Submission

A lamb does not complain when it is slain inasmuch as it is destitute of the elements of personality. Old Testament lambs were dragged to the altar. Christ, however, was not an unwilling victim. He gave Himself as our ransom. The world has witnessed many kinds of death, as, for example, of covenanter, hero, and martyr; but these men were liable to die. Our Lord Jesus Christ, on the other hand, chose death. Death did not claim Him. He was born in order that He might die. We often say that if we had known what would face us, we could never have lived, but the Lord Jesus knew every step of the blood-red way and walked the whole road with bleeding feet until He reached the cross. His whole life was one of voluntary sacrifices. Sacrifice, for Him, commenced at His incarnation and culminated at Calvary.

Just as a lamb exists for others, so the whole of Christ and His work are for us. A lamb gives its wool, and we have clothing; its flesh, and we have sustenance. From God's Lamb likewise we receive both covering and food.

Think of His Deity

Our Lord was no ordinary man. The Jews could bring any lamb to the altar, providing it fulfilled certain conditions. With God's Lamb it was different. There was none other who could die for man's sin. "There was no other good enough to pay the price of sin." He who was good enough gave virtue to what He did. The blood He shed was the blood of God (Acts 20:28) as well as the blood of man. Since Christ was the God-Man, His sacrifice was efficacious, seeing that deity was joined to humanity. The blood has transcendent power owing to its unique character. The Lamb was God and of God. And it is just here that we can mark the difference between Christianity and the religions of the world. In pagan religions man provides a sacrifice for his god. In Christianity, God provides a sacrifice for man; and the mystery of mysteries is that God gave Himself! God is the source of our salvation. It was *He* who loved the world and, in His beloved Son, died to reconcile it to Himself.

The Revelation is essentially "The Book of the Lamb." Within it Christ is only once referred to as a Lion, but twenty-eight times as the Lamb. While there are various ways of approaching The Revelation, the most dramatic book of the Bible, it is conspicuous as the Lamb-honoring book. The Greek word used in The Apocalypse is *arnion,* meaning "the little lamb," and not *amnos,* as in John 1:29. Over against the arrogance and wickedness of the beast, the false lamb, John placed the meekness and innocence of Christ, the little Lamb. Such a title combines the almightiness and invincibility necessary for the full and final subjugation of all evil forces.

The Revelation, then, is essentially the Book of the Lamb. The entire volume revolves around Him. He is the center and circumference of this mystic and glowing book. It is also to be noted that Christ is always presented as the Lamb that was *slain.* The scepter of universal sovereignty will rest in His pierced hand. His cross wins Him the crown. Government is founded upon His grief. His reign as sovereign is His as one of His redemptive rights. His wounds, evidence of His past sufferings and token of our present unworthiness, are also precious in that they forecast His vengeance upon His foes. His Calvary marks form the ground of coming judgment. His pierced hands and feet are a source of comfort for His own (John 20:20), but will strike terror in the hearts of His enemies. Those sacrificial scars, declaring Christ's willingness to be slain rather than submit to sin, cannot possibly compromise with iniquity and are, therefore, alone worthy to dispense righteous judgment.

There are many serviceable outlines of The Revelation, but, thinking of the way in which the Lamb dominates the book, we can divide its chapters thus:

1. The Vision of the Lamb (1)
2. The Church of the Lamb (2-3)
3. The Adoration of the Lamb (4-5)
4. The Wrath of the Lamb (6-19:6)
5. The Marriage of the Lamb (19:7-10)
6. The Reign of the Lamb (19:11-22)

Classifying John's references to Christ as the Lamb, we recognize these aspects:

The Lamb and His Eternal Wounds

Two pregnant phrases call for attention: "a Lamb as it had been slain" (5:6) and "the blood of the Lamb" (7:14). Here we have reminiscences of His "blood, sweat, and tears" on our behalf. When Winston Churchill promised the British people this trinity of anguish, did he recall Byron's use of it in the memorable lines?

> Year after year they voted cent for cent
> Blood, sweat, and tears—wrung millions—
> Why? for rent.

It is interesting to note that for the word translated "slain" John uses a word that means "newly or freshly slain." Further, Christ as the slain Lamb implies that He carries the scars of sacrifice. In heaven, those "rich wounds, yet visible above" eternally remind the saints of all that they owe to Christ, who became both victim and victor. Faith has no

442

difficulty in believing that the glorified body of Christ bears the indelible scars of the cross (John 20:20-27). Memories of Calvary are treasured in heaven. On earth we see the Lamb wounded and slain; in heaven He is the center of power and glory.

John turned to see a lion but beheld a lamb. Christ is both. Majesty and mercy are combined in Him. But the Lamb that John saw was not nailed to a cross or even sitting, but "standing" between the throne and the elders. He is about to assume His redemption-inheritance. Now He is seated at the Father's right hand (Heb. 1:3; Rev. 3:21; Ps. 110:1), but patience is ended. The Lamb vacates the throne to take unto Himself His power and reign. "Sitting" is a state of rest; "standing" bespeaks readiness for action. How we love the sight of the scarred, standing Lamb.

> Dear suffering Lamb, Thy bleeding wounds
> With cords of love divine
> Have drawn our willing hearts to Thee
> And linked our life with Thine.

We are thrice blessed if we have the mystic robes made white by the blood of the Lamb. His scars are our only right of access into the holiest of all. The blood alone can make saints, whether they be of this present age or of the Tribulation. Trials and tribulation make sacrificial sufferers of saints.

The Lamb and His Worship

All within creation are stirred to the depths as they come to worship the Lamb. Angels adore the Lamb, yet they cannot praise Him as the redeemed of earth love to do, for the saints alone can sing the new song.

> They sing the Lamb of God
> Once slain on earth for them;
> The Lamb, thro' whose atoning blood
> Each wears his diadem.

The Lamb, the bleeding Lamb, is the theme of the new song, which is the only theme worth singing about. The cross is the grandest fact of all time. Without it Christ would have been in glory alone and sinners would have had no deliverance from the guilt and government of sin. But the suffering, conquering Lamb of God has all intelligences ascribing praise and honor to His name (Rev. 5:8-14).

While He was on earth God's Lamb was silent before His shearers. No word of rebuke or reproach fell from His lips as He willingly endured all the contradictions of sinners against Himself. He never exercised His inherent power to save Himself from all who put Him to shame. Now all is changed. He no longer stands amid the godless horde, silent and alone in His holiness, in His calm dignity, with spittle and blood covering His face. Universal adoration is His. He is acclaimed as the object of heaven's worship. Once patient in His agony, this is now the Lamb's supreme moment, when all are prostrate before Him.

Around the throne we have the redeemed of all ages, with angels forming the outer circle. Having taken the seven-sealed book, thus accepting authority and government, the Lamb is now worthy to receive every mark of distinction that it is possible to confer upon Him. He is praised for the perfection of attributes He can now manifest (5:12; 7:12).

Power: This is first named, for the Lamb is about to exercise power in its widest, most comprehensive character.

Riches: All wealth, whether material, moral, or physical, is His due. As the Lamb who gave His all, He claims our best.

Wisdom: This comes as the personification of divine wisdom and, being made unto us wisdom, He will manifest highest wisdom when He comes to reign.

Strength: Here we have the quality which enables Him to carry out all He determines to do for His own, and for the earth as He comes to reign.

Honor: As the Lamb, He died dishonored. Religious leaders caused Him to die as a felon on a wooden gibbet. Now deserved recognition is His.

Glory: He is also worthy to receive all public glory. Now the Lamb can be glorified with the glory He had with the Father in the dateless past.

Blessing: All forms and characteristics of blessedness or happiness are to be His. Full contentment will be the Lamb's.

What exaltation is His! The tide of praise gathers force and volume until the whole universe ascribes honor to the Lamb.

> The Lamb is all the glory
> Of Immanuel's Land.

The Lamb and His Wrath

John writes as an eye-witness of the act of the Lamb opening the seals containing the sore judgments of heaven for earth. The Lamb is related to the seals; the angels to the trumpets; God to the vials, or bowls. In his Gospel, John reminds us that God has given His Son the necessary authority to execute judgment (John 5:27) and now in The Apocalypse, John depicts Christ as the Lamb about to exercise all governmental and civil authority. All must bow to Him when the great day of His wrath is come (Rev. 6:17).

What a vivid emblem of terror the last section of chapter 6 presents! How staggering it is to read about "the wrath of the Lamb." The Lamb! The One who is noted for meekness, gentleness, and patience now is swept along by a fearsome, righteous indignation. It is very seldom that a lamb gives way to anger or disturbed feelings. When it does, we are told it can be most ferocious. Thus will it be when the Lamb of God comes to execute judgment upon the godless of earth. The outburst of His concentrated anger will be terrible in the extreme, causing the rebellious to seek shelter in caves. How grateful we should be that, through the experience of the cleansing blood of the Lamb, we shall never need to bear the wrath of the Lamb!

Divine and satanic anger form another profitable study of The Revelation. Not only does John speak of "the wrath of the Lamb," but twice over we read of "the wrath of God" (14:10, 19). God and Christ are one in their determination to rid the earth of all beast-worshipers. Such a scene, depicted in the fall of Babylon, fulfills the prophecies about "the day of vengeance" (Isa. 63:4; Matt. 25:31-46).

Then there is the "great wrath" of Satan (Rev. 12:12). Exiled from his domain in the heavenlies, he realizes that his time is short and indulges in one final outburst of rage and destruction. That these will be terrible days when Satan is here in person can be gathered from John's warning: "Woe to the inhabiters of the earth and of the sea." Deposed as the prince of the power of the air, after his war with Michael and his angels, the devil will be more diabolical than ever.

The Lamb and His Sovereignty

Christ, as the Lamb, is often associated with a throne in this climactic book of the Bible. He is on a throne and also in the midst of a throne (7:10, 17; 22:1). The sacred head once crowned with sharp cactus-thorns is to bear many a diadem. Rejected by earth, He is to rule over it. Regal glory is to be His. With all His sorrows and sacrifices past, the strength and security of the throne are the Lamb's.

Exercising all dominion and power from the midst of a throne, He is able to meet every need of His own, conquer all His foes, and dispense salvation in its most comprehensive sense to Jews and Gentiles alike. This is why the throne is the prominent object in the last part of the vision granted to John. The saints also are to reign with Him. They are to be sharers of His royalty.

It must not be forgotten that it is as the Lamb that Jesus Christ is to reign. Thus, when He climbed those bloody slopes leading to His cross, He secured more than deliverance from the penalty and power of sin. Certainly He died as the sinless substitute for sinners. But more than salvation was provided by His death. With it came His sovereign rights as the King of kings. In a Messianic psalm we read: "Say among the nations, The Lord reigneth" (Ps. 96:10, RV). Some of the old versions of the Bible have an addition: "Say ye among the nations that the Lord reigneth from the tree." *From the tree!* Ah, yes, those scars of the Lamb mean sovereignty as well as salvation. The Redeemer is to reign. In virtue of His cross, the slain Lamb will exercise His kingly prerogatives. Because of the tree, He is to have a throne. The royal diadem is to adorn the brow that cruel men crowned with thorns. Instead of a mock coronation, unsurpassed majesty will be His when, from "the throne of God and of the Lamb," He reigns in righteousness.

The Lamb and His Register

While various registers are mentioned in The Revelation, there are two specific references to the Lamb's roll-call: "The book of life of the Lamb" (13:8) and "the Lamb's book of life" (21:27). This register contains the names of those who have been washed in the blood of the Lamb, inscribed in the sacred volume before the foundation of the world (Eph. 1:4-5). None of these names will ever be erased. Once we become the Lord's, we are His forevermore. "What God doeth is forever." It is different with the book about which we read in a previous chapter: "I will not blot out his name out of the book of life" (3:5). This is a record of professors and possessors. All who make a Christian profession, true and false, make up this register. The true are those who have had their names written in the book of life from the foundation of the world (17:8). But in this particular register the names of the unsaved do not appear, for this is the book of the redeemed. "Whosoever was not found written in the book of

447

life was cast into the lake of fire" (20:15). Only those whose names are written in the Lamb's book of life (21:27) are delivered from eternal separation from the Lamb and enter into the eternal blessedness of the holy city. Thus the question of paramount importance for each of us to face as we think of the Lamb's register is: "Is *my* name written there?"

Commenting on the solemn declaration of John, "If any was not found written in the book of life, he was cast into the lake of fire," William R. Newell says:

Let us mark certain facts here:

1. It is not the absence of good works in the book that dooms a person. It is the absence of his *name*. Only names, not works, are in that book.
2. It is not the fact of evil works. Many of earth's sinners have their names in the book of life.
3. All whose names do not appear in the book, are cast into the lake of fire.
4. All names there found in that day will have been written before that day. There is no record of anyone's name being written into the book of life upon that day, but rather the opposite.

"If any man was not found written." How overwhelmingly solemn this is!

The Lamb and His Firstfruits

Chapter 13 presents the false lamb and his followers, for whom there is nothing but doom. In chapter 14, John brings us to the true Lamb and His followers. By the 144,000 we understand the spared Jewish remnant, the tribe particularized in chapter 7. These Israelites are loyal in their witness to God and the Lamb, and are now publicly owned by heaven. Many of these Jews are depicted as sealing their testimony with their blood. Others are spared through the sor-

448

rows of the Tribulation and share the seat of royalty. They pass from tyranny under the beast to triumph with God. From the scene of suffering they go to the seat of sovereignty.

The divine estimate of these faithful followers of the Lamb is full of spiritual instruction for our own hearts. Apart from participation in the new song, they are described as walking in virgin purity. They were also obedient to the Lamb, following Him whithersoever He went, and that in spite of surrounding idolatry. Multitudes were giving their loyalty to the beast, but this godly remnant gave the Lamb undivided heart affection. Theirs was a "magnificent obsession." We are also told that no guile was in their mouth, and that they were without fault before the divine tribunal (14:6-8). What a reputation to have! Beast worshipers, deluded by his false claims, believed a lie; but no lie was found in any mouth of this godly company. They acknowledged the Messiah to be the true One, refusing to conform to the blasphemous edicts of the beast.

No wonder these redeemed ones are spoken of as being "the firstfruits unto God and to the Lamb." Priority in time and blessing is theirs, and they form the earnest of a more glorious harvest. William R. Newell says of them:

> They are the firstfruits of the millennial reign. They connect the dispensations—somewhat as Noah did, who passed through the judgment of the flood into a new order of things. Therefore, the Lamb is seen standing on Mount Zion (*before He actually comes there,* as in Revelation 19 and Psalm 2), that with Him may be seen this overcoming host, who will very shortly share His actual reign there.

The Lamb and His Victory

What jubilant overcomers are before us in the issue of the

war in heaven: "They overcome him by the blood of the Lamb" (12:11)! Satan, as the prince of this world, heads up imperial powers on earth, just as he controls all evil spiritual powers as the prince of the power of the air. All saints, however, are victorious as they seek the shelter of the blood, representing as it does the empowering virtue of Christ's death and resurrection. The cross was Satan's Waterloo. Pleading that cross, we conquer him. We often sing about marching on to victory. Is it not true that we are marching on *from* victory, even the victory of Calvary? Deliverance from all diabolical machinations will be experienced by the devil-driven Jews as they plead the abiding efficacy of the blood. Along with this evidence of victory, we also see prophetic witness and willing martyrdom. Released from satanic oppression, the accused brethren rejoice. Are we among the singing victors?

Later on in The Revelation we see the victorious Lamb Himself: "These shall make war with the Lamb, and the Lamb shall overcome them" (17:14). This conquest brings us to the final act of the beast and his allies, and the conflict between the Lamb and these satanically inspired forces is more fully described in chapter 19. Here, in chapter 17, the war is anticipated and victory is assured. The Lamb is the mighty conqueror, exercising all vested authority. As the Lion-Lamb, He is to reign, combining tenderness and power (5:5-6). The victor of Calvary is to take the throne and, when He does, earth's sin, sighs, sobs, and sorrows will cease. "The Lord shall be king over all the earth" (Zech. 14:9). Inflexible righteousness will characterize His reign. There will be no more contention between right and wrong, truth and error, peace and war. "He shall be a priest upon his throne" (Zech. 6:13). How glorious will be His reign as He manifests priestly grace and kingly authority! What ultimate triumph will be His! All His enemies will be routed, and His church will be entirely free from all blemish and the antagonism of sin and salvation.

The Lamb and His Bride

As we have several glimpses of the church under the figure of the bride, it may prove profitable to gather them together under this section. Some there are who affirm that Israel, and not the church, is the bride. The Scriptures, however, are explicit on the point that Israel is the adulterous wife of Jehovah. Those who reject the church as the bride affirm that she cannot be the bride and the body at the same time. But why not? It is no more incongruous to think of the church as a bride and a body than it is to speak of Christ as the Priest and as the Lamb. Yet He is both, is He not?

First of all, we have the marriage of the Lamb (19:7, 9) which takes place in heaven amidst rapturous scenes of joy. Here the bride is spoken of as the wife for the simple reason that as soon as a marriage is completed the bride becomes the wife. "The 'bride' speaks of her deep place in the affection of the Bridegroom," says Walter Scott. "The 'wife' intimates the established relationship existing between the Bridegroom and the bride."

This celestial marriage precedes the assumption of the kingdom by the Lord. Because of the relationship existing between the Bridegroom and the bride, the latter is to share the former's glory and reign with Him while occupying her special place in His heart's deep love. In chapter 21:9, the bride, as a city, is shown to Israel in her millennial glory. The church is the city of millennial and eternal days. A city represents an organized system of social life, united interests, activity of government, all of which the church will experience.

The bridal robes of the wife (19:8) are in sharp contrast to the gorgeous attire of the harlot (17:4). The glorious clothes of the bride speak of character, of a righteousness provided and practiced. The deeds of the bride are appraised at their true value in heaven. The bride, clothed in pure white linen, as beautiful as her trousseau will be, will not eye her garments but "her dear Bridegroom's face."

451

The guests are distinguished as friends of the Bridegroom (19:9) of whom John the Baptist will be the most honored one (John 3:29). All saints not incorporated within the church will be among the invited guests to the marriage of the Lamb.

Presently the Spirit and the bride are united in their desire for the Lamb to return (22:17). It is not merely the Spirit *in* the bride crying: "Come!" Both cry as one. The Lamb will appear as the Bright and Morning Star when He comes to claim His bride. For Israel, He will appear as the Sun of Righteousness in all His noonday splendor. No one can meditate upon the revelation granted to John without realizing something of the glorious heritage awaiting both the church and Israel.

The Lamb and His Song

Two songs are united since they both celebrate redemption—one, redemption by power; the other, by blood. "They sing the song of Moses the servant of God, and the song of the Lamb" (15:3). The first song celebrates the marvelous deliverance that God gave to Israel at the Red Sea. The second song magnifies the Lamb for the redemption that He provided from sin's guilt and government. The one was an earthly redemption; the other is a spiritual redemption. The song of Moses speaks of triumph over the power of evil by divine judgment. The song of the Lamb is taken up with the exaltation of the rejected Messiah. It is the song of the faithful remnant, sung in the midst of the unfaithful, apostate Israel; the song of martyred victors.

The theme of the song is the Holy One of Israel. What a tower of strength we have in the combination of titles given (15:3-4). He is great and marvelous; just and true and holy. He is the King not only of the saints but of the nations, as the Revised Version expresses it. When the Lamb appears on the earth, it will be as the sovereign of His redeemed ones of

Israel and of all the nations of the earth. "Who would not fear thee, O king of nations? for to thee doth it appertain: forasmuch as among all the wise men of the nations, and in all their kingdoms, there is none like unto thee" (Jer. 10:7).

What a day that will be when the Lamb is lauded as the world emperor! What a relief for our blood-soaked earth it will be when, with Satan imprisoned in the pit, Christ takes the throne as King of the nations! Are you not grateful that, having the assurance of having been washed in the blood of the Lamb, yours will be the joyful privilege of joining in the glorious "Hallelujah Song" as Christ takes the throne?

The last reference to the Lamb, in the Lamb-exalting Book of The Revelation, is in its concluding chapter: The servants of the Lamb shall serve Him (22:3). Note that which all lovers of the Lamb are found doing:

They serve Him. We are not to idle eternity away playing harps. Highest and holiest service will be ours.

They are to see Him. What soul-thrilling rapture will be ours to see His face and eternally to behold it!

They are to bear His name. This means that we are to reflect His character. "In their foreheads" implies in the place easily seen.

They are to bask in His presence. Natural and artificial lumination will no longer be necessary. The Lamb will be the light of our world.

They are to have His eternal provision and guardianship. The enthroned Lamb is to feed and lead His own forever (7:15-17). Through all eternity He will shepherd, protect, and illumine His followers.

Through the ageless future we shall not be able to repay Him. We shall be the Lamb's dear debtors forever. He will be our guide and glory in Immanuel's land.

Dr. Herbert Lockyer spent nearly three decades as a pastor in England and Scotland before coming to the United States, where he conducted a ten-year lecturing ministry under the auspices of Moody Bible Institute. He is the author of more than fifty books including the well-known, fifteen-volume All series.